FAT

FAT

Culture and Materiality

Edited by
Christopher E. Forth
and Alison Leitch

B L O O M S B U R Y

LONDON · NEW DELHI · NEW YORK · SYDNEY

Bloomsbury Academic
An imprint of Bloomsbury Publishing Plc

50 Bedford Square	1385 Broadway
London	New York
WC1B 3DP	NY 10018
UK	USA

www.bloomsbury.com

Bloomsbury is a registered trade mark of Bloomsbury Publishing Plc

First published 2014

© Christopher E. Forth and Alison Leitch, 2014

Christopher E. Forth and Alison Leitch have asserted their rights under the Copyright, Designs and Patents Act, 1988, to be identified as Editors of this work.

British Library Cataloguing-in-Publication Data
A catalogue record for this book is available from the British Library.

ISBN: HB: 978-0-85785-616-6
PB: 978-0-85785-509-1
ePub: 978-1-47252-018-0

Library of Congress Cataloging-in-Publication Data
A catalog record for this book is available from the Library of Congress.

Typeset by Apex, CoVantage LLC
Printed and bound in India

CONTENTS

NOTES ON CONTRIBUTORS

Trudie Cain is a research manager in the College of Humanities and Social Sciences at Massey University, New Zealand. She received her PhD in sociology from Massey University and contributes to papers on research methods, globalization, and New Zealand culture and identity. She has published in the areas of migration, particularly on issues of social cohesion and labor market outcomes, and embodied reflexivity. Her research interests include gendered, sized, and migrant identities; qualitative research methodologies and ethics; and the materiality of everyday lives. She is particularly interested in the negotiated spaces of the clothed body.

Kerry Chamberlain is professor of social and health psychology at Massey University in Auckland, New Zealand. He is a critical health psychologist whose research focuses on health and the everyday, with specific interests in medications, media, materiality, mundane ailments, food, disadvantage, social and cultural process, and innovative qualitative research methodology. He has published widely on health issues and qualitative research and methodologies.

Ann Dupuis is associate professor of sociology and regional director of the College of Humanities and Social Sciences at Massey University's Albany Campus in Auckland, New Zealand. She has a long-standing interest in inheritance and the meanings associated with inherited possessions, whether in the form of money from housing, wealth inheritance, or special gifts. She has published extensively in the area of the meanings of home and the connection between home, home ownership, and ontological security; urban intensification; and private urban governance.

Nadine Ehlers teaches in cultural studies at the University of Wollongong, Australia. She is the author of *Racial Imperatives: Discipline, Performativity, and Struggles against Subjection* (2012) and has published in journals such as *Social Semiotics*, *Patterns of Prejudice*, and *Culture, Theory, and Critique*.

Christopher E. Forth is the Howard Professor of Humanities and Western Civilization and professor of history at the University of Kansas, United States. A specialist in the cultural history of gender, sexuality, and the body, his books include *The Dreyfus*

Affair and the Crisis of French Manhood (2004) and *Masculinity in the Modern West: Gender, Civilization and the Body* (2008), as well as several edited collections, including *Cultures of the Abdomen: Diet, Digestion and Fat in the Modern World* (2005). He is currently completing a cultural history of fat in the West.

Anna Lavis is a medical anthropologist and research fellow at the University of Birmingham. Within the multidisciplinary context of the Department of Primary Care, she conducts research into psychosis. Also focused on individuals' lived experiences of mental illness, Anna's doctoral thesis explored pro-anorexia, and she continues to work on eating disorders, food, and eating. With Emma-Jayne Abbots, Anna has recently edited *Why We Eat, How We Eat: Contemporary Encounters between Foods and Bodies* (2013) and founded a research network entitled Consuming Materialities: Bodies, Boundaries and Encounters. As a research associate in the Institute of Social and Cultural Anthropology at the University of Oxford, Anna is currently collaborating on projects investigating media representations of obesity.

Alison Leitch teaches in sociology at Macquarie University in Sydney, Australia, and has a PhD in social anthropology from the University of Sydney. She has conducted long-term ethnographic fieldwork in the Italian marble-quarrying community of Carrara. Among her publications are the journal articles "Slow Food and the Politics of Pork Fat" (*Ethnos*), "The Life of Marble" (*Australian Journal of Anthropology*), "The Materiality of Marble" (*Thesis Eleven*), and "Visualizing the Mountain" (*Journal of Modern Italian Cultural Studies*), as well as the chapter "Carrara: The Landscape of Stone" in *Australians in Italy* (2010). She has coproduced a sound documentary *Carrara: Primo Maggio Anarchico* (*Vox Lox*) and is currently working on a book about women sculptors working with marble.

Anne Meneley is associate professor of anthropology at Trent University in Canada. She has published articles in *American Anthropologist, Cultural Anthropology, Ethnos, Food, Culture and Society*, and *Middle East Report*. She is the author of *Tournaments of Value: Sociability and Hierarchy in a Yemeni Town* (1996) and is the coeditor of two collections of essays, *Fat: The Anthropology of an Obsession* (2005) and *Auto-Ethnographies: The Anthropology of Academic Practices* (2005).

Jennifer-Scott Mobley is a visiting professor of theater at Rollins College, Winter Park, Florida. Her article "Tennessee Williams's Ravenous Women: Fat Behavior Onstage" appeared in the inaugural issue of *Fat Studies: A Journal of Research* (Routledge). Her performance and book reviews have appeared in *Theatre Journal, Theatre Survey*, and *Shakespeare Bulletin*. She is currently completing a book-length manuscript tentatively titled *Enter Fat Actress: From Lillian to Lena, Female Bodies on the American Stage*.

Brad Weiss is professor of anthropology at the College of William & Mary, United States. He is the author of three books and numerous articles on Tanzanian culture and society and served for ten years as an editor of the *Journal of Religion in Africa*. Weiss is currently the president of the Society for Cultural Anthropology. His current research explores contemporary American interests in transforming the industrial food system by examining the social and cultural significance of pasture-raised pork in North Carolina. Weiss's works develop a phenomenological approach to embodied experience and the production of value in sociocultural worlds.

FAT

Country towns are full of it.
The suburbs are awash with it.
Acidic molecules consort with glycerol,
Adopt another name, move into cells and hang out there.
It cushions heels, grows big around the waist and other parts
When glands play sport, unlike their hosts.
It sashays through arcades where it leans heavily
On trolleys stacked with meat. It makes its pilgrim way
To packaged sacraments on supermarket shelves.
Around the globe, a billion factories work around the clock to keep it sleek.
Motel chains and airlines do not make life easy for it
And its feedlot children bobbing in its wake.
It cannot bear to see so much it yearns for going spare:
It plugs a void. It loves a pick-me-up, a snack:
It keeps its strength up in lacunae between meals.
It lards the littoral, is unflagging in its interest,
Offers shares to politicians, corporations, come who may.
It flattens springs of king and queen-sized mattresses,
Beats single beds to pulp. It tries to fit itself in dinky chairs
In theatres, restaurants and cars; twin-sized men and women
Manifest it on the margins of school playgrounds,
Cheering jumbo-sized descendants oscillating round a ball.
Some of its exemplars are renowned for stepping light,
And pirouette like graceful zeppelins at play.
It is the cynosure of classrooms, office towers, is imposing
On a stage. It pauses to consider stairs and hills;
It keeps strange pets who share its appetites and shape.
It goes on convoy in vast vehicles that sigh as it steps in.
No end of artists celebrate it. Rubens loved it;
Joseph Beuys wrapped it tenderly in felt.
It wages war with buttons, belts. It builds a verandah on the toyshop,
And amuses tiny friends to whom the wonder is it replicates itself.

—From Michael Sharkey, *The Sweeping Plain* (2007).

INTRODUCTION: MATERIALIZING FAT

Christopher E. Forth

In today's world, where warnings of an "obesity epidemic" are regular front-page news, it is impossible to escape the ways in which fat is framed as a problem, and most often as a crisis (Saguy 2013). Yet despite the medical jargon used to measure body mass and height, calories and pounds, all of which present the need to slim down as a simple but urgent matter of health and self-control, our prejudices against fat are often accompanied by a powerful emotion that is anything but detached or disinterested. "If one were forced to come up with a six-word explanation for the otherwise inexplicable ferocity of America's war on fat," Paul Campos writes in *The Obesity Myth*, "it would be this: Americans think being fat is disgusting. It really is, on the most important cultural and political levels, as simple as that." He argues that our current stigmatization of fat has exploded in a world in which the stereotyping of traditional minority groups has become generally unacceptable. "Fifty years ago, America was full of people that the social elites could look upon with something approaching open disgust: blacks in particular, of course, but also other ethnic minorities, the poor, women, Jews, homosexuals, and so on" (Campos 2004: 67).

What Campos writes about the United States could easily apply to other cultural contexts, and of course disgust is by no means the only emotional reaction that fat may elicit. As we will see throughout this book, in various societies across time and place fat has been capable of generating a broad spectrum of responses, positive and negative, across a range of cultural registers. Yet it is the disgust response that is commonly observed by scholars who think critically about contemporary encounters with fat bodies,[1] and probing this emotion raises certain questions about what it is about fat that is capable of eliciting such a reaction. Like most people who analyze fat stigmatization, Campos (2004: xxiv) approaches disgust as an emotion elicited "by the sight of people who weigh anything from a lot to a little more than our current absurdly restrictive cultural ideal." While this privileging of the visual makes sense in our highly mediatized culture, it is equally clear that stereotypes about bodies, especially those that rely on strong visceral sensations for their potency, are not constructed out of visual cues alone. Rather, they elicit and mobilize a range of sensory responses that often stigmatize their objects as revolting and contaminating. In fact, when it comes to disgust, vision is not the primary sense at work. Summing up recent work by anthropologists and psychologists, the philosopher Martha Nussbaum argues for the central role of *tactility* in the generation of disgust insofar as "the key idea is that of crossing a boundary from the world into the self." As such "disgust would thus be closely connected to all three of the senses that the philosophical tradition regards as 'tactile' senses rather than mediated or distance senses: i.e., touch, smell, and taste, rather than sight or hearing" (Nussbaum 2004: 92). Disgust is thus brought into being through a range of senses, and even when one sense is central, they are nevertheless capable of being synesthetically transposed (Durham 2011). This is how visual information is capable of evoking tactile and other sense impressions that may generate feelings of alarm and revulsion at the very thought of coming into contact with a specific form of matter. In other words, as Margat (2011: 18) proposes, when certain "visual sensations" seem to provoke disgust it is better viewed as "a fear resulting from an anticipation of [tactile] perception." So when Lee F. Monaghan (2008: 68) observes that fat today is "routinely discredited as female or feminizing filth," the situation he describes is at least as much about fears of contamination as it is about representation.

An analysis of disgust thus suggests that processes of stereotyping are complex multisensory phenomena evoking synesthetic responses that may rely on tactile, olfactory, and auditory impressions as well as visual ones. We can see this multisensory process at work in the irrational fears of blacks, Jews, women, homosexuals, and the poor, which have been shown to consist of strong reactions to the smell and touch (as well as the sight and sound) of people associated with these groups (Alcoff 2006; Corbin 1986; Gilman 1991; Smith 2006). We also encounter it in the experiences of anorexics, whose aversion to food has long been explained as an exaggerated response to dominant standards of female beauty and slenderness. Megan Warin's (2010) ethnographic research convincingly reveals the extent to which anorexic girls and women are often less obsessed with thinness per se than with an avoidance of fats (corporeal and noncorporeal), which they have come to associate with impurity and to which they may respond with feelings of disgust. Here, in what many see as the *nec plus ultra* of fat phobia, the object of anorexic dread may be less visual than a conventional focus on appearance is prepared to acknowledge. If the emotion of disgust is largely prompted by "contact" senses, then we need to investigate what exactly people are worried about coming into contact *with* when they express worry about fat. A discussion of fat and disgust is therefore useful for the light it sheds on the properties attributed to a substance rather than only on the visual appearance of bodies.

So what, then, *is* fat in cultural and material terms? This question requires interdisciplinary answers that *Fat: Culture and Materiality* seeks to provide. This volume shows that, above and beyond its status as an adjective referring to a certain state of the body, *fat* is also a noun denoting a materiality rich in properties as well as possibilities. Capable of being perceived and applied in a variety of ways, fat is literally as well as conceptually slippery. By focusing on the complex and often ambiguous *material* and *experiential* dimensions of a problematic substance, *Fat: Culture and Materiality* suggests that our wider cultural engagement with fats and oils has implications for the lived experience of fatness both as an identity and as a way of being in the world.

FAT, BODIES, MATTER

Given that today vision seems to overshadow the other senses, it is perhaps unsurprising that the materiality of fat tends to be sidelined in many critical discussions of "obesity." This is especially true in the field of fat studies, where scholars are often more concerned with how representations and experiences of fat are determined by culture and are therefore arbitrary in relation to the substance itself (see, for example, the essays in Braziel and LeBesco 2001). As Krista Scott-Dixon (2008: 24) explains, scholars adopting this social constructionist view of fat often manifest a "distrust of direct engagement with the body's material" because, in their view, referring to "the material structures of physiology might even be deemed evidence of [a] biological essentialism" that downplays the formative role of discourse in how certain bodies are perceived and experienced. As a method of engaging critically with biomedical discourses that pathologize fatness, many fat studies scholars focus their attention less on the body as such than on the positioning of fat subjects within "contingent systems and structures." For them *fat* refers less to a material reality with inherent properties and tendencies than to "a fluid subject position relative to social norms." It becomes a matter of identity politics in which the word *fat* is itself reclaimed as a term of "pride and identity" (Cooper 2010: 1021). Consequently, a large number of scholars, especially during the early years of the field, focused on the ways in which fat bodies seemed to be doubly "revolting" (LeBesco 2004) in their dual defiance of aesthetic norms and social expectations. As Natalie Anne Cowley (2006: 105) sums up the conventional wisdom, "it is generally not FAT as a substance that is detrimental to individual well-being, but FAT as a signifier." In such claims the materiality of fat is acknowledged only to be overshadowed by the near determinism of representation.[2]

Despite the usefulness of engaging with fat stereotypes with reference to reigning aesthetic standards, the limitations of this focus on representation were clear to some during the early days of fat studies. Viewing the situation from the perspective of human geography, Rachel Colls (2002: 219) warned of the dangers of "textual overload" in which a strong emphasis on representation reinforced "the need to take the (fleshy) body seriously." To others a reluctance to explore the substance of fat reflected a troubling disregard for the role of materiality in the construction of the person, thus reinforcing ideas about decorporealized subjectivity that resonate widely in modern Western culture. We see this dematerializing tendency in a variety of contexts. Participants in Christine Durif-Bruckert's (2008) French study of how "corporeal well-being" is experienced, for example, described the ideal body as one that was "lived" as light, clean, and silent, a state in which one is not reminded that one even has a body. Similar fantasies of separating the self from the fat body are evident in Karen Throsby's (2008: 119) study of how people undergoing weight-loss surgery tend to describe the "pre-transformation body as discordant with the true self" and as a "true self trapped in the wrong body." From such perspectives fat seems to represent an especially insistent reminder of a corporeality that is already imagined as being incompatible with the disembodied subjects we often imagine ourselves to be (Leder 1990). A tendency to dismiss the materiality of fat—or, indeed, of the body as such—as inessential to personhood not only plays a role in the disgust feelings aroused by obesity but even surfaces among fat activists who—in their otherwise admirable campaign to promote size acceptance—end up drawing distinctions between the fat body and the person "within" (Murray 2008). As Le'a Kent asserts, in Western culture "[t]he self is never fat. To put it bluntly, there is no such thing as a fat *person*." As a result of this decorporealizing conceit the fat body is made to "bear the full horror of embodiment" (Kent 2001: 135).

Despite this tendency in the field to reproduce mind/body dualisms that have retained currency in the West for centuries, some fat studies scholars have begun to take the materiality of fat seriously. In a groundbreaking article Colls (2007: 355) proposes that investigating the "intra-active capacities" of fat as a substance should encourage a shift in focus from "what fat represents, to what matter is capable of doing." Drawing on the insights of Judith Butler (1993) and Julia Kristeva (1982), among other theorists, Colls (2007: 358) submits that fat may be viewed as "a form of bodily matter that is not only impinged upon by outside forces but has its own capacities to act and be active" in ways that, depending on one's perspective, may be viewed positively or negatively. Thus, even when fat is framed as deviant or abject in the wider culture, the properties and capacities of fat as a substance necessarily offer other possible ways of living the subjective experience of fat. Thus fat may be seen to roll or "gather" on the corpulent body, to hang, flow, or even "dance" in ways that may be experienced as pleasurable and comforting rather than shameful and degrading. Thus, as Colls argues, if "fat bodies exceed the iterative norms that produce them," it is because matter itself is always "implicated in the processes of its materialisation" (363, 364). Rather than necessarily being experienced as a repulsive substance that one must continually expel from one's conception of oneself—as in Kristeva's (1982) concept of abjection—the properties of fat also offer possibilities for a more affirming response to what, following Robyn Longhurst (2005), we might call "corpulence."

Colls's important intervention in the largely discourse-centered field of fat studies offers useful ways of thinking about the materiality of fat as necessarily bound up with the experience of embodiment. However, by pressing her analysis a bit, we may be able to consider other ways in which the materiality of fat may be approached. For instance, Colls (2007: 358) rightly acknowledges that fat is "ambiguous" because it is "placed simultaneously under the skin yet materialised as a substance in and of itself." Insofar as she views the skin as a more or less reliable envelope that prevents fat from leaking out as other problematic fluids do, Colls concludes that fat is similar, but not identical, to the substances normally associated with abjection: "Fat does not seep out of the body and traverse the skin as blood and faeces do. Therefore, its existence is less permeable and more enduring" (358).

While Colls is certainly right when contrasting fat with blood and feces, these do not exhaust the pool of abject bodily materials capable of generating disgust, nor does such a perspective acknowledge the other forms that fat may assume. After all, fat is often conceptualized with reference to certain cognate substances that are believed to share some of its qualities. Sweat, for instance, has long been imagined as being closely associated with fat, so much so, in fact, that the notion that exercise is to some extent a process of burning or melting fat away through the pores has been durably entrenched in our culture since antiquity (Onians 1951). While sweat may not generate the same level of alarm as blood or feces, its fluctuating connection with concepts of filth and immorality means that it cannot be viewed as a neutral or unproblematic fluid. In fact, unsecreted sweat and other bodily effluvia were for centuries thought to be a *cause* of fatness, which may be one reason that fat bodies have been so closely linked with excrement in the West (Forth 2012).

Moreover, in modern culture, the stereotypical fat person is often depicted as sweating—uncontrollably (supposedly because he or she is exhausted by the slightest effort) but also inappropriately (that is, outside of gyms and playing fields). In its manifestation as corpulence, fat may indeed be approached as "matter out of place" (Douglas 1966)—as flesh that exceeds what our culture considers to be the aesthetically acceptable limits of body size and shape—but the same is also true of fat's mitigated appearance in the liquefied form of sweat. Occurring at the wrong time and/ or in the wrong place, sweat could be imagined as "fat out of place," capable of eliciting feelings of shame and disgust (Fusco 2004; Ravenau 2011; Shove 2003) as well as other emotions. As opposed to the unsolicited perspiration of the corpulent, sweat that is deliberately coaxed out of the body may be celebrated for the proof it offers that one is fighting the good fight against fat. Hence the fitness slogan "Sweat is fat crying," which one may find on posters and T-shirts in Britain and North America, stands as a reminder of the near equivalence of fat and sweat today as well as the debased, if not outright culpable, status of the former. The apparent transformation of "bad" adipose tissue into "good" sweat through the alchemy of exertion reveals another way of approaching the materiality of fat.

Contrary to Colls's claim, then, we do *not* consistently assume that fat is only something neatly contained within the skin. This may seem like a trivial point for those who equate fat with corpulence, but by drawing attention to this fact we may begin to approach the ways in which fat has a cultural status whose meanings are not exhausted by its reduction to the human body. Indeed, not only is fat considered to be capable of seeping from the bodily interior into the world, but it is commonly believed to migrate from outside to inside. If we explore cultural associations between fat and dirt, dietary fats provide perhaps the most intuitive example of how corpulence is imagined with reference to fats outside of the body. Nutritional discourses have fostered a commonsense correspondence between fatty foods and corpulence, giving rise to the commonsense notion that "fat makes fat," even when many physicians and nutritionists place greater emphasis on the fattening potential of carbohydrates.[3] Yet the *incorporation* of fatty and greasy foods may be perceived and experienced with a level of alarm that goes beyond medical concerns about health and fitness. Among Durif's (1992) French respondents, animal fats in particular evoked impressions of "heaviness," "invasion," and "rotting" as opposed to foods that were admired for being "light," "useful," and "*dégraissé*" (trimmed, skimmed, or degreased), which were often paired with bodily comportments suggesting a preoccupation with almost immaterial lightness. Similar perceptions were registered in Deborah Lupton's study of Australian attitudes toward nutrition, where participants typically distinguished "clean," "light," and "healthy" foods from those they perceived as "heavy" and "stodgy," while greasy and sticky fare was often aligned with the slimy and repellent. One respondent registered obvious fears of contamination when he contemplated "all that gooey, oily stuff" lurking within a particular kind of bread, while another described chicken and salad as "a very clean meal, very fresh, very colourful and no grease." Structurally opposed to the "clean" and "healthy," in this alimentary imaginary grease and fat are aligned with the "dark," "slimy," and "dirty" as well as the "unhealthy" (Lupton 1996: 82).

There is an obvious class dimension to such perceptions: since at least the 1960s perceptions of fatness, as well as the experience of ingesting fats and carbohydrates, have registered differently as one moves up the social ladder. Asked how they felt after eating a rich meal full of starches and fats, French respondents gave different answers according to their socioeconomic level, with agricultural and manual laborers far more likely to report sensations of being "full" or of "regaining strength." Among white-collar professionals such a repast was more likely to produce feelings of "heaviness," "nausea," and "drowsiness" and the sensation of being "weighed down" (Boltanski 1971). Such kinesthetic sensations have been readily translated into social taxonomies. This is why, as Pierre Bourdieu (1984: 178) observes, the bourgeoisie could be culturally primed to see in the popular classes a kind of "congenital coarseness" and in so doing to manifest a "class racism which associates the populace with everything heavy, thick and fat."

Today it is widely recognized that the popular classes tend to consume fattier foods, often out of economic necessity, and also tend to be fatter on average than elite groups who have more time and money to eat well and exercise regularly. Social distinctions are thus interarticulated, as they have been for centuries, with fears of coming into contact with a spectrum of aberrant substances, especially those that seem to have the capacity to rub off on and penetrate bodies. One of Durif-Bruckert's (2007: 154) informants even insisted that eating fatty foods was less disturbing than the idea that, after being ingested, such substances would be "in contact with me on the inside." Implicit in some of the overtly aesthetic and medical rationales that may prompt individuals to seek to lose weight, this fear of contamination by unctuous matter counts among the motivational techniques employed in the world of fitness and dieting. Monaghan (2008: 101) tells of a British gym instructor who would smear greasy food on a mannequin and "then ask members to visualize what their bodies would look like if their dietary intake was similarly visible." In this ostensibly visual exercise the possibility of physical contact with unctuousness is used to elicit the feelings of self-disgust that are the bread and butter of numerous fitness programs. As if to bring such images (literally) closer to home, a recent weight-loss plan calling itself the "My Pet Fat" program sells anatomical replicas of adipose tissue to display inside one's refrigerator as a means of discouraging people from overeating (Hardy 2013).

With fat positioned as a kind of "intimate other" that both is and is not part of the body, it is not surprising to find that anxieties about contamination are particularly acute among anorexics. Warin (2010: 106) found that the properties of certain greasy foods can be especially alarming to eating-disordered women, "not simply because of their fat content, but because of their form, their ability to move and seep into the cracks of one's body." Consider the example of Elise, a respondent who was not only anxious about the "dirty" feeling she experienced when coming into contact with butter but also "so concerned about oily substances being absorbed through her skin and congealing in her body that she stopped using hand creams, wouldn't wash her hair with shampoo or use lip balm to moisten her lips. Her rationale at the time was: 'Well, where does it go? It disappears into your body, and then what?'" (123; see also Lavis, in this volume).

If such highly charged reactions to various forms of fat blur the line between anxieties about weight gain and a more generalized fear of contamination, there remains a tacit yet durable association between fat as a question of morphology (i.e., corpulence) and the various fats and oils that exist within and outside of the body. In the United Kingdom and North America fat is even implicated in long-standing analogies drawn between the structure of the human body and that of the city, particularly in regard to the fats, oils, and grease that congeal and accumulate in sewers. As Simon Marvin and Will Medd (2006: 314) observe, fat not only "flows" through cities but also solidifies and hardens, causing blockages and immobility as well. Urban bodies and cities are thus sites of "multiple metabolisms." This co-formation of bodies and places has since the eighteenth century leveled attention at the noxious role of "toxins" in the body that may produce or be lurking within excess fat, with the excretory functions of the body likened to the sewer system of a city (Forth 2012), but it also resonates with contemporary claims that environmental toxins or "obesogens" (Saguy 2013) are the real culprits behind weight gain around the world. Hence a recent book promises to teach readers how to become *Clean, Green and Lean* (Crinnion 2010) by putting their bodies as well as their homes on diets. By widening the ways in which bodies are implicated in the built and lived environment, this perspective includes, but also goes beyond, Longhurst's (2005: 256) appeal to scholars "to write fat bodies *geographically.*" The richness of fat's materiality cannot be reduced to the corpulence of the human body.

So far this discussion has revolved mainly around the various ways in which fat is cited for its capacity to elicit disgust. Yet all of this talk of fat as dirt, pollution, and even excrement should not distract us from the richer potentialities of fat as a substance, many of which are not negative at all. As Colls (2007) shows, no matter how corpulence is perceived today, *fat* in its broadest sense remains expansive enough to retain many of its positive features. Despite our contemporary obsessions with thinness, and the near-skeletal slenderness of many fashion models, few people consider extreme emaciation to be an especially beautiful condition. Moreover, in some cases it is the pronounced *absence* of body fat that elicits discomfort and even disgust. This is relevant today among anorexics, whose food avoidance may produce disturbingly gaunt physiques, as well as HIV-positive individuals, who may experience disrupted fat distribution (lipodystrophy) due to certain drugs used to fight HIV (Graham 2005). The surgical technique of fat transfer (grafting unwanted fat from one part of the body to another) further suggests that aversion to body fat is also a matter of location. Thus the proverb that one "can never be too thin" doesn't entirely hold true.

Arguably it may be less fat per se that offends our aesthetic sensibilities than the appearance and even the sensation of fat "out of place" or in the wrong form.

Appreciation for fat does not end here, though. In gustatory terms mouthfeel, taste, and a sensation of satiety count among the most appreciated experiences associated with the ingestion of dietary fats, and in recent years the pleasurable qualities of lipids have come to be viewed as especially important in understanding weight gain. Several studies have shown how laboratory rats display a seemingly insatiable appetite for fats, which they would eat excessively if given an endless supply. More recent research even suggests that an ability to detect fattiness must be added to the other qualities we usually attribute to taste, alongside the sweet, sour, bitter, and so on. The ability to provide this luscious sensual experience, preferably without recourse to potentially unhealthy additives, is the aim of many food manufacturers (Bourne 2002; Mouritsen 2005). Thus the very gustatory enjoyment that fats offer—the sensual qualities that often encourage us to overindulge—seem closely bound up with their capacity to elicit disgust.

But there is still more to fat than this. If we acknowledge that fats may be viewed as "frozen oils" (Pond 1998: 6), then we clearly encounter them in liquid forms as well. Consider the essential oils prized in aromatherapy (Garreta 1998), the often exotic fats used in skin care products, or the array of oils and lubricants marketed for massage and other purposes. Notwithstanding contemporary aversions to saturated fats, even cooking oils can be considered "good" on nutritional and gastronomic grounds, especially when one considers the growing connoisseurship connected with extra-virgin olive oil in recent years (Meneley 2007). In such practices it is often the "purity" of the fat that enhances its appeal. Such appreciation even extends to the auditory realm, where music lovers may relish bass tones that are described as "fat" or "phat" because they are satisfyingly deep and rich. As a complex substance fat oscillates in interesting ways between the poles of purity and pollution, pleasure and disgust, evincing an inherent ambiguity that makes it an especially rich substance to think with.

All of this suggests that the problem of fat both *is* and *is not* a matter of corpulence as such. Rather, fat also pertains to a cluster of substances and qualities, ideals and anxieties, that trigger a range of reactions in our culture, both positive and negative. Scott-Dixon (2008: 29) is thus partly right when she describes fat as a "thing and idea [that] radiates outward from the tiny point of the adipocyte through individual body processes and experiences, through local communities and public structures, diffusing itself finally into global interconnected practices and systems of power." Rather than endorse such an anthropocentric approach to materiality we might equally propose that, as a substance and an idea, fat also resonates through material entanglements with a wide range of substances in which bodies and minds are implicated (Hodder 2012). Thus, in order to properly engage with the materiality of fat we must be open to the subtle interconnection between—and the properties of—these substances as they have been perceived and inflected at various times and in different contexts, both within and outside of bodies. But how do we approach such properties without leaving ourselves open to charges of materialism or essentialism? To what extent do the physical properties associated with fat structure the ways in which corpulence has been imagined?

CONCEPTUALIZING MATERIALITY

Materiality is a term that is used in a variety of ways in academic writing today and that means different things in various disciplines. Some approach materiality from the largely constructivist position of Judith Butler (1993: xviii), who argues for the discursive production of the material, or "*a process of materialization that stabilizes over time to produce the effect of boundary, fixity, and surface we call matter* [italics in the original]," in conjunction with "the materializing effects of regulatory power." What makes Butler's approach less useful for understanding the materiality of fat relates, as Pheng Cheah (1996) points out, to the fact that her conception of materiality refers almost exclusively to human bodies, and matter as such appears almost superstructural in relation to the discourses that seem to have a determining power over it. Aside from its apparent privileging of the cultural over the material, Butler's somatocentric approach seems less suited for the study of substances that exist both inside and outside of human bodies.

While Colls (2007) argues that matter and discourse are so mutually implicated that neither has a privileged determining status over the other, others approach fat as a substance that not only evades cultural determination but may be capable of structuring thought to some degree. In his very suggestive book *The Anatomy of Disgust*, historian William Miller (1997) suggests that there are limits to the extent to which culture can shape our experience of certain substances and aptly points out that bodily "excreta" (such as sperm, menstrual blood, feces, and urine) typically resist being arbitrarily lumped into innocuous categories except under special circumstances that are usually recognized as being exceptional. Contrary to Mary Douglas's (1966) well-known insistence on the role of cultural classification in the generation of responses to matter, Miller argues for the capacity of certain substances to motivate culture in their own right.[4] He could easily have added fat to his list of problematic substances, for it too has been historically viewed as a bodily excretion explicitly likened to urine and feces and, in some cases, described as one of their effects. "Like powerful masses in space," Miller (1997: 44) contends, such potent "substances have a gravitational attraction that bends social and cognitive structures along their lines of force." Miller uses fat as an example of this. Explicitly grounding his phenomenology of disgust in the experiences of Americans of his own social class, Miller discusses the sensation of having overindulged in fatty and sweet foods as both an instance of disgust as well as an experience capable of structuring thought: "Fat, oil, and syrupy sweetness structure the concept of cloying. . . . We believe our system not to be particularly efficient as a self-purifier with things that cloy, the very word attracted by alliteration to sister concepts of 'clinging' and 'cleaving unto' that make things hard to get rid of. Fat and sweet stick like glue and like the host of other nauseating things we think of as greasy and sweet. . . . Grease and fat conjure up images of indolence, otium, weak-willed lethargy, sliminess, unctuousness" (60–63).

Acknowledging that the potentialities of fat are richer than this, Miller (1997: 44) notes that the "gravitational attraction" of substances capable of eliciting disgust may also result in fascination, comfort, and even pleasure. This ambiguity is not germane only to fat. Carolyn Korsmeyer (2011: 8) has recently examined the curious "magnetism or allure" that even apparently "disgusting" objects may generate, especially in food and art. So too does Miller (1997: 121–22) concede that, despite the negativity that such substances may evoke, "the greasy and the sweet continue to allure us with their taste. They have the capacity to make us eat more of them than we wish; they are will-weakening or will-deviating." Examples of fats' capacity to exercise a kind of agency can be multiplied. The fatty acids in certain foods, for instance, have been shown to alter moods, decreasing sadness and promoting a sense of well-being implied in the notion of "comfort foods" (Oudenhove et al. 2011). Arguing from a vital materialist theoretical position, Jane Bennett (2010: 41) takes this emphasis on the tendencies of fats a step further to remind us that "certain lipids promote particular human moods or affective states," with effects ranging from a reduction in violence among prisoners and learning improvements among certain schoolchildren to diminished memory (at least in laboratory rats). Rather than using this information to bolster a reductive or mechanical causality, as is common in nutritional science, she proposes that we approach the human encounter with lipids as a complex "assemblage in which persons and fats are participants" (42). By affording these substances a degree of agency, then, Bennett leaves room for "the strivings and trajectories of fats as they weaken or enhance the power of human wills, habits, and ideas" (43).

On one level such analyses support Colls's (2007: 355) call for an "intra-active" perspective that "shifts the focus from what fat represents, to what matter is capable of doing." Yet while in apparent agreement with Colls's statement that fat "has its own capacities to act and be active" (358), Miller and Bennett emphasize the life that fat has outside of its relationship with human bodies and culture. This way of thinking about materiality resonates with recent work on material culture generated in anthropology and archaeology. While conceding the obvious relevance of social constructionist ideas, many scholars in these fields would agree with Nicole Boivin (2008) that the physicality of the material world is not simply a "text" to be interpreted but a reality with properties and dimensions that cannot be completely reduced to social determinants. Indeed, Boivin (2008: 47) writes, "[I]n many cases, ideas and cultural understandings do not precede, but rather are helped into becoming, by the material world and human engagement with it. . . . Human thought has not only used the world as a prop for expressing itself, but has, in fact, often been enabled by that world." This suggests that material symbols are not completely arbitrary in relation to the concepts they signify but refer as well to "a physicality which resists and enables" (Boivin 2004: 6) and which plays an active role in the construction of meaning (Strang 2005). To borrow Ian Hodder's (2011) felicitous phrase, then, we might conclude that the body does not engage in "material entanglements" only with objects but also with substances (both of human and nonhuman origin) that are on some level considered to be at once part of, yet at the same time somewhat dissimilar to, the body.

If material culture studies offers useful ways of conceptualizing fat as a physical reality, the traditionally object-oriented nature of this field renders the study of fat somewhat unusual. The structure and substances of living bodies are rarely objects of analysis in this area, where the focus is largely restricted to the analysis of human remains and nonhuman artifacts and objects. Joanna Sofaer (2006: 67–68) takes issue with this state of affairs: "If we take on board the general point that physical qualities and material consequences are an inseparable dimension and defining parameter of semiotic significance, and we accept that bodies do have such significance, we might ask why an exploration of material qualities should apply only to objects and not to bodies, especially since objects can be regarded as bodies and bodies as objects." Jean-Pierre Warnier (2007: 11n5) seconds this view, pointing out that "most, if not all, of our gestures are propped against, and shaped by, the objects and substances we are in contact with in motion and agency." Of course, being without definite form, substances like fat are not quite "objects" like those ordinarily studied as material culture (Hahn and Soentgen 2010), and substances in general have not yet received their due in anthropology (Carsten 2004, 2011). However, fat does count as a *thing* in Hodder's (2012: 7) broad definition of the term: it fits into the category of contained entities that "create bundles of presence or duration in the continual flows of matter, energy and information." Despite its lack of form, then, fat participates in the broadest sense of objectness when we consider that the word *object* is derived from the idea of "throwing in the way." Objects thus are not merely formed matter but are things with the capacity to assert themselves, to resist or "object" in their relationship with subjects. Fat thus shares in the overall "objectness, the stand-in-the-wayness to things that resists, that forms, that entraps and entangles," as Hodder puts it (13).

Like all substances fats and oils possess a nearly "infinite richness" of properties and tendencies (Hahn and Soentgen 2010), and one of the challenges of dealing with the materiality of fat is that the term does not refer to a single stable substance. When broadly understood, fat shares many of the qualities that are semiotically bundled together in olive oil, including luminous, permeable, cleansing, and warming properties (Meneley 2008; on qualisigns, see Keane 2005; on qualia, see Chumney and Harkness 2013). Yet many of the qualities of olive oil are also present in other fats derived from human, animal, and even plant sources, which encourages us to identify olive oil as an especially valued exemplar of a wider set of fats and oils (Forth, in this volume). The materiality of fat is thus complex and ambiguous, presenting a wide range of properties and tendencies that are capable of being pressed into any number of social, cultural, and political services. Fat, as well as things designated as being fatty, are located within as well as outside of the body.

Fat: Culture and Materiality is therefore a deliberately cross-disciplinary volume. Like the substance that constitutes its main focus, it defies easy categorization and takes on a number of forms. Following chapters on the politics of Palestinian olive oil and the attractions of artisanal fatty pork in North Carolina, it considers the material sources of ancient stereotypes about fat people as well as the function of fat as a healing substance in the artworks of Joseph Beuys. Two central chapters shift the focus onto contemporary bodily terrain as fat is examined as a threatening agent in the embodied experiences of anorexics but also as a substance with biovalue when unwanted fat cells are surgically grafted from one bodily area to another. The final two chapters examine the experience and representation of bodily fat in the lived sartorial experiences of plus-sized women and in spectacles of celebrity weight loss in which the lost materiality of fat is dramatized and prized as a means of erasing specters of one's former self.

Despite being a collection of individual studies of fat, this volume does not quite qualify as a work of fat studies in that it approaches issues of materiality in ways that are, as of yet, unusual in the field.[5] Yet even though these chapters examine aspects of materiality, few of them really qualify as material culture studies either, not least because, at the moment, when that field addresses "the body" it is generally as human remains rather than as the substances and capacities of living bodies (Sofaer 2006). By expanding the ways in which the study of fat is usually approached, this volume makes a somewhat unique contribution both to fat studies and to material culture studies, as well as to the critical study of the body, where scholars in a range of fields generally prefer to view flesh and bone through their representation in culture (Cheah 1996). Agreeing with Daniel Miller (2010: 6) that "we too are stuff," we may take Warnier's (2001: 10) point that since "there is hardly any technique of the body that does not incorporate a given materiality," there are no reasonable grounds to "divorce material culture studies from the study of the body, and vice versa, as is largely the case at present." By approaching fat as a substance that is neither neutral nor passive in relation to culture, this collection explores ways of approaching living bodies as both engaging with and constituting forms of material culture.

If the material richness of fat defies casual attempts to simplistically denigrate this substance, then perhaps there is a way beyond the disgust that so often colors our views of fat bodies today. In *Vibrant Matter* Bennett (2010: 12–13) proposes that one path to human happiness is "*to raise the status of the materiality of which we are composed* [italics in the original]" so that, by accepting that each human is composed of "wonderfully vibrant, dangerously vibrant, matter," we might achieve a situation in which "the status of the shared materiality of all things is elevated." To achieve this frame of mind, of course, means accepting the complexity of human being in all of its rich materiality.

1 THE QUALITIES OF PALESTINIAN OLIVE OIL

Anne Meneley

Olive oil is a fat, an ancient fat, one that has been valued across time and space but not always in the same way. This diversity of values arises from the materiality of this fat, which gives it a powerful semiotic potential. This chapter builds on my previous investigation of how the sensuous materiality of olive oil affords substrates for various potential meanings. As Webb Keane (2003) argues is the case with all material objects, olive oil bundles together a semiotic surplus of sensuous qualities. In any given case, some of these qualisigns become meaning and belong to the object's life as a sign, and others remain mute and belong to the object's life as a thing but retain a potential for mediating the career of the object as a sign or as a thing. In the case of olive oil, the relevant bundle of qualisigns includes luminosity, liquidity, the capacity to cleanse, the capacity to seal or preserve, the capacity to insulate, the capacity to burn, and a lack of miscibility in water. In my previous work on the topic (2008), I focused on how these various sensuous qualities made olive oil such a prominent substance in ritual practices in the circum-Mediterranean religions. I suggested that olive oil might, in certain contexts, be a material diagnostic of the sacred (2008: 305). Olive oil, of course, does not have a universal or unitary meaning that remains unchanged throughout time or space, but the various qualisigns of olive oil allow different aspects of the same substance to become meaningful in this or that religious context, with the net result that the substance in general, with all its material potentialities, rather than any specific quality of the substance, comes to be associated with the sacred across a wide range of different religions.

This chapter examines how the protean nature of olive oil and its sensuous qualities (here its luminosity and capacity to cleanse, seal, and preserve) are politically charged in contemporary Palestine. In addition, I note that in contemporary discourses there is a shift from olive oil and its properties to the tree that produces it, particularly the qualities of rootedness and durability. Theoretically, this chapter draws on my earlier work on the qualisigns of olive oil, which afford, but do not determine, certain meanings and practices. Somewhat counterintuitively, I also draw on earlier work on foie gras production, in which my coauthor Deborah Heath and I used the work of animal ethicist Temple Grandin, who proposes an idea, and attendant practices, of an "ethics of care" whereby humans and nonhuman actors are seen as coproducers in food production (Heath and Meneley 2011). I draw on the work of amateur ethnographer and medical doctor Taufik Canaan, particularly his book *Mohammedan Saints and Sanctuaries in Palestine* (1927). In his work, we see very much an ethics of care between humans, olive trees, and saints in early twentieth-century Palestine. While in the post-1948 period, after the Nakba and the establishment of the state of Israel, the Jaffa orange was the symbol of the exiled Palestinian refugees, until the early 1980s the olive tree (singular) came to stand for the Palestinian people (singular) in nationalist discourses. As the Palestinians began to transform their olive oil production beginning in the 1990s, the oil from the nationalist tree became bound up with particular images of the "Palestinian farmer" as it is itself transformed in a new production practice that is destined for the palates of sympathetic consumers abroad. Key to the marketing of this new oil is the highlighting of the depredations that have been visited on Palestinian olive trees of late.

OLIVE OIL IN THE MEDITERRANEAN

Olive oil, cultivated since the Bronze Age, has long been central to the devotional practices of the monotheistic traditions, such as Judaism, Christianity, and Islam, and has also been a central culinary element for the members of these traditions who resided in the Mediterranean region. It has been, and could be, a unifying element among peoples of different religions, a shared polysemy afforded by various material qualities of olive oil that flowed between the cracks of different religions. In the Muslim tradition, members of all three monotheistic religions are described as *Ahl al Kitab*, or "Peoples of the Book," implicitly recognizing their common roots. In Islam, olive oil is referred to as *zayt nur Allah* ("oil is the light of God"). Olive oil is used in Christian rituals to facilitate one's entrance into the world (baptism) and exit from it (extreme unction). Olive oil was central to the ancient Israelites, as the first pressed oil was given to the priesthood and used to light the menorah in the Jerusalem temple (Porter 1993: 35; see also Frankel, Avitsur, and Ayalon 1994: 22). A shared Mediterranean valuing of olive oil for ritual, cure, beautification, and nurture was effectively torn asunder with the establishment of the state of Israel in 1948, when the separation of the monotheistic Peoples of the Book and the question of who owns the land came to the forefront in a fashion that surpassed the centuries of competition for the Holy Land. Several decades later, the question of who "owns" olive oil and the olive tree began to surface as a point of contention. The religious and ritual use of olive oil and olive trees have become fused in the contemporary political context. This chapter focuses on how the qualities of this ancient fat, which was one of the world's first commodities, and the tree from which it is derived, have become politicized.

Olive oil was and is central in the everyday religiosity of Palestinians, both Muslims and Christians. The olive tree is known as *shijara mubaraka* (the blessed tree) and *shijara an-nur* (the tree of light). Canaan's (1927) *Mohammedan Saints and Sanctuaries in Palestine* discusses how in the past, shrines of Christian and Muslim saints dotted the landscape, often on hilltops, accompanied by sacred trees, often olive trees. Olive oil was offered at saints' shrines and in churches more than any other substance in exchange for the granting of a vow. The worldview described by Canaan transcended or underlay more formal religious practices and distinctions and was shared by Muslims and Christians as well as by local Jews (Tamari 2009: 93–112). Canaan was dedicated to recording the traditions of Palestinian farmers and to establishing connections between biblical and contemporary Palestinian religious practices. Canaan's book was published by the Palestine Oriental Society, whose journal that lasted exactly as long as the British Mandate in Palestine. Canaan's dual role as a medical doctor and amateur ethnographer put him in a position to see some tragic ironies as the British Mandate Palestine died with the birth of the state of Israel, or as the Palestinians call it *Al-Nakba* ("the disaster"). Canaan was at that moment the head of the leprosy clinic in Jerusalem. Almost immediately, the Israelis decided that the Palestinian lepers were to be expelled from their fellow suffering Jewish lepers as their religious affiliations were deemed more important than their status as generic outcasts resulting from a disease famed in biblical lore. As the noted Palestinian sociologist and historian Salim Tamari points out, this little-known and absurd move was a signal for the kind of policies of separation and exclusion that have become yet more pronounced in contemporary Israel and the occupied West Bank (2009: 93–94). For the purposes of this chapter, I examine the material qualities of olive oil that made it such a prominent feature in the religious rituals of the monotheistic traditions in the Mediterranean.

ABSORBING AND PENETRATING

The two qualisigns of olive oil that make it particularly effective for carrying blessings between the material and immaterial worlds are its capacity to absorb and its capacity to penetrate into porous surfaces, like skin. Olive oil swiftly absorbs smells, which makes it an ideal compound for making perfume as well as for anointing and for cooking, as in the flavored oils of the culinary world. Canaan's many examples indicate that olive oil was the ideal substance for absorbing *baraka* (benevolent power) from holy places, that is, saints' tombs where oil is given as part of religious vows. Canaan refers to the capacity of substances and objects to absorb the holy as "contact magic," which bears a strong resemblance to James Frazer's notion of "contagious magic," which depends on proximity to the sacred. It is indexical as opposed to iconic, as is Frazer's "sympathetic magic," which depends on mimicry. However, as I have argued elsewhere (Meneley 2008) it is a material quality of olive oil, specifically its absorptive capacity, that makes it an ideal vehicle for conveying the sacred. For instance, Canaan, in describing how olive oil was used in saints' shrines, says, "From the oil of the lamps, which may be used to rub one's hands and face, one receives a more lasting barakeh" (1927: 94). The quali-sign of permeability, olive oil's capacity to penetrate porous surfaces, facilitates the transference of the sacred to the person as a blessing. It can also be used as a cure. Olive oil absorbs the sacred by its proximity to it, and sometimes this endows the oil with curative powers; rheumatic or neuralgic patients, referred to as suffering from *asabi* (nervous and mental disorders), rub their foreheads and joints with oil from shrines (106, 112).[1]

ILLUMINATION

One of the visual effects of olive oil is its capacity to produce light. Canaan's (1927: 8) work shows how, in the early twentieth century, the light of olive oil lamps was central to daily devotional practices, as offerings in various Christian and Muslim saints' shrines. He notes the ubiquity of oil lamps scattered about in the saints' shrines. In order to produce light, olive oil must change its form. A key qualisign of olive oil is its combustibility: it is a fluid, a material, and through the process of combustion becomes dematerialized to form light and smoke. Alfred Gell (1977) argues that smoke has the capacity to connect the material and the immaterial in its transformative process. Olive oil in an oil lamp is halfway between thing and energy, between liquid and light, evoking a merging of the material and the transcendent (Meneley 2008: 312) Despite the sometimes unsightly effect of oil stains on the walls of the *qubba*, or shrine, which Canaan notes, it is also the *performance* of religious acts, such as making oaths or vows, lighting lamps, and burning incense, that makes a place holy and indicates that it is indeed inhabited by a holy person (1927: 12, 46).[2] So there is a reciprocal effect: the oil is able to absorb the holy by its proximity to the shrine, but the vows, oil offerings, and lamplighting are practices that themselves *verify* that a holy being—a saint or a shaykh—inhabits the shrine.

The Palestinians of the early twentieth century were engaged in an ethics of care that included people, saints, trees, and olive oil in a series of exchange relationships that were guided by concepts of respect and reciprocity. For instance, petitioners would make a vow to offer a jug of olive oil to the saint's shrine if their child recovers from an illness or if a long lost son returned home safely from North America (Canaan 1927: 137). If a petitioner wanted to take oil infused with baraka from a shrine, it had to be replaced with new oil; "if this is neglected, the holy oil may produce a result opposite to that intended" (113). There were also exchanges between the shrine's visitors: a donor of an olive oil lamp might also leave matches to allow unknown petitioners the opportunity to light oil lamps too, as a form of charity for which the donor would be rewarded. Even the wicks of spent olive oil lamps in a shrine could have curative powers; women would sometimes swallow them in an attempt to cure infertility (112). People created moral selves out of appropriate comportment, which took work: relationships with the saints, like those with other people, did not just exist but needed constant attention. Sometimes people brought oil even if they had not made a vow, as "[i]t [the gift without a request] is believed [to] please the saint, who favours the giver" (145). Although most people at that time may not have been able to afford it, "animal sacrifice please[d] these holy men because so many of the poor are fed in their names" (172). One person's offering to the saint became a collective good in an ethics of care that is social as well as individual.

Improper behavior, like urinating in the shrine, could be punished. Taking oil without replacing it was regarded as stealing and could involve a warning, as is evident in the following anecdote: "A wayfarer took oil from a shrine to fry his eggs, but as soon as he poured it in the pan, it turned to blood so he returned the oil which was once again simple oil" (Canaan 1927: 255). The saintly oil itself, in this instance, was thought to display agency.

"Olive trees enjoy special honour in Palestine," notes Canaan (1927: 108), as does the "*shijarah mubaraka*," which comes from Paradise "and is the most noble among all the plants" (Fahr er-Razi quoted in Canaan 1927: 31n5). People swore "by the life of the Tree of light" or "by that one [God] who put the oil in the olives" (Canaan 1927: 143). Trees were often associated with shrines and holy places and were sometimes depicted as actors themselves. And the trees themselves were often venerated by extension: votive rags were often fastened on a holy tree associated with the shrine, and these became infused with baraka, which would pass on to a person who took the infused rag along on a journey. Through the shrines and the holy trees, individuals could access the divine. Cutting down a holy tree for a pragmatic purpose, such as for making charcoal, was another offense that would provoke the saint to wreak vengeance (36). Taking olives from a saint's olive tree without permission would cause retribution, as in Canaan's anecdote about a boy who stole olives from the trees of the saint, causing thunder and lightning, which so scared the boy that he threw the olives back and his mother immediately vowed to bring a gift to the saint as recompense (255).

In the early twentieth century, Canaan notes that the things vowed and offered were most often for upkeep, decoration, and repair of the shrines. "Most of the offerings which belong to this group are so simple and cheap that even the poorest peasant is able to offer something" (1927: 142). Olive oil with its qualities of combustibility was then, and still is, the perfect offering for making contact with the sacred. As Canaan notes, "Olive oil is vowed and offered more than anything else. Peasants and townsmen, Christians and Mohammedans, rich and poor vow oil, and it may be offered to any sort of sanctuary" (142). Canaan is speaking of the community in Palestine at the time, where access to the sacred was relatively egalitarian in these forms of practices, since the poor as well as the rich had access to olive oil, and the uneducated as well as the educated could make a vow and an offering. Canaan is speaking of a time when most families had olive trees that produced the fat, olive oil, which was considered essential not only for physical health but also for spiritual well-being. As I discuss below, with the confiscation of Palestinian land and the destruction of their olive trees in recent years, the physical as well as the spiritual well-being of Palestinians has been jeopardized.

LUBRICATING, STRENGTHENING, CLEANSING, SEALING, PRESERVING

Just as it does for oil lamps, olive oil provides fuel for humans for work and for sex. Olive oil is also implicated very intimately in the physical as well as the social reproduction of the family. One of my Palestinian consultants, a jolly man with a great laugh, said that olive oil is particularly important for sex, as sex requires energy. Explaining that it was particularly important for men with two wives, he related a funny anecdote about how his friend had told him that after sex with one wife, he would drink a cup of olive oil, which goes straight to his knees, to allow them to become strong (*qowi*) again. My consultant said he did not know whether this was true or not because he didn't have two wives! He also said that it used to be customary for a mother to give her virginal daughter a cup of olive oil on her wedding night to use as a lubricant. Again, eyes twinkling, he said he couldn't empirically verify this himself because he was not a virginal daughter. The products of sexual unions, newborn babies, were also treated with olive oil: their induction into the social world was lubricated by massaging them with oil for the first seven days of their lives, when they were referred to as "the oiled" (*mazayit*). Olive oil was at the center of an ethics of care between farm animals and their owners, who depended on them for milk or meat. I was told by one consultant, a veterinarian, that a cow's vagina would be massaged with oil if she was having difficulty giving birth. A mixture of salt and oil was used for stomach troubles in animals (salt to disinfect and oil to lubricate), and the same mixture was used for surface wounds as well. I learned of other proverbs at an animated meeting with consultants who are passionate about olive oil: "Oil is the centerpost of the house" (*zayt imad al-bayt*) and "Oil strengthens the structure (of the body)" (*zayt masaamir al hasab*). Olive oil is perceived as itself intimately bound up with the biological and social reproduction of Palestinian households and families and healthful, strong bodies. So central to the reproduction of human and animal life, olive oil production is now under threat. It is this strengthening capacity of olive oil that makes it a central image of Palestinian resistance to the Israeli occupation, often referred to as *sumood*, or steadfastness.

Indeed, olive trees are often spoken of as kin, the older trees as grandparents and the younger ones as children, for which one would care as if it were one's own child. People spoke of their trees with great affection, especially the long-lived ones, which are often given names and serve as orienting markers in olive groves. In one interview, an olive oil professional with a great interest in the way in which the nature of the olive tree is embedded in culture, told me of an old proverb (using the voice of an olive tree): "If you want me to be more productive, you'll keep my sisters away from me." He explained that under Palestinian environmental conditions olive trees produce more fruit when well spaced. However, what I found interesting was not the functionalist interpretation of "agricultural advice in a proverb" but rather the interpolation of the olive tree as an actor, a kind of coproducer of its own care. It also represents a reciprocity between tree and farmer, an ethics of care that goes beyond material gain, cogenerating productivity and well-being for both people and tree.

CLEANSING, SEALING, STRENGTHENING, PRESERVING

The cleansing quality of olive oil is evident in the practice of many older Palestinians, who drink half a teacup of olive oil every morning as it is believed to help cleanse and keep the digestive tract regular or treat constipation. The capacity to cleanse is not evident only in the use of olive oil for the interior of the body; it is also used on the body's exterior. Olive oil is used to make olive oil soap, for which Palestine is famous, especially for that from the mountainous Nablus region. The place it plays in the popular Palestinian imagination is evident in the following proverb: "That guy is so dirty, all the soap in Nablus won't clean him," implying not only physical filth but also moral corruption. For centuries it was an important commodity in regional trade networks (Doumani 1995). It even reached farther sites: olive oil soap from Nablus was reputed to be the favored soap of Queen Elizabeth I (1533–1603), daughter of Henry VIII. Olive oil soap from Nablus now has a different trajectory: like extra-virgin olive oil, it now travels abroad as a fair trade commodity.

The production and consumption of olive oil in Palestine goes far beyond a subsistence strategy, but it is important to remember the oil's contribution to the Palestinian diet as it provides calories and nutrients. Long before there were scientific claims about the nutritional benefits of olive oil, it was considered a nutrient that, according to a Palestinian consultant, keeps one in good health (*sahaa*). As noted above, olive oil is said to strengthen the body. Canaan (1927: 144) invokes a proverb that illustrates how olive oil was considered superior to even expensive, valued fat like *samna* (clarified butter):

> The following story will illustrate the belief that olive oil strengthens the body more than melted butter (samneh). A wife had a son of her own and a step son. Both were shepherds. Every day before they drove the animals into the fields she gives her own son—who was always preferred—bread and samneh, while the other received no more than bread dipped in oil. After finishing their meals both used to wipe their hands by rubbing them on their sticks. The stick of the son was soon hollowed out by weevils, while that of his step-brother became harder and stronger.

Once again, we see the strengthening and preserving capacity of olive oil highlighted. Olive oil is particularly important to poorer farmers as most of them have olive trees, which provide a nutritionally rich fat that is far superior to the cheap cooking oils that (like other food products) are packaged in Israel and flood the Palestinian market. Palestinians are forced to use these inferior oils, which do not have the sacred associations that olive oil does, if their olive trees are confiscated, cut down, or burned and they cannot afford to buy olive oil. One of the Palestinians I talked to said that if they have oil and bread, they can survive anything; others add the beloved aromatic herb mix *za'atar* (composed of wild thyme, sumac, and sesame seeds), which is often served with oil and bread, to the list of essential survival foods. Another qualisign of olive oil is its immiscibility in water. This quality made it important in preserving pickles of various kinds and cucumbers. The oil floats on top of the water and prevents any fungus from entering the pickles and ruining them.

Erasures

Canaan (1927) notes that early in the twentieth century, the fame of localities was established by the local saints and their tombs, which were visited to make oil offerings.

For instance, Qalandiya was known for its saint, Es-shaykh Imbarakeh (1927: 61). Now it is known for the Israeli checkpoint that cuts Ramallah off from Jerusalem. It is a site of humiliation for West Bank Palestinians; it "steals" their time (Peteet 2008) and their productive energy and prevents the flow of their agricultural goods, including olive oil, into Jerusalem. Similarly, in Canaan's time, the village of Deir Yassin was famous for the tomb of Es-shaykh Yasin, but this reputation was replaced by its more dubious fame as the site of the 1948 Israeli massacre of 254 Palestinians, led by Menachem Begin and the Stern Gang, a moment that, in the words of the Israeli historian Ilan Pappé (2007: 90–92), was central to the "ethnic cleansing of Palestine."

This is more than a Weberian "disenchantment of the world." Rather, it marks a more violent and hardened confrontation between an ethics of care that is sensitive to seasonal and ritual time and a profoundly unethical exertion of technologies and bureaucracies of control over the Palestinian population by the Israelis; this is resulting in what Beshara Doumani (2004: 10), a historian of olive production in the once-wealthy Nablus district, calls "the slow and cruelly systematic asphyxiation of an entire social formation."

Canaan's rich ethnography bears witness to prior meanings and practices enabled by the material qualities of olive oil. These meanings are now being erased by the threatened disappearance of the substance itself, Palestinian olive oil, and particularly by the destruction of the trees that produce it and mark the land of the producers. To move from the fat, olive oil itself, to the tree from which it is produced is a logical transition as the land itself is under threat. Loss of oil indexes loss of land and loss of the trees that produce the oil: in short, it indexes the contemporary plight of the Palestinians. Attention shifts from the oil to the tree. Palestinians who have their land confiscated, or their trees uprooted or poisoned, lose a means of livelihood and also a means of accessing the sacred through engaging in offerings of olive oil for spiritual benefit. Under the current conditions of occupation dispossessed Palestinians become delinked from the sacred, their land, their food, and their fellow Palestinians. This is particularly true in Bethlehem and Bayt Jala. Bethlehem is the long-standing center of olive wood carving in the West Bank, a notable source of souvenirs from the Holy Land. For centuries tourists have been purchasing olive wood crèches, olive wood figurines of camels and sheep, and olive wood crosses and rosaries as religious commodities that carry the cachet of the Holy Land. Olive wood is hard, durable, and beautifully veined. When freshly cut it retains quite powerfully the scent of the oil.[3] Yet over the past two decades, especially during the 2000s, Bethlehem has been severely hit by land confiscations for settlements, the Separation Wall, and the checkpoint leading to Jerusalem, as well as various army outposts that are now slated to become settlements. Up to 70 percent of the land in the Bethlehem district is now under Israeli control.[4] I was told by an olive wood carver whose family had been in Bethlehem for five centuries that most of his land had been confiscated to build the checkpoint. Some of his trees are still there (for now), but his family cannot harvest them or they will be shot by the soldiers at the checkpoint. Because of the confiscation of land and trees, olive wood for carving has become scarce. Small vials of oil from Bethlehem have similarly been sold for centuries (this is an ancient practice for bringing home blessings from the Holy Land [Coleman and Elsner 1995: 85]), but now the olive oil comes from a Christian village, Zababda, in the Jenin district, as Bethlehem oil is so scarce. For most Bethlehem families, once self-sufficient in olive oil, the confiscation of land and trees has meant that they do not have enough olive oil to see their families through the year until the next harvest. As my olive wood carver friend told me, "We still must give oil to the church," to burn in the lamps of the Church of the Nativity, which should never go out. The poor are the most vulnerable to the loss of olive oil not only as food but also as a spiritual donation. Thus, the Israeli land confiscations have had an effect not only on the Palestinian diet but also on the capacity of Palestinians to interact with the sacred via olive oil. Antwan, whose family owns some of the most valuable olive oil–producing land in Palestine, told me that his first obligation was to provide his family with olive oil, the second obligation was to give olive oil to the church, and the third was to give olive oil to the poor in the community. The latter is considered an obligation, but it is an obligation that brings God's blessings in return. This was very important to Antwan but might soon be a moot point. Several years ago, the Israelis rezoned his land, located in the valley underneath the illegal settlement of Gilo, to become part of Jerusalem, meaning that he needs special permission from the army to access his trees.[5]

DURABILITY AND ROOTEDNESS

There are certain qualisigns of the olive tree that appear in Palestinian nationalist discourse in a way that is different from the kinship or religious imagery that was evident in the early twentieth century. Indeed, in nationalist discourses it is the qualities of the tree itself, rather than the oil it produces, that are highlighted. In such discourses the *durability*, *longevity*, and *rootedness* of the olive tree, not its holy status, are foregrounded. The semiotic link between the olive tree and the qualities of the people is a relatively recent development. Nasser Abufarha (1998) notes that up until the 1982 expulsion of the Palestine Liberation Organization from Lebanon, the lemon trees of Jaffa had been the key symbol of the Palestinians in exile who led the resistance. After that the resistance movement looked inward to the occupied West

Bank and found the olive tree as a symbol of Palestinian nationalism. It appears as a symbol of "steadfastness" (sumood), standing for Palestinian rootedness on *their* land, and as a symbol of political resistance to the occupation and confiscation of the land.[6] It is associated with steadfastness against oppression, and the qualities of the tree become associated with qualities of persons. For instance, when Sari Nusseibeh, now the president of Al-Quds University in Jerusalem and a member of one of the famous old families of Jerusalem, was imprisoned by the Israelis, he was described by a fellow prisoner and nationalist as "the steadfast olive tree" (Nusseibeh 2007: 333). The qualisigns of durability and rootedness figure prominently in the semiotic metadiscourses that insert olive trees squarely into nationalist discourses. Under normal circumstances, olive trees can live thousands of years. Their presence on the terraced land of the West Bank, terraces that are clearly man-made structures that required considerable labor to build and maintain, gives the lie to the Zionist myth of a land without people. The olive tree's deep roots and its capacity to throw up shoots even after the tree has been cut down provide a vital symbol of Palestinian rootedness in the ground (Abufarha 1998). The fact that olive trees are reemerging decades later in former Palestinian villages destroyed in Al-Nakba (which had been planted over with pine trees) is celebrated as the indomitable spirit of the olive tree and the steadfastness of the villager (Pappé 2007: 227–28). Evidence of the olive tree's presence in Palestine can be traced back to 8000 B.C.E. (Rosenblum 1997), and thus, according to Abufarha (1998), it became a prominent symbol in the student movement in the 1970s and 1980s, which focused on Palestinian nationalism, along with the revival of long-lapsed Palestinian folklore. This version of the nationalist movement looked for forebears, the Canaanites, who according to the Bible preceded the Hebrew prophets.[7]

THE NEW OLIVE OIL

A new Palestinian olive oil has emerged since the Second Intifada that began in 2000, when Israel implemented yet more severe policies of closure in the West Bank. Low-skilled jobs were once plentiful in Israel, but now permits, checkpoints, and the Separation Wall have meant that there has been a kind of re-ruralization of Palestine (Tamari 1981). With few other options, people are turning back to the land to try to make a living. Olive oil has proven an obvious choice. Again the quality of durability is key: olive oil is relatively durable in the sense that it can withstand longer delays at borders than agricultural produce like fruits and vegetables. The need to export olive oil was met by a need to find markets for Palestinian olive oil as traditional export markets disappeared. Jordan closed its borders to Palestinian oil several years ago. The export of Palestinian oil to the Gulf states more or less dried up with the mass expulsion of the large expatriate Palestinian community following the Iraqi invasion of Kuwait in 1990. The once-vibrant trading connections between Palestinian cities and Amman, Damascus, and Beirut have been truncated and determined by the Israelis' military actions and their stranglehold on borders and what kinds of commodities, as well as people, can cross them. The current markets available for Palestinian oil are further afield: Britain, the European Union (EU), the United States, Canada, Australia, New Zealand, and Japan. The most successful of these initiatives has been fair trade Palestinian olive oil; in the promotional material the dire situation faced by the Palestinian farmers is outlined in detail. Even for the fair trade market, however, the quality of the oil must be extra-virgin. Experts, mostly French, Spanish, and Italian, funded by foreign aid, have been advising Palestinians and providing infrastructural aid to transform their production practices to produce olive oil that will accord with international standards. Extra-virgin Palestinian olive oil is expensive (in part because of the myriad fees that are required to get it through Israeli ports), and consumers who pay $15 to $20 for it want a quality product. The other factor is that North Atlantic tastes for olive oil have been cultivated by the international standards set by the International Olive Oil Council, which ranks very low-acidity oil as the prestige extra-virgin olive oil.

As noted above, olive oil was used traditionally to treat gastrointestinal blockages. It is ironic that now it is fair trade Palestinian olive oil that is used to "treat" the blockages of the occupation: despite all the obstacles, fair trade olive oil manages to circulate, albeit less than smoothly, to customers in northern Europe, North America, Japan, and Australia. This commodity's circulation is facilitated by imaginaries of sympathy with the suffering of the Palestinian people. *Extra-virgin* is a legal and bureaucratic term, not one that is in common usage in Palestine except among the new olive oil professionals. The determination of a single qualisign, "extra-virgin," has technical, scientific, and aesthetic aspects. Extra-virginity is now primarily determined by a chemical test for acidity level: legally, the term *extra-virgin* can be used only to denote an olive oil that has less than 0.8 percent acidity.

Yet there are consequences for this transformation of olive oil. In the production of extra-virgin olive oil in Palestine for export, uniformity and conformity to international and EU standards are a must. In speaking of olive oil, people will refer to the distinctive oil of Bayt Jala or Nablus or Jenin. But as Palestinian oil is exported under fair trade nongovernmental organizations, the local specificity and the individual farmer get lost in the oil's evocation of "Palestine" and the "Palestinian farmer." A semiotic flattening happens when focus is put on the importance of the production of olive oil as staking a claim to the land that Palestinians already own but that is under continual threat of confiscation. Symbolic meanings have been flattened in favor of highlighting another form of materiality: olive oil's monetary worth on the market, enabling the livelihood of the Palestinian farmer. A grade of extra-virgin also ensures that an oil can be sold at a higher price, which has an important pragmatic effect for Palestinian farmers, who have few wage-labor opportunities after the construction of the Separation Wall. This has meant a dramatic transformation in the qualisigns highlighted in contemporary Palestinian olive oil: to be salable abroad, olive oil must be determined to be extra-virgin, a quality that does not refer to the spiritual world but rather to an internationally recognized domain of connoisseurship. It has also meant a transformation in how value is determined: technoscientific chemical analyses and international organoleptic tests now determine an oil's value. In the past, an oil's value was closely connected to its belonging to a family, grown on their land. As I have joked with Palestinian friends, every Palestinian farmer thinks his own olive oil is the best. So we see a movement from bodily memory and taste, from family meals enhanced by the thick, dark green, high-acidity oil, to formal organoleptic and chemical testing, focusing on qualities that are valued by virtue of expert intervention and scientific expertise.

In the marketing of Palestinian olive oil, the conditions of production under the Israeli occupation are highlighted. These conditions are not palpably discernible in the taste of the oil itself, which conforms to international standards. Rather, the consumer needs to be informed discursively. In an interview with me in 2006, a Palestinian olive oil producer, holding aloft a bottle of Holy Land Olive Oil, said,

> This is very expensive oil. Expensive because a farmer risked being shot by an Israeli settler to pick his olives. Expensive because the farmer may have been kept from his land by the Separation Wall. Expensive because of what we had to go through to export it.

The religious meanings of olive oil are dismissed by the Palestinian olive oil professionals as "important to some people, maybe the old, but not to us." The blood, sweat, and tears in a bottle of Palestinian olive oil, which are discursively conveyed to the consumer, are a kind of secular baraka as consumers witness, and try to ameliorate, the harsh conditions Palestinian people face. What is welded together is a discourse of gustatory distinction with political distinction. The consumers may be more than "politically correct foodies." After the 2008–2009 bombardment of Gaza, the sale of fair trade Palestinian olive oil rose dramatically. Purchasing of Palestinian oil may be a way for supporters to get involved; it appeals to many who cannot quite envision themselves standing in front of an Israeli bulldozer as Rachel

Corrie did.[8] It should be noted that this extra-virgin fair trade olive oil scarcely has a market in Palestine because of the homogeneous taste and the price. Many Palestinians prefer the taste of their own oil, from their own trees, grown on their own land.

CONCLUSION

Oil in its nutritious capacity is envisioned as the center of Palestinian gastrointestinal, religious, and social health. Olive oil is central to interactions with the sacred, as its qualities of combustibility allow people to connect with the sacred through olive oil lamps. The quality of permeability also lends itself to communing with the sacred, as olive oil in shrines is thought to absorb the sacredness of the saint and provide blessings to the petitioner who rubs the infused olive oil into his or her skin. The blessed olive tree, from which the valued oil is produced, is central to cultural, religious, and political imaginings of Palestine; the taste and smell of olive oil evoke embodied gustatory memories of home and homeland. Therefore, the Israeli attacks on land, water, and olive trees strike with a threefold prong into the heart of the individual, the social and religious practices, and the nation of Palestine. Customers abroad are drawn into purchasing and consuming Palestinian olive oil because of Palestinian pain, a peculiar kind of commodity fetish indeed. But what is happening here is that the sensuous qualities of the olive oil are not foregrounded. Indeed, the olive oil that is being exported as fair trade extra-virgin oil is not the same kind of oil at all; traditionally produced Palestinian olive oil is thick and dark green in color, with a very high acidity level. The compassion of the consumer abroad comes at a high price in terms of what they expect from a product, even one that is bought out of solidarity and in sympathy.

At the same time as attention shifts from the oil to the tree, the very materiality of Palestinian olive oil as it is marketed abroad changes in such a way that the substance itself is no longer the same, reconfigured technoscientifically as a cosmopolitan extra-virgin olive oil, no longer comparable in its material properties to traditional Palestinian olive oils. Although denatured in terms of its sensuous properties, the oil becomes discursively attached to the properties of the Palestinian producers. The secular properties of the human producers—their blood, sweat, and tears—are transferred to the oil in a manner that parallels the way that sacred properties, the baraka of saints and shaykhs, were transferred to the oil in the past.

In the poetry of the late and widely mourned Palestinian poet Mahmoud Darwish, we see that the Israeli occupation has not eradicated the connection between person and tree, the binding of emotion between them, and the imaginative animation of the trees. In his words, which appear on the label of the Zatoona olive oil, "If the olive tree knew of the suffering of its owner, its oil would turn into tears." Yet the quote suggests a new disconnect between person/owner and olive tree, which suggests an old intimacy grown dormant, as if the trees cannot yet know the true extent of the devastation of the Palestinian people.

2 IN TASTES, LOST AND FOUND

Remembering the Real Flavor of Fat Pork

Brad Weiss

In the late 1980s the U.S.-based National Pork Producers Council inaugurated its campaign to promote pork as "The Other White Meat." What is this "other" white meat? Why is it "white"? What are its material qualities? And what might "white meat" that is also pork taste like? One way we might think of this American campaign is that it is designed to make pork appealing *not* on the basis of its taste but for other valued qualities: its lightness, simplicity, healthfulness, or convenience. Pork is extolled, in fact, as a ready analogue to the ubiquitous chicken breast.[1] It is worth noting that this campaign also invokes the materiality of pork in very specific ways. The whiteness of this other meat not only promotes an association with chicken breasts but further depends on the physical and biological remaking of pork and pigs. For in order to turn pork into white meat, pigs must be raised to be long and lean, with as little fat as possible in their high-priced tender loins, the cut most often marketed as white.

This well-known advertising campaign encapsulates many of the themes addressed in this chapter. To begin with, the ambiguous materiality of fat is, in many ways, the very object of the Pork Council's advertising. As the council itself puts it, "The goal of the campaign was to increase consumer demand for pork and to dispel pork's reputation as a fatty protein" (National Pork Council 2012). This attempt to recast pork as white focuses on this persistent conception of pork as something problematic and locates that problem in pork's fattiness. Moreover, this concern with the reputation of a protein, and the attempt to address this problem by reclassifying pork as white, using descriptive terms reserved (in the American lexicon) for poultry, suggests that fat is not simply a physiological feature of pigs and their (un)desirable meat but is also a socially and culturally symbolic form.

In this chapter I consider fat as a symbolic form, and I focus, in particular, on the ways that the *taste* of pork fat conveys or carries sociocultural significance. I also ask, "How might we describe the materiality of taste?" Taste, in both its prescriptive and descriptive versions, is often assessed as primarily a discursive form. There are all sorts of ways that taste can be understood as a representation, a commentary, or a moralized point of reference for securing the bonds of commensality or demonstrating potent sources of social distinction. In many critical assessments "taste," as Carolyn Korsmeyer puts it, "invites philosophical interest" (1999: 144) when it is situated within what she calls "narratives of eating." Such approaches to taste (e.g., Appadurai 1981; Bourdieu 1984; Korsmeyer 1999; Robertson Smith 1972 [1887]; and Stoller 1989; to name but a few) raise a host of compelling questions and have cast remarkable light on the significance of food as a sociocultural form. But at a perceptual level, taste has its own specific qualities that are not just narratable or referential but felt. And it is these felt qualities within lived experience that merit even closer consideration. Such a consideration of pork fat as a symbolic material form with sensible and sensuous properties leads me to understand this substance in terms of the qualisigns it exhibits. Charles S. Peirce's (1955) discussion of qualisigns has received a good deal of attention in certain anthropological quarters (Fehérváry 2009; Keane 2003; Meneley 2008; Munn 1986), as a way of bridging the divide between the conceptual and material dimensions of signifying practices. Qualities, in Peirce's terms, are primary experiences, feelings, or immediate sensory characteristics (e.g., whiteness, redness, heaviness, lightness). These properties have the potential to convey significance and so to serve as qualisigns across the different material forms in which similar qualities are embodied. Thus, the fattiness of pork has the potential to suggest, for example, unctuousness of character, smugness, and immoderation but also humility, sincerity, and modesty. How these various qualisigns convey any of these actual meanings is an open question that can be determined only within concrete contexts of practice and discourse (Keane 2003: 419).

Critical attention to fat in these terms is warranted, in part, because the felt qualities of taste so frequently motivate people to pursue particular foods and, in pursuit of them, to engage in a whole host of social projects. And yet the question remains very much open: What *is* taste, and how do we recognize those distinctive qualities that make it a discernible phenomenon that is not simply reducible or equivalent to the discursive meanings of consumption, dining, or cuisine? While taste is, undoubtedly, a dimension of each of these, the vocabulary that we need to describe taste itself,[2] and the perceptual qualities particular to it, deserve further inquiry.

Considering the taste of pork fat and fatty pork, I argue that the taste of such fat is critical to understanding different registers of value that are available when eating pork. The taste of fat is occasionally proffered as a distinctly different "basic taste" worthy of the same primacy of importance as salty, sweet, bitter, sour, and the "fifth taste," *umami*. I will address these claims in my discussion of contemporary meat science. But my primary focus, even in consideration of these scientific assessments, is on the ways that they reveal how the taste of pork fat has certain phenomenological as well as political economic qualities. These qualities can be discerned when we look more concretely at contemporary social movements in the United States that are attempting to transform the way that pork is produced and brought to the public and are working to advance alternative models of meat production—embraced as simultaneously "new" and "old-fashioned" methods of animal husbandry. These alternative models, and the kinds of pigs they promote, often privilege the taste of fat as a critical feature of that innovative social and cultural practice. Taste is framed in these efforts as a matter both gustatory and political, and a more nuanced appreciation of what taste is might, then, reveal matters of broad relevance to contemporary social practice.

A SENSE OF MEMORY: ANTHROPOLOGICAL APPROACHES TO TASTE

Within the Western sensorium, we might note that taste presents a paradox. At once evanescent and palpable, taste can elicit nostalgic reminiscence of bygone pasts, at the same time that it seems to be really available to us only when we have tactile contact with some material form. Seeing is believing; a touchstone, something we can get our hands on, confirms the concrete presence of the world; and the aromatic stimulates the erotic. The place of taste (to turn *terroir* on its ear) in this array of associations, its slot in the taxonomy of senses, is its complex evocation of memory. In the course of this chapter I inquire into what taste is, or can be, and how we can know it, or at least make shared, meaningful claims about it. Evocation, recollection, and nostalgia are the canonical modes of remembrance allied to eating. More specifically, in asking about the relationship between taste and memory, I am interested in the various ways that gustation can formulate relations between the past, present, and future. In keeping with Karl Marx's enigmatic assertion that "The *forming* of the five senses is a labor of the entire history of the world down to the present" (1988: 109), I explore the historical possibilities of gustatory tastes by examining a particular taste's history.

The evocative character of taste has been noted often in the anthropological literature. David Sutton's (2001) celebrated account of alimentary practice in the Aegean offers a cogent theoretical and ethnographic illustration of a Proustian anthropology's efforts to capture cuisine's ability to formulate and incite recollection, commemoration, and nostalgia. In his recent review of the literature, Jon Holtzman (2009) demonstrates that memory is often the implicit subtext of ethnographic examinations of food and that considerations of such memory-constructing processes as commodification, urbanization, and ethnogenesis often fix on things culinary as apt illustrations of social transformation. He also makes the provocative point that the sensuous interconnection of cuisine and remembrance is often *celebrated* as a sensuous mode of fond recollections, a sensuousness that overlooks the ways that meals, both bitter and insipid, can recall hardship, illness, and—of course—hunger.

Nadia Seremetakis's notable invocation of the peach variety known as "the breast of Aphrodite" offers a well-known illustration of the characteristic mode of capturing memory through taste (and the senses more generally). Her work highlights "the complicity of history and the senses" (1994: 4). But what is truly critical in Seremetakis's work is less a concern with what that peach *tastes* like ("a bit sour and a bit sweet, it exuded a distinct fragrance"; this is the sum of her description of this peach's taste [Seremetakis 1994: 1]) than an interest in contemporary Greek nostalgia for "the peach," which is no longer grown, it seems, anywhere in Greece. The peach itself is not recognized for its (perhaps indescribable) taste; the peach's *absence* is what is remarkable about it. "The absent peach became narrative" (2). The absence of the peach then becomes a way of recalling, and therefore of remembering, history. Its taste remains strangely inaccessible.

Judith Farquhar's (2002) magisterial account of post-Maoist banquets in China describes opulent feasts in which newly wealthy businessmen and bureaucrats indulge in newfangled appetites in highly poetic ways. In one instance, amid the dishes of three-in-one duck, artfully carved root vegetables, and barrels of white liquor that grace any banquet, are an assortment of mossy plants with fried and roasted insects—the very foods of hunger that barely sustained these very same eaters during the depths of the Cultural Revolution (Farquhar 2002: 134). Here Farquhar shows the complexities of memory in relation to shifting ethical demands in a society where it has become "glorious to get rich," as contemporary Chinese subjects keep alive their recollections of collective immiseration by transforming them into modes of exquisite refinement and, of course, distinction.

These anthropological assessments are valuable touchstones for exploring the taste of fat and its connections to history and memory in this chapter. In the specific history that I discuss here, there is, as we'll see, a discourse of tastes that are "lost" and so subject to being "found," revitalized, and reproduced in the present. What intrigues me most about this formulation is that, like Farquhar's exquisite banquets, these ways of grasping tastes do not merely register the passage of time but posit its trajectory; they comprehend a past from which the present has not just emerged but deviated, even declined. Such taste claims, then, are ways of evaluating temporality, and—insofar as values induce strong feelings, motivate subjects, and compel action—attention to these culinary claims might allow us to understand taste as a means of making history.

TOWARD AN UNDERSTANDING OF THE SIGNIFICANCE OF TASTE

It is interesting to note, in respect to these questions, a kind of paradox in Aristotle's hierarchy of the senses. For if taste is a quintessential "proximal sense" that can only encounter and confirm its object in the intimate interiors of the body (which makes it less noble and more bestial in Aristotle's view), our *accounts* of taste characteristically make reference to locations distant in place and time. This is as true for the Classical tastes of foods whose concrete qualities are grounded in the humoral stuff of the universe itself (Shapin 2010), as it is for contemporary claims about the bacterial profiles of cheeses and their molecular counterparts in grassy hillsides and thistled pastures. The Tanzanians I've eaten with routinely describe the tastes of stewed plantains as heavy, satisfying, and wet, like a farm replete with vegetation, and the cassava porridge they consume only in the absence of plantains as dry and pallid, like the exposed grassland where it grows. A food of hunger, then, tastes like the social condition itself. Indeed, the general amenability of taste to connote potent memories and, as I'll suggest, to call forth others suggests that taste's proximity belies its eminently social character. Again, the evaluative efforts of food artisans of all stripes puts food into the making of history, recuperating what's been lost and calling forth new ways of tasting

To ask the question again: What *is* taste (to say nothing of the taste of tasty pork)? Is our ability to attribute a *temporal* character to tastes, such as the nostalgia or commemoration regularly invoked in anthropological accounts of taste, akin to the temporality of other modes of perception—as when we offer a new vision for the future or capture the ancient tones of a musical genre? My premise, which stems from my phenomenological predilections, is that taste is not just a sensation, the product of a stimulus formulated by various flavor precursors targeted to human receptors, but rather a mode of perception, and so a form of being in the world. Taste is simultaneously part of who we are, in body and mind, and the world we inhabit, both an opening to and embedding in reality for us. It is, then, a way of both making and acting on existence, a way of inhabiting the world.

Consider a comprehensive review essay entitled "The Taste of Fat." It offers a summary of how meat scientists characteristically understand taste, or "gustatory mechanisms":

> Gustation (informally often referred to as "taste" or "flavor perception") is a form of direct chemoreception in the taste bud that is bathed in saliva. The taste bud is composed of sensory taste cells surrounding a central pore, and has several layers of support cells on the outer region of the taste bud. . . . The superior

laryngeal branch of the vagus nerve innovates the epiglottis and larynx and the
posterior one-third of the tongue. Different sensory signals from ortho-nasal,
retro-nasal odour and gustatory receptors may integrate in the higher centers to
give "flavor" cognition. (Dransfield 2008: 38)

Evaluation of the taste of fat, so critical to meat flavor, requires attention to this che-
moreceptive process, the coordination of lipid-derived volatile compounds, saliva,
sensory cells, and neural innovation. But note as well that this same paper begins
with the observation that the perception of fat, and therefore of meat quality, is not
entirely comprehended by these mechanisms:

> The evaluation of fat by the consumer comprises elements of the fat itself (its
> amount and quality), as well as the consumer's sensory capacities, cultural back-
> ground and concerns about environmental and ethical considerations in meat
> production. (Dransfield 2008: 37)

This characteristic object-subject (and, we might add, nature-culture) divide has provided a methodological agenda for meat scientists in the field, as a spate of recent
studies propose to study the difference in the taste of meat from pasture-raised as
opposed to conventionally raised animals. Not surprisingly, given the ties of meat
science programs to industrial producers, these studies often attempt to discredit the
claim that, for example, grass-fed beef tastes better than grain-fed beef, or to attribute such claims to subjective biases or cultural factors, like the consumer's country
of origin. I have no reason to doubt the validity of physiological claims about chemoreception, or the levels of linoleic acid in consumer-preferred meats, or the role
of fatty acid transporter proteins in the mechanics of taste. But it remains an open
question as to how these mechanisms are articulated as the *experience* of taste or why,
for example, the mere presence of these acids, proteins, and physiological structures
should not just register as a flavor sensation but be evaluated as, for example, tasty
and rich rather than cloying and heavy. These questions about evaluation and quality, to say nothing of the role of "cultural background and concerns about environmental and ethical considerations in meat production" in consumer preferences,
indicate that taste is a feature of how we make our worlds.

Giorgio Agamben offers an apposite and characteristically eccentric discussion
of what taste might be through the illustrative example of what taste *isn't*, in the
Umwelt, or environment-world, of a tick (2004: 45–47). Here he relies on the ecolo-
gist Jakob von Uexküll's notion of an environment-world, characterized as a welter
of what Uexküll calls "carriers of significance," which form an integrated system
of features that correspond to the bodily receptors of the organism that inhabits
this world. There is, then, no objective environment with fixed features, or abstract

body with discrete sensory capacities. Rather, Uexküll describes the correspondence between "carriers of significance" and bodily reception as a musical unity, "like two notes 'of the keyboard on which nature performs the supratemporal and extraspatial symphony of signification'" (Agamben 2004: 41).

And what of the tick? The tick, says Uexküll, has an Umwelt with three carriers of significance: (1) the smell of mammalian sweat that attracts it, (2) the hairy surface of the mammalian body to which it clings, and (3) the temperature of 37 degrees Celsius, which corresponds to the blood of mammals. The life of a tick is united to these three elements; indeed, says Agamben, the tick *is* the relationship among these elements. And it is no casual observation to note that what is not present as a carrier of significance in the Umwelt of the tick is the *taste* of blood. Indeed, Uexküll observes that the tick can carry out the fullness of its existence without benefit of the taste of blood, for ticks will attach themselves to any suitable surface and absorb any liquid beneath that surface that is at the proper temperature (picture warm, hairy water balloons). Agamben moves right along from this observation, but it raises interesting questions for me about the possibilities of taste as a kind of *attuned engagement* in the world, and what it might mean to have it. What kind of carrier of significance is taste, and how do we attribute significance to it?

The questions derived from this perspective of engagement, in my view, raise problems for the standard models of stimulus and response that inform much of the discussion of taste perception, and of the perspectives and protocols of meat science intended to disclose the machinery of taste. If taste is a carrier of significance to which we are attuned, it would not seem readily reducible to any such mechanistic framework. In what follows I elaborate an understanding of how this process of significance unfolds and is expressed in affect, language, and memory. Meat science itself often offers some clues to this signifying process, for it both proposes and records the words used to describe the taste of meat in sensory panels. "Flavour," reports one respected article, "was the attribute that the focus groups discussed the most and found relatively hard to describe" (Meinert, Christiansen, et al. 2008: 312). Indeed, it is notable how wide-ranging accounts of taste are when they are offered in reports on tasting panels. The very same meat sample, for example, can be described in some instances in the exact same terms (as, for example, "intensive" and "acidic") but either preferred or rejected for those attributes (e.g., one panelist reports, "Good flavor; A little acidic," while another says of the same sample, "Sour, a little boring in flavor"). Conversely, the same sample can be described in exactly the opposite terms (e.g., "very meaty taste" or "not really meat flavor"). Rather than saying that there's simply no accounting for taste, we might look directly at some of the language used in the sensory analysis of pork. Consider the following table as a not-atypical example of how sensory attributes are described in pork tasting:

	Sensory attributes	Description	Reference
ODOUR	Fried meat	Fried pork aroma	Fried pork schnitzel
	Burnt	Charred pork crust aroma	Well done fried pork schnitzel
	Roasted nut	Roasted nut aroma	Roasted walnuts
	Piggy	Piggy aroma	Melted pork fat
	Acidic	Acidic aroma	Leavened fresh milk
FLAVOUR	Fried meat	Fried pork flavour	Fried pork schnitzel
	Burnt	Charred pork crust flavour	Well done fried pork schnitzel
	Sweet	Sweet taste	Sucrose (1%)
	Acidic	Acidic taste	Citric acid (0.1%)
	Salty	Salty taste	NaCl solution (0.001%)
	Piggy	Piggy flavour	Melted pork fat
	Metallic	Metallic taste	Copper coin

Source: Data from Meinert, Tikk, et al. (2008: 252).

The series of replications across these categories—the "roasted nut" quality that smells like "roasted nut aroma" as found in "roasted walnuts"—suggests, at a minimum, the challenge of disarticulating perception, objects, and language when it comes to taste. In spite of the mechanical reduction of taste to chemoreception and volatile compounds in meat science, things in the world (or perhaps in the world of meat) seem to *be* what they *are*, in both our ability to taste them and our ability to express the qualities of those taste perceptions. This isomorphism between language, subject, and object on matters of taste was further suggested to me in a conversation I had with a chef about the breed of chicken she was using at her restaurant. The tasting panel she convened had preferred an organically raised free-range local bird for the "really deep flavour" it had. "It really *tasted* like something," she said. And what, I asked, did it taste like? "It tasted like chicken!"

How might this lamination of world, perception, and language with respect to taste have implications for the pronounced associations of taste and memory and, in particular, the notion of pork having a "lost taste" that could be recuperated? Consider one of the more intriguing sensory attributes from these meat-tasting descriptors: pork that smells and tastes "piggy." At one level, this looks like the example par excellence of the unity of subject and object characteristic of taste—a taste that is the quintessence of the thing in itself. At the same time, this clearly is *not* what is entailed in the category of piggy, which implies a certain off or excessively intense flavor and odor. "The distinct pork-like or piggy flavor noticeable in lard or cracklings and in some pork," according to the text *Food Chemistry*, "is caused by *p*-[para] cresol and isovaleric acid that are produced from microbial conversions of corresponding amino acids in the lower gut of swine" (Fennema 1996: 249). The terms *pork-like* and *piggy* as mere signifiers might seem evidence of the inadequacy of language to express the complexity of taste, but as sociolinguistic elements in a *community* of speakers, they are terms that can have specific meanings. And, therefore, they are available for diverse meanings as those communities shift across time and space.

My cursory examination of the meat science literature and the tasting panels convened by meat scientists indicates that "piggy" is a quality solicited and reported primarily (but not exclusively) by Danish researchers. The Danish Meat Association extols their industrial farms by reporting that chops from pigs fed a 100 percent organic diet have a more piggy and metallic odor than chops from conventionally fed pigs (Søltoft-Jensen 2007: 3). Given that pork is truly pervasive in Danish cuisine (Buckser 1999) and that Denmark regularly competes with Canada and the United States as one of the world's leading pork exporters, it's perhaps not surprising to find a general public that can discern such flavors as the aggressiveness of too piggy pork-like pork. But note as well that pigginess is a flavor that is increasingly being *promoted* by advocates and connoisseurs of pastured/local/heritage breed pork. In a taste comparison of artisanal British charcuterie, the *Guardian* critics described one brand of *coppa* (air-dried ham) as "oversalted, not enough piggy flavour" or "strong, dry, piggy, not bad" (*Guardian* 2010). In *The Times*, a pork pie is extolled as being "full of piggy flavour," while a Vietnamese *banh mi* luncheon meat is dismissed for lacking "the true Viet depth of sticky, piggy flavour" (O'Loughlin 2010). In such instances, pigginess is celebrated as an esteemed "deep" feature of real pork.

I do not think that the taste of *pigginess*, as it is used by these British advocates of pork, is identical to the Danish perception of pigginess, although given the vagaries of the lexicon, I am really not certain of this distinction, either. What matters, though, is that the perception of taste is elicited in identical language that can be valorized in opposing ways. In each instance, pigginess, the taste that confirms the presence of the thing in itself, is a carrier of significance that conveys the intensity and force of the animal in question. But is that quality of intensity a form of overpowering excess, or is it evidence of the true, authentic character of the animal, well cared for and naturally raised? As a tangential but not unrelated point, I'd note that male pigs raised for meat as opposed to breeding are almost uniformly castrated in both conventional and pastured farming in the United States, a measure that prevents their meat from acquiring what is called a "boar's taint." There are, however, a very few consumers I have spoken with who have eaten "intact" boar's meat and have a preference for this "tainted" flavor, which they describe, in a parallel fashion, as "aggressive," "deep," or simply "strong." This evaluation of depth or intensity as a signifier with a range of available meanings is also, as I hope to show, an indication of how tastes can be "lost and found."

PIEDMONT PIGS AND PORK FAT: A REGIONAL TASTE HISTORY

One of the intriguing things about pork (especially in the United States, in recent years) is that it hasn't always been obvious that pork has a taste or—perhaps—that taste is the quality most relevant for pork producers and consumers. The research I've been doing in the Piedmont of North Carolina with pasture-raised pig farmers, chefs, food activists, and eaters of all kinds is, in part, an investigation into just how the taste of pork—and fatty pork, at that—has come to be relevant to and, in many ways, exemplary of flavor and taste more generally; as well as iconic of the potent, robust pleasures of eating for the locavores, artisans, and foodies who have embraced pastured pork production in this region and across the country.

At the same time, as I have indicated, appeals to taste, like those made by advocates for local foods and the virtues of terroir, or a "taste of place" (Trubek 2008; Weiss 2011), are ways of evaluating temporality, and so attention to taste affords us an important (perhaps even privileged) perspective on processes of making history. And making history through fat pigs is very much what many food activists, chefs, farmers, and consumers have in mind in the contemporary United States. I have been engaged in ethnographic work with participants in this food movement, in fields, farmers' markets, and restaurants (as well as classrooms and agricultural extension offices) across the Piedmont of North Carolina, a region that extends from the Triad (formed by the cities of Greensboro, Winston-Salem, and High Point) in the west to the Coastal Plain in the East. A dedication to pork and the pigs that possess it has a very concrete material history in the Piedmont. Here's how the story unfolds: From a high of over 600,000 hog farms in 1980, the number of hog farms in the United States fell to 200,000 by the mid-1990s and to less than 70,000 by the early 2000s. Simultaneously, the average annual output of hogs per farm increased from 1,000 in 1980 to 400,000 in 1999. Plainly, the agricultural dictate of Earl Butz (secretary of agriculture under Presidents Nixon and Ford) to "get big or get out" was most fully realized in hog production. Confined animal feeding operations (CAFOs) and corporate contracting became the infrastructural technologies that facilitated this wholesale transformation. Nowhere has this process been more rapid or pervasive than in North Carolina, home to Smithfield Foods, the largest meat packer in the world.

This industrialization was accompanied by the National Pork Producers Council's campaign to promote "The Other White Meat," described at the beginning of this chapter. This national campaign (1987–2005) was surprisingly *unsuccessful* in many ways. While the Economic Research Service of the U.S. Department of Agriculture suggests that pork sales rose by 20 percent in the first five years of this campaign, longer-term assessments indicate that pork consumption in the United States has remained at a relatively stable level since the 1910s. Moreover, since 1998 the production of the live animals has been unprofitable. In 2009 hog farmers who market their pork in the United States are losing about $20 per pig (National Pork Producers Council 2009). Industrial pork, like most American industrial agriculture since the 1970s, survives through tax breaks and direct subsidies (Blanchette 2010). Nonetheless, the model of vertical integration based on the consolidations of economies of scale continues apace. These industrial processes, as I indicated above, radically transform the very biology of pigs and the taste of pork. The industrial process breeds a long and lean hog, which maximizes the marginal returns available to pork growers and encourages the sale of such innovative, higher-priced products as "lean bacon" and "tenderloin" (as opposed to simply tenderized loins or other cuts of pork), which are notably free of fat and quintessentially exemplify the "other white meat."

In a host of ways, these historical transformations in North Carolina offer a microcosm of wider rumblings in the American food system. Moreover, these dramatic changes have attracted a wide range of critics who decry all aspects of this intensified process of industrialization, from the cruelties inflicted on pigs through the confinement system, to the environmental degradations wrought by the industry, to the dangerous, often criminal nature of labor exploitation in factory farms and processing facilities (Kaminsky 2005; Kenner 2009; Morgan 1998; Niman 2009). In addition, critics of such industrial agriculture often lament the tastes of the food it produces; with respect to pigs and pork, it is the absence of fat that is often decried. And, indeed, bringing fat back into pork has been one of the ways that advocates for change in the industrial system have both worked to bring about transformations and demonstrated the clear superiority (in their view) of alternative production methods. In an interview I conducted with one such chef committed to promoting these alternative methods, I asked him what qualities he was looking for in the "local pork" he featured at his restaurant. Was it some specific breed of pig, I wondered, or perhaps healthier meat derived from a pig raised outdoors and unconfined? He told me simply, "I was looking for a pig with some fat on it." No "other white meat" for him! One of the most popular pork products sold at the farmers' markets throughout the Piedmont, provided by farmers dedicated to methods of animal husbandry that are today embraced as both innovative and old-fashioned (that is, raising pigs outdoors in unconfined "pastures"), is bacon. Bacon procured from a "pig with some fat on it," as such pastured animals inevitably are, is no ordinary bacon, for it is self-evidently exceptionally fat. It is so fat that at the market stall where I work each weekend we make sure to tell each of our new customers to cook their bacon at a low heat (preferably in the oven at 325 degrees Fahrenheit for 15 minutes) lest its fat burn up in the pan. Indeed, these fatty bellies are found on restaurant menus across the Triangle (formed by the cities of Raleigh, Durham, and Chapel Hill).

Our market stall has customers who come each week asking for what one of them calls our "life-changing bacon." This term (while somewhat idiosyncratic), and the more general popularity of bacon (which at $12 per pound is roughly two to three times the price of industrially produced bacon), suggests the ways in which bacon as a cut of pork—an especially fatty one at that—is iconic (in the classic Peircean sense) of this alternative food movement. That is, not only are the pigs raised by techniques that oppose the perils of confinement operations, but the fatty bacon they produce also has characteristics that exhibit the virtues of—and in this way resemble (like all iconic signs [Peirce 1955: 101])—this transformed production process. That is, bacon, with its distinctive fattiness, possesses the qualisigns of value (Meneley 2008; Munn 1986) of artisanal, pastured, healthy pig production, which counteract the qualisignificance of the industrially produced, confined, "inhumane" processed pork that is best embodied in what is marketed as healthy, white, lean meat. Bacon and loins are each icons of the productive processes that generate them (pastured and industrial, respectively), and their distinctive qualisigns of fat and lean are embodied in materially meaty form.[3]

In order to elaborate on how this fattiness is (re)generated in pigs, and with what consequences for the taste of pork, the phenomenology of memory and political economy allow me to draw on the history of one particularly salient pig-breeding scheme in the North Carolina Piedmont. The history describes a pig that was literally revitalized as a heritage breed by virtue of its exceptional and excessive fat. In the early 1990s, an animal scientist, Chuck Talbott, at North Carolina A&T (a prominent historically black college in Greensboro), dismayed by the devastating effects of CAFOs on both the animals and the farmers who are increasingly ensnared by this production system, began to look for alternatives to this system of pig production. He is, by his own account, driven primarily by economic concern for farmers no longer able to operate under the onerous terms of those pork contracts. For Talbott this concern stems not from some nostalgic appeal to a disappearing way of life but from questions of food security and environmental degradation. And it was only relatively later, toward the end of the 1990s, that he hit on the idea that *taste* might be a significant factor in farmers' ability to market pork raised on pasture rather than in confinement.

Talbott told me that he came to this realization when he read Edward Behr's summer 1999 edition of "The Art of Eating." This "quarterly letter" was entitled "The Lost Taste of Pork" and focused on the efforts of Paul Willis, a pig farmer in northern Iowa who was committed to raising his pigs outdoors, in straw and hoophouses, even as outdoor pig production declined precipitously in Iowa through the 1970s and

1980s. As a literate piece of foodism, Behr's essay draws special attention to the ways that pigs raised in this fashion produce delectable pork. Behr's first experience eating Willis's pork came when eating a "thick chop . . . roasted before a wood fire" at Chez Panisse, which inspired his pilgrimage to Iowa. In his letter, Behr offers a thorough survey of the techniques of outdoor production and its advantages over confinement for both the health of the pigs and the environment, a point he makes by repeated reference to the horrific stench of CAFOs. His elaboration of Willis's farming expertise redounds to the taste of the pork produced. As Willis puts it, "If something tastes good . . . I think it reflects the health of whatever it is you're eating. Allowing the pig to behave as naturally as possible is enhancing the eating quality" (quoted in Behr 1999: 12). "It tastes like the pork I had when I was a little kid" is how one of Willis's neighbors describes it (quoted in Behr 1999: 18).

Upon reading Behr's essay, Talbott contacted Willis about how to promote the same production practices and cultivate consumers and markets more generally across North Carolina. By now, Willis was the pork manager for Niman Ranch, a company that markets meats raised by a network of farmers and ranchers who raise animals according to a variety of welfare and environmental standards. And so Talbott sought to promote pastured pork production by providing opportunities for pig farmers to market their meat through Niman Ranch. This strategy was further supplemented by subsidies, not from the farm bill, but from the tobacco buyout (Golden Leaf Foundation 2011). Funds from the tobacco settlement in the early 1990s were made available to help tobacco farmers convert to other kinds of crops. In this environment, Talbott developed the Golden Leaf Project targeted to "under-resourced" small farmers who had less than ten acres devoted to tobacco in order to fund their conversion to outdoor pig production. These farmers would be educated in outdoor pig farming techniques by Talbott's staff in the swine husbandry department of A&T and would have their facilities and—ultimately—the quality of their pork certified by Niman representatives. The pork raised on this pasture would be sold under the Niman brand, largely through Whole Foods and direct sales to chefs.

This set of material, institutional arrangements—"marginal" farmers, capitalization from the tobacco buyout, a branded network of high-end meat producers, and the scientific expertise of swine husbandry in a historically black college— fundamentally reshaped the market for pasture-raised pork in central North Carolina. And, for our purposes, it is especially important to recognize the vital role that *taste* played in motivating these actors. According to one of the extension officers who worked on this project, Talbott became, in effect, a meat scientist, driven by an interest in the ways that pasturage, feed, and behavior produced the taste attributes prized by discerning consumers. In pursuit of these discerning consumers and the pigs they preferred, Talbott travelled across southern Europe, looking at varieties of pigs that were, as he put it, "part of the whole way of life" in little towns and villages where pork production and provisioning are integrated into the seasonal round, the very paragon of Slow Food's "Ark of Taste." Upon returning to North Carolina, Talbott found that an insular group of pigs on Ossabaw Island (a Sea Island near Savannah, Georgia), with ancestral ties to Spanish Iberian *pata negra* (black foot) pigs, was being culled by the Georgia Department of Natural Resources because they threatened the ecology of the island, most specifically, the endangered loggerhead turtles that nested there. Given these Ossabaw hogs' ties to the celebrated Iberico pigs that Talbott had encountered in Spain, Talbott and the swine husbandry team at A&T became extremely excited about the prospects of raising a herd of Ossabaws as a niche-market heritage breed (certified by the American Livestock Breed Conservancy). Today, the Ossabaw Island Hog is raised by small but growing number of farmers across the Eastern Seaboard and in a few places in the Midwest.

It is also important to note that the Ossabaw—and other types of pigs that have been revitalized as heritage breeds—are materially different from industrial hogs in ways that go beyond their production techniques. In addition to the ancestral connection of Ossabaws to Iberico pigs, for example, the physiological adaptations these hogs had acquired through 400 years of island life are also important to their viability—and materiality. As an insular breed of pig, Ossabaws are adapted to the resource limitations of their island territory. As feral pigs, they became smaller, a process called "insular dwarfism," and further developed the capacity to drink brackish water. But what makes the Ossabaw Island hogs especially suited to pork production is the unique biochemical system of fat metabolism they developed. The "thrifty gene" these pigs developed enables them to store a larger proportion of fat than any other hog. Indeed, Ossabaws have the highest percentage of body fat of any nondomestic mammal (Watson 2004: 114). This remarkable ability also produces a tendency to develop type 2 diabetes, which made these hogs of interest to medical researchers. In 2002 a group of twenty-three pigs that had served as animal models in an National Institutes of Health research study in Columbia, Missouri, were "rescued" from being "sacrificed" and were donated to Talbott and his program in swine husbandry at A&T (Kaminsky 2005).

TELLING THE TASTE OF FAT

But what is the taste of the Ossabaw and its characteristic fat? How does its taste connect it to the Spanish pata negra with which it shares ancestry, or with other heritage breeds raised by similar methods of swine husbandry across this region and elsewhere? How might this taste be implicated in the complex and varied narratives—of heritage, adaptation, cultivation, ecology, and connoisseurship—by which this domesticated American breed comes to be? This chronicle is further informed by more general claims about the "lost taste of pork," where fat replaces lean, and the capacity of these animals to not just taste good but recuperate taste. What I can further show is that that such recuperation is also a form of innovation that brings with it, not surprisingly, a new taste of pork.

How can such tastes be told? Recall that in my consideration of meat science's approaches to taste, the ambiguity of terms like *piggy*, *off*, and even *strong* suggested that the very same terms could be used to describe (the same?) tastes that some found desirable and others found repellent. The consumers of pasture-raised pork in central North Carolina confirm some of these disparities, expressed less as positive and negative evaluations of the same flavors than as different perceptions of what is widely agreed to be some very tasty pork. The pig farmers with whom I'm working serve a wide area of central North Carolina. This region is remarkably, and increasingly, diverse in demographic terms (North Carolina is the fastest-growing state east of the Mississippi), and consumers of pastured pork—more commonly called local pork—reflect that diversity. It's well known that purveyors of such artisanal "slow" foods are often perceived to be catering to a foodie elite that can afford, for example, pork chops that cost $10 per pound. But what's also clear is that consumers have different tastes that shape their purchasing decisions. In very rough terms, the Triad is part of a Southern rustbelt, an industrial group of towns that were once dominated by textile and woodworking mills that have in living memory departed for cheaper labor in Latin America and East Asia; in turn, the Triangle is an epicenter of high-tech corporate enterprise, from big pharmaceutical companies to software engineering firms, facilitated by proximity to academic research centers. Among the farmers I know who sell in both regions, the Triangle is known as a region of avid customers, eager to try new things and pay for them. As one beef farmer put it, "Three years ago when I first started processing cattle, I kept a flank steak for myself figuring it would never sell. I must have had fifteen customers at the Durham Farmers' Market ask me for a flank steak! I haven't eaten one since then." Along the same lines, a pig farmer with the same Triangle clientele told me, "I'd make a fortune if I could figure out how to raise a pig with four bellies" (a sign as well of the qualisignificance of belly-providing bacon). These customers also crave personalized attention and narrative accounts of "heritage" (like the one I've recounted above) along with their farmers' market purchases. In contrast, the customers in the Triad are thought of as reluctant to try new things, and it's a hard sell to get them to pay the premium prices that pastured pork commands. As a result, small packs of ground beef and breakfast sausage are the biggest sellers at the Greensboro Farmers Market.

Moreover, while both sets of customers are, by their own accounts, drawn to the taste of pastured pork, my ethnographic inquiries have found that each apprehends taste in rather different ways. In a customer survey I conducted, Triangle customers described the taste of their preferred pastured pork in terms like these:

"The taste is so different, so superior to mass-produced meat products!"
   "Pork that tastes like pork, not 'the other white meat.'"
   "The taste—so yummy and *different* than any other bacon I've ever had."
   "The taste is superior to all of the commercial pork products I used to buy. In addition I like knowing where my food comes from, that it was raised with care for both the animal and the environment, and in buying it I am supporting values I believe in."
   "The meat tastes excellent—but it's not just the sensual flavor of the meat, it's the mental knowledge that what they do is responsible, for the planet, people, and animals."

Triad customers speak much less frequently in such terms of "ethical consumption"; rather, they are inclined to appreciate pastured pork for recapturing the tastes they recall from a bygone era. "Tastes like the best meats I have had as a child, that was home grown and free-range"; "the pork tastes the best, like what Grandfather used to have when he had a farm down in Florida where the pigs had lots of pasture." One of the most renowned barbecue pit masters, Ed Mitchell, who (until recently) offered pastured pork at his Raleigh restaurant, sums up this appreciation of its taste this way:

The pork knocked me down. It tasted like the barbecue I remember from the tobacco days; juicy, and full of flavor. I knew that was the pork my grandfather ate all his life. I knew that was the old-fashioned pork we lost when near about everybody went industrial. (quoted in Edge 2005: 54)

Here, in short, are tastes both lost and found, an appreciation of innovation, pork unlike any other. Such pork is unique and laden with *distinction* in its methods of "responsible farming" and nonindustrial/commercial qualities; and, at the same time, as farmers stereotype Triad consumers preferences, it is "pork that tastes like my granddaddy used to raise," redolent of concrete times and places and connections to both kin and personal experience.

As I indicated in my discussion of the iconic status of bacon, these tastes of both innovation and nostalgia are embedded in the fat of the pig. That is, when consumers and chefs extol the virtues of this simultaneously "new" and "old-fashioned" pastured pork, they inevitably are drawn to its fat as evidence of these virtues. Note

Mitchell's discussion of the "juicy" pork he prefers, the fat that could be found in "the pork my grandfather ate all his life." If taste is a way of evaluating carriers of significance, then much of the significance of pork is carried in its fat. Fat exhibits, to return to my original point, qualisigns of ambiguity, for it exemplifies—all at once—a traditional, forgotten experience rooted in kinship and loss, as well as innovation, superiority, and ethical environmental practice.

CONCLUSION

Let me turn briefly to two examples (both of which I've discussed elsewhere; see Weiss 2011, 2012) of attempts to narrate the taste of heritage pork that further detail this complementary dualism of tastes lost and found. The American Livestock Breed Conservancy has introduced evaluation and tasting protocols (in coordination with Slow Food and Chefs Collaborative) for the meat from heritage breeds of animals, which call for "Renewing America's Food Traditions" (RAFT Alliance 2013). This language of renewal and tradition is unsurprising, but consider the results of one intriguing evaluation. Chuck Talbott, along with Peter Kaminsky of the *New York Times*, convened a professional tasting panel in order to assess and codify the taste of acorn-finished Ossabaw. Acorn consumption recalls, again, the historical narrative of these pigs, whose Iberico relatives are finished on acorns before their hams are cured as *jamon iberico de belota* (*belota* is Spanish for acorn). The panel found that "forest-finished" Ossabaw has a "deeper, more complex flavor" than the meat of animals finished on grain. They also report, to a high degree, what is called (by pork industry standards) an "off-flavor," a category labeled "dark turkey meat" in meat science. To reconcile this apparent discrepancy (pork that tastes so good that it tastes bad, or off; the technical term for this in the food taste business is *funky*), Charles Talbott et al. (2006: 189–90) determined that "[f]or niche-market applications, a new 'On Flavor' classification may be required to distinguish differences in conventional sensory models." The lost taste of mast-fed pork, then, demands new modes of description, perhaps even new models of taste.

The other example has to do less directly with tasting than with ways of cooking these chronicled pigs that similarly combine innovation and nostalgia. "Renewing Food Traditions" has also renewed interest in dishes that make use of all manner of interesting, formerly icky bits of pig. Such snout-to-tail cookery is part and parcel of the Slow Food agenda and is especially apparent in the dishes served in the restaurants across the Piedmont that offer pasture-raised pork (Weiss 2012). Not always content to serve up good ol' Carolina barbecue, local chefs are promoting their skills, and tempting their customers, with applications like grilled pig tails, pork belly confit, and headcheese. Headcheese, in particular, is embedded with traces of paradoxical experiences. Once eaten in North Carolina as "souse" (and sometimes still eaten), this boiled and congealed *gelée* of pork trimming is recalled as a food of hardship, a bit of meat—often eaten at breakfast—providing a hearty energy source for agricultural labor. This ethos of economizing is certainly praised by the Slow Food chefs and many of the consumers who are so taken with snout-to-tail cookery. But, of course, their own experience of consumption—and so, perhaps, of the taste of headcheese—has little to do with hardship, or even with nostalgic recollections of repasts gone by. Most of them describe such dishes as what they call "*real* food," a culinary offering, then, that values authenticity rendered material.

This difference is telling and, I would argue, consistent with the claims made by professional panels about the taste of heritage pork more generally. That is, such foods are modes of renewal, evocations of the past (occasionally, but not always, for those who actually did eat this way in their own past), and simultaneously innovative techniques of preparation, provisioning, and marketing of these tastes. The once-lost and now-renewed past is offered, in both instances, not simply as a documentary representation but as an evaluative claim about the past—its complexity, character, and "realness"—as a resource for creating the present and future. To understand taste as a mode of perception with a privileged relationship to memory is (or so I have argued here) to ask about the character of complex alignments of past, present, and future. In this way, taste is a way of making the world, of evaluating the qualities of the past that are felt to contribute to the present, and of further cultivating those qualities one hopes to secure in the future. Creating history in these perceptual ways requires us to grasp the sensory character of the world and our place in it as laden with carriers of significance, mutual attunements beyond stimulus and response. Taste is both of the world and in us; we have taste, and tastes grab us. The particular flavors of pastured pork can reveal how taste offers us a kind of potential, diverse possibilities for aligning historical processes. Pigginess as "excess" or "authenticity" is iconic of these possibilities. So, too, are lean loins and fatty bellies and bacon, each of which embodies qualisigns of the very different processes of production through which they come into being. In this regard, they also exhibit the divergent historical potential of taste, as this sensory significance divulges thoroughly different orders of labor, ecology, animal welfare, and agriculture more generally. In this way, the qualisigns exhibited by iconic forms conjoin the sensory and the political economic. Tastes in memory are lost and found, heritage and innovation, firmly bound to time and place, as well as unique and unprecedented. This plenipotentiality of pastured pork—life changing and extra-fatty—demonstrates how tastes assert the significance of the changing worlds that produce not only pigs but ourselves as the consumers of their pork and the bearers of the tastes by which we perceive the worlds we inhabit.

3 THINKING THROUGH FAT

The Materiality of Ancient and Modern Stereotypes

Christopher E. Forth

Given our current obsessions with the health and beauty issues that are so often connected to "obesity," this chapter begins with a perhaps counterintuitive question: why should historical reflections on something as complex as fat be narrowed to fit our contemporary preoccupations with fat and thin *bodies*? In addition to functioning as an adjective used to describe corpulent physiques, the word *fat* is also a noun denoting a substance located *within* bodies as well as *outside of them*. While various kinds of fat have numerous practical applications in everyday life—for example, in nourishing, cooking, heating, healing, sealing, and preserving—fat's protean characteristics, notably its ability to change readily from a solid to a liquid and even a vapor (Meneley 2008), have excited the human imagination, often mobilizing other, more intense, symbolic and metaphoric associations across time and space. Linked in various contexts to ideas about fertility, vitality, increase, or transformation, fats and oils participate in the ambivalence that often attends such concepts. They are thus ambiguous substances capable of eliciting reactions of pleasure and fascination as well as fear and disgust. The fact that, historically speaking, "excessive" amounts of fat in the body have also occasioned ambivalence invites us to investigate the ways in which the materiality of fats and oils has at times inflected cultural perceptions of corpulence. This chapter is therefore concerned with understanding, from a historical perspective, what this thing we call fat actually is. What has *counted* as fat at various times and places, and *where* have such things been located? Moreover, it asks what, culturally speaking, is fat *made of* that it can elicit such a range of powerful reactions, both positive and negative, in our culture? And how were these qualities made to resonate with the physical, mental, and moral characteristics attributed to "fat" people so that they became entwined with the very idea of fat personhood?

To engage with these questions this chapter examines perceptions of fat in classical and biblical texts, which are not as disconnected from contemporary issues as some might think. While acknowledging the growing centrality of vision in the formation of physical ideals in the modern world, I propose that neither visuality nor aesthetics fully accounts for some of the negative images of fat personhood that have circulated in one form or another in the West. This is not to suggest that matters of morphology and proportion were *irrelevant* in antiquity or that fat's capacity to enhance or "deform" bodies went without comment. Rather, this chapter suggests that, at various historical moments, many negative stereotypes about the corpulent were complemented and perhaps even informed by perceptions of fat as a material substance with definite properties and qualities. Consider, for instance, how frequently fat people have been described as sweaty, smelly, or greasy, as if their very flesh is rotten or corrupt; or perhaps how often fat people's weakness of willpower and muscle is attributed to their supposedly soft minds and bodies. One may also reflect on the foolishness or stupidity that has for centuries been attached to the corpulent, as if the workings of their minds are somehow dulled by the supposed insensibility of their flesh. While stereotypes of corrupt, weak, and stupid fat people have circulated since the early modern era, their ideational roots extend to classical antiquity and the Hebrew Bible. We thus need to look beyond appearances if we are to make sense of such vivid images. In an effort to understand these three long-standing stereotypes about corpulent people this chapter submits that the material properties of fat—particularly its unctuousness, softness, and insensateness—have played important roles in motivating some of the responses this substance has generated with reference to both human bodies and their material worlds.

As Janet Carsten (2004: 110) points out, anthropologists have traditionally assumed close links between conceptions of substance and ideas about personhood, but in so doing they have exaggerated the differences between non-Western perceptions of substances and persons as "inherently fluid and transformable" and Western views that emphasize immutability and, in the case of persons, boundedness. As we will see, classical antiquity viewed fat as a protean, transformable, and even detachable by-product of the body's "concoction" of nutriment into blood, semen, and milk, something that defined male and female bodies in specific ways. Most important, the fatty qualities of the body were conceptualized as being analogous to those observed in nature generally, revealing the extent to which bodies were profoundly implicated in the wider environment. The latitude with which fat is analyzed here seeks to capture some of the many levels on which the substance has been perceived historically, even if our understanding of the term today is considerably circumscribed by aesthetic and medical concerns. Thus we will find fat residing in (or extracted from) animals and vegetables as well as deposited beneath the human skin, and will even encounter it lurking within the soil and its products, suggesting a once-common holistic relationship between humans, animals, plants, and the body of the earth itself. Due to the conceptual slipperiness of fat in its various forms (whether "frozen" as a solid or liquefied as oil or grease), this analysis tracks the ways in which the properties connected to this substance have been perceived across these registers, revealing the surprisingly mercurial and ambiguous ways in which fat has been understood. To be sure, many perceptions of fat and corpulence have clearly positive connotations, but because the focus of this chapter is on the material formation of fat stereotypes, the following discussion foregrounds ambiguity and negativity. It also makes no claims to completeness. Insofar as substances generally manifest a wide range of manifest and hidden or unexpected properties and tendencies (Hahn and Soentgen 2010), fat is far too rich a substance to be fully savored in the space of a chapter. This analysis thus necessarily skims the surface of a much more complex phenomenon.[1]

Approaching fat personhood in this way entails a rapprochement between constructivist theories of the body and recent scholarship on materiality. In agreement with the growing number of anthropologists and archaeologists who argue that the physicality of the material world is not simply a "text" to be interpreted, Nicole Boivin (2008) has written eloquently of the need to overcome the rigid social constructionism that depicts material things as mere props for culture and language. Of particular relevance to the present analysis is the way in which certain sensuous qualities of substances may be bundled together and mobilized within systems of value that privilege certain qualities over others. Rather than *determining* culture in any direct way, these material qualities "remain available, ready to emerge as real factors" in various contexts and at different times (Keane 2005: 194). Ian Hodder uses the term *resonance* to describe the process "by which at a non-discursive level coherence occurs across domains in historically specific contexts" (2012: 126). By examining the ways in which unctuousness, softness, and insensateness have moved back and forth between the material and social registers, as well as across the vegetable, animal, and human worlds, this chapter probes the ways in which the qualities of fat may offer "a series of potentialities for signs" (Meneley 2008: 305) that resonate in various ways to the present day. However fat has been perceived, its qualities seem to motivate, without actually determining, some of the ambivalence with which corpulent people have been perceived at various historical moments. If there is now ample evidence that "humans think through material culture" (Hodder 2012: 35), then thinking through fat is at once an exercise in historical reconstruction and an attempt to identify the material sources of some rather durable cultural stereotypes.

UNCTUOUSNESS

If a range of dissimilar things were described as fat in antiquity, it was not always because they displayed plump, bloated, or fleshy qualities but because they shared a certain unctuous property that had more to do with tactility than visuality. It was this greasiness that formed the basis for the analogies that often resonated across the registers of animal, vegetable, and human. Examining the unctuous qualities of fat thus opens up a range of potential meanings that may shed light on the ambiguous responses this substance has elicited. Among early peoples fats derived from plant and animal sources were used for a variety of artistic, culinary, and ritual purposes. In addition to being used as food and in religious rituals and burial practices, they were employed as illuminants, sealants, lubricants, polishes, binders, varnishes, and bases for perfumes and medicinal and cosmetic ointments (Evershed, Mottram, and Dudd 1997). The unctuousness of fats also implied the related qualities of inflammability and luminosity. The stone lamps used in Paleolithic times employed animal fats as fuel, thereby allowing humans to remain active at night and thus facilitating cave painting, tool making, and other cultural advances (Beaune 2000). This burning of fat for illumination revealed another quality: through the process of combustion fat can seem to dematerialize into smoke and light (Meneley 2008). In a process strikingly similar to alchemy, fat may be transformed from a state of "gross" or "dull" materiality—which is how it has also been described (see below)—into something subtle and even transcendent. If fat seemed to *symbolize* light and life, then it was because such qualities were considered intrinsic to the oily substance itself. Fat seemed to contain rather than merely represent such powers (Bille and Sørensen 2007).

Fat is therefore an intrinsically mutable and ambiguous substance, one capable of switching between solid and liquid as well as between matter and "spirit." This may be one reason that fats and oils could be viewed as almost magical in the past. Some believed they could divine the future by watching how oil interacted with water through the practice of lecanomancy, or by gazing for long periods at the luster produced by oil rubbed on a smooth surface, a practice known as *scrying* (Bilu 1981; Daiches 1913). The Hebrews usually used the word *šemen* to refer to oil, almost always that pressed from the olive, which was a dietary staple and considered a blessing from God. As such it served as a metaphor for life, fertility, and purity. When oil was rubbed on the face, skin, and hair, its luminosity could make them shine, but oil also possesses penetrative tendencies that were thought capable of transforming the character and status of an object or person. The capacity of penetrative substances to elevate or contaminate partly explains the ambiguity with which oils could be perceived, for bodies penetrated by oils could have their status either enhanced or diminished in some way. Thus, while the oil used to anoint high priests or kings in

Israel partly facilitated their change in status, in other contexts the contaminating potential of oils could make them seem dangerous. Drawing on the purity codes found in Leviticus (11:33–38), the Jewish sect known as the Essenes viewed oil and other fluids as transmitters of contamination if they came into contact with impure things. They thus avoided oil altogether and were careful to keep their skin dry (Baumgarten 1994; Ringgren 2006; Sommer 2009).

Viewing fats as containing some of the vital power of their plant and animal sources, the ancient Greeks believed that some of that power could be imparted to the human body. Olive oil was used to anoint the bodies of athletes because it might give them greater strength while also tanning and softening the skin, causing it to shine with a luminosity that made the body seem divine (Lee 2009; Sansone 1992; Vernant 1991). For the Greeks, though, there was also an implied connection between the oil that one applied externally and the fat and sweat of the body itself. The healthy functioning of the body required one to replenish oil that was secreted and washed off of the skin— for an athlete to scrape the excess oil and sweat from his skin without reapplying oil was to rob the body of something essential. This is why it was considered bad luck to dream about a bathing scraper without an accompanying oil flask since such a device would "scrape off one's sweat and add nothing to the body" (Artemidorus 1990: 67). This belief in oil's capacity to revive flagging vitality was based on personal experience, and nonathletes also reported feelings of rejuvenation when oil and water were rubbed on their bodies after a period of fatigue (Aristotle 1953; Theophrastus 2003). This tacit link between oil and sweat in classical texts led Richard B. Onians to propose that the main function of anointing the body with oil after a bath was "to feed, to introduce into the body through the pores, the stuff of life and strength, which appears to come out through the pores in the form of sweat" (1951: 210).

This intimate and homologous relationship between human and nonhuman fats warrants closer examination. Not only did Aristotle (1953) draw a distinction between aqueous moisture, which easily evaporates, and the unctuous sort, which is separated from matter only with difficulty, but he even likened the life of the body to a lamp in which the flame slowly consumes its oil. While the simile of life as an oil lamp recurs in several cultures and would endure in the West for nearly 2,000 years, Aristotle also contended that unctuous moisture was in fact present in all matter, organic and inorganic, and that it was responsible for lending objects and substances their specific shape or consistency as well as whatever inflammable capacities they might have. In this very broad sense fatty matter was the stuff of the entire world. Steven Connor sees more reasons why fat could have been validated as the very stuff of life itself. "That the fat of the body should have the power of furnishing light, rather than being rendered down into ash like the bones and flesh, might seem to confirm the idea that fat contains the life of the body" (2004: 190).

Agricultural writers generally corroborated such claims, at least insofar as they pertained to the relative "fatness" of agricultural land. For much of Western history soil has been described as being fat or thin, as well as loose or dense and wet or dry, oftentimes in combinations of these qualities. Aristotle's successor at the Lyceum, Theophrastus (1916), was just one among many Greeks who drew distinctions between "fat" and "lean" soil, applying a taxonomy that was shared by the Romans and that would persist in the Western imagination well into the nineteenth century. According to the Roman writer Varro, the first thing a farmer must determine is whether a given soil is "thin or fat or moderate" because that will indicate which sort of farming one can do (1978: 32). Since fat soil had a distinctive texture and consistency that experienced farmers recognized, touch was considered one of the most reliable methods of judging soil. Virgil maintained that one could always tell which soil was fat (*pinguis*) because "never does it crumble when worked in the hands, but like pitch grows sticky in the fingers when held" (1978: 132–33). Since the tactile attributes of such soil called to mind the viscous and pliable qualities of oil or grease, describing a field as fat was no simple metaphor. Rather, there was something palpably unctuous about fertile soil, as well as a kind of swelling tendency that could be discerned through other means. After removing a handful of soil to test for unctuousness one had to pay close attention to what happened when reinserting the sample into the hole one had made in the ground: "if there is an excess as by some sort of leavening, it will be a sure sign that the soil is fat; if it is insufficient, that it is poor; if it makes an even fill, that it is ordinary" (Columella 1968: 121). The "increase" made possible by fertile soil did not refer solely to agricultural yield but to the inherent tendencies of this particular kind of matter.

The viscous and oily qualities that farmers understood as tangible evidence of fertility were not figments of the ancient imagination. Recent analyses of medieval soil composition reveal the biomarkers of fatty acids or lipids contained in the manure used to fertilize arable land (Bull et al. 1999; Simpson et al. 1999). Nor were such perceptions restricted to Greek and Roman culture. Similar observations about the oleaginous qualities of soil were registered among the Hebrews, for whom abundant crops and livestock were examples of the fat (*hēlebh*) of the land (see Genesis 45:18).[2] In Hebrew culture fat was used metaphorically to refer to the best part of something, especially the choicest fruits of the harvest as well as the fertile land that produced them (Münderlein 1980). The fat cattle and ears of corn of which Pharaoh famously dreamt in Genesis 41 have been repeatedly cited in the West as a way of illustrating this connection between fat and abundance. Yet this metaphor seems to have been also connected to the physical properties of fertile soil. It has been argued that the oft-repeated biblical reference to a "land flowing with milk (*hālāb*) and honey" may, when read in consonantal Hebrew (*hlb*), be more correctly rendered as a "land flowing with fat (hēlebh) and honey" (Dershowitz 2010). Isaiah 34:6–7 even suggests that insufficiently fertile soil could be enhanced through the introduction of animal fat. In one of his righteous fits of violence Yahweh declares his sword to be "gorged with fat" and dripping with blood from the slaughter of countless animals, so that when the gore drops on the ground the "soil [shall be] made rich with fat." The fat that so abundantly and poetically enhanced and flowed from the soil infused everything with its richness, from crops and animals to those humans fortunate enough to revel in its flow. One of the Dead Sea Scrolls even foretold a time when bodies would swell luxuriantly in tandem with the land: "all who shall po[sse]ss the land will enjoy and grow fat with everything enjoya[ble to] the flesh" (Martínez and Tigchelaar 1999: 343). Unctuous richness thus provided quite tangible ways of thinking about increase, in terms of both agricultural yield and bodily growth.

Of course, in Hebrew culture not all fat was permitted for human consumption, not least because in sacrificial rites—where substances symbolizing life were circulated between the divine and human realms—the best part of the animal (hēlebh) was reserved for Yahweh just as Yahweh had given humans the fat of animals and vegetables (Marx 2005: 87). Hence the injunction "All fat is the Lord's" (Leviticus 3:16), which chiefly referred to the layer of suet that wrapped the kidneys, organs long thought to be connected to the genitals and therefore to reproduction and sexual desire (Kellermann 1995). Perhaps because this suet was considered especially tasty—and thus could propel people to excess (Hill 2011)—this substance was forbidden to the Hebrews: "It shall be a perpetual statute throughout your generations, in all your settlements: you must not eat any fat or any blood" (Leviticus 3:17). So imaginatively interwoven were the respective fats of lands, animals, and people that, centuries later, the Babylonian Talmud would tell of a certain Rabbi Sheshet who believed he could, through the act of fasting, offer his own body fat as a proxy for the more traditional animal sacrifice: "Now I have sat in a fast, and so my fat and blood have become less. May it be pleasing before you that my fat and blood that have become less be received as if I had offered them up before you on the altar and so be reconciled with me" (Neusner 2005: Chapter 2, Folio 17A).

The Greeks, Romans, and Hebrews thus shared an admiration for oily richness, but this should not distract us from the other tendencies of fat, not all of which were positive. It is worth remembering that the substances that helped to make a particular soil fat also tended to consist of rotten matter as well as feces, substances that are typically viewed as ambiguous even if they yield beneficial results. Columella (1968) described "the very best soil" as being "fat" (*pinguis*) owing to its oiliness as well as "rotten" (*putris*) due to the dead and decaying organic matter it contained (110–11). Fertile soil thus gives life precisely *because* it is comprised of greasy and decaying matter, thus achieving that state of "fecund putrescence" (Tétart 2004) that is the middle term of the organic process of death and rebirth.

It was moderation that kept the relationship between fatness and fertility within manageable bounds, though this link could be short-circuited when too much fat was present. Thus, despite his praise for the fat and putrid, Columella warned that whereas very lean soil tends to become barren, "the fattest and most fertile soil suffers from rankness of growth [*luxuria*]." To make this point he drew an important analogy between fields and bodies: "There is need . . . of much intermixture among these so different extremes, as is requisite also in our own bodies, whose well-being depends on a fixed and, so to speak, balanced proportion of the hot and the cold, the moist and the dry, the compact and the loose" (1968: 306–7). Through such distinctions, especially the one separating hot from cold soil qualities, Columella revealed his reliance on the humoral model of the body that, based on Hippocratic precedents, would structure European medical thinking through the seventeenth century (Winiwarter 2000). Rather than a simple borrowing from medicine, the communication of ideas between the agronomic and medical domains moved in both directions. Just as agricultural authors borrowed insights from physicians, the Hippocratics derived a great deal of their knowledge of human nutrition by observing what took place in plants (Schiefsky 2005).

In animal bodies fat's connection to fertility could be disrupted if it was present in large quantities. Aristotle noted that in fat animals "what needed to go from the blood into semen and seed is converted into soft and hard fat" (2001: 26), which among humans meant that fat males and females will be "less fertile than those who are not fat, the reason being that when the body is too well fed, the effect of 'concoction' upon the residue is to turn it into fat" (Aristotle 1943: 87). Fat was thus viewed as having been concocted from blood and from the nutriments that helped to create blood, but insofar as the normal itinerary of blood was to be turned into sperm in the male and milk in the female, the presence of large amounts of fat in the body could militate against fertility. As a residue of other vital bodily substances, fat enjoyed a double status as both a vehicle of vitality and a form of surplus that could be viewed as literally "excremental" in that it was secreted from the body and might represent a form of waste. Obviously, such ideas are culturally specific. As opposed to African cultures, where fatness can be deliberately cultivated as a means of storing up the forces of life and reproduction (Popenoe 2004; Warnier 2007), Western societies have tended to emphasize the idea that the production of fat and the production of sperm are in a state of tension. This prompted Françoise Héretier-Augé to assert that "[i]n our cultures fat is considered as a deviation of that which should be devoted to sexual activity" (1991: 507). Conceived as a specific concoction of blood, in the West fat tends to be haunted by projections of what it could have been.

Classical sources generally support Héretier-Augé's claim while differing in some respects. Medically speaking, fat was one of the most conspicuous signs of the moist female body. Hippocrates (1957) famously wrote that the great fatness and moistness of the bodies of Scythian women made it difficult for their wombs to absorb the seed of the men (1957: 125–27), though this may have referred to a blockage caused by excessive amounts of the substance rather than the properties of the substance itself (Hippocrates 1959: 171). Indicating that bodies could be imagined with reference to trees as well as land, the great compiler of ancient knowledge, Pliny the Elder, described the fat that is located between the flesh and the skin as being "fluid like sap" (1947: 96). Here, too, excess could result in sterility and decay: "All fat animals are more liable to barrenness, in the case of both males and females; also excessively fat ones get old more quickly" (Pliny 1983: 567). Sustaining an association between plant and animal anatomies, Pliny contended that both suffer from "hunger and from indigestion, maladies due to the amount of moisture in them, and some even from obesity [obesitate], for instance all which produce resin owing to excessive fatness [pinguitudine] are converted into torch-wood, and when the roots also have begun to get fat, die like animals from excessive adipose deposit" (1971: 153).

Analogies between crops and minds had been the stock-in-trade of educational theory since fifth-century Athens (Kronenberg 2009), and when extended to bodies they formed the basis for a set of tropes that would proliferate in the West well into the modern era. The luxuria, or "rankness of growth," that Columella said was a consequence of overly fat soil referred to excessive organic increase that must be cleared away lest the land become unproductive. A term used to describe organic excess that threatened to result in decay and loss, luxuria was more widely used to describe a primary cause of personal and social corruption in Rome (Gowers 1996). The greasy qualities that helped to explain agricultural abundance were also capable of giving rise to more negative consequences: overgrowth, rottenness, and barrenness instead of moderation and fertility. Whether occurring in fields or bodies, corruption and decay represented the furthest reaches of abundance. This way of thinking about bodies—especially those of women—that would remain operative in the West at least through the Middle Ages (Bynum 1995).

SOFTNESS

Depending on the context and circumstances, then, the positive connotations of fat and oily things were capable of being reversed. This may be one reason that the Romans, despite having adopted the Greek custom of rubbing themselves with oil, retained a certain distrust of a practice they often associated with luxury and effeminacy

(Bowie 1993). Yet unctuousness is not the only culturally relevant quality that fat possesses. When contained within the bodily envelope, greasy and sticky fat enhances the softness of soft tissues, fills in potentially unsightly concavities, and blunts the hard edges of bones. This erasure of the most telling signs of the skeleton—an unpleasant reminder of human mortality—may be one reason that varying degrees of plumpness have functioned in many cultures as evidence of health, youth, and vitality. As we will see, however, the yielding capacity of fat did not remain a simple tactile impression but was analogically related to other forms of softness, which were seen as being in some respects the cause or effect of corpulence. While some of this softness pertained to qualities attached to females, who were typically seen as being colder, fatter, and moister than males (Dean-Jones 1994), it also denoted organic decay as well as corruption in general. This slippage between the feminine and the rotten is a common feature of the softness that fat has manifested in Western culture (Bynum 1995; Tétart 2004).

As was the case with the unctuousness of fat, some of this softness was explained with reference to different physical environments, where climate and terrain were thought to mold bodies and character in definite ways. While space limitations do not permit a full discussion of the ancient associations between corpulence and moisture, the Hippocratic authors maintained that people residing in fat and moist lands were more likely to have similar features in their bodies and characters. This cluster of textures was freighted with moral significance. "For where the land is rich, soft, and well-watered . . . there the inhabitants are fleshy, ill-articulated, moist, lazy, and generally cowardly in character" (Hippocrates 1957: 137). This more or less geomorphic perspective facilitated a mesh of mutually supporting qualities within which fatness was entangled with physical and cognitive traits. In addition to being prone to "slackness" and "sleepiness" such people would lack the "hard" and "taut" articulation of joints that distinguished men from women, warriors from farmers, and Greeks from Asiatics (Kuriyama 1999: 142). Instead, they would manifest an overall laxness in their lifestyles and characters that aligned them with slack effeminacy and corruption. This was the kind of softness implicit in the Greek word for luxury (*tryphē*), which has origins in the idea of receptiveness or nonresistance that is at odds with the "hard" virile ideal publicly celebrated in Hellenic and Roman culture (Dench 1998; Foucault 1990). Thus Herodotus could declare that "[s]oft lands breed soft men; wondrous fruits of the earth and valiant warriors grow not from the same soil" (1969: 301). Commentaries on very corpulent rulers in Egypt and Asia Minor (Athenaeus 1933) provided strategies for moralizing about the "effeminate" luxury that seemed to categorize Asiatic societies, the moral and physical softness of which were presented as a sharp contrast to the imagined virtue and hardness of Rome (Dalby 2000).

Along with moistness, the tactile properties of fat thus played an important role in constructing the moral category of the soft as well as the gendered distinctions that it enabled. The discourse of muscularity that arose at some point between the Hippocratic and Galenic periods reinforced this cultural validation of the hard and taut, establishing a connection between muscles and volition that, according to Shigehisa Kuriyama (1999), has shaped our Western sense of the self ever since. As a substance whose properties include the soft and flabby, fat has functioned since antiquity as the moral and physical "other" of muscle and sinew, whether this tension has been manifested literally, in the validation of hard and taut bodies over soft ones, or figuratively, through references to a softness of character and a lack of willpower. No doubt there was an important visual dimension to such ideals: according to the ancient art of physiognomy, excess flesh, especially if it was soft and flabby, could speak volumes about the character of a person. Appropriated by sculptors as a way of representing how inner ideas of human excellence were popularly believed to be manifested in the external traits of the male body, physiognomic wisdom cast in bronze its assumptions about fat, muscularity, and proportion (Stewart 1990). Yet fat was never simply a matter of aesthetics and appearances. The same logic that compelled Greco-Roman observers to link fat lands to soft characters—and to compare animal and human physiques and character traits—offered a potent way of combining these qualities with reference to fat people.

For example, while corpulent bodies were certainly capable of being admired, in classical antiquity it was also possible to depict them as being physically and morally soft, unable to assume a firm or hard stance in relation to external stimuli or their inner desires. In addition, as we will see below, they could also be seen as insensate, as if the fatty layer under their skin rendered them mentally or emotionally dull. Each of these qualities further aligned such individuals with a spectrum of "lesser" life forms that seemed docile or unintelligent (such as domesticated animals) or those whose apparent raison d'être is to be consumed, whether figuratively, in the case of women (sexual desire has been described since antiquity as a form of hunger, just as females have been metaphorically likened to food), or literally, as in the case of domesticated or hunted animals. After all, the bounty that fat fields and fattened animals could provide *for humans* was grounded in the fact that plants and animals were meant to be consumed or *devoured*, and thus necessarily must have been *mastered* on some level, whether by being gathered, harvested, hunted, or slaughtered. This is the source of the tradition of seeing large bodies as evidence of wealth, status, and happiness but also of the popular tendency to describe certain individuals or groups as fearsome predators who "devour" or "grow fat" off of others.

This impression of fat mastery was nonetheless highly unstable and subject to reversal. According to classical models of appetite the act of consumption could easily drift from the moderate enjoyment of sensual pleasures to excesses reflecting a slavish submission to one's desires. Moreover, situations in which one's control over the process of consumption might be called into question—as in the case of fattened animals—could imply very different qualities. Varro had no doubt about the subordination that fat entailed for barnyard fowls: "These are shut into a warm, narrow, darkened place, because movement on their part and light free them from the slavery of fat [*quod motus earum et lux pinguitudinis vindicta*]" (1934: 481–82). Impressions of fat subjection were further complicated by suspicions of emasculation. Domesticated male animals, as every farmer knew, tended to grow fatter once they had been castrated, with the result being that their flesh became more tender and palatable while their dispositions were said to grow softer (Vialles 1994).

The much-detested eunuchs associated with "Asiatic" courts were a prime example of this, but even when castration was not implied, ancient moralists often registered contempt for those who seemed to emulate the more placid of beasts. Plato (1980: 196) wondered what people would be like in a society that freely provided basic necessities and eliminated the need for vigorous effort to obtain them: "is each of them to live out his life getting fattened up, like a cow?" In his view such people had become fit for slaughter by stronger and harder types: "it's appropriate that an idle, soft-spirited, and fattened animal usually is ravaged by one of those other animals who have been worn very hard with courage and labors" (197). The Stoics extended these ideas in their sharp criticisms of luxuries that threatened to reduce men to ignoble beasts. Seneca described how dissolute fat men who kept late hours and got no exercise were like birds being fattened for the slaughter, except that—unlike animals that had been captured by humans—such men were personally responsible for the fact that "their idle bodies [were] overwhelmed with flesh" (1979: 412–13). Thus, Plutarch admired the Spartan practice of having men dine in common messes, a practice that prevented them from "reclining on costly couches at costly tables, delivering themselves into the hands of servants and cooks to be fattened in the dark, like voracious animals, and ruining not only their characters but also their bodies by surrendering them to every desire and all sorts of surfeit" (1914: 233).

The specter of ignoble animality haunted ideas about fattening in antiquity and, arguably, much of Western culture ever since. Indeed, as a consequence of the methodical and even forced ingestion and incorporation of edible things, the process of fattening carried the troubling reminder that humans, too, are edible and may be "devoured," literally or metaphorically, by those more powerful than they. The softness of fat was thus readily extended to a range of moral qualities and bundled up with several others, which is why corpulence was an ambiguous sign of social privilege that could be celebrated or denigrated, depending on the circumstances. To *grow fat* through good living could signify agency, status, and enjoyment. It could even indicate a predatory role in which a person might "devour" others in a manner commensurate with his or her power. But this impression remained haunted by another possible interpretation: that such a person had abdicated self-mastery by succumbing to more powerful appetites, thus bringing about an internal reversal of power relations, resulting in a sort of *self-fattening* that was considered ignoble and demeaning. To *be fattened* by someone else, in the manner of a pig or goat, could suggest mindless passivity and a resemblance to livestock destined for the chopping block or, centuries later, females fattened to satisfy male sexual appetites (Forth 2012a, 2012b).

INSENSATENESS

In addition to its connections to greasiness and softness, since antiquity fat has been viewed as a dull and insensate material capable of disrupting perception and cogitation. Arguing that blood itself lacks perception, as does anything (like fat) concocted from blood, Aristotle speculated that "if the entire body were to become fat, it would lack perception entirely" (2001: 26). The Romans adopted a similar perspective. Explaining that "greasy fat has no sensation, because it does not possess arteries or veins," Pliny (1983: 567) declared that most fat animals are more or less insensitive: "it is recorded [by Varro] that because of this pigs have been gnawed by mice while still alive." It was due to this insensateness that "the son of the consular Lucius Apronius had his fat removed by an operation and relieved his body of unmanageable weight." The third-century writer Aelian tells the story of the tyrant Dionysius of Heraclea, whose habitual gluttony and luxury caused him to gain so much weight that he found it difficult to breathe and, out of shame, held audiences while seated behind a chest that concealed all but his face. His physicians recommended passing long needles into his ribs and stomach while he was in a deep sleep to discover where his fat ended and his flesh began. The idea was that his fat "was insensitive, and in a sense not part of him," so that the slumbering tyrant would awaken only when the needles hit something "not transformed by the excess of fat" (1997: 291). Dionysius's fat could be cut away because, strictly speaking, it was a form of surplus that was not bound up with his body in the same way as a limb or organ.

Along with the related qualities of unctuousness and softness, the insensateness of fat was readily extended to the characters of individuals burdened with such dull materiality. If the softness of fat could denote excessive yielding, its insensate thickness suggested a kind of insulation through which stimuli pass only with difficulty. The insensateness of fat thus reminds us of its status as an object that, as Hodder reminds us (2012: 7), functions as an obstacle and thus also "objects." In the fourth-century B.C.E. *Physiognomics*, which was erroneously attributed to Aristotle, insensitivity was closely bound up with bodies in which "the distance from the navel to the chest is greater than the distance from the chest to the neck." People with such physiques are "gluttonous and insensitive [*anaisthetoi*: insensate]; gluttonous because the receptacle into which they admit their food is large, and insensitive because the senses have a more cramped space, corresponding to the size of the food receptacle, so that the senses are oppressed owing to the excess or defect of the food supply" (1936: 118–19). In such persons the capacity for emotions and even perception itself is diminished through the constriction of those regions of the body in which the senses are located (Martin 1995). Insensateness was also coupled with the qualities attributed to animals domesticated for human consumption and thus deliberately fattened through restrictions on diet and movement. Thickness and sluggishness of bodily movement thus found parallels in the torpor and clumsiness of the mind: animals with very large abdomens also happened to be "less clever" than those with smaller ones (Pliny 1983: 559). Boxers were often said to grow fat because it prevented them from feeling the full force of their opponents' blows, and no one ever credited boxers with being the cleverest of men.

The insensateness of fat thus seemed to enable cognitive insensitivity as well as motoric sluggishness, both of which would form durable stereotypes about corpulent people that would transmitted through jokes and proverbs. While sometimes admiring fat bodies as evidence of wealth and status (Smith 1997; Varner 2004), the Romans also suggested that intelligence and corpulence were mutually exclusive. As a joking reference to the goddess of intellect, a popular means of denoting dim-wittedness was to say that such a person had a "fat Minerva" (*crassa* or *pingui Minerva*), thus suggesting an unbridgeable gulf between corpulence and wisdom (Plaza 2006). The physician Galen even claimed that the dullness and slowness of the very fat were common knowledge, citing a popular saying to back up his claim: "And this is chanted by almost everyone, for it is one of the truest of all things, that a fat stomach does not bear a subtle mind" (Galen, quoted in Drysdall 2005: 133). If insensateness could move from the literal to the figurative as well as between the animal and the human, it was equally capable of being bundled together with the other qualities of fat. This is how all of those soft and cowardly inhabitants of fat lands could be relied on to be "thick-witted, and neither subtle nor sharp" (Hippocrates 1957: 137). The high living that might contribute to corpulence—and therefore moral and physical softness—could just as easily bring insensateness with it. Railing against the ruinous luxury he saw all around him, the first-century Roman poet Persius described a particularly villainous man as being "numb with vice" because "prime fat has overgrown his heart" (*fibris increvit opimum pingue*), as if the substance had worked its way into his very innards (quoted in Plaza 2006: 94).

None of this was exclusive to the Hellenistic tradition, for the Hebrews, too, registered concern about fat's desensitizing effects on the person. In biblical texts words like *hēlebh* take on negative implications when observed in the human body, especially for the well-to-do, whose enjoyment of "fat things" could lead to arrogance, selfishness, or financial ruin (Berquist 2002; Kottek 1996; Ringgren 2006). Insensibility was a primary trait of wealthy people who showed no compassion for the needy, for they had been rendered insensate and dull by their own prosperity and suffered the ill effects of fat regardless of their actual corpulence: "They close their hearts to pity [literally: they are enclosed in their own fat (hēlebh)]; / with their mouths they speak / arrogantly" (Psalms 17:10). In a number of biblical passages fat is synonymous with being mentally slow or "thick" and is manifested most often among the prosperous: "Their hearts are fat [*taphash*: unreceptive or stupid] and gross [hēlebh]" (Psalms 119:70; Brown, Driver, and Briggs 1974). Such people become obdurate, suffering from a hardening of the heart, which was also considered the seat of the mind. In Deuteronomy 32:15 Moses recites the words of God to the Israelites, explaining how, after being provided with the bounty of the land, Jacob became complacent and turned his back on God: "Jacob ate his fill; / Jeshuran [i.e., the people of Israel] grew fat [*šemen*], and kicked. You grew fat [šemen], bloated, and gorged!" Even if abundance and good living had caused these bodies to become grotesque to the eye, the Hebrew tradition was more concerned with the spiritual and cognitive effects of this fattening.

CONCLUSION

Once incorporated into early Christianity the Hebrew concept of the "fat heart" and the Greco-Roman alignment of softness with corruption and effeminacy were woven into the Western imagination. Variations on the ancient theme of the insensate, decadent, uncaring, or stupid fat person survived into the Middle Ages and beyond. First recorded in 1250, the English epithet *fathead* (*fetthed*) captured the gist of this idea, and the proverbs that have circulated since then have further propagated this stereotype: "a belly full of gluttony will never study willingly," "a gross belly does not produce a refined mind," and so on (Strauss 1994: 1:18). If, as several scholars suggest, fatness did not necessarily signify gluttony in the Middle Ages, it was quite often seen as a prime symptom of folly. The modern West thus inherited from antiquity a view of fat as a sign of vitality and fertility that, when present in excessive quantities, could produce opposite effects. We may thus concur with Susan Hill that, rather than being an unequivocally good substance or habit of the body, in the premodern world fat "spills over conceptual binary boundaries and functions much like a cultural trickster, connecting with both life and death" (2011: 13).

What is striking about the qualities of fat is the extent to which they resonate in a range of stereotypes throughout Western history. Let's consider one example from physiognomy, an ancient form of corporeal knowledge that, along with the pseudo-science phrenology, was discredited by medical specialists while remaining popular among Americans into the twentieth century (Griffith 2004). In a work that appeared in new editions through the 1920s, Mary Olmsted Stanton drew direct parallels between the properties of fatty tissue and the characters of fat individuals. Muscle and fat are "two classes of tissues [that] create and exhibit two distinct and opposite kinds of character" (1890: 75). Whereas muscle reveals the power of the will, "[f]at is yielding, without the ability either to withstand or to overcome. It is negative in its nature, utterly unreliable, except where we find it in combination with a good bony structure and considerable muscular development" (93). From the properties of fatty tissue Stanton inferred a range of personal characteristics, notably selfishness and a lack of empathy. While warning readers against looking for any single sign of such traits, Stanton declared that "[t]he excessively fat are usually quite selfish, for fat is a tissue which is *negative* in its nature and is not endowed with *feeling or sensitiveness*" (262, emphasis in original). A fat person is simply "too busy looking after his own comfort to think of others, and too weighty and bulky to *move actively* in those acts of friendship and benevolence which require personal effort" (262, emphasis in original). Here, then, on the cusp of our modern obsessions with slenderness (Stearns 1997), ideas about fat personhood resonated with the physicality of the fatty substance even as they were updated to function in novel contexts.

This chapter has argued that the unctuous, soft, and insensate qualities of fat have been bundled together in Western culture through centuries of "semiotic regimentation and stabilization" (Keane 2005: 195). Part of this regimentation revolves around an unstable yet resilient and durable hierarchy of substances, textures, and consistencies that tacitly mobilizes methods of characterizing the social world and the people who inhabit it. To the extent that modern stereotypes about fat personhood are permeated by premodern ideational content, it seems likely that the qualities of fat have continued to impress themselves on our language and culture well into the present (Forth 2012b). None of the preceding purports to reveal a deep-seated cultural repugnance for fat bodies that somehow explains or validates our contemporary misgivings. The will to see in classical antiquity pre-echoes of our own modern obsessions is as problematic as the desire to completely divorce our current concerns from the distant past, as if prejudices against fat are either distinctly modern or purely visual. Rather, there is an ongoing dialectic between past models and present applications, between those elements of the past that fall into oblivion as well as those that are resurrected and reimagined to serve novel agendas. If our contemporary anxieties about corpulence reflect more modern changes in our society, they may also be viewed as being inflected by a cluster of much older ideas that circulate in the present in subtle ways. Although further research is needed into how such ideas are transmitted and reworked over time, Anne Brumley may well be right when she notes that "fatphobia is entrenched firmly, and often invisibly, in every English speaker's heritage" (2010: 126).

4 JOSEPH BEUYS

Shaman of Fat

Alison Leitch

It is the transformation of substance that is my concern in art, rather than the traditional aesthetic understanding of beautiful appearances. If creativity relates to the transformation, change and the development of substance, then it can be applied to everything in the world and is no longer restricted to art. . . . Then there is the fat inside the tub, lying there like a moulding or sculpting hand of the kind which lies behind everything in the world. By this I mean creativity in the anthropological sense, not restricted to artists. The relationship is with realities rather than artifacts.

—Joseph Beuys (in Tisdall 1979: 10)

In a provocative essay, anthropologist Tim Ingold (2007) asserts that scholars working on the materiality of social life have paid far too much attention to the materiality of objects at the expense of a deep understanding of materials. Inspired by the work of James Gibson (1979) on visual perception, Ingold presents what might be seen as a deep ecological position on the ways in which human beings are immersed within material worlds that are in a constant state of transformation and regeneration.[1] Materials, Ingold insists, *occur* rather than simply *exist* (2007: 14). Human beings are literally immersed within an "ocean of materials," within a world that is in continual flux involving ever-present "processes of admixture and distillation, of coagulation and dispersal, of evaporation and precipitation" (7) in which the basic elements of life—water, rain, sun, daylight, fire, and even air—are also essential mediums (7–14). Just as humans play a part in the transformation of materials, so too, Ingold insists, do other creatures, for example, insects and plants. Thus, for Ingold, far from being the inanimate stuff typically envisioned by modern thought, materials are active constituents of a world-in-formation in which all living organisms are enmeshed. And while this defense of "materials" as opposed to "materiality" might appear overly dismissive of the wide-ranging and increasingly sophisticated field of thinking about human entanglement with inanimate objects in social analysis (see, for example, Bennett 2010; Hodder 2012), the call to take materials more seriously as active forces in human, animal, and biological lifeworlds certainly provides a stimulating platform from which we might rethink the ways in which substances resonate in everyday aesthetic and cosmological domains across time and space.

This chapter takes up Ingold's challenge in relation to the work of the enigmatic postwar German sculptor Joseph Beuys. Long considered a controversial figure within contemporary art worlds, Beuys has been regarded suspiciously by some as a charlatan showman (Buchloh 2001, while others have viewed him much more positively, as a visionary shaman (Kuspit 1995; Walters 2010). But regardless of how he is portrayed, Beuys's use of materials in the sculpting process shares, I argue, something of this general concern with substances and their relationship to more general ecological processes. Just as Ingold suggests that the properties of materials tell stories about what happens to them as they flow, mix, and mutate in natural and social worlds, Beuys is equally engaged with the "transformation of substance": with what materials can tell us about human life, natural ecologies, and their emergent energies through works of art.

Beuys used fat as well as felt in many of his works. He thought of fat in particular as a supremely alchemical material, the archetypal *prima materia* to be transformed into *ultima materia* "in Paracelsus' words, the *quinta essentia* of the 'life spirit' that can cleanse a man's life" signifying ideas of transformation and renewal (Kuspit 1984: 350). Taking fat as a key element in Beuys's aesthetic, this chapter will tease out the various ways in which the artist focused on the resonate power of substances to promote a form of ecological and spiritual healing of trauma in the modern world. In tracing these themes, the chapter will take a closer look at a number of Beuys's works, for example, *Tallow*, in which Beuys chose a "sick" spot in the urban environment of Münster to cast a twenty-ton block of animal fat, the "negative" of the wedge-shaped space under an access ramp to a pedestrian underpass, and *Fat Chair*, one of Beuys's most enduring assemblages that plays with the idea of chaos.[2]

Love him or hate him—and it appears that the artist provokes vehement reactions in both directions—there is no doubt that Joseph Beuys is one of the major figures of postwar European art. There is an enormous literature on Beuys and about his work even though it is difficult to categorize him within any specific art tradition or movement. Throughout his life Beuys adopted many different media, from drawing to sculpture. But, like Marcel Duchamp,[3] his work is viewed as a major breakthrough in rethinking the purpose of art in the twentieth century. So singular and exemplary is his art-making practice and philosophy that the literary philosopher Gregory Ulmer (1984: 21) even likened Beuys to the "Derrida" of performance art. Outside of Germany, his work is perhaps best known in the United States, where he conducted a lecture tour entitled "Energy Plan for Western Man" in 1973[4] and gave one of his most provocative one-week performances in 1974, entitled *Coyote: I Like America and America Likes Me*. This action was held at the Réne Block Gallery in New York, where Beuys famously locked himself into a cage in the gallery with a coyote for three days.[5] And in 1979 a much-discussed major retrospective for Beuys was curated at the Guggenheim Gallery in New York.[6]

Beuys was a member of the neo-Dadaist art movement known as Fluxus between 1962 and 1965, alongside figures such as George Macinus, John Cage, Nam June Paik, Yoko Ono, and Allan Kaprow, but eventually broke his ties with them because he apparently believed Fluxus had no program for effecting real change in the world (Taylor 2012: 20). He has also been associated with a loose group of avant-garde artists whose work the Italian art critic Germano Celent labeled as *arte povera* (literally, "poor art") and promoted as a revolutionary genre that attempted to break down the barriers between art and life in the heated political atmosphere of Italy during the late 1960s and early 1970s. But Beuys's vision went far beyond this group's interest in the magical nature of the natural world, material substances, and the utilization of found objects in their assemblages and performance art. While he was similarly engaged with a critique of the contemporary art world and modern rational systems of thought and social organization, Beuys's ideas on art making drew much more specifically from nineteenth-century German romantic poets and writers (for example, Johann Wolfgang von Goethe and Friedrich von Schiller), as well from German idealist philosophy and other, more idiosyncratic spiritual, mystical, and esoteric influences, such as early speculative alchemy.

Many scholars have noted the huge influence of Rudolph Steiner's anthroposophy on Beuys.[7] David Adams observes, for example, that "Beuys began to shape his artworks out of the anthroposophical understandings of the spiritual qualities or activities of substances, plants and animals in nature—not as symbols of these activities but as direct manifestations of them composed into meaningful signs" (1998: 198). And the religious philosopher Mark Taylor also argues convincingly that it was indeed Steiner who provided the bridge "that would enable [Beuys] to join his explorations of mythology, shamanism, and alchemy on the one hand and, on the other, philosophy, Christianity, and art" (2012: 29). Since the 1980s Beuys's reputation has waxed and waned, but more recently he has been the subject of a number of critical reassessments (e.g., Foster 2011; Mesch and Michely 2007; Novero 2010; Taylor 2012; Thompson 2011; Walters 2010) and many new major international exhibits.[8] As Taylor (2012:14) notes, in this historic period where reality itself is becoming more and more virtual, many artists are returning to media that are insistently material: rethinking the ways in which art reconnects us to more spiritual dimensions of human and social life, to the threshold of the visible and invisible realms of our increasingly fragile lifeworlds.

Although Beuys was profoundly interested in the transformative nature of the material world and the material qualities of substances, such as fat, he was probably not familiar with the wider ethnographic evidence on the healing powers of fat and its symbolic meanings in cosmological worlds both within and outside Europe. Yet, surprisingly, far from being the negative substance that it has become in contemporary times, often evoking ideas of disgust (Forth 2012; Forth, in this volume), in many other cultural contexts fat is often thought of as a healing and life-enhancing material. Historically, for example, ideas about fat have changed quite dramatically throughout European history. In a particularly nuanced account, the cultural historian Christopher Forth excavates a range of meanings attributed to both fat bodies and fatty substances as he details the historical sources of modern European perceptions of fat. Among other things, he observes that in many ancient European texts fat was linked to ideas of fertility and viewed as the stuff of life, of vitality and strength, in both human and natural worlds (2012: 87). Although these ideas on the life-enhancing nature of fat and fatty substances jostled with other, more ambivalent ideas from the early modern period on, Forth also documents the ways in which fat—even human fat—was seen as a healing substance and commonly used for medicinal purposes until well into the nineteenth century.

Forth's cultural history of the changing meanings of fat is firmly based within recent work on materiality that has emerged in anthropology and archaeology (Boivin 2008), as well as in semiotics (Keane 2005; Meneley 2008), that insists on the ways in which the meanings attributed to things and substances are embedded in and engage with the physical properties of the material world. Fats and oils, Forth suggests, are "slippery substances both materially and conceptually" (2012: 92), but this slipperiness, he would argue, is partly due to fats' material properties: their capacity to readily change their form, enabling them to take on new meanings depending on the cultural and historical context. And as I have already suggested above, Beuys also engaged closely with fats' material properties in his art-making practice and philosophy.

Beuys sometimes referred to his project as an "anthropological" one. As I later explain, the artist used this term specifically to refer to the critical nature of his art-making practices in the context of debates about the impact of art more generally on the human condition. But while Beuys certainly drew on an eclectic range of premodern ideas of substances as malleable materials, ideas that were useful to this critical project, he was not really interested in any wider cross-cultural ethnographic research about fat's transformative properties. In the concluding section of this chapter I will turn to a detailed examination of the healing and transcendent power of fat in traditional Australian Aboriginal societies. This is not meant as an exercise in ethnographic diversion. In highlighting this material, my intention is simply to allude to some possible links to the use of fat more generally in human life. These examples, I suggest, not only bear some uncanny resemblances to the ideas of fat that Beuys refers to in his work but are useful in bringing us back to a focus on fat's more universal material qualities that may well encode ideas of death and rebirth, fertility and decay, as well as spiritual transformation: both bodily and worldly across time and space in many different cultural contexts.[9]

ORIGIN STORIES

My own fascination with Joseph Beuys has evolved quite circuitously through other research projects that have little to do with art history or criticism. For many years now I have been working on a landscape memoir of people and place in the marble-quarrying region of Carrara located in central Italy, and I have been agitated by the phenomenology of marble, not fat (Leitch 1996, 2010). However, during the first period of this research, between 1986 and 1989, I became equally intrigued with a particular local specialty—*lardo di Colonnata*—a type of cured pork fat made in a remote mountain village located at the end of a narrow, winding mountain road traversing one of the three main marble valleys of Carrara. A festival dedicated to this culinary specialty used to be held each year over three hot days in late August, with thousands of visitors descending on the tiny village of Colonnata to consume copious quantities of unctuous, salted pork fat, scantly adorned—if you were lucky—with a slice of raw onion and a piece of bread. My interest in the subject of lardo was thus first piqued by these Dionysian gustatory displays of sheer pleasure associated with tasting fat and by the local reverence toward what appeared to be such an obviously proletarian and elsewhere despised food, associated, for example, with the notion of fat as "poison" in modern American diets (Klein 1996; Rozin 1998).

As I later discovered, not only was pork fat a "proletarian hunger killer" (Mintz 1979) viewed as a key source of calorific energy in the quarry worker's diet—at least in the past—but it was also considered to be a potent healing substance and was used as a cure for any number of health ailments, from an upset stomach to a bad back. One local restaurateur and lardo maker, nicknamed Ometto, or the "little man," was a mine of information on the subject. As he put it, when one went to the butcher and asked for lardo, "everyone knew there was someone ill at home" (Leitch 2000: 107). Later, I went on to document the ways in which lardo di Colonnata became appropriated as a key symbol of an "endangered food" for the Slow Food movement (Leitch 2003), and it was while writing up this research that I first came across the work of Joseph Beuys. It surprised me at the time that no matter how fleeting the conversation or how detached the social context, Beuys was constantly mentioned to me by other scholars and sculptors in Carrara during subsequent discussions about my pork fat research. I began to wonder what prompted people to talk about Beuys whenever fat was mentioned. Why did Beuys, as well as fat, incite such agitated responses?

Although Beuys worked with a number of different materials—including felt, wax, rubber, dead and live animals, blood, copper, honey, and bones—fat was arguably one of his most provocative and misunderstood materials. Indeed, Beuys himself often commented on how surprised he was at viewers' strong reactions to the use of fat in his work. Rather than clay or plaster, Beuys chose fat as a modeling medium partly for its protean properties—its ability to change its form in response to warmth and cold—as well as for its symbolic qualities: its connection to the idea of spiritual warmth linking visible and invisible levels of reality. Fat not only played a crucial role in Beuys's idiosyncratic material imagination that linked substances to the development of form in the natural as well as the human world but was also his favorite metonym for the human body and the human condition: "his antidote to the 'Nazi armored body'" and the wounds of modernity (Chametzky 2010: 163).

In this respect Beuys's insistence on the healing power of fat is also related to his own biography: mythical, psychological, and actual. Famously, Beuys created an origin myth of his birth as an artist when talking about his near-death experience during the war as the Stuka plane in which he was flying crashed over the Crimea in the winter of 1943.[10] According to his own account, Beuys was saved by the prompt actions of local people, the Tartars, who smeared his horribly burned flesh with animal fat and wrapped him in felt. In the catalog prepared for the 1979 Guggenheim retrospective of his work, Beuys recollects the incident as follows:

> Had it not been for the Tartars I would not be alive today. . . . Yet it was they who discovered me in the snow after the crash, when the German search parties had given up. I was still unconscious then and only came round completely after twelve days or so, and by then I was back in a German field hospital. . . . The last thing I remember was that it was too late to jump, too late for the parachutes to open. That must have been a couple of seconds before hitting the ground. . . . My friend was strapped in and he was atomized by the impact—there was almost nothing to be found of him afterwards. But I must have shot through the windscreen as it flew back at the same speed as the plane hit the ground and that saved me, though I had bad skull and jaw injuries. Then the tail flipped over and I was completely buried in the snow. That's how the Tartars found me days later. I remember voices saying "*Voda*" (Water), then the felt of their tents and the dense pungent smell of cheese, fat and milk. They covered my body in fat to help it regenerate warmth, and wrapped it in felt as an insulator to keep the warmth in. (in Tisdall 1979: 16)

Whether or not this story is an outright fabrication, as one of Beuys's most scathing critics, Benjamin Buchloh (2001), initially asserted, or merely a creative embellishment of the actual wartime accident, Beuys's account of the event undeniably served as a powerful creation myth of the artist's rebirth in the wake of the horror of Nazi rule and its devastating aftermath. This was a period of history that, as Buchloh also remarked, annihilated cultural memory and "left mental blocks and blanks and severe psychic scars on everybody living in this period and the generations following it" (2001: 203). Whether intended or not, this extraordinary experience "became the 'stuff' of Beuys's art" (Taylor 2012: 21). It was also a legend—the "Story," as Peter Nisbet dubbed it (2001: 7)—that would haunt his critical reception inside and outside of Europe for years to come.[11]

Less well known, perhaps, is the more intimate connection to fat that recurs throughout Beuys's early biography and his family background, as well as in the wider generational concerns of the body politic. Born in 1921, Beuys grew up in Kleve (Cleves), a provincial town located in the Lower Rhine region of Germany, adjacent to the Dutch border. The town was "an anomalous Celtic-ethnic and strictly Catholic enclave tenuously attached to a Germanic and Protestant country" (Moffit 1988: 127), with rich mystical traditions dating back to the Middle Ages. Beuys's parents were devout Catholics who apparently subjected their son to a strict religious upbringing, against which he rebelled. According to one of his biographers (Stachelhaus 1987), the Lower Rhine, with its flat, expansive landscape, replete with Celtic myths and legends of medieval kings, left a strong mark on Beuys's personality and no doubt contributed to his lifelong interest in Celtic mythology and his idiosyncratic version of Christianity. As a young boy, Beuys demonstrated a love of nature, jotting his observations about trees, grasses, and herbs in notebooks and keeping botanical collections, as well as maintaining a small zoo and laboratory in his parents' house (Stachelhaus 1987: 12). Interestingly, in light of Beuys's future love of costuming in his performance art, Stachelhaus also notes that during his adolescence Beuys went around "pretending to be a shepherd, with an imaginary flock and a genuine shepherd's crook—which he later transformed into *Eurasian Staff* in one of his Actions" (1987: 12).

Shortly after the Nazis assumed power in 1933, Beuys defied his strict Catholic family and, like many of his peers, joined the Hitler Youth. After graduating from high school, he enlisted in the military and joined the Luftwaffe, piloting the now-infamous Stuka dive-bomber, in which he was injured five times before his critical wounding in the winter of 1943. But after the war his parents wanted him to pursue a much more mundane occupation rather than becoming an artist. As Beuys recalls, "After my time as a prisoner of war . . . [my] parents would have preferred to see me—and here is something superficial—going into the lard factory at Cleves.

Because we have in Cleves one of the largest factories for butter, margarine, and lard" (quoted in Chametzky 2010: 189). Fat, then, could be said to affirm Beuys's complex, indeed ambivalent, connections to his family and to the bountiful landscape and culture of the Lower Rhine valley, as well as his struggle to escape the physical and psychological scars of the past.

It is interesting to note as well the way in which fat in all its forms figured as a highly valued yet scrupulously controlled item in German diets during the war years: an item that, as art historian Monika Wagner points out, is "historically laden" (quoted in Chametzky 2010: 190) and has multiple meanings and associations. On the one hand, Wagner observes that fat was associated very positively with cultural ideas of individual good health, as well as happiness and well-being, and during the war years the Nazi government even devised a "fat plan" for delivering fat to its hungry population and troops.[12] Yet alongside these very positive ideas, more negative meanings were attached to fat in the aftermath of the war. According to some writers, both fat and felt became associated with the collective trauma of Auschwitz: as the by-products of the state killing apparatus, human fat was reputedly rendered from the murdered bodies in the gas chambers to be used for the production of soap, and hair shorn from victims was shipped to factories to be made into felt. But although the historian Gene Ray (2001) has argued quite persuasively that many of Beuys's objects, particularly those using fat and felt, referred directly to the experience of Auschwitz, Beuys never explicitly acknowledged this connection, as Ray also admits. Indeed, Beuys actively resisted the idea that his work could be interpreted simply symbolically, stating in 1968 that "I do not want to interpret, because then it would seem that the things I do are symbolic, and they are not" (quoted in Foster 2011: 54).

In a brilliant review of major German twentieth-century art movements, Peter Chametzky describes one of Beuys's performances in 1964 that may shed some light on where he stood, at least in relation to the question of the collective wounds of the Nazi era. The event took place at the Fluxus group's Festival of New Art at Aachen University and was timed to coincide with the twentieth anniversary of the July 20, 1944, attempt on Hitler's life. The action involved Beuys and another performance artist, Bazon Brock. While Beuys stood idly by, melting his Rama brand margarine on hot plates in cases, Brock began broadcasting Goebbels's infamous 1943 speech recorded after Germany's defeat at Stalingrad, in which the propaganda minister exhorted his listeners to die in what appeared to be an increasingly hopeless cause, with the phrase "Do you want total war?" With the soundtrack of Goebbels raging in the background of the theater, Brock stood on his head while calling out to his audience, "Do you want total life?" The event was apparently too provocative for some of the more right-wing students, who stormed the stage and punched Beuys on the nose. A photograph was subsequently circulated depicting a wounded Beuys, bleeding from the nose, holding in his left hand a sculpted crucifix, with his right hand also held aloft in "an incantatory gesture that alluded both to blessing and to the Hitler salute" (Chametzky 2010: 183). As Chametzky astutely suggests, it was precisely "by incorporating his personal history into his work not only as metaphor, but also as material and public wound bearing performances, [that] Beuys repositioned himself and his art on the side of the victims" (184).[13] Just as Beuys was healed, metaphorically or actually, through these materials, fat and felt, the world, he seems to suggest, could be healed through his art.

FAT PROVOCATIONS

Fat in all its forms—whether liquid or solid, soft or hard—is without any doubt a provocative material even in everyday contexts. Greasing and sliding fats act on the world, facilitating other actions and transformations. When heated they produce other kinds of substances, like smoke. Fats elicit smell. Transporting taste, they whet the appetite; their unctuous qualities combine, recombine, and react with other materials to produce myriad forms of other kinds of deliciousness. Oozing out of their receptacles in unpredictable ways, fats cannot be easily contained. They spill. They stain. They spot. Easing friction, fats may lubricate silence, but they also have sounds. They hiss. They sizzle. They spat. Yet fat is also often associated with ideas of excess and waste, viewed as aesthetically unappealing, as something to be trimmed, excised, or eradicated. Fat, then, attracts but also easily arouses immediate reactions of disgust.

Consider, for example, one response to the 1979 major retrospective for Beuys at the Guggenheim Museum in New York. Beginning her review with one of Beuys's more controversial works, Janet Danto (1979) wrote:

> "Bathtub," a child-size white metal tub on a stand with Band Aids taped randomly about the outer walls, inaugurates the first major retrospective of German born artist Joseph Beuys at the Guggenheim Museum. On closer view, the work "Bathtub" contains a shallow pool of liquid in the basin. Floating in this liquid is a lump of fat wrapped in gauze and tied to a string which extends to the opposite end of the basin like a tadpole's tail The fat, lumpy and yellowish, looks like an aborted fetus lying in the remains of its amniotic fluid. Bathtub invites two reactions: Disgust and wonder that this hideous highly unaesthetic assemblage has made its way into the upper echelons of the New York art world.

Key here to Danto's critique is the idea that fat is clearly abject, out of place in the context of a high-end art gallery, and Danto was certainly not unique in her revulsion to the use of fat in Beuys's installations. But in the catalog for the exhibit, the curator, Caroline Tisdall, offers an alternative interpretation. *Bathtub*, she explains, is a seminal work. It is

> [t]he tub in which he was bathed as a child, extended in meaning through sculptural additions: sticking-plaster and fat-soaked gauze. The plaster indicates the wound, while fat suggests a less physical level, Beuys' metaphor for spirituality and the passage from one state to another. Fat can appear in solid or liquid form, definite in shape or chaotic in flow, according to the temperature . . . here it indicates change, transformation and substance—like the act of birth. (1979: 10)

And Beuys confirms this interpretation, adding:

> My intention with this work was to recall my point of departure . . . It acts as a kind of autobiographical key: an object from the outer world, a solid material thing invested with energy of a spiritual nature. You could call this substance, and it is the transformation of substance that is my concern in art, rather than the traditional aesthetic understanding of beautiful appearances. If creativity relates to the transformation, change and the development of substance, then it can be applied to everything in the world, and is no longer restricted to art. . . . The idea of contact with material implies this wider concept of art and of human work and activity in general, and that for me is the meaning of this object. It suggests initial contact with elements like water—moving life—and heat. Some people say "Beuys is crazy, his bath water must have been too hot". Such old sayings have deep roots and some unconscious truth. Then there is the fat inside the tub, lying there like a moulding or sculpting hand of the kind which lies behind everything in the world. By this I mean creativity in the anthropological sense, not restricted to artists. The relationship is with realities rather than artifacts. (in Tisdall 1979: 10)

What does Beuys mean when he suggests that his work is concerned with "realities rather than artifacts"? In order to unpack this question we must first turn to a brief discussion of what Beuys meant by his expanded concept of art.

As many scholars have already argued, Beuys clearly worked against traditional aesthetic ideas of what art is or should be. For Beuys art was not "merely retinal" (in Harlan 2004: 14) but had a wider therapeutic and healing purpose: it was concerned with loss of meaning and a withering of the senses in modern society (Borer 1997). It was concerned not only with the wounds of the immediate past, the Nazi era, and the subsequent division of Europe during the Cold War, but also with more general wounds related to the nature of modern capitalist societies and the human condition in general. The function of art, said Beuys, was to heal, but in order to effect a cure the artist believed, it was necessary to return to elementary, forgotten knowledge and things: "to focus our attention on what exists, but is not always visible and seen, not because it is impossible to see but because our attention is focused elsewhere" (Foster 2011: 55). Beuys was interested in exploring substances and materials used in everyday life, for example, honey, beeswax, and copper, which he believed were already endowed with spiritual essences.[14] He also enlisted animals such as the hare or the coyote as allies in his action performances, while selecting other materials that were clearly categorized as nonaesthetic in his assemblages. As we have already seen, these were often discarded things: the detritus of society, such as gauze and bandages, old cardboard boxes, a rusty bathtub, and bleached bones, as well as ordinary materials, such as fat and felt, that the artist nevertheless believed possessed particular qualities that could effect some sort of transformation of human society in an alchemical way.[15]

For example, in the catalog accompanying the 1979 retrospective, the curator comments on Beuys's use of fat and felt, which appeared and reappeared in many of his works. She notes:

> **Fat** infiltrates other materials, is gradually absorbed and brings about a process of INFILTRATION; **felt** absorbs anything with which it comes into contact—fat, dirt, dust, water or sound—and is therefore quickly integrated into its environment. Unlike the filter, it does not let things pass through it but soaks them up into its centre, becoming tighter and denser in the process, and therefore even more effective as an insulator: FAT expands and soaks into its surroundings. FELT attracts and absorbs what surrounds it. (Tisdall 1979: 74, bold in the original)

Fat and felt were thus clearly "empathetic" materials that intermixed with the environment that surrounded them (Kuspit 1984: 351). For Beuys, fat embodied the vital force of nature, movement, and the flux and flow of energy that was linked to his conception of art. Its protean qualities—its ability to change its form, to liquefy, solidify, and even evaporate as it comes into contact with other substances and actions—represented the idea of human creativity: "action in the imagination" (Borer 1997: 21).

As Beuys explains:

> I just worked with substances. I brought substances into a particular configuration, in this case fat. Fat, in itself, represents warmth, for it arises through the warmth process in organic growth processes in the plant, in the process of seed formation. Fat is plastic, flexible mass, still very close to the fluid condition, because the moment any external warmth is applied, even the hand, the blood's heat, then it turns back into oil. And this susceptibility to be reshaped is effected by warmth alone; it doesn't even need a physical encounter. One can also make clay very flexible and warm, so that the lightest fingerprint is imprinted on it,

including the lines. But I wanted a still greater flexibility, and in this great flexibility of the material I wanted to be able to express the very nature of sculpture in the most fundamental sense. (in Harlan 2004: 47)

Beuys's sculptural use of these materials began in the early 1960s with a series of *Fat Corners* (1960–1962) and *Felt Corners* (1961–1963) and with his more well-known *Fat Chair* (1964). As Beuys himself notes, when he first started using these materials, especially fat, he was quite surprised at audiences' reactions:

[And] when I spread the first fat corners—sometimes they were only so big—into a corner, people immediately hit the roof [laughs]. Yes, so you see, I was really lucky, or quite cunning, or quite insightful. I had more or less counted on these fat corners provoking something, calling forth a reaction. And lo and behold, it worked. But then, I didn't just sit back and say: See what's here! Fat corners. Instead I straightaway took this further and attempted, in fact formulated the significance of fat corners: why fat corners, why corners at all, and why the other actions with fat, why not simply a pool of fat? (in Harlan 2004: 47)

Beuys's works in fat and other materials were designed to provoke thought about what sculpture could do. His intention was to appeal to the viewer's inward level of experience. Thus, rather than a conceptual or verbal dialogue about his art, the artist tried to establish an "energy dialogue" with his audiences: a dialogue in which, through images and other actions, he attempted to convey the forces and energies of the natural world and their interactions with the human psyche (Adams 1992: 26; Adriani, Konnertz, and Thomas 1979: 257). In using nonaesthetic materials such as fat, Beuys thus intended both to stimulate discussion and to illustrate his theory of sculpture.

In its most simple form this theory expressed the idea that all processes of transformation in the human and natural world potentially involve a continuous movement between order and chaos, warmth and cold, as well as undetermined and determined states. Both fat and felt were ideal materials to express these ideas, as Beuys observes:

Fat, for example, was a great discovery for me. . . . I was able to influence it with heat or cold. . . . In this way I could transform the character of fat from a chaotic and unsettled state to a very solid condition of form. In this way the fat underwent a movement from a very chaotic condition to a geometrical context at its end. I thus had three fields of power and, there, was the idea of sculpture. It was the power over a condition of chaos, over a condition of movement, and over a condition of form. In these three elements—form, movement and chaos—was the indeterminate energy from which I derived my complete theory of sculpture, of the psychology of humanity as the power of will, the power of thought, and the power of feeling: and there I found it—the schema adequate to understanding the problems of society. (quoted in Taylor 2012: 41–42)

So, for example, in *Fat Corners*, Beuys explores the transformation of substances by placing the most malleable of materials—fat—in a very tight and constricted space: a right-angled corner. *Fat Chair*, on the other hand, plays with the idea of chaos. In this piece a rough triangular wedge-shaped piece of fat is placed on a chair, and a more elementary connection with human transformative processes is made through a pun on the German word *Stuhl*, which can mean "chair" or "excrement/shit." As he describes the work we also glean a sense of Beuys's considerable humor:[16]

> The fat on the **Fat chair** is not geometric as in the **Fat corners**, but keeps something of its chaotic quality. The ends of the wedges read like a cross-section cut through the nature of fat. I placed it on a chair to emphasize this, since here the chair represents a kind of human anatomy, the area of digestive and excretive warmth processes, sexual organs and interesting chemical change, relating psychologically to will power. In German the joke is compounded as a pun since **Stuhl** (chair) is also the polite way of saying shit (stool), and that too is a used and mineralized material with chaotic character, reflected in the texture of the cross section of fat. (in Tisdall 1979: 72, bold in the original)

In *Fat Chair* fat is the material embodiment of chaos, the reserve of energy from which form emerges. As Taylor (2012: 38) observes, understood like this, fat demonstrates what sculpture meant for Beuys. Sculpture, here, is no longer an object but represents for Beuys the idea of formation—*Gestaltung*[17]—and the creative process.

This is also the sense in which Beuys adopts an anthropological definition of art: the idea, in other words, that "everyone is an artist" (1986: 39). But by coining this phrase, Beuys explicitly did not mean that everyone should *become* an artist, for example, a painter, a musician, or a sculptor, but rather that all human beings have the capacity for creativity: the ability to transform themselves and their immediate social environments. The slogan "Everyone is an artist," says Beuys, "refers to the re-shaping of the social body in which every single person both can and even must participate so that we bring about that transformation as soon as possible" (1986: 39). Thus, for Beuys, society itself can be seen as subject to form-giving processes like any other material, and social life can, indeed should, be a site for experimentation, transformation, and self-healing. "Everything," Beuys concludes, "is sculpture" (1986: 57).

Ultimately, Beuys saw his role as an artist as a shamanistic one: a healing vocation in which the principles of what he called "social sculpture" became the cure, the basis and precondition for any healthy living form. However, as other scholars have noted (Kuspit 1993; Walters 2010), Beuys was, apparently, emphatic that in his work he was not interested in resurrecting shamanic practice in any literal sense. As he explained:

> My intention is obviously not to return to such earlier cultures but to stress the idea of transformation and of substance. That is precisely what the shaman does in order to bring about change and development: his nature is therapeutic. . . . So while shamanism marks a point in the past, it also indicates a possibility for historical development. . . . When people say that shamanistic practice is atavistic and irrational, one might answer that the attitude of contemporary scientists is equally old-fashioned and atavistic, because we should by now be at another stage of development in our relationship to material. . . . So when I appear as a shamanistic figure, or allude to it, I do it to stress my belief in other priorities and the need to come up with a completely different plan for working with substances. For instance, in places like universities, where everyone speaks so rationally, it is necessary for an enchanter to appear. (in Tisdall 1979: 23)

Nevertheless, many of Beuys's works focused on "trauma points" in modern life and were attempts to effect a symbolic healing.[18] Some also involved the use of fat. For example, in 1977, in response to a call to several well-known sculptors to create site-specific sculptures in the city of Münster, Beuys created *Tallow*. For this piece, Beuys sought out a "wound"—a "sick" or "sore" spot in the city—and found a modern "architectural folly," as Tisdall called it: a deep wedge-shaped acute angle that collected nothing but dirt in a desolate concrete section of an underground passage on the way to a new auditorium at the university. Making *Tallow* was a massive effort. To enact his cure Beuys built a huge mold of the exact space, measuring five by sixteen meters (52 by 17.5 feet), into which he poured a liquid mixture of twenty tons of molten mutton fat granules and beef fat. All of this was carried out at a concrete factory on the outskirts of the city, where Beuys apparently worked day and night, pouring vat after vat of fat into a plywood mold that even had to be reinforced after it burst under the enormous pressure of the molten liquid. After letting the material cool for several months, the artist used another "warmth process," cutting the wedges of tallow into various sections with wire. He then transported the giant wedges to the courtyard of the Westphalia Museum, where they were eventually displayed looking like "majestic icebergs" (Tisdall 1979: 253). Tisdall refers to Beuys's efforts in making *Tallow* as "an extraordinary example of absurd artistic licence put to didactic and provocative use, a critique of the soullessness of our environment transformed into a survival battery of warm energy: a reserve of fat" (253).

As he played with the power of substances, Beuys brought to light new ways of thinking about the animate nature of the material world and the processes of human creativity. Indeed for art historian Donald Kuspit, Beuys's work possesses unique qualities that render it "resistant to codification as art" (1984: 347). Describing his first experience of viewing Beuys's objects in their display cases at the Darmstadt Museum, Kuspit remarked that the work appeared to him as having a primal, almost primordial charge: more ethnographic than "high culture" in import. In this palatial space with its high ceilings and slightly melancholic light the artist's work reminded Kuspit of the power of art in human consciousness, or rather the power of "what art can be" (347). He writes:

> Existing as relics of life, looking as though they were archeologically excavated from some strange site of experience, Beuys's objects seem at once familiar and unfamiliar, all too human yet from a world of foreign experience. As such they exist not just esthetically, but with an uncanny intimacy, for they seem at once the residue of and lure towards a possible experience of being. (347)

Keeping in mind Kuspit's evocation of the anthropological power of Beuys's art as a "lure towards a possible experience of being," in the following section I am going to make what might appear, at first, a very odd detour into an entirely different imaginative world: the meaning of fat in Australian Aboriginal cosmologies. As I already indicated at the beginning of this chapter, my purpose in incorporating this material is not simply to add another exotic layer of ethnographic evidence around the meanings of fat but rather to suggest that Beuys was perhaps not at all unique in thinking about the power of fat as a transcendent and transformative substance. As we have already seen, Beuys drew inspiration for his ideas about fat from a variety of early modern and premodern European sources, and there is little doubt that Beuys was unfamiliar with the examples I am about to discuss. Yet, strangely, Beuys's insistence on the need to understand the energetic substance of the material world and the potentiality of substances, such as fat, to encode ideas of spiritual transformation, both bodily and worldly, resonates here quite profoundly. This example, I hope, might bring us back to the wider discussion about the importance of thinking about substances more generally: to what we might learn from materials and the "vitality of matter" (Bennett 2010)—the capacity of nonhuman things and materials to affect the social world—and to what, following a Beuysian logic, we may have forgotten, want to avoid, or do not see.

THE LIFE OF FAT

A number of researchers have noted the cultural significance of fat in traditional Aboriginal communities of northern and central Australia (Devitt 1991; McDonald 2003; Redmond 2001; Redmond 2007; White 2001). Like anywhere, fat has of course many practical uses in Australian Aboriginal everyday life, but it is also a highly symbolically laden material. Not only is fat still a sought-after food linked to ideas of health and physical attractiveness, but it is also seen as a source of energy, endowed with spiritual power and associated with positive ideas, such as happiness, strength, health, and fertility, as well as danger (White 2001). For example, writing about the Ngarinyin people of the North Kimberley region, Tony Redmond (2001; 2007) notes that the high caloric value of fat combined with the strong taste and ease in swallowing that it imparts to meat has made the term *proper fat one* the highest accolade that Ngarinyin people give to food. Indeed, fishing and hunting patterns are still largely determined by the season in which various species are known to be "fat." Fatness is also highly valued in newborn babies as an index of strength, and the possession of kidney fat from a frill-necked lizard may even bring good luck to avid cardplayers. These ideas about the deliciousness of fat, as well as the particular potency of particular kinds of fat, are replicated in many other contemporary Aboriginal communities; for example, among the Yolngu of northern Arnhem Land, seasons are marked by various food sources becoming *djukurrmirr* (fat possessing). In the months before the arrival of the wet season, the glistening green turtle fat is particularly prized, along with the oysters and stingrays that have likewise become fat and prime for hunting (Jennifer Deger, July 1, 2013, personal communication).

Yet, Redmond insists, the mobilization of fatty substances, at least in Ngarinyin cosmology, is not just about the taste of fat or its functionality. It concerns much deeper imaginative processes in a world composed of ancestral substances and energies where fat is deposited in the land, in the bodies of humans, and in animals and plants and is transformed into other things. For example, in the Ngarinyin imaginary, diamonds and other kinds of crystallized rocks or "greasy stones" are seen as the congealed fat arising from the bodies of ancestral beings. Similar "stones" may also occur within human bodies, while in the hands of an effective healer they apparently become malleable and pass from one body to another, becoming soft and hard again as they move through different media. These greasy stones are also said to characterize Ngarinyin country, a legacy of the original jellylike nature of the world that allowed its features to be molded by the travels of the autochthonous Wanjina, or original ancestral beings.

There is no doubt, of course, that like many other communities contemporary Australian Aboriginal people suffer from high rates of obesity, heart disease, and many of the other illnesses of modernity as they have moved away from more traditional diets to those based on overconsumption of processed foods, sugar, and saturated fats. Indeed, as Heather McDonald (2003) points out, some these problems may derive to a certain extent from the failure in these communities to distinguish between good fats—bush fats—and the fat derived from domesticated animals and other plant oils. However, if we look at the research on traditional Australian

Aboriginal diets, we see that in stark contrast to modern Western ideas about the deleterious effects on the body of eating too much fat, having a constant supply of animal fat, at least in the past, was mostly thought of as very beneficial, although here, too, fat could be seen as too powerful or potent for certain people.[19]

Much of the literature on traditional Australian Aboriginal diets cites the idea of fat as a powerful ancestral medicine that not only enhances emotional health and social ties but also maintains internal bodily health and keeps the body clean (McDonald 2003).[20] McDonald notes, for example, the way that in some parts of the East Kimberley's, in Gija and Jaru physiology, fat is seen as melting in the stomach as it flows through a network of channels in the body, along with other bodily substances, such as blood and breath. Thus, fat not only provides individuals with an energy source to enable physical activity, plumping out the skin to prevent the body from drying out, but also replenishes other fats and fluids that are lost from the body through exertion and sweating. It is perhaps not surprising, therefore, to learn that fat harvested from native animals such as kangaroos or goannas was—and is—commonly used as an external medicine to anoint and smooth the skin and to treat rashes and sores. But in the context of our wider discussion of the ways in which fat circulates more broadly as a life-enhancing substance and is, without any doubt, a profoundly transformative material in traditional Aboriginal life, I think it is worth reporting here a particularly dramatic contemporary case.

While conducting fieldwork on Warlpiri women's art-making practices in the central Australian desert in the late 1980s, the anthropologist Jennifer Biddle contracted a series of very painful boils—golden staph—known locally as *winjini*. Like the greasy stones that Redmond writes about in the Kimberley's, for Warlpiri people *winjini* live within both human bodies and the landscape and are similarly typified by country; in this case boils are associated with plant materials and prickles, from which they are said to derive. Biddle insists that for the Warlpiri, boils are not a disease of modernity but rather have distinctive histories, distinctive narratives, associated also with powerful ancestral forces. Biddle's vivid account of her own experience is instructive. She writes:

> [W]hen I had that first *winjini*, all those years ago, that first one on my back brewing up a pain unbearable in its throbbing insistence pressure cooker lid explosive before it breaks. Then, my mothers, aunties stayed awake all night with me singing, rubbing my *winjini*, my breasts, my stomach and thighs, time and again with special *marparni jaku*—oil, fat, emu and/or kangaroo sometimes still, olive oil or Crisco from the local shop *more better* yet—the same oil, fat they use on their bodies in ceremony, that same oil that transforms the skin into a mark . . . for imprintation, for transubstantiation, for bringing the surface somatic border of the body to the impregnable fleshy world of the Ancestral, ground, body, canvas. (2008: 98, italics in the original)

From this rather primal encounter, Biddle further develops an analysis of the relationship between *winjini* and painting, observing that it is not just the content of the designs that should be considered. She argues that equally important to understanding this art form are the techniques of painting, particularly the priming of the canvases before the designs can be imprinted. And just as bodies are oiled before ochre is applied in ceremonies, canvases are oiled, painted, and smoothed before marks can be applied. Like the skin of the human body, the canvas of the painting is thus seen as a porous surface—a contact zone between the ancestral and human beings—and once again we see that it is *fat*, or oil, that facilitates the transference of ancestral energy to humans: an energy that reflects again the idea of a living sentient landscape—a malleable force/matter—that responds in a variety of ways to the interventions of human, animal, and ancestral beings.

CONCLUSION

What can we learn from paying attention to the materiality of life and these ideas of fat (and other substances) that I have outlined in this chapter? And what might these ideas have to do with the wider argument I have attempted to outline here on the importance of thinking about the materials that artists, such as Beuys, mobilize in their work? Even though he is inspired by entirely different intellectual sources, I find in Beuys's discussions about fat a striking similarity to some of the ethnographic material on the circulation of ideas about fat in traditional Australian Aboriginal cosmologies. Here we see that fat takes on a variety of symbolic meanings that are deeply connected to its material qualities and its practical use in the everyday but that also bring to life other, less obvious imaginative processes, illustrating more profound ontological conceptions of an animated world where humans and ancestral beings, plants, and animals are all engaged with the processes of creation. This example serves to remind us, as well, of the more universal and sedimented meanings of fats and their "slippery" qualities, which enable them to take on many meanings— their links to both fertility and decay, to transformation and renewal, to birth, death, and spiritual transcendence—which tend to surface and resurface, spreading across time and space (Forth 2012).

Beuys's own cosmology also resonates with the discussion that began this chapter: Ingold's call to think about social analysis not just in terms of objects but also in terms of the vital nature of substances. When Beuys says he is interested in "realities rather than artifacts" he is making a similar distinction: in his case between substances, such as fat, and works of art. Just as Ingold evokes a world in motion— where substances in the material world mix, coagulate, and disperse, undergoing continual processes of formation, regeneration, and transformation—so, too, does Beuys insist on a metamorphic imaginary, in his case a "spiritual alchemy" where substances, such as fat, are imagined through processes of continuing formation and transubstantiation. And just as Ingold insists on the intersubjective nature of the human relationship with the natural world and its material makeup, Beuys also argues, albeit from an entirely different and idiosyncratic perspective, that there is no possibility for human expression except in relation to thinking about materiality and human entanglement with matter.

In summing up his work many scholars have suggested that for Beuys "thought is sculptural," but even "thought," says Beuys, can be expressed only through the materiality of the human body and its sensory organs. As Beuys once remarked, again in an interview with Harlan:

> Yes, there is absolutely no possibility for a human being, as long as he is one, to express himself to someone else except through a material process. Even when I speak I use my larynx, bones, sound waves, for instance, and I need the substance of air. You have to have a membrane in your ear otherwise you wouldn't hear my speech at all. There's no possibility of conveying one's meaning except through imprinting it in a particular material. . . . In other words, conveying information between people is not imaginable without materiality. (in Harlan 2004: 56)

Clearly, for Beuys, materiality matters. Beyond his obsession with fat and other substances, Beuys reminds us here of what we might learn more generally from artists as they transport us into a deeper connection with the elements of life. For, as Gaston Bachelard also tells us, poetic images draw from matter; "[t]hey emerge through a 'material imagination' that learns from fundamental elements" (1983: 11). Material reverie, Bachelard urges, "inlays its objects; it carves them out of the depth of substances" (113). Here we might say, then, that the work of Joseph Beuys in particular—and sculpture in general—could be seen as a solid demonstration of such reverie: a concrete manifestation of our "dreams of will" (Bachelard 2002) and pan-human engagement with matter.

5 ENGROSSING ENCOUNTERS

Materialities and Metaphors of Fat in the Lived Experiences of Individuals with Anorexia

Anna Lavis

> I think there's . . . there's . . . symptoms and effects of the anorexia, which manifests itself in a physical form, or whatever and therefore is seen like an illness and maybe, yes, the weight . . . the low weight is an illness in itself . . . yes, that's what it's like; the low weight's the illness but the mental thoughts are me.
>
> —Claudine, inpatient, 2008

"A dread of fatness and flabbiness of body contour" (World Health Organization 2007: F50.0) is part of the diagnostic criteria of anorexia nervosa (see American Psychiatric Association 1994). It is why "anorexia has low weight as a criterion" (Palmer 2005: 2), which differentiates it from bulimia nervosa. Across disciplines anorexia has frequently been viewed as an extreme modality of achieving a "slender body" (Bordo 1993), which frames self-starvation as a practice aimed at an end goal of thinness. Yet by drawing on ethnographic participant observation and semi-structured interviews conducted during anthropological fieldwork in an English eating disorders inpatient unit (2007–2008) and on pro-anorexia websites (2005–2013),[1] this chapter explores anorexia by paying attention not to thinness but rather to fat(ness). Tracing threads of metaphor and materiality in informants' experiences of *fat* on plates and bodies in order to think about an illness more habitually saturated with reflections on *thin*, offers insights into the meanings that anorexia may have for those living with, through, and inside it.

This chapter has developed from the recognition during my fieldwork in both the English eating disorders inpatient unit and on pro-anorexia websites that thinness was not a frequent focus of informants' interviews. When it did arise, it ebbed and flowed through wider, more complex discussions, which revealed anorexia to be enacted *with* the body but never to be simply *about* the body. This suggests that to enhance our understanding of lived experiences of anorexia, it is necessary to think beyond the illness as a future-orientated quest for thinness and to question " 'bodily obsessed analyses' in which fat phobia and body image distortion are esteemed as the universal driving force behind food refusal" (Katzman and Lee 1997: 386–87). Yet, in both fieldwork spaces, many informants did talk about fat—as well as eating, food, and anorexia. Thus, by turning its attention to the particular ways in which fat is discussed, pinched, conceptualized, and avoided by individuals with anorexia, this chapter asks, if this illness is not *about* thin, then what, if anything, is the relationship between anorexia and fat?

That body fat is, in Euro-American culture, highly stigmatized is clear. Prevalent discursive formations position it as both "abject" (see Kent 2001), where that signifies a "danger issuing from within the identity" (Kristeva 1982: 71), and yet also as external and "inessential . . . an excrescence, a corruption of the flesh" (Klein 2001: 27). As scholars have argued, "the fat body is read as the corporeal presencing of other, presumably more intrinsic, incorporeal qualities or characteristics" (LeBesco and Braziel 2001: 3), and these range from laziness to lasciviousness, and from excess to gluttony (see Braziel and LeBesco 2001; Farrell 2011; Gilman 2010; LeBesco 2004; Rasmussen 2012; Throsby 2012). Work that has critically examined, and sought to counteract, such discursive formations has primarily done so by (re)-theorizing fat embodiment (e.g., Murray 2005a). This chapter complements those valuable discussions by instead exploring how fat is lived, imagined, and (dis)embodied by individuals who do not inhabit socially determined "larger" bodies but to whom fat is potent with meaning. I examine how such meanings both draw on and also "interfere" (Haraway 2008) with wider cultural constructions. Connotations such as excess are delinked from, and relinked to, fat by informants in ways that speak of day-to-day practices of being anorexic and even of doing anorexia through not eating.

Looking beyond cultural constructions of both fatness and thinness is not an attempt to dis-embed anorexia from the cultural context. Rather, it is to consider how anorexia and culture touch edges in intricate ways as particular affective spaces, modes, and contexts give anorexia a value in and of itself—for what it does as well as how it looks. It is in relation to the threads that bind anorexia and personhood that subjectivities and conceptualizations of fat emerge, and this context of relationality is key. The chapter traces how self-starving processually maintains and reproduces an illness that many informants describe as a friend (see also Lavis 2011, 2013). It is from anorexia's friendship that social personhood emerges; informants describe the illness as offering them a way to move through, and withdraw from, the worlds around them. This dynamic entangles fat's material properties with informants' subjectivities of both their anorexia and sociality. Comprising a temporal duality, body fat both visually attests to a loss of the personhood made possible by anorexia and also comes to act in the present in surprising ways. Adding materiality to George Marcus's call to "follow the metaphor" (1998: 92) in ethnographic investigation, these discussions trace the seepages and moments of encounter between fat, anorexia, and personhood.

In its attention to "being anorexic" (Gooldin 2008)—to the practices, meanings, and subjectivities of anorexic individuals themselves—this chapter forms a dialogue with other recent works that have looked beyond thinness in anorexia (e.g., Warin 2010). However, to recognize that anorexia is valued, and even actively maintained, by some informants is not to ignore the distress or ambivalence many also feel; nor is this to deny that anorexia is a dangerous illness—one that, as John Evans writes in his memoir, may be "dark and dangerous and [leave] a shell of a human being in its wake" (2011: 19). Yet, while acknowledging this enormous suffering and also that informants' agency and values (see Tan, Hope, and Stewart 2003) may be affected by anorexia, I also do not assume that their embodied experiences are entirely circumscribed by illness—that the "anorexia is talking" (Tan 2003). As such, this chapter traces the "mattering of matter" (Hayes-Conroy and Hayes-Conroy 2010: 1275), that is, of fat, in informants' narratives. In so doing, the discussion also signifies a mattering of lived experiences of anorexia for individuals for whom the illness may constitute a way (albeit a painful one) of being in the world.

The first half of the chapter explores individuals' relationships with anorexia. Taking account of these demonstrates how fat and thin come to be important or, rather, highly feared in the context of existing anorexia. They have a particular temporal positioning as markers of the presence or loss of the illness and, thus, of the personhood it "holds" and protects. To move the discussion beyond fat as a visual index, and take account of how its materiality enters informants' subjectivities, there is an interlude between the two halves of the chapter, which focuses on the material properties of fat in foods. To informants, fat is at times cloying, lumpen, and static, as in donuts. At others, it is mobile and seeping, as in melted butter. By tracing dynamics of affect mapped along bodily perimeters, the second half of the chapter then explores informants' conceptualizations of how personhood metonymically takes on these material properties of fat. To informants, an increase in body fat not only renders them vulnerable to the worlds around them but also causes them to affect these in undesirable and even harmful ways.

PART ONE: FAT ATTESTS: EATING, RELATIONALITY, AND "KEEPING OTHER PEOPLE AT BAY"

To explore fat as it manifests in the narratives of anorexic informants, this discussion begins not with bodies or fatty food on plates but with lived experiences of anorexia. By beginning here, this section situates itself at a particular temporal moment, one that we might term *in anorexia*. Here fat is potential, and to understand the fear that accompanies this potentiality, it is necessary to pay attention to individuals' relationships with the illness. In their interviews many informants, both in the eating disorders unit and on pro-anorexia websites, described anorexia as an illness replete with physical and emotional pain, often using words such as "horror" and "hell." Yet many of the same informants also described anorexia as a "friend" that they actively maintained and "looked after" by not eating. For example, Tara,[2] who was now in her thirties and had been affected by anorexia for twenty years, explained in her interview, "It's been a friend to me for a long time." It has previously been recognized that "core features of eating disorders can be highly valued" (National Collaborating Centre for Mental Health 2004: 6.5.5) by those affected and also that this value is linked to a subjectivity of relationality; that the illness may be experienced as a friend is explored in discussions from the anthropological (Warin 2006) to the psychological (Colton and Pistrang 2004; Serpell et al. 1999) and is common in memoirs of anorexia. In her account of illness, treatment, and recovery, for example, the British television celebrity Nikki Grahame writes that "anorexia was my best friend, my only friend" (2009: 309; see also Hornbacher 1998, 2008). In his memoir, John Evans (2011) goes further than this to ambivalently describe his relationship with anorexia as like a "marriage."

During my fieldwork many reasons were offered for why anorexia felt like a friend; common to these were descriptions of anorexia as "helpful." In his interview on the eating disorders unit, Laurie said, "It's a friend, definitely a friend. It keeps me company . . . and it helps me . . . you know? It does help me." Likewise, another informant, Shanice, said:

> The first thing that comes to my mind about anorexia is it's like a friend. It's like sort of . . . I dunno . . . yeah, more of a person rather than an illness. It's more of a friend, a close friend, rather than having an illness. Because, when it came along I was going through a really bad time and I was feeling quite depressed and it just sort of came along and rescued me in a way. It's always there for me. It doesn't abandon me, when the going gets tough. It'll always step in for me in a fight.

Although Shanice's discussion of anorexia's help frames the illness as an active agent that "steps in," underlying this is something shared with many other informants, which is the sense of anorexia as in control. In her interview, Jumela, a participant on pro-anorexia websites, wrote, "Speaking as someone with anorexia, I can say that anorexia is in no way connected to wanting to look like models or movie stars. It's a way to have some control in your life." During their interviews, informants described how they shared their agency with, or relinquished it to, anorexia at times when they felt that they needed help. That anorexia may offer control has been recognized in discussions of the illness as "a functional coping strategy in which control of eating serve[s] as a means of coping with ongoing stress and exerting control" (Eivors et al. 2003: 96). As such, the "use of anorexia nervosa to avoid dealing with other problems" (Cockell, Geller, and Linden 2002: 77) has been highlighted. However, it is less recognized that allowing anorexia to take control and, paradoxically, gaining control through this process centrally underwrite this friendship with anorexia. Moreover, existing work has tended to regard a dynamic of control as intrasubjective, related to how starvation dampens emotions. This has led to discussions of how "the emotional life of people with eating disorders centres upon food, weight and shape" (Treasure 2012: 430; see also Espeset et al. 2012; Kyriacou, Easter, and Tchanturia 2009). However, while a dampening of affect and sense of numb protection do form part of informants' descriptions, anorexia's "help" also emerges as something relational and spatial—as much external as internal, social as individual.

In her interview Kate echoed many other informants when she described anorexia as "my space to go into." To her, the illness was both something into which to retreat, where she "[didn't] have to feel," and also something that stood between her and the world, mediating its impact. Or, as Paula put it in her interview, "anorexia keeps other people at bay," which is particularly illuminating when read alongside Miriam's statement that "with anorexia I'm not alone." What has been seen in the psychological literature as an "an illness of the emotions" (Treasure, Smith, and Crane 2007: 73) here emerges as a protective external other that stops the inflow of the world. In its offering of shelter, stillness, and calm, anorexia resembles anthropologist Ellen Corin's discussions of "positive withdrawal" on the parts of individuals recovering from psychosis. She describes this as the construction of a kind of "psychic skin that parallels the social skin" (2007: 283). Here anorexia is a psychic *and* social skin; it is, Kate said, "safe," but she also described how "it keeps me safe." Another informant, Cally, when describing how anorexia helped her in difficult social situations, said, "It's there so I don't have to be." There is thus a duality here that has resonated throughout this discussion of help and friendship; anorexia offers informants a retreat while also, itself, "coming out" to act in the world in their place. It is a presence, and it is necessary to recognize the ambivalence of this. Anorexia here is a safe way of being, but it is also clearly a way of disappearing, or perhaps of *being disappeared*. As such, to trace the dynamics that underpin informants' attachment to their illness is not to gloss over their concomitant fear and distress. Describing how anorexia allowed her moments of calm in which she could forget the pain that various life events had caused her, Claudine said, "You just sit there and sometimes it manifests itself in a sort of numbness and I'll just lie on my bed, stare into space and I'll sleep a lot or something like that. I just want to stop thinking and you do almost zone out as it were." Yet her smile disappeared when she described how much pain her anorexia had also caused her and her family. During these discussions on the eating disorders unit, Claudine would repeatedly smash her fist into her head and scratch her face.

Thus, while I recognize the palpable suffering that anorexia causes, it has also become clear that informants' friendships with the illness are both inter- and intra-subjective in the sense that anorexia is at once both an *other* and yet also a part of, and intrinsic to, personhood. In informants' accounts, it is integral to how "the everyday is produced" (Tucker 2010: 526). By "helpfully," albeit ambivalently, medi-ating how informants encounter and convene with their surrounding social worlds, it offers them a modality of contextually moving through, interacting with, or with-drawing from these. Such dynamics of reordering and producing the everyday allow a particular personhood to emerge *within* and *through* anorexia. As such, practices of self-starvation undertaken by informants maintain a personhood that not only is "held" by the illness but also "unfolds" (Curtin and Heldke 1992) with it. Infor-mants' narratives thereby evince their "intersubjective fusion" (Jackson 2002: 340) with anorexia. In her interview Kate said, "Anorexia's mine. It's just mine. I just think 'I don't want to share this with you' and you know, it's my little . . . it's me. It's how I do things. You do it quietly, you do it on your own." She also said, "I don't want to open myself up because I don't want people to be able to get . . . to get to me, if you know what I mean? If I keep it [anorexia] secret, they can't get to me either." It is clear from Kate's words that protecting oneself and protecting anorexia are always necessarily two parts of the same process. And both of these depend on a continu-ing self-starvation. In her interview Leila said of anorexia, "Well, it helps you so you help it," and helping it, she said, meant not eating. In informants' narratives anorexia emerges both as the practice of not eating but also, as is clear from the above ac-counts of friendship and personhood, as an entity that is *maintained by* not eating; to informants it is a presence that depends on but is greater than starvation practices. I have written in more detail elsewhere (Lavis 2013) about the ways in which not eat-ing "keep[s] anorexia close," as John Evans puts it in his memoir (2011: 83). What is key to the current discussion is the position of fat in this dynamic process. Given that one must eat to stay alive, and also stay alive to continue to be anorexic, while also maintaining anorexia through not eating, the illness is a precarious friend. Its presence must be continually monitored, especially after eating, to check that each threatening mouthful has not allowed anorexia to slip away out of reach. Informants check this by assessing their relative thinness.

In her interview Milla described "patrolling [her] perimeters" by encircling her arms and measuring her thighs with her hands. This "knowing where the perimeters of my body are," as she put it, was Milla's way of reassuring herself that anorexia was still there to offer her retreat and convene with the world for her if needed. Likewise, in her interview Miriam said:

> If you put on any weight it's like . . . "what did you do wrong? What did you do yesterday? What's gone wrong? Why are you putting on weight? Why, why are you doing this? What's going on? How on earth . . . Why, why . . . why did you have that? What was wrong with you? What's going through your mind? You don't need that! Now your weight's gone up and you know, you're giving up and you're just being weak and pathetic." And . . . you know, you've got to be strong, you've got to keep going, keep ploughing on.

Narratives such as Miriam's elucidate the importance of taking account of the particular temporality through which fat and thin come to be central to informants' subjectivities of anorexia. Thinness is not an end goal; rather, it *becomes* important as a marker of the continuing presence of anorexia's protective friendship in opposition to the destructive power of eating. In her interview Eva said, "For me it was never about losing weight, I never wanted to lose weight. I just thought I'd put on weight if I ate more than I had the day before. . . . It's never been about losing weight, it's always been about I will get fat!" This "intense fear of gaining weight or becoming fat" is part of the diagnostic criteria of anorexia nervosa in the *Diagnostic and Statistical Manual of Mental Disorders IV* (American Psychiatric Association 1994), and it is widely recognized that for those with anorexia, "weight gain can be a terrifying experience, not just mentally but also physically" (Treasure and Ward 1997: 107). However, the context of relationality and an "anorexic personhood," just discussed, shifts our understanding of why body fat may be terrifying. If thinness marks a presence, fatness indexes loss. Any increase in body fat felt by encircling arms or quantified by self-weighing comes to attest that one has not sufficiently "looked after" anorexia; it signifies failure. In her interview Nina said, "If I eat I feel fat, disgusting, dirty and a failure," and Jumela, likewise, described her horror at "the awful fat that you can see all over you."

This discussion of fat and thin as important to informants *after* or *in* anorexia, rather than as initial driving forces of self-starvation, challenges the frequent "spectacularization of the anorexic subject position" (Allen 2008), which positions fat simply as the failure of a body-centered project aimed at achieving thinness. Here the temporality in informants' accounts demonstrates thinness and fatness to be usefully quantifiable indexes of anorexia's presence or absence. As such, although it is clear that anorexia is not focused on the body but, rather, maintained *through* the body by self-starving, there is also perhaps a paradoxical "spectacularization" to the way in which corporeal perimeters become central. This process might seem to render the body a two-dimensional index lived only through its visuality. Samantha Murray has explored the "hypervisibility" (2005b) of fat, as body fat is, like anorexia, frequently discussed in purely visual terms that take no heed of its embodiment. However, while I acknowledge that bodies are relational—that their "boundaries material-ize in social interaction" (Haraway 1991: 201) and through the gaze of others—visuality is intriguingly positioned here. It is clear that informants' own gaze turned on the body takes on importance, as is demonstrated by statements such as "video-tape yourself and watch it to see how fat you look whenever you want to eat," which is a self-starvation tip on a pro-anorexia website. Yet what the gaze monitors is not visuality itself. Rather, this is co-opted to stand for subjectivities of how self and world encounter one another.

Many informants found being told by family, friends, or clinicians that they were "looking better" profoundly distressing. As Abigail put it, "How stupid are they, don't they realise that better just means fat?" and fat, she reminded me, means "alone." If, to informants like Abigail, fat marks a dual loss—a slipping away of both friendship with anorexia and the personhood made possible through that friend-ship—then it is clear how it signifies being unprotected. Informants in the eating disorders unit in particular, who experienced an ever-increasing weight gain and loss of anorexia through the enforced eating of treatment, described themselves in ways that suggested a loss of their "social skin" (Corin 2007: 283). Not only is the "safe space" of anorexia lost through eating, but so too is the illness that "stepped in" between informants and their surrounding social worlds. As such, "feeling fat" is not simply a description of unwanted visible corporeal change but also of a lived and felt vulnerability. In her interview Michelle said, "One of the things that my anorexia is about is feeling overwhelmed by life and the world. It really helps me by limiting choices and it helps me keep control." And it was this word "overwhelmed" that reemerged in her descriptions of how she felt when she experienced anorexia to be slipping away from her during treatment. Like other informants, Michelle described how other people's voices, thoughts, and feelings began to "flow into" her in uncon-tained, uncontrolled ways. About this Michelle asked, "How do you say, 'well, that's not my problem, that's other people's problem, I can't control that'? I can't control the economy, I can't control even the things that are going on in this hospital—other people's problems, I can't control that." It is clear from Michelle's words that there is a resonance between this experience of others' emotions and the way in which anorexia was seen above to control informants' own emotions, and this has been noted in psychological literature (Kyriacou, Easter, and Tchanturia 2009; Warren and Cooper 2011). Yet Michelle's narrative also elucidates that it is sociality more widely that is experienced as threatening. Other people come to be too keenly felt when anorexia no longer stands between informants and their worlds. The word that Paula and some other informants used to describe this was "suffocating." This word offers a glimpse into how fat not only indexes these dynamic processes of sociality but also plays a part in them. To understand this and also, importantly, to see how this flow between informants and sociality is not unidirectional, we need to begin to think about fat's materiality. Tracing how fat is "ambiguous; placed simultaneously under the skin yet materialised as a substance in and of itself" (Colls 2007: 358) will offer insights into how fat not only attests to loss and induces vulnerability but also "comes out" in anorexia's place in undesired ways. The following interlude therefore reflects on fat as matter before Part Two explores the links between this and the personhood that informants feel arises when fat is gained and anorexia lost.

INTERLUDE: BETWEEN PLATE AND BODY/ METONYMY AND SUBSTANCE

In the English eating disorders inpatient unit where I conducted fieldwork, boxes filled with hundreds of one-portion cubes of butter spoke of institutional life, individual struggle, and the need to "fatten" to save lives. But butter was also the subject of the most subversive stories about avoiding this clinical food-as-treatment paradigm. Butter was smeared into hair, under chairs, and on clothes—all activities aimed at avoiding both the ingestion of and any contact with fat. This avoidance was also clear in many other contexts on the unit. Cooking Group was held once a week in the fading light of Wednesday evenings. This was attended by a few patients nearing the end of their admissions, who had been directed by their care plans to come together with the occupational therapist to prepare meals under supervision. Each patient planned, shopped for, and cooked dinner, and then everyone participating in that week's Cooking Group ate together in a room separate from the main dining room. The occupational therapist and participants generously let me join them on many Wednesday evenings, during which the usual atmosphere of Cooking Group was a mixture of chat, music, and gallows humor. Yet, in contrast to the free ebb and flow of laughter and words, participants often expressed anguish at touching food. Some would hold serving utensils by the tip, as far away as possible from the cooking food, and would jump back hastily if a drop of mashed potato or rice pudding slid off the spoon. Others would wash their hands frequently, not only after contact with food, but sometimes even after stirring the saucepan. During the cooking, utensils were continually placed in the sink and new ones got out for each stir. Some participants also held their noses and hid their faces from cooking smells. The constant resurrection of boundaries against food is part of the processual protection of anorexia, which keeps one's friend and one's personhood present in opposition to eating, as explored in Part One. However, what became particularly clear in Cooking Group was the specific positioning of fat in this process; fat was more frequently described as "contaminating" and "dangerous" and aroused more fear than other foods. Informants' conceptualizations of this substance centered on two contrasting material properties; it was seen as static, engulfing, and cloying as well as mobile, sneaky, and uncontainable.

During one week's Cooking Group Claudine and I made a risotto. Claudine found it difficult to place the "cleaner" food, which to her was the drier food, such as rice, in the pot with the oil. She described feeling that the oil sullied the rice but also, importantly, trapped it. Her horror focused on the way in which the oil entirely coated the rice, engulfing it with a threatening permanence. This sense of stifling stasis was also present in informants' discussions of how oil, butter, and grease coated hands, lips, and the insides of their mouths. In conversation about the therapeutic enforcement of meals, which is inherent to the treatment of eating disorders, certain foods arose with the greatest frequency, and one of these was donuts. Informants' explanations of why they objected to being made to eat donuts focused not only on their capacity to add fat to patrolled bodily perimeters but also on donuts' material properties. As one inpatient informant, Elle, told me, they *were* fat. Elle qualified this by describing how donuts do not—cannot—break into crumbs; instead, they "squodge," with the fat maintaining an internal coherence to their parts, which cannot be separated. As informants turned bits of donuts over in their fingers, trying to reduce them to disposable dust during the communal mealtimes, these simply coated their hands with oil. It was while attempting to do this—and avoid eating— that another informant, Chloe, suddenly screamed during one mealtime, "I'm not eating this shit again!" before slamming her untouched donut onto the communal table, reducing it to a stodgy squash of jam and sugar. Chloe then ran from the room in tears. Donuts, like other foods, induced fear and revulsion in informants like Chloe because of their cloying, engulfing fat, which we saw in Claudine's horror at the coating of rice with oil. Yet the ways in which Claudine talked about fat's progression through the pan to coat each rice kernel not only resonated with a sense of entrapping, enforced connection but also evinced a second aspect of fat's horrifying materiality. As well as lumpen and seemingly indestructible, fat was also described by informants as mobile and seeping.

It was also the uncontrollable and uncontainable nature of the oil's trajectory toward the rice that Claudine winced at and recoiled from. In her ethnographic explorations of anorexia, Megan Warin has also explored this quality of fat. She suggests that for her anorexic informants "foods that glistened (such as melted cheese on top of a pizza), or those that left remnants of oil behind . . . were considered dangerous, fatty, and dirty" (2010: 117); fats and oils, moreover, were "most dangerous . . . because of their ability to move and seep into the cracks of one's body" (106). This latter aspect—informants' conceptualizations of fat's movements within as well as outside the body—is clear when we reflect on a particular way that anorexia is maintained by not eating. During my fieldwork a practice undertaken by some informants to test whether they were "looking after the illness properly" was "chewing and spitting." Informants recounted how they would take mouthfuls of food and chew it carefully before spitting it out. This is advocated on pro-anorexia websites as a way of testing one's mettle to self-starve; by refusing food *through* the body, this is part of the day-to-day maintenance of anorexia. Yet discussions among my informants and more widely on pro-anorexia websites also highlight that chewing and spitting is precarious; it is frequently mired in failure, and the reason for this is fat. One website participant described why chewing and spitting is counterproductive, saying, "The fat slides down your throat anyway." Just as fat was seen to move across the pan in Cooking Group, it seeps uncontrollably across the body's boundaries. Melding the two interwoven conceptualizations of fat—as static and dynamic—one participant to a pro-anorexia website wrote in 2011 about chewing and spitting: "The grease (totally yuck) gets stuck on your tongue and the inside of your mouth you still eat the fat and leave out all the nutrients." Chewing and spitting therefore reminds us how much eating constitutes a failure to maintain anorexia, and the precariousness of this as an enterprise, while also illustrating that fat is perceived as breaching boundaries in the present as well as attesting to their rupture in the past.

In this second conceptualization, thus, fat is seen to move in ways that show it to have vitality. "Vitality," Jane Bennett suggests, is "the capacity of things—edibles, commodities, storms, metals—not only to impede or block the will and design of humans but also to act as quasi-agents or forces with trajectories, propensities or tendencies of their own" (2010: viii). As Karen Barad likewise states, "[M]atter is not a fixed essence; rather matter is a substance in its intra-active becoming—not a thing but a doing; a congealing of agency" (2003: 828). The congealed stasis of fat and, particularly, its sneaky mobility weave through informants' conceptualizations of personhood *after anorexia*. Now that we have reflected on fat-as-matter in informants' accounts, we are able to explore the second of the dual temporalities of fat. To informants, fat expanding and rupturing their carefully patrolled bodily perimeters does not only index a loss of anorexia's protection and hence an open vulnerability to the world. The substance itself is also felt to alter personhood so that this metonymically comes to take on the cloying and seeping material qualities of fat.

PART TWO: FAT ACTS: BODIES, PERSONHOOD, AND MEDIATED CONNECTION

In her interview Kate described eating by saying, "I just feel like, when I've got something in my mouth, no matter how small the piece is, it just expands and it fills my mouth completely. I feel like I've got hamster cheeks full, full of food." This sense of food expanding was recounted by many other informants and was linked in their narratives to ways in which food becomes fat. During a sunny afternoon in an otherwise damp English summer, Abigail and I left the eating disorders unit where she was an inpatient to dawdle our way across the scrubby grounds of the psychiatric hospital. Having just had Afternoon Snack, which that day was carrot cupcakes covered in thick, creamy icing, Abigail was becoming increasingly anxious. She had an overwhelming desire to, as she put it, "run off the cupcake." Abigail explained how she could feel it in her body, expanding and moving through it; the cupcake breached her boundaries, forcing layers of fat to appear under her skin, stretching it outward. Abigail demonstrated this by pinching her upper arm, thereby making an as-yet imagined—or, perhaps, potential—expansion tangibly material between her thumb and forefinger. There is a clear linearity to the translation—or transubstantiation, perhaps—of eaten food into fat in both Kate's and Abigail's narratives, which was echoed by other informants. For example, Eva said:

> After every meal, after every time I eat, I think it's there already. I feel like, I have this weird. . . . I know it's irrational but I think that the weight's gone straight to my stomach and I've put on weight already . . . the second after I've eaten, I've put on weight, I've put on weight. It's not, I don't see it as . . . even if I had to put on weight from eating that meal, it wouldn't show straight away, like that! Do you know what I mean? But I'll start clawing at my stomach to test how much fat's on it. For me it's always been about my stomach. I don't look at my arms or legs or anything . . . well, I do a bit but more than anything it's my stomach.

As the "site of incorporation" (Carden-Coyne and Forth 2005: 1), Eva's stomach is where two temporalites coalesce. On the outside, its expansion signifies shamefully to Eva that she has eaten and therefore failed to protect her anorexia. On the inside, it is where Eva feels food to transmute immediately into fat. As food is "literally made into flesh" (1), this is where eating and therefore the loss—or active disappearing—of anorexia traced through Part One take place. Fat is made manifest, and anorexia threatened, by a hyperawareness of each morsel ingested as these are felt to settle and solidify on body contours. The linearity and immediacy of this process show the struggle between anorexia and fat to be embodied, in the sense of being utterly felt through the body. Yet it is also, paradoxically, in this process that the body most becomes materialized metaphor. Abigail's and Eva's narratives, like the discussions of visuality in Part One, remind us that thinking about bodies here "has to be done carefully" (Grosz 2001: 26) and in tandem with an engagement with informants' accounts of the many intersubjective entanglements of personhood and anorexia. Having explored the "vibrant materiality" (Bennett 2010) of fat as it moves across and congeals on plates, we are now able to comprehend how this linear relationship between eating and becoming fat not only conceptually remaps vectors of digestion and metabolism but also echoes, and enacts through the body, notions of seepage, transgression, and contamination in informants' experiences of fatty foods. The uncontained movement of the cupcake through Abigail's body signifies the beginning of an unwanted, and literally viscerally felt, remapping of personhood through the unwilling embodiment of fat's material properties. To trace this we first need to think about informants' discussions of their bodies "expanding" beyond their carefully patrolled "perimeters" and "taking up space."

When I asked Abigail what was so frightening about putting on weight during treatment, in addition to describing her fear of being, as she put it, "without anorexia," she said, "Well the immediate thing, the selfish thing, is getting bigger." This word "bigger" occurred in many other informants' narratives, as did accounts of "expanding" and "taking up space." Clearly redolent of wider discursive formations of fat bodies as "out of bounds" (Braziel and LeBesco 2001), taking up space resonates with a sense of excess. Yet we must be careful not to link informants' narratives too closely to these cultural imaginings of fat as excess; this not only could return us to a superficial focus on the visuality rather than the embodiment of fat; it also risks categorizing informants' subjectivities of fat simply as culturally prescribed reactions. We therefore need to hold in one analytical space the seeping of the oil into the rice in Cooking Group, the mobility of the cupcake through Abigail's body, and the threatening inward flow of sociality that follows the loss of anorexia's "social skin" (Corin 2007). This triangulation takes us beyond a neat relationship between informants' subjectivities and dominant cultural tropes. Instead, we might say that informants "borrow, displace and transform cultural signifiers in their attempts to name and tame an elusive sense of themselves and the world" (277). Getting bigger, in informants' accounts, is not a statement only about the body but, rather, a way of articulating a sense of oneself *through* the body. The body and its perimeters here sit on the threshold between the material and the metonymic, as well as between culture and an intimate lived individuality. This is because, as bodies come to be felt to be taking up more space through weight gain, especially in treatment, personhood too is experienced, felt, and lived differently. Informants describe how this assumes the material qualities that they attribute to fat—on both plates and bodies. As such, informants' bodies and their personhood are almost more connected in this temporal moment *after anorexia* than they were *inside* it, when the body served more as a visual index. By drawing on a culturally pervasive codification of fat as "evidence of the body's capacities to extend beyond any established limits" (Colls 2007: 360), informants articulate the feeling that both their bodies and their personhood are uncontained and uncontrolled.

By many of those interviewed, a feeling of "taking up space" after weight gain was contrasted to how anorexia itself was a "space." When exploring this in Part One I suggested that retreating into the space of anorexia was, to a certain extent, about disappearing. In tandem with this, anorexia "came out" to stand between informants and the worlds around them. In her interview Milla explained why anorexia's delineation of her perimeters, which we saw her patrol by measuring her thighs and encircling her arms earlier, was so valuable. She said, "It's about keeping a really tight check on yourself and it started like that before it started with food. I never had . . . it never started as a losing weight thing. It was a sort of general crackdown." Milla's words suggest that the personhood that emerged through and within the illness enacted her desire to not affect the world around her. In her interview Josie, a pro-anorexia website participant, also evinced this when she said, "When I'm very ill then I feel like a living shadow and being emaciated is like being a living shadow and that is sometimes what I aspire to be." She described being a shadow as something that allowed her to be in the world in a way that engaged with it but did not leave an imprint on it. To her it signified not being "too present" or "too visible." Likewise, Elle described how the act of allowing anorexia to convene with the world in her place enabled her to pass through it almost "without touching it." Michelle, likewise, explained that she wanted to avoid "having any effect on other people." In contrast to these statements, after weight gain, once personhood is still mapped along corporeal perimeters but no longer through anorexia, it is not anorexia that "comes out" into the world for informants. With the containment provided by anorexia gone, informants find themselves enacting a particular way of being that "comes out," unwanted, at anorexia's loss.

As such, "feeling fat" is, we might say, doubly dual; as well as referring to both the body and personhood, it also speaks of both vulnerability and a feeling of being, as Paula put it, "too much." The first half of this chapter ended by arguing that a loss of the personhood made possible through anorexia is both indexed and induced by body fat; fat attests to and produces an absence, thereby leaving informants vulnerable. When anorexia no longer stands between informants and their worlds, others' voices, emotions, and words are felt to flow overwhelmingly inward. Yet, in an intertwining of affect and materiality, narratives of "getting bigger" and "taking up space" have offered insight into how there is also a flow, seepage, or transgression in the opposite direction; "affect arises in the midst of in-betweeness"

(Seigworth and Gregg 2010: 1), and it is therefore about acting as well as being acted on. Narratives of "feeling fat" and "getting bigger," elucidate that, to informants, both directions of the flow between self and sociality embody and enact threat and contamination. Expanding on what she meant by "keeping a really tight check on yourself," Milla said:

> You just want to draw everything back into yourself and that's a way of making yourself compact and at the same time it's a way of stopping yourself having an effect on anybody else because it's so easy to just say "bluh, bluh, bluh" and really hurt somebody's feelings. You don't know when you're going to actually hit on something that's going to damage someone for life. So that is sort of a way I have . . . I keep telling myself, you know, "stop talking, stop talking" but in the absence of that, then I find it very difficult to shut up but I feel like if there's less of me physically, then I kind of feel like there is less of a ripple effect on the rest of the world.

Thus, as the new uncontained personhood seeps out into the world in ways uncontrolled and undesired, not only are individuals with anorexia vulnerable to sociality, but their surrounding social worlds are also vulnerable to informants. Milla was not alone in describing herself, with distress, as undesirably affecting the world around her and even as causing harm through this "ripple effect."

Paying attention to how not "taking up space" can be about connecting to the world in ways that do no harm—that touch edges rather than infiltrate, perhaps—illuminates that for many informants anorexia is not only about the safety of retreat; it is also a paradoxical mode of connection. The illness signifies to Milla and others a particular kind of "held-in" mediated connection that is not only about not being engrossed, and therefore needing to "keep others at bay," but also about not wishing to encounter the world in engrossing ways. If we think back to anorexia as a "social skin" (Corin 2007), this is not as surprising as it may at first appear. As Michel Serres reminds us, skin is dual; "in it, through it, with it, the world and my body touch each other, the feeling and the felt, it defines their common edge" (2008: 80). Skin, he argues, not only closes off but also "intervenes between several things in the world and makes them mingle" (80). As such, as one's safe anorexic personhood is replaced by a personhood felt to be unknown and harmful, feeling fat and taking up space articulate a rupture of connection as much as enforced connection. Such phrases describe a sense of isolation as informants may find themselves unable both to enact a desired personhood and to feel in control of that which is out there in the world. That Milla described wanting to, as she put it in her interview, "fold herself back in" also illustrates the circularity and entrapment to these processes of interaction between fat and anorexia. Milla's sense of how this new personhood after anorexia is harmful leads her to try harder to rid her body of fat so that she might know, once again, "where [her] perimeters are." This was a cycle described by many informants and one that evinces how holding onto anorexia can slip from a desire to maintain one's friend into a need to hold onto a crumbling sense of self. It also elucidates how anorexia, as a way "to live with what would otherwise be unendurable" (Fischer 2007), may become increasingly important to informants on the continual reemergence of the unendurable that is signified by expanding bodily perimeters. As such, as they patrol their bodies and self-starve, individuals with anorexia may oscillate between two profoundly distressing ways of being, with anorexia marginally less painful than fat.

CONCLUSION

In this chapter fat has not only seeped across plates and through bodies but also oozed through, and plumped up, imaginings and narratives, social worlds and affective sensations. Tracing such metonymic layering and synecdoche has offered an alternative way to reflect on an illness that is diagnostically circumscribed as fat phobia and yet is most pervasively discussed in terms of an extreme desire for bodily thinness. A focus on fat as matter has offered insights into the multiplicity with which anorexia, fat, and bodies are conceptualized by informants, all being delinked and relinked in complex contextual ways. It has, moreover, illuminated individuals' lived experiences of sociality and their embodied ways of being in the world both in spite of and through anorexia. The chapter began by exploring informants' relationships with anorexia. Against this background, thinness arose less as a goal and more as an indexical marker of the continuing presence of the illness. I explored how this presence is looked after by informants through not eating because of the help it is felt to offer. Providing a sense of stillness in the face of painful emotions or interpersonal interactions, anorexia is described as a space into which to retreat as well as an other that "steps in" between informants and their worlds. Yet paying attention to the material properties of fat as these manifest in interview narratives illustrated a two-way flow. As personhood after anorexia's loss continues to be mapped along corporeal contours, fat not only induces vulnerability but also embodies a feeling of moving through the world in harmful, excessive ways. In contrast to these, therefore, anorexia signifies a paradoxical mode of connection as much as it does disconnection; to informants it comprises a way of being in, but not affecting, the worlds around them. Tracing these threads between personhood, anorexia, and fat has illustrated moments of encounter between subjectivity and cultural formations, as well as between materiality and metaphor. As the second half of the chapter in particular demonstrated, wider stigmatizing cultural denigrations of body fat do enter into, and come to shape, informants' experiences of their own bodies and of particular foods. It is difficult to disentangle the complexities of how anorexia and such cultural tropes touch edges and to fully comprehend the ways in which each informs how fat comes to stand for a loss of protection and a loss of self for informants. Arguably, a linear linkage of eating and fat is culturally wider than my informants' narratives, and notions of individual responsibility and self-blame in their accounts of looking after anorexia also echo discursive formations and media coverage of "globesity" (Delpeuch et al. 2009). This chapter, however, has not been about making judgments that might have risked "heaping reaction formation upon reaction formation" (Butler 2000: 20). Rather, it has endeavored to listen to "whatever, or perhaps to whatever it is that matters" to individuals themselves (Grossberg 2010: 160) by ethically navigating lived experiences and cultural discourses in ways that have allowed ambiguity. This has illustrated that, for individuals with anorexia, fat may come to matter in ways visceral as well as discursive, affective as well as symbolic.

6 FAT IS THE FUTURE

Bioprospecting, Fat Stem Cells, and Emergent Breasted Materialities

Nadine Ehlers

In dominant Western power/knowledge systems, fat is viewed negatively: as surplus, as waste. Fat is often rendered synonymous with "the offensive, horrible, or deadly aspects of embodiment" and, consequently, as that which is abject and must be expelled (Kent 2001: 130). Materializations of fat are disavowed in this cultural context, and fat bodies, as Le'a Kent argues, are "fragmented, medicalized, pathologized, and transformed into abject visions of the horror of flesh itself" (2001: 132).[1] Fat, however, has no ontological status: it is given meaning—and made to signify— through specific meaning-making systems. The way fat signifies, and the status of fat, necessarily depends on the *domain* in which it exists. This chapter focuses on medico-technical deployments of fat and the various economies of the body and new material ontologies for/of the body that these deployments enable.

My specific interest is the domain of breast reconstruction following breast cancer surgery, which offers a range of salient examples of the reordering, revaluing, and instrumentalization or operationalization of fat. Looking to this domain is particularly fruitful because, in the context of breast cancer, it becomes evident that certain forms of fat are considered desirable and good: the fat (adipose) tissue that is a key component of breast morphology (along with glandular tissue) is what gives contour to the female body and signifies femininity.[2] When this tissue is either completely or partially removed in what is considered life-saving surgery, notions of corporeal wholeness and integrity are threatened, in turn potentially threatening or destabilizing gendered subjectivity. Under such conditions of loss, breast reconstruction technologies aim to return the contours of what is viewed as "feminine embodiment" by refashioning breast morphology.[3] Precisely because fat has become central to this endeavor, it seems imperative to consider what fat can be made to do in the context of these reconstruction technologies. This analysis, however, is not directed toward women's material experience of these forms of reconstruction or the ways in which these procedures come to be embodied by subjects. Rather than pursuing an analysis of the subject or the personal, I am more concerned with how possibilities for the body are shaped by biomedical technologies. Thus, I move toward a consideration of how fat is put to work—the *labor of fat*—in the domain of breast reconstruction and the various material possibilities that fat can engender. To these ends, this chapter asks, what are the capacities of fat, what biomedical technicities can animate these capacities, and how might these technicities remake dominant conceptualizations of fat? Thinking about fat in this way allows for the recognition that fat does not simply exist in the realm of—and as a property of—the subject. Instead, it becomes evident that any analysis of fat must always be attentive to the ways this substance has become part of a broader bioeconomy and technical intervention.

In many breast reconstruction technologies, fat is deployed and operates in/as what Catherine Waldby and Robert Mitchell (2006: 31) have called a "tissue economy," a term that points to the idea that tissue—and in this case fat tissue—is productive and is able to be ordered or valued in various ways. A tissue economy, specifically in the context of Western biomedical technological advances, maximizes the productivity of tissue and organizes or adjudicates its value. Within a tissue economy, human tissue that has traditionally been designated as *waste* can be *reordered as value*:

> Waste material which may appear as the very opposite of value in one context can become the starting point for the generation of significant degrees of value in another. Hence one of the fundamental movements of any successful form of economy is the circulation of waste objects from unprofitable to profitable contexts where they can be resignified and redeployed. (Waldby and Mitchell 2006: 84)

Within the circuits of dominant knowledge systems, regimes of value, and traditional biomedical ordering, "human tissues are more likely to be classified as waste as they lose . . . status" (84). Thus, tissues that are seen as essential to the body's functioning and integrity—such as skin, bone, organs, and limbs—acquire status or significance, while tissues that are regularly expelled from the body are either constructed as neutral (hair or nail clippings) or repugnant (pus, feces, or urine). Fat would fit into this last category: while not routinely expelled from the body, it is *designated* as that which *should* be expelled and as corporeal material that can be *wasted*. This waste, however, is relocated to other regimes of value in breast reconstruction technologies: in these technologies fat/waste is recuperated and reanimated as a therapeutic substance, and thus its status shifts from valueless "garbage" to value-laden "gold." This, however, is not a simple reversal of status. As Waldby and Mitchell (2006) make clear, it is only because a tissue is designated as waste—a part of the body to be expelled—that it can be put to another use. In the case of fat, it is only because it is classified as surplus and as a substance that can be wasted that it can be redeployed and epistemologically reevaluated in another context. Put another way, value is facilitated by the tissue being categorized as waste.

Fat undergoes such a change in status in many breast reconstruction technologies and becomes a tangible form of biovalue.[4] In a general sense, as Nikolas Rose (2007: 32) argues, the term *biovalue* can be used to "refer to the plethora of ways in which vitality itself has become a potential source of value: biovalue as the value to be extracted from the vital processes of living processes." The vitality of fat—its live-ness, malleability, and capacity—is extracted in certain breast reconstruction technologies and redirected *in order to promise a return to wholeness* after breast cancer surgery.[5] *Wholeness* here refers to the post-Enlightenment paradigm of a closed, complete, and invulnerable subject whose body functions in line with the normative conventions of controlled embodiment. The "whole" body is understood as singular, unitary, defensible, and complete with all anatomical parts in their proper places (Cohen 2009; Shildrick 1997). Moreover, the "whole" body is marked by a sense of bodily consonance, or a seamlessness of bodily experience.[6] The loss of a body part, such as a breast, interrupts the possibility of experiencing the body seamlessly and instead represents a state of bodily dissonance, where the body is viewed as disorganized or in a state of disarray or lack. But such lack can be recuperated through breast reconstruction—so the logic goes—and deploying the vitality of fat as biovalue has become key to this process. Fat, then, becomes enabling in the context of such loss. However, while deploying fat in breast reconstruction might seemingly inaugurate a return to normative embodiment, I have argued elsewhere that this would be too simplistic an interpretation, one that often leads to conceptual gridlock (Ehlers 2012).[7] Instead, it seems more productive to consider how using fat in breast reconstruction might compel particular *contingent and emergent materialities* (ones that undercut the promise of wholeness) and how such use of fat may represent a new future in terms of how we understand subjectivity, the body, and life.

This productivity of fat has been enabled only through the development of particular innovative biotechnologies. In what follows, I focus on four of these biotechnologies and their accompanying tissue economies. First, *fat transfer*—known as autologous reconstruction—understands and deploys fat as capital, with certain "fatty" parts of the body outsourced and rearranged to make new (and organic) breasts. Second, *fat grafting* repurposes unwanted body fat and, through lipofilling, is used to add volume or correct a breast contour problem after lumpectomy or reconstruction. Third, *fat autogenesis* uses fat stem cells to regenerate tissue damaged through radiation or removed through mastectomy, effectively growing new fatty tissue–based breast material. And, finally, *fat banking* enables extracted fat to be preserved for future use, either to be used in subsequent reconstruction procedures or to await new biomedical possibilities. Through these biotechnologies fat enters into the organizing logic of biomedicine, a logic underpinned by "the myth of technocratic transcendence" of the limits placed on the human by nature (Davis-Floyd 1994). This possibility of technocratic transcendence plays a particularly important role in our contemporary age, when the medical terrain has become a key site wherein individuals are expected to organize themselves around "the norms of enterprising, self-actualizing responsible personhood that characterize 'advanced liberal' societies" (Novas and Rose 2000: 488).[8] The way these new "fat biotechnologies" are talked about by the medical practitioners and individuals who partake in them highlights that they have become a way to deliver the promise of transcendence—over biological shortcomings or the surgery to correct biological shortcomings, such as cancer—*and* seemingly a means through which individuals can enhance, transform, and customize their bodies as part of broader neoliberal culture.[9]

The biotechnologies that I list above instrumentalize fat in divergent ways and operate on two registers. The first register works through the *redistribution of fat*, in that fat is taken from one area of the body and moved to another. The second register operates through the *morphogenesis of fat*, whereby certain processes of fat emergence or growth are encouraged.[10] Thus, while fat is instrumentalized in both registers in/ as a tissue economy with demarcated biovalue, the way it is put to use, the things it is made to do, and the value that is attributed to it are distinct, depending on the register. In both registers, however, the materiality of fat is harnessed and harvested; the promise of wholeness that accompanies the procedures or processes at work can fail, and this promise is paradoxical, in that the body can be made whole again only by disaggregating it.

FAT AND THE ART OF REDISTRIBUTION: "ENOUGH TO MAKE TWO GOOD-SIZED C'S"

In a web forum dedicated to breast reconstruction, one participant revels in her supposedly excess belly fat, stating that she has "enough to make two good C's." Another participant exclaims that "it's possible I might only have just enough belly fat to make a pair of B's at MOST (almost NO more muffin top unless I sit slouched, and even when I slouch, the muffin is small)!" What these women refer to here is their capacity to participate in the breast reconstruction technology known as autologous, autogenous, or living-tissue reconstruction. This procedure can be thought about as a mammary organics, in that fat from a woman's own body is harvested, redistributed, and repositioned to construct a new breast. Autologous breast reconstruction is by no means a new invention. For over a century, surgeons have used patients' own fat, muscle, and skin to enlarge and reshape breasts. The first documented breast reconstruction using such methods was performed in 1895 by the German physician Vincent Czerny, who transplanted a lipoma (a benign tumor comprised of fat tissue) from the lumbar region to reconstruct a breast (Del Vecchio and Fichadia 2012). In recent years, autologous reconstruction has become a primary form of breast reconstruction and is heralded as providing a more natural/whole aesthetic result than reconstruction using alloplastic implants.

There are several forms of this surgery, and while each of them instrumentalizes fat in order to facilitate a return to wholeness, they each also carry with them some level of corporeal risk that delimits that promise. The pedicled TRAM (transverse rectus abdominis muscle) flap is the standard model of autologous reconstruction in the United States; it uses a fat, muscle, and skin flap from between the belly button and pubic area that is tunneled through the body to make a breast. To be a candidate for this form of reconstruction, a woman must have adequate (and what is usually thought of as excessive) lower abdominal fat tissue to create one or both breasts (as reflected by the statements of the women quoted above). Other forms of autologous reconstruction using abdominal fat include the DIEP (deep inferior epigastric artery perforator) procedure (which uses an artery from the upper abdominal region to maintain the harvested abdominal fat; see Gill et al. 2004), the SIEA (superficial interior epigastric artery) procedure (using an artery from the lower abdomen), and the free TRAM flap (where fat tissue is used to create a breast shape without having to be tunneled under the skin; see Nahabedian et al. 2002). For women with less abdominal fat reserve, other parts of the body are sought for this harvesting: the TUG (transverse upper gracilis) flap utilizes the fatty tissue of the upper inner thigh, the GAP (gluteal artery perforator) flap surgeries take fat from the buttocks (see Blondeel 1999), and the LAT (latissimus dorsi) flap uses fat, muscle, and skin from the back to make a reconstructed breast.

These procedures operationalize fat in order to model norms of the breast, in that the autologous breast can appear more "naturally" shaped than those produced with the use of implants. Also, because it is usually made wholly of live tissue, it is warm to the touch (unlike implants) and resembles the tactility of breast tissue, an achievement enabled only by using fat tissue in addition to muscle and skin. However, this form of reconstruction challenges the possibility of a return to wholeness and normality in that the reconstructed breast will have no or little sensation. The donor site might also be compromised through weakness and additional scarring and might be marked by dog-ears (large bulges at the edges of scars). Beyond these factors, autologous reconstruction evidently involves a highly invasive surgery requiring significant recovery time, and complications can include partial or total flap loss, fat necrosis (where large portions of the tissue turn black, die, and must be removed), and abdominal bulge or hernia (Nahabedian et al. 2002: 466). At the level of appearance, the use of fat in these procedures may enable the body to visually register as having achieved the norm, for the reconstruction is often imperceptible to an onlooker. Regardless of the possible social ontology that might be generated, however, the material ontology of this reconstructed breast is that it is dismantled fat taken from the stomach, back, leg, or a portion of the buttocks and redistributed to be *made* breast.

Another breast reconstruction technology that puts fat to work by redistributing it is the procedure known as fat grafting. In this procedure, excess body fat is identified, harvested, processed, and then moved to another part of the body—the chest. This fat is harvested through lipoaspiration, treated through repeated saline washing or centrifugation and refinement (to remove all gross blood products), and then transferred back into the body through various injection techniques. As a reconstruction technology, fat grafting is primarily thought of as a supplement to primary reconstruction (such as with implants) and is used for aesthetic augmentation, the correction of symmetry or deformity, and the provision of soft tissue coverage for implants (Coleman and Saboeiro 2007; Spear, Wilson, and Lockwood 2005). For instance, if a woman has reconstruction with implants and the edges show or there is a lack of upper pole fullness to the reconstructed breast, fat can be injected using this technique to address the imperfection. In other cases, fat grafting has been used as the primary reconstruction technique: for example, in a recent Italian case, plastic surgeons used fat grafting to entirely rebuild a woman's breasts following a mastectomy and radiation (Panettiere et al. 2011). In this procedure, the lipoaspirated fat was injected over a period of eight months, with the fat acting as both the expander (of the radiated skin) and the filler (of that skin). Once the fat is injected, the aim is to have it become vascularized in order to ensure its survival.

Fat grafting, then, is a *structural technology*, in that it labors to return the structure of the breast and, through this, return the sense of corporeal wholeness. Several factors threaten such a return, however: like with fat transfer, there can be donor site deformity (borrowing from Peter to pay Paul), there may be inadequate or not enough donor sites (with the patient not being fat enough!), the fat can fail to become vascularized and lead to tissue death or fat necrosis, or the fat can be reabsorbed by the body (requiring further grafting touch-ups, over and over again). Additionally, this procedure can result in infection, cellulitis, calcifications, and oil/fat cysts, and many plastic surgeons have questioned the efficacy and ethics of such a procedure, because some of these side effects—such as calcification in the breast—can interfere with subsequent breast cancer detection.

The economy of fat at work in both autologous fat transfer and fat grafting involves establishing *where* fat *is* on the body, how *much* of it there is, and what method will be used to *move* it. The underlying assumption of such procedures, then, is that fat exists as surplus or excess, and—with the idea of the "whole body" as the teleological end point—the more fat one has, the better the chances of materializing new breasts and thus achieving wholeness. Identifying this supposedly surplus fat becomes a form of bioprospecting: the search for new and available bioresources—in this case, fatty tissue that is demarcated as unwanted waste on one part of the body—that can be sacrificed, exploited, and redirected to a state/site of value. Such divisibility or disaggregation of the body represents, then, an understanding of the body as comprised of certain spare parts that can be rearranged.

Both fat transfer and fat grafting engage in what I am calling the art of redistribution, a way of instrumentalizing fat that is marked by several key features. First, these technologies are organized around the logic of moving and then reproducing given forms: *the existing form* of flesh and fat is transplanted *to make a breast/form.* Importantly, here, the pregiven form of the flesh and fat found elsewhere on the body will determine the form that the reconstructed breast will take (most particularly with fat transfer technologies), *and* the transplantation is predicated on reproducing the standardized form/norm or structure of breasted morphology. In this register, fat is understood as that which can give form—fat here is morphological—but that form is imposed from the outside: it is either transferred or injected *into* the body (albeit from another part of the body). Second, these technologies view the body in a mechanistic sense and pursue a point-to-point substitution, with the various tissues seen as interchangeable. As Melinda Cooper (2008: 110) argues, in transplantation surgeries, "[o]ne organ can substitute for another, just as one prosthetic equivalent can take the place of an organ, as long as the essential relations between form and function are preserved." Obviously, however, these forms of breast reconstruction do not involve substituting like for like, because what is transferred is not a breast but a tissue made to *become* breast. Third, these technologies focus on achieving tissue survival, integration, and stasis: thus, the energies of the body are directed at fighting possible infection or tissue rejection in order to maintain the reconstructed breast form over time and, importantly, discourage change/instability. The overriding imperative in these technologies seems to be, then, to reproduce or recuperate standardized form or the norm: of the breast, of female corporeality. However, it becomes evident that more than this is going on. Instead of simply reproducing the norm, these procedures highlight customization of the body, where multiple norms might be imagined and pursued through techniques that commodify fat; certain failures or limitations that are presented in the quest for corporeal wholeness; and the fact that achieving the norm might be a fraught enterprise, precisely because these procedures compel the subject to experience the body as transitional and conditional, due to either those failures or the corporeal traces these technologies leave.[11]

FAT AND THE ART OF MORPHOGENESIS: BREAST-MAKING GOLD, HIDDEN IN A PAIR OF LOVE HANDLES

While fat operates in the tissue economy of breast reconstruction on the register of redistribution, it also works on a second register involving what might be thought of as an art of morphogenesis. In this register, particular technologies, techniques, or technicities put fat to work by *growing* it—through processes of autogenesis—in order to make new breasted materialities. These technologies are significant in that they highlight the instrumentalization of growth processes in the domain of breast reconstruction, show a further refinement of the customization of matter (enabled via the malleability of fat), and demonstrate efforts to initiate and harness the capacities of the morphogenesis of form itself.

One of the ways this morphogenesis of fat is evident is in the practice of women growing their own fat for future breast reconstruction. This might take place when a woman has inadequate fat to make two C-cup breasts, for instance, and so puts on enough weight over a specific period of time in order to be able to harvest the amount required for the reconstructive surgery. In other instances, women might have had implant reconstruction but have a contour problem or rippling to the implants. In these cases it might be necessary to generate more fat in order to harvest it for lipofilling. A participant on one web forum, for instance, talked of being instructed by her plastic surgeon to gain twenty pounds so that he would have enough material to work with. In such a case, the subject becomes her own "fat farm," in that she grows fat as a bioresource. I want to draw a distinction between this practice and that of simply extracting existing fat from the body. What is particular about this kind of activity is that women *strategically* and *tactically* enhance their body's fat reserve—by growing more—in order to yield a greater return and, thereby, maximize the possibility of producing a sense of corporeal wholeness. Such a practice becomes possible, however, only because fat has been revalued in this tissue economy and because fat (as it is attached to skin and muscle) is the material substance used to recreate breasted embodiment. Other forms of corporeal loss cannot be regenerated in this way: the subject cannot grow a new kidney or a new arm—or a prosthetic supplement—but she can "grow a new breast" through deploying fat as a bioresource.

Again, such a strategic customization of fat materiality becomes possible only because stomach, hips, thighs, and buttocks can *become* breast, a possibility that, in turn, is predicated on the malleability of fat.

This circular orgy of possibility is perhaps interrupted only by the implications of fat growth for the health of the subject. To grow fat—to amass body weight—is contrary to dominant dietary protocols for patients diagnosed with breast cancer, particularly those with estrogen-positive cancers (which is the most common form of breast cancer). Most patients with this kind of breast cancer are advised to limit their fat intake and actively reduce their body-fat mass because fat increases the estrogen levels in the body and, thereby, elevates the chances of the cancer recurring or metastasizing. One oncological study found, for example, that doubling one's fat intake, from 20 to 40 percent, was associated with a 15 percent increase in breast cancer risk.[12] In light of such statistics, the activity of fat autogenesis can foster a growth that kills.[13]

These tangible risks aside, it is important to note that a very specific economy of emergence is at work in this form of fat autogenesis: a sense of self and breasted embodiment that is facilitated by the strategic enhancement—through fat—of the body's bioresources. Such a process, however, is ultimately recuperated back into the first register of the breast reconstruction tissue economy that I discussed above, in that this grown fat will be deployed in breast reconstruction techniques that are governed by the logic of redistribution. Here again, tissues represent a certain form of limit (and limit of form), and will be subjected to structural technologies that *mold* harvested material into particular *predetermined forms*. As Cooper (2008: 113) argues, in these kinds of surgeries "active form [will be imposed] on formless matter." Or, as Sharon Begley (2010) has put it, "the doctor squeezes and smooshes, and moves tissue to fill in divots and missing quadrants and, with luck, turns what might have been reduced to an A cup during a cancer operation [or removed completely] into a match for the B or C on the healthy side."

However, the relatively recent discovery of stem cells in fat tissue has reworked these prior understandings of fat as holding only limited material capacities and potential. Identifying these fat-derived stem cells (what are known as adipose derived stem cells [ADSC]) has been a eureka moment in bioprospecting and biotechnological developments, where new possibilities for embodiment and human life have been found "hidden in a pair of love handles," as one plastic surgeon noted (Begley 2010). What is so promising about this discovery is that fat-derived stem cells can be used in tissue-engineering technologies—in the field of regenerative medicine—to grow not only new fat tissue but also new bone and muscle, and to generate a new blood supply.

In order to map out the possibilities that this new ADSC technology represents, it is first essential to understand that there are two primary forms of stem cells:

embryonic and adult stem cells. Adult stem cells have been found in the liver, the male and female reproductive systems, bone marrow, the brain, skeletal muscles, skin, teeth, and now fat. Both forms of stem cells renew themselves in a process called self-renewal (or morphogenesis) and can transform into a variety of other kinds of cells. Where embryonic stem cells are pluripotent, or what could be thought of as "blank" cells that can give rise to *any* type of cell, adult stem cells are multipotent, meaning that they can give rise to different (but specific) kinds of cells in their home tissues. Despite the fact that adult stem cells have a particular physiological function in vivo and do not normally generate cell types outside their particular tissues, they can be manipulated in vitro to act more like embryonic stem cells: they can be re-programmed to become what are known as "induced pluripotent stem cells," which are then exposed to signaling molecules so that they differentiate into specific kinds of tissues. It is this technology that is now enabling fat-derived stem cells to not only *become* fat tissue but also be induced to differentiate into three distinct lineages: bone and cartilage, muscle, and neurons (Fraser et al. 2006; Zuk et al. 2001).

Stem cell tissue engineering, as it is combined with regenerative medicine, can be thought of as the second generation of earlier biomedical technologies of prosthetics and transplantation (Cooper 2008: 103). But where first-generation technologies were preoccupied with the transplantation or *substitution of form*, this second-generation technology is concerned with the *genesis of form* itself, with the goal of achieving corporeal self-renewal. And while stem cell research using embryonic tissues has raised significant controversy, ADSC technology has been able to rise to the forefront of applied stem cell tissue engineering. This is due to two primary factors: not only does using stem cells from fat circumvent the ethical minefield associated with using stem cells derived from embryos (because fat is seen as inconsequential material), but it also commodifies and capitalizes this tissue that is often readily available and usually wasted. As Begley (2010) notes:

> In 1999, Marc Hedrick, then assistant professor of surgery at UCLA, was doing yet another liposuction, and not a little suck-out-a-few-ounces-around-my-thighs-please-doctor procedure, either. He vacuumed 8 liters—more than 2 gallons—of fat from his patient. Scientists had long wondered whether fat tissue might contain stem cells. "If it does, then here we are, stupid plastic surgeons, doing the stupidest procedure on the face of the earth. . . . I'd just taken 8 liters out of some woman and dumped it in the trash."

Rather than remaining waste (and being wasted), this tissue was reimagined as "breast-making gold," with breast reconstruction using ADSC therapy becoming the first applied fat stem cell therapy. That ADSC therapeutics has developed here, in the context of breast reconstruction, might be because breasts are seen as inconsequential to the "laboring body"; that is, breasts are not required to "work" in order for the body to survive. It is easier, then, and strategic, to clear scientific and regulatory hurdles through conducting stem cell research in relation to breasts rather than other tissue. As Begley (2010) notes, "Breasts simply aren't as necessary as other organs, so the bar proving to regulators that the technology works will be lower." However, while breasts might be designated as relatively unimportant in the larger taxonomy of supposed corporeal significance, this technology represents a bright new horizon in how subjects might rethink and materialize their bodies after breast cancer surgery: once animated by these technicities, fat and the stem cells it contains become the means by which to produce an emergent breasted materiality. In stating this, I mean on the one hand that this technology initiates and materializes the enfleshment of a new breast—one that arises or emerges from the genesis of cells and the interaction of these cells within the biological organism of the human. On the other hand, I also refer to the idea that, for the subject undergoing this form of reconstruction, a new material breast literally emerges from the body: growing, moving, and developing sensation from the complex generation of new nerve endings, fat, and flesh.

The U.S.-based Cytori Therapeutics is one of the key companies now conducting research into this form of breast reconstruction. In doing so, they employ adipose tissue as a speculative asset, a point I return to later. Cytori has created what they call the Celution system—a magic box—that isolates the stem cells from liposuctioned fat, processes them, and concentrates them into a pellet. This pellet is then added to some of the liposuctioned fat cells and injected into the lumpectomy site, the missing breast quadrant, or the empty skin pocket from a mastectomy.[14] Within forty-eight hours, this tissue will become stabilized, with new capillaries entwining through the new cells, supplying oxygen and the necessary nutrients for tissue survival. Another company, Neopec, which is based in Australia and funded by the Victorian state government, uses a similar technology to "entice a woman's own regenerative capacity to grow living fat" for breast reconstruction (Neopec n.d.). This technology is slightly different from Cytori's, in that a biodegradable synthetic chamber is inserted into the mastectomy site and blood vessels from the patient's underarm are redirected into this chamber, which is then injected with the stem cell–rich lipoaspirate, which grows into the space of the chamber.

Regardless of the particularities, these technologies imagine the refashioning of breasted morphology and a return to normative embodiment in ways that are very distinct from the technologies that involve the redistribution of fat. Where redistributive technologies impose form, these technologies involve the *animation* of form. Where redistributive technologies require tissue stasis in order for the reconstruction using fat to survive, morphogenic technologies are predicated on the processes of transformation and growth. This "technicity works with and exploits the active responsiveness of living tissue, its power to affect and be affected and to change in time" (Cooper 2008: 113). Thus, the economy of the body is altered in morphogenic technologies, in that its labor/energy is directed not to fighting and survival but to vitalism. And where redistributive technologies reproduce the standardized norm, these morphogenic technologies instead *regenerate the transformable*—the emergent stem cell—to inaugurate a form of biomimesis, where fat is provoked to mimic the morphological coding of breasts.

What makes this technology work, however, is also what makes it a threat to corporeal well-being and any sense of corporeal integrity. For the success of this technology is based on the continuing ability of cells to transform, grow, and morph in ways that can't be predicted. The risk here is that these cells will grow or proliferate *too well*, and it is this kind of autogenesis that enables metastatic cancers to grow. The first signs of life—cell growth—can instead herald the first signs of death, where the body is, as Cooper (2008: 125) notes, "overcome by a surplus productivity that is indistinguishable from a surplus of life—that is, crises of overproduction or . . . dangerous, excessive vitality": the material emergence of cancer. Perhaps in light of this risk, the U.S. Food and Drug Administration has yet to approve the Cytori technology, although doctors are still able to use it and clinical trials are under way.[15]

BANKING (ON) FAT: COMMODIFICATION AND BIOFUTURITY

Despite these possible complications, ADSC technologies are hailed as the future not only of biomedicine but also of the human and what we know as life.[16] This biofuturity—the future of the biological enabled via these medico-technical advancements—offers the possibility of extending and enhancing our given understandings of the limits of the human by helping the body rebuild and, indeed, regenerate itself. In the service of this quest, fat becomes an investment in the future, one that people are increasingly banking on. There are two primary ways this investment is currently occurring, one that operates more at the level of the individual and another that works at the level of the health of the population—in terms of the projected use of fat in regenerative medicine.

Individual investments in fat can be seen explicitly in the practice known as fat banking, a recent phenomenon whereby people literally store their own fat—as wet biological material—for later use. With this practice, excess or unwanted fat is harvested, stored/frozen, and reanimated for various therapeutic uses, such as repeated breast reconstruction revisions, or kept while people await new biotechnological developments in ADSC research (this, then, is a storing of promise or possibility that is deferred to the future). In what has become an autologous economy, donors of this fat come to use their body's own regenerative capacities for self-renewal, representing what Waldby and Mitchell (2006: 56) have referred to as a "gift of self to self." Such a biotechnology is made possible only because a tissue surplus has been identified in the body/self and because this tissue—fat—has been revalued within the current biomedical domain of reconstruction and regenerative medicine. Additionally, such a practice holds particular neoliberal appeal, enabling individuals to invest a part of the body in their own future and rely on their own body for that future. Banking for the future does not come cheaply, though, with retrieval and storage costs carrying a significant yearly financial burden. As Waldby and Mitchell note, then, the irony here is that subjects are now being called on to "pay good money to buy back . . . [their] own bodily waste after it [has] . . . been processed through the infrastructure of capitalism and commodity culture" (83). Such a commodification of fat is clearly visible in the fat bank called Liquid Gold (registered with and approved by the Food and Drug Administration), whose marketing strategy explicitly frames fat within the language of finance and value: viewers of the website are greeted by an image of a piggy bank (the pun on fatness intentional?) and the caption "invest/save/withdraw" (Liquid Gold 2013).

Fat is not being banked and banked on only for individual purposes, however, as there is a concerted push toward using fat for the greater good, or the welfare and health of the population. Corporations thus employ adipose tissue as a speculative asset, and the stem cells this fat contains "acquire their value," as Waldby and Mitchell note (2006: 127), in a "virtual realm, in projections of . . . possible new repertoires of activity and agency." Liquid Gold, for example, expects that ADSC technologies will be used for life-saving treatment (and markets the bank with this in mind), and Cytori aims to introduce stem cell therapy to the mass market in the near future, using their ADSC technology. The anticipation here is that while this technology is currently being used only to regenerate new breasts, it will "be the *key to every ischemic disease,*" in which tissues die from inadequate blood supply (Begley 2010, my emphasis). The idea is that by increasing the blood supply, stem cells found in fat will be able to enhance, heal, and rebuild a range of damaged tissues (such as those affected by a heart attack or kidney injury) and treat various diseases, such as chronic heart disease and incontinence. This projected use becomes possible in ways that embryonic stem cell technologies do not, because excess fat is abundant and because fat is so accessible and malleable. So, for instance, adipose tissue contains 2,500-fold more stem cells than bone marrow and can be extracted through simple liposuction rather than a painful and detailed procedure.

The applications seem endless, and in a world full of this now-valuable tissue, fat perhaps represents the ultimate Promethean dream. Its deployment most certainly highlights Susan Merrill Squier's claim that, through contemporary biomedical innovations, human existence is no longer "defined by its unique temporal and spatial coordinates: one body, one life, in a specific space and time. Instead human life is increasingly defined by the agential, instrumental deployment of resources for bodily renewal, both its temporal and spatial context subject to extension or translocation" (2004: 183). What is inarguably occurring is that new markets of and for the body are being imagined and inaugurated, conjuring into existence new corporeal materialities through fat. But while it might be tempting to imagine a new form of endless value production via fat, what must also be kept in mind is that such a promise cannot faithfully model the Promethean tale of endless renewal: the fount of fat is not endless (the body contains only so much); the capacities of fat are not endless (for instance, fat stem cells cannot infinitely transform), and the body must be disaggregated to enable these capacities (through the literal rearrangement of body parts or through a disaggregation that occurs at a molecular level); and fat growth can lead to an excess of life that can cause death. The medico-technical deployment of fat, then, raises questions about boundaries *in the very promise* of excess, boundlessness, and regenerability. And, ultimately, this promise—of reimagining the terrain of body, the capacities of that body and, indeed, bodily ontology through fat—inevitably still depends on questions of *when* fat can be valued, what *domain* it operates in, and which *body* it is associated with.

7 BOUND BODIES

Navigating the Margins of Fat Bodies and Clothes

Trudie Cain, Kerry Chamberlain, and Ann Dupuis

The provocative book on fat identity *Revolting Bodies?* begins with a question: "Are fat bodies revolting?" (LeBesco 2004: 1). In posing this question, the author introduces the dominant discourse of the fat body as the abhorrent body, while simultaneously creating space for understanding the personal and political struggles associated with fat identity in contemporary Western society. Clearly, and unsurprisingly, people think about fat in different ways. In our research, when we asked the seemingly simple question, "what is fat?" we received a wide range of responses: "it's the stuff that sets on the top of the leftovers in the fridge"; "fat? It's this" (giving her "love handles" a jiggle); "it's the wobbly stuff that hangs over my jeans"; "it's what keeps me going to the gym"; "it's an ugly word . . . an insult"; and simply "me." Such varied responses not only speak to the subtitle of this book, *Culture and Materiality*, but also reveal the multiple meanings of fat itself. Congealed fat on cold food is an objective reality that can be identified, skimmed off, and potentially discarded. Even "love handles" and "wobbly stuff" have tangibility, although they may be qualitatively different from a slick of fat on the surface of food. Although "what keeps me going to the gym" does not accurately define fat, it does, nonetheless, speak to the sociocultural practices that have become closely intertwined with fat(ness) and, in particular, resistance toward fat's settlement on the body. The single-word answer—"me"—gets to the heart of the matter and, importantly, the heart of fat experience.

Fat itself is intriguing. As a substance, it exists outside of the body (leftovers on a plate in the fridge), it exists within the body (settling itself around thighs and hips, hearts and lungs), and yet fat also exists on the surface of bodies, appearing as cellulite, saddlebags on the thighs, and wobbly wings on arms. Fat is matter that matters: "fat is ambiguous; placed simultaneously under the skin yet materialised as a substance in and of itself" (Colls 2007: 358). We can eat fat (indeed, we need fat), but we can also *be* fat. Fat can be a state of being, an identity claim. Fat is *outside* of the body, *in* the body, *on* the body, and *of* the body. Fat crosses the boundaries of both substance and experience.

This chapter, however, is not only about fat. It is also about clothing, and clothing is important for understanding the experience of fat. In a social and cultural sense, clothing serves as a mechanism for making the body culturally available to others; through clothing we mark ourselves as members of a given group—"buying and displaying the tribe-specific paraphernalia" of that group (Bauman 1990: 206). Clothing offers individuals the materials with which to "try on" identity for size (Andersson 2011; Sweetman 2001), and through clothing we can display our private selves to a public world. Here, the communicative capacity of clothing is emphasized, its materiality serving as a conduit between the self and others.

The suggestion that clothing is a powerful signifier of identity has some traction. However, as Webb Keane (2005: 182) so eloquently states, "signs are not the garb of meaning." Underlining the communicative capacity of clothing fails to fully capture the reciprocal relationship *between* clothing and wearers as they are located within a particular time and location. Umberto Eco (2007 [1973]: 144) wrote, "I am speaking through my clothes," but we would argue that wearers and clothing operate *together* in a given spatial and temporal context. Central to this is the idea that the dressed self is embodied (Attfield 2000; Entwistle 2000; Hansen 2004). Clothing is not only a material object but a lived garment (Miller 2005), in possession of its own interconnected narrative—stories and histories woven into the fabric that connect an item of clothing to particular moments, imaginings, and practices of wearers. Indeed, the meanings of clothes are not fixed. Rather, they are multiple, renegotiated at the moment of each articulation, moment of remembrance, or moment of dressing (Cain 2011). As such, clothing possesses the capacity to evoke and "mediate emotions, relationships and identities" (Attfield 2000: 121), producing multifaceted understandings of the self. Such multiplicity is exacerbated by the way that clothing both reinforces and challenges boundaries: clothing "frames the body and serves both to distinguish and connect self and 'Other' . . . clothing is, then, both a boundary and not a boundary, . . . it is ambiguous and produces a complex relation between self and 'not self'" (Cavallaro and Warwick 1998: back cover).

In this chapter, we take the notion of boundaries (boundaries of bodies and clothes as well as boundaries of place) as a starting point for our discussion. To introduce an empirical element, we draw on data generated from a research project that examined the everyday clothing practices of ten (self-identified) larger women[1] who participated in a study about fat clothed identity, which was undertaken between 2008 and

2009 (Cain 2011). Given the problematic way in which fatness is discursively constructed in contemporary Western society (Kent 2001; LeBesco 2004; LeBesco and Braziel 2001; Longhurst 2005b), and taking as a starting point the assumption that fatness is embodied (Carryer 2001; Colls 2007; Murray 2008), the research aimed to find out how larger women responded, through their various clothing practices, to the problematic construction of their bodies.[2] Of particular interest were the participants' experiences of *everyday* occurrences: getting dressed in the morning, going shopping for clothes and trying on clothes in the changing room, and going about their normal everyday work and leisure routines.

In order to capture the mundanity of everyday life, the study involved a number of research methods. First, participants were asked to complete a clothing journal for one week, recording every time their clothing, or their body as it related to their clothing, intruded on their thoughts or actions. Conversational interviews were conducted later to expand on the journal entries. Second, participants opened up their wardrobes to the researcher, sharing experiences and stories of their clothing. Third, participants each went shopping for clothes with the researcher, many of them trying on clothes and purchasing clothes. This research stage was designed to find out how larger women navigate a clothing market that largely ignores them. The fourth research stage asked participants to take photographs of their "clothed worlds," capturing images that conveyed something about their understandings of their body, their clothes, or the relationship between them. The fifth and final stage of the research asked participants to take part in one of two group discussions where they were provided with the opportunity to share their experiences of clothing their bodies, examining their stories for points of commonality and departure. Each meeting was audio-recorded and relevant material transcribed verbatim and analyzed critically. Underpinning the research foci, and the research methods chosen, was the assumption that what happens on an everyday basis can reveal something extraordinary about our individual lives and the community and society in which we belong because "when we are at the everyday is when we are at our most cultural" (Turner 2003: 2).

Overall, the research showed that the participants' experiences of their clothed bodies were complex, resulting in ambivalent understandings of self that were both temporally and spatially situated. Indeed, the situatedness of their experiences was a recurring theme, underlining the importance of place for understandings of the fat clothed body. On closer analysis, the conceptual notion of boundaries and, in particular, boundaries of bodies, clothes, and geographic sites, gained traction as it became clear that the participants found themselves located within a field of bounded sites that had to be continually navigated. The remainder of this chapter works through conceptual notions of boundaries and is divided into two broad parts. The first examines boundaries as a theoretical and conceptual tool. The second fleshes out the ideas raised by drawing on empirical data.

BOUNDARIES . . . AND BEYOND

Boundaries are always important. To frame this chapter, we explore three distinct notions of boundaries. First, we consider the boundaries of the fat body itself and, especially, the way in which the boundaries of the fat body are tenuous and troublesome in their fleshy folds and rolls. Second, we consider the boundaries of clothing, clothes' role as a marker that separates one person from an "other," and the way in which clothing can categorize people, generating socially constructed boundaries between groups. Third, we consider the boundaries of geographic sites in which people might be excluded or included and the place of the fat woman's clothed body within those sites.

Boundaries of the Body

Applied to the body, the notion of boundaries is particularly useful. Certainly, the skin marks the boundary between one person and another. However, the specific boundaries of the body are not fully clear. There are parts of the body, such as hair and nails, that are not firmly located either inside or outside the body (Cavallaro and Warwick 1998). Also, although skin contains the body and its contents, ensuring the inside of the body cannot leak across the border, elements of the body, such as sweat, fail to be fully contained, transgressing the body's borders.

These ambiguous borders are important when considering the fat body. Fat can be consumed, moving from the outside to the inside of the body. However, fat also settles within the body. When fat settles, it is as though the margins or boundaries of the body have been breached, the world excessively entering the corpulent body (Huff 2001). This is particularly the case given the problematic construction of fat as a food source in the Western world. In this context, fat is largely constructed as an impurity or pollutant that is inherently threatening to the internal machinations of the body. Yet fat also settles on the body, appearing on the body like "barnacles on a ship" (Huff 2001: 44). The way in which fat resides, at once, *within* the body while also being visible *on the surface* of the body complicates the fluid and indeterminable boundaries of the fat, fleshy body. The social and discursive construction of fat and its occupation of the "in-between, the ambiguous, [and] the composite" space (Kristeva 1982: 4) means that the (breached) boundaries of the fat woman's body are encapsulated by uncertainty and ambiguity. Further, the lack of solidity to material fatness (Longhurst 2005b), and its propensity to wobble, quiver, and jiggle, gives rise to perceptions of fat bodies as unruly and beyond the control of both the individual and society.

Crucially, the uncontrolled (and uncontrollable) body is perceived as dangerous, given that it defies social order. Judith Butler (1990: 168) contends that "all social systems are vulnerable at their margins, and . . . all margins are accordingly considered dangerous." The foundation of Butler's comment—indeed, underpinning the notion of corporeal boundaries more generally—is Mary Douglas's work on boundaries and dirt in *Purity and Danger*. In this seminal text, Douglas argues similarly that margins are dangerous and that what is regarded as "dirt" in any given society is what may be considered "matter out of place" (1966: 36). Douglas posits that dirt is

> never a unique, isolated event. Where there is dirt, there is a system. Dirt is the by-product of a systematic ordering and classification of matter, in so far as ordering involves rejecting inappropriate elements. (36)

The relevance of Douglas's work for this chapter is clear. The materiality of the fat body stands in as the abject "dirty" body; it is a symbolically polluted corporeality that defies social order. Fat and their "folds of soft flesh disrupt the solidity of things . . . [thus] fat bodies can be seen to occupy a borderline state that disturbs order by not respecting 'proper' boundaries" (Longhurst 2005b: 256). The conceptualization of fat as analogous to dirt and pollution serves as another form of social control (Huff 2001), the result of which is the reification of hegemonic discourses that position fat women on the margins (or boundaries) of society. Thinking through the fat woman's body in this way constructs the fat body as intrinsically problematic and potentially threatening.

Boundaries of Clothes

The conceptual notion of boundaries is raised once again when considering clothing. Clothing "lies at the margins of the body and marks the boundary between self and other, individual and society" (Entwistle 2001: 37). Clothing is at once intimate, residing against the surface of the individual body, and social, indicating social categories. Clothing has individual functions, such as keeping the body warm and preserving modesty, but also serves a social function by marking an individual as a member of a given social environment or group. Thus, clothing is the matter that transforms the private and individual body into a sociocultural entity to be recognized by others; clothing inscribes meaning on the body (Grosz 1994).

The materiality of clothes serves as a physical boundary that marks one person as separate from another. However, given the capacity of clothing to transform biological matter into social matter (Entwistle 1997) and imbue the self with socio-cultural meaning, clothing also serves as a symbolic boundary. To put it another way, clothing acts as a transitional object that transforms the private body into the public body (Entwistle 2000; Woodward 2007). In doing so, clothing can mediate the wearer's social membership as, through the act of dressing, we invariably consider the views of those we might encounter on entering the public realm (Woodward 2005). Through clothing, we reveal aspects of ourselves to others, such as our ethnic group (Barnes and Eicher 1997; Eicher 1995), our religious affiliation (Gies 2006), our sexuality (Clarke and Turner 2007), our moral and political leanings (Parkin 2002; Wilson and de la Haye 1999), our social status (Barthes 2006; Bourdieu 1984), and even our competence within the workplace (Glick et al. 2005). Clothing makes us socially, publicly, and "culturally visible" (Wilson and de la Haye 1999: 2).

Despite the utility of clothing to mark people within (or without) social groups, the boundaries between clothing and the body itself are troublesome. At what point does the body end and clothes begin? Certainly, the boundaries of each are prob-lematized further when considering the textural porosity of fabric. The body is not wholly contained. Rather, it seeps and leaks, with fabric providing a ready net. The body's secretions—blood, sweat, and tears, for example—defy the boundaries of the body, marking clothes with the body's interior. In this way, it is as though clothes serve as the "final frontier" (Wilson 1987: 3) between the body and the outside world as what was once internal to the body becomes part of the cloth.

The body and clothes cannot be considered in isolation, for the two interact dia-lectically; "dress works on the body and imbues it with social meaning and the body is a dynamic field which gives life and fullness to dress" (Entwistle 2000: 327). At the moment of dressing, the two, body and clothes, converge on the same space, bringing the other into being in intimate reciprocity. When the body is dressed, clothing lives alongside the body, following its contours and simultaneously shaping, constraining, concealing, and revealing it. The body can no longer move without being shadowed by the clothes. This shadow self is both self and not self; the space between represents the most intimate of relationships. There is, it seems, corporeal and sartorial synchronicity of the clothed body.

As suggested earlier, the boundaries of the (fat) body are ambiguous. The bound-aries of clothing are equally ambiguous. Although clothing may be considered an adjunct to the body and, as such, is worn on the surface of the body, clothing is also *of* the body. In a social sense, at the same time as clothing frames the body, separating it out from others, it also connects the self with others in a multiplicity of ways. As Elizabeth Wilson explains:

> Clothing marks an unclear boundary ambiguously, and unclear boundaries
> disturb us. Symbolic systems and rituals have been created in many different

cultures in order to strengthen and reinforce boundaries, since these safeguard purity. It is at the margins between one thing and another that pollution may leak out. Dress is the final frontier between the self and the non-self. (1987: 2–3)

Wilson's comments echo the earlier comments of Douglas (1966) with regard to the polluting potential of insecure boundaries. The multiply ambiguous relationship between clothing and the body is accentuated when one considers the fat, fleshy body. The boundaries of fat bodies are not as clearly delineated as those of smaller, firmer bodies. Fat flesh gives under pressure and yields to physical constraints, and their "folds of soft flesh disrupt the solidity of things . . . [thus] fat bodies can be seen to occupy a borderline state that disturbs order by not respecting 'proper' boundaries" (Longhurst 2005b: 256). Further, fat bodies take up more space than they are allocated (Adam 2001), and their "excess" flesh spills, for example, beyond the confines of a chair and, importantly, beyond the confines of clothing.

Boundaries of Place

Recent decades have seen a renewed interest in place within the social sciences. No longer are places considered simply sites of geographic location. Rather, they are theorized as "processual, relationally ordered systems" (Löw 2006: 120), the boundaries of which are changeable and dynamic (Stokowski 2002), "contested, fluid and uncertain" (McDowell 1999: 4). The boundaries of place are not innocent. They serve particular interests, and, importantly, they include and exclude (McDowell 1999).

Returning again to the work of Douglas, societies possess "external boundaries, margins, [and] internal structure" (1966: 115). The operational boundaries of society mark one group from another and potentially carve society into discrete categories, effectively defining a person's social position as either inside or outside a bounded social group (Douglas 1996). Furthermore, groups on the boundaries or margins of society, such as larger women, are considered risky by those in the center (Tulloch and Lupton 2003). This exacerbates their construction as other and their potential as pollutants.

Clearly, bodies are an important feature of this process of inclusion and exclusion given that the "social body constrains the way the physical body is perceived" (Douglas 1996: 65). When one considers the fat body this is particularly evident. The dominant discourses available for speaking of fatness construct the fat individual as problematic and intrinsically objectionable. The medicalization of fatness frames fat as both a disease (Jutel 2006; Tischner and Malson 2012; Wray and Deery 2008) and a morally based social problem affecting the individual and society (Jutel 2005; Rail, Holmes, and Murray 2010). In addition, the suggestion that fat bodies are "site[s] of undisciplined flesh and unmanaged desires . . . unhealthy, deviant, and defiant" (Murray 2005: 265–66) becomes accepted over time as the truth of the fat individual. Deeply embedded within the contemporary Western psyche, it has even been suggested that prejudice against fat women is the last existing socially sanctioned prejudice to exist (Breseman, Lennon, and Schulz 1999; LeBesco and Braziel 2001; Longhurst 2005b). Expanding recently to include anyone fat, these negative constructions of fatness and the unavoidable visibility of fatness ensure being (publicly) fat is experientially problematic.

The dressed body is always situated within a particular context, and, as such, clothing is important for generating and mediating the meanings of public places. Within public sites, and at any given time, there are clothing rules and regulations of engagement. At times, these are embedded within regulatory frameworks, such as an employer's insistence that a uniform be worn. However, more often, clothing rules are informal, with social and cultural norms that are enforced through socializing techniques that reinforce accepted behaviors and practices. For example, mourners at a funeral usually wear somber colors, typically black (Bedikian 2008; Harvey 1995), and despite a postmodern shift toward diversity and difference, the white wedding gown remains de rigueur for reinforcing the ideology of heterosexual romantic love (Ingraham 2008). While the rigidity of social norms may be shifting (Pringle and Alley 1995), such clothing practices remain part of social knowledge and practice.

Clothing rules and regulations do not apply to all people in the same way. Unwritten yet codified rules of dress exist for different people in different places. These rules of dress are certainly gendered. However, equally, they are sized, and numerous informal, socially constructed, and socially enforced rules of dress specifically apply to fat women. Everyday evidence is readily apparent. For example, bloggers can be found complaining about fat women "drilling for oil" in stiletto heels and making onlookers "want to hurl" by wearing miniskirts and revealing cleavage, and skinny jeans are seemingly out of the question unless a larger woman wants to look as though she has "sausages for legs." Taking a less overtly judgmental approach, reality television style gurus Trinny and Susannah have plenty of advice on how to reduce the appearance of body fat with their "magic bum, tum and thigh reducers," "tummy-flattening bikini briefs," and "body smoothers." Tellingly, much of their advice around clothing the body is primarily about reducing the appearance of body fat, and only secondarily about establishing codes of sartorial conduct linked to body shape. These normative rules of dress determine what should and should not be worn, and by whom. As such, they serve as a powerful way in which social control and social order are attained and maintained, as breaching these rules can potentially result in public censure (Cain 2011).

THE FAT BODY CLOTHED AND BOUND

This section places yielding folds of flesh firmly at the center of inquiry by considering the "fleshy materiality" (Longhurst 2005b: 256) of fat women's bodies and their clothing. In particular, we consider the situated, corporeal and cultural boundaries of the fat body and clothes, and the fat body in place, through an empirical examination of the everyday clothing practices of larger women.

Between Bodies and Clothes

The materiality of clothes is obviously distinct from the materiality of the body (Entwistle 2000), but these seemingly obvious distinctions become troublesome when considering the fluid boundaries of the fat body. For the women who took part in our study, the relationship between clothes and the body was often experienced as ambiguous and not clearly delineated, as each intruded on the space of the other. A number of participants spoke of clothing leaving its mark on their bodies by "digging into," "biting," "rubbing," and "chafing" the surface of the skin. Indeed, clothes were also capable of leaving behind a permanent reminder of their presence. For example, as a result of wearing bras to accommodate her larger (and heavier) breasts, Mary now sports permanent shoulder indentations where bra straps have dug into her flesh over an extended period of time. Effectively, the materiality of the bra has permanently etched its way into the materiality of the body.

As clothing moved unbidden around the participants' bodies, their bodies were exposed in unwanted ways. As a result, there was a persistent mindfulness of the place of clothes against their skin and a perpetual checking of clothing's placement.

> I'm constantly making sure that it's [clothing] where I want it to be. I'm always conscious of the fact. Has my top ridden up? . . . Is it down over my bottom? Or is it down over my stomach? . . . I would constantly be checking . . . and I do it unconsciously. I don't realise I'm doing it. . . . Can I pull this down? Rearrange it better. (Rose, Clothing journal interview)

Driving the habitual practices of rearranging clothing was the desire to conceal the surface of a body that was understood to be socially problematic and unruly. Further, an awareness of the fat phobia that exists in society ensured that the larger-sized participants in this study were conscious that bodily revelations must be avoided and their bodies hidden from view. As Beth explained, she was "very aware" when her top rode up over her back as she did not "want to show bare skin" or her "spare tyre."

The fraught relationship between the participants' fat, fleshy bodies and their clothing was captured by Rose in the photo elicitation task. Rose's photograph of a vine wrapped around a tree sought to capture the intimate tension that exists between her clothing and her body, discussing how the vine (clothing) does not simply fall around the tree (body). Rather, it wraps itself around the tree, confining, strangling, clinging, restricting, and constraining.

Rose's image denotes the fraught relationship between the boundaries of larger bodies and clothing. However, while clothing can be used to conceal the body, clothing can also be used to smooth the boundaries of the body. The normative construction of the female body, at least in contemporary Western society, is not only slim but also streamlined and controlled. In contrast, the boundaries of the fat, fleshy female body are not. In the present study, clothing was often used as a mechanism to smooth the surface of the body. Georgie, for example, sought to smooth her body by wearing either a one-piece swimsuit or an all-in-one control undergarment underneath her outerwear. This, she found, was the ideal antidote to her "lumps and bumps" as the swimwear "held all these bits in and gave me a flattering figure." Similarly, while Beth had her "standard underwear," she also had "magic knickers" that were "kind of meant to be . . . the answer to every large woman's problems." Although the magic knickers were "hot" and "tight" and "not overly comfortable" to wear, Beth wore them at times as they "iron[ed] out" the creases of her body:

> When you're wearing a particular dress . . . and you want to just iron out the creases a little bit . . . the magic knickers . . . come right up to your chest, but they will smooth, they will flatten . . . they don't flatten my tummy, they just hold it firmer. I mean they don't make it go away and it doesn't make it any smaller, it just holds it steadier. (Beth, Clothing journal interview)

Beth's comment alludes to the *movement* of the fleshy body. This is an important point. While the slim, toned, athletic body is firm, the fat, fleshy body jiggles and wobbles. This movement challenges normative constructions of controlled feminine corporeality and also affects the way the body rubs up against clothing. As the body moves, and the flesh moves, clothing does not always stay in place as expected; clothes slide and ride into the body's crevices, chafing the skin's surface and cutting into soft flesh. Clothes found their way (uninvited) into the fleshy crevices of their larger bodies. In response, habitual practices were often employed by the participants to negotiate the troublesome space between their bodies and their clothing. Such practices included pulling across the edges of cardigans to disguise the stomach (Beth) and scooping up the front of tops to cover the cleavage (Charlotte). Rose reported finding that T-shirt material found its way into the folds of her waist. In response, she developed a "little flicky thing" to flick the fabric out of the "groove[s]" of her waist when she was walking around. Although the habit reportedly "drives [her] insane" and she is "constantly conscious that [she's] doing it," she continues to do so in order to successfully negotiate the boundaries of her body and her clothes and put each in their proper place.

Engaging in such habitual practices allowed these larger-sized women to mediate unwanted revelations of their bodies and tempered the problematic boundaries of their clothed bodies. These routinized practices put clothes back into order and their rightful place, and ensured that private bodies remained private by ensuring that clothing "behaved." At such moments, tacit knowledge was carried, or lodged, in the body as these women demonstrated their awareness of their bodies' failure but also of the practices required to (partially) remedy that failure. In doing so, they realigned (momentarily) the tension-filled space between their clothing and their larger bodies.

The Fat Clothed Body on the Margins

Not only must fat women negotiate the fluid boundaries of their bodies, they must also negotiate the gaze of others, a gaze that positions them on the margins of society. In the present study, all participants reported awareness that their bodies were deemed socially problematic and, as such, were the object of others' negative attention. An entry from Rose's clothing journal specifically attests to this understanding:

Being judged
Observing what others are wearing, even when I feel OK
My message can quickly turn into, not being "right"
Not good enough, I don't fit in
Being out in the public eye, feeling I'm being watched
Who is the watcher?, what are they looking for?
Back 'n' forth thing, observing others
Being observed, like a game of tennis
Meeting the other, eye to eye
Turning away

Women learn very early in their lives that their bodies are flawed (Hartley 2001), and for fat women this is especially true as their bodies are observed through the lens of negative fat stereotypes. It is telling that Rose turned away from the gaze of others. As her body was caught within this exchange, it was transformed and marked as problematic. Although Rose explained that she was better able to resist these glances when she was "confident and whole within [her] edges," for the most part, to meet the other "eye to eye" entailed directly facing an image of herself for which she was ill prepared. In contrast, "turning away" ensured she never had to fully face the social construction of her body as problematic and misplaced.

The fat body was not the only recipient of the judgment of others. The participants also reported that their clothing choices were also the target of others' judgment.

> I feel like I'm being judged on what I wear because that doesn't suit a bigger person. I mean I always dress how I like to feel but sometimes it is as a bigger woman, why are you wearing that? . . . It's what can I get away with and not offend. (Annette, Clothing journal interview)

Processes of judgment about fat bodies and their clothing do not come only from the other. Many of the participants "liked to check out" other larger-sized women themselves, casting judgments on both body size and clothing choices. Although there were certainly occasions when this process of judgment was negative, there were also occasions when witnessing other large women who were "well turned out," who "looked good" and had clearly "done alright" (Beth) with regard to their clothes, provided them with the confidence or knowledge to try out new styles. In Beth's words, the "fat lady done well" also served as "kind of an affirmation that big ladies can do okay," despite "always [being] told we can't." In this way, the positive assessment of others provided a source of inspiration that extended their own clothing repertoire. However, Beth's final comment indicates the inherent tension therein. Although she gained inspiration from the "fat lady done well" (perhaps even against the odds), she remained mindful of the broader social judgments attached to her own larger body and its location on the margins and, in this way, remained complicit in her own marginalization.

These examples demonstrate the extent to which fat women are positioned on the margins of society and, equally, the extent to which they are contained within bounded sites. For the participants taking part in this research, their task was to negotiate their way in, through, and around these symbolic boundaries. One of the key motivations for doing so was the attainment of corporeal and sartorial invisibility, not drawing attention to oneself. As an everyday occurrence, negotiating public encounters often involved an interplay of revealing and concealing the body in the attempt to attain invisibility. Beth, for example, spoke of her upper arms as a part of her body that she refused to reveal in public.

> Went to pub with friends. It's cold and wet so need something warm. Wore jeans, animal print top and big woollen [sic] cardi. The top has short sleeves so I will not be taking the cardi off however hot the pub gets. Would rather melt than expose upper arms and midriff. (Beth, Clothing journal excerpt)

In the journal interview with Beth about this excerpt, she explained that she was firmly committed to keeping her "big woollen cardi" on irrespective of the temperatures reached. She was mindful of the way her body appeared in public, and she felt an environment such as the pub exacerbated the social judgment she could potentially face. Given the unavoidable visibility of larger women's bodies (Murray 2005), Beth did not wish to draw further unwanted attention by revealing her "fat arms."

This example is indicative of a symbolic exchange that results in the perception of exclusion. However, in other public spaces, such as the shopping mall, the experience of exclusion is far more tangible and structural. During the shopping trip stage of the research, a number of participants chose to visit a local mall. However, their experiences of the mall were underpinned by exclusionary practices that problematized their bodies and placed them further on the margins. While shopping with them, it became apparent that large parts of the mall were metaphorically closed to them because of their larger body size. Charlotte described her experience of this exclusion as "pressing your nose up against the window of a party you're not invited to." The majority of the clothing stores within the mall were framed as out of bounds in the minds of the participants, as Beth so clearly elucidated:

> There's no point going in there, I've never been in there . . . there'd be no point going in there 'cause there'd be absolutely nothing . . . very frustrating so out of this whole great big mall I can say [department store], [plus-sized clothing store], and [department store] would be the only places I could buy something. The rest from my point of view would be completely redundant. (Beth, Shopping trip)

Similarly, during the shopping trip, Jen explained that she "wouldn't even bother going into so-called ordinary shops 'cause I know that they wouldn't have clothes that would fit me." The shopping mall is an enclosed space with clear practices of inclusion and exclusion; despite its appeal to the mass market, groups considered undesirable can be easily excluded. Certainly, fat women are not directly excluded from the shopping mall; no one bars their entry. However, the limited number of clothing stores offering to accommodate larger-sized bodies illustrates the structural constraints imposed on larger-sized women. This is a puzzling imbalance given the number of fat people in the Western world. Moreover, this systematic failure to account for fat women (and their disposable incomes) certainly fails to fit the economic model of supply and demand.

Yet shopping malls do carry some clothing lines in large sizes. Shopping with the participants revealed that one department store located within the mall carried two clothing ranges for larger women representing two distinct styles and reflecting two different price ranges. Outside the shopping mall, participants also chose to visit occasional boutique stores that incorporated a separate clothing line for the larger woman. However, in both the department store and the designer store, these garments were placed, quite literally, on the margins. In the department store, the two available product lines were situated in the farthest back corner, the sartorial equivalent of a restaurant table by the toilets. Jen was fully aware of where she could locate clothing to fit her:

> Usually the large are at the back. They want to get us out of the way [laughs] . . . you don't even know it's happening and it's just unconsciously you know "oh yeah my stuff's down the back of the shop." (Jen, Shopping trip)

Although Jen had never visited the mall and department store before, she intuitively knew she would find the larger or plus-size clothing "down the back of the shop," well beyond the store frontage where she could be seen by others. Similarly, the larger women's clothes in the designer store were constructed as a "special" line with a different label, beyond the primary clothing line. They were also positioned apart from the main body of clothing and, as Ann described, separated out on a "little rack" in the corner:

> I walk into the shop and the first thing the lady says to me is "oh the bigger racks are over there" [laughs] . . . I guess we're quite sensitive as bigger ladies and we want to be like everyone else you know [laughs]. So we don't want to have a little rack over in the corner for us . . . why can't they put those ones in amongst the others? Why do they have to be separate? (Ann, Wardrobe review)

The structural boundaries of sites of consumption act to position fat women on the margins. Specialist plus-size clothing stores are often referred to as "outsize" stores. However, the term *outsize* suggests that which is beyond the norm. Not only does it sound audibly similar to "outside" (Adam 2001), but as a spatial metaphor it clearly positions the shopper who frequents these stores as beyond the margins of normativity and, thus, beyond legitimacy (Colls 2006). Indeed, it is not only the clothing that is constructed as marginal in these places; the women who buy the clothes are similarly constructed. Clothing stores are not in the business of producing and selling clothes only; they are also in the business of constructing normative models of gender. Through the creation of "special" clothing labels that are spatially marginalized, the larger wearers of those clothes are socially marginalized. In the process, the larger woman as shopper is simultaneously constructed as marginal and "beyond the margins of intelligibility" (Butler 1990: 132), the very margins within which smaller-size women find their legibility.

The lack of available clothing stores and the marginalization of larger clothes within stores mean that fat women are effectively excluded from the sphere of fashion. Arguably, this exclusion may reside with designers and company heads who maintain clothing is at its best when worn by smaller women ("Skinny White Runway Models" 2007). Betsy Breseman, Sharron Lennon and Theresa Schulz argue that designers consider that having their clothes made in larger sizes could be "fashion poison," damaging their brand and potentially insulting smaller women who may be "confronted" with a fat person in the same outfit (1999: 181). Describing the fat woman as poisonous is reminiscent of Douglas's (1966) commentary on the polluted, and potentially polluting, body, discussed earlier. Irrespective of the reason, the failure of clothing stores to accommodate fat women's bodies directly excludes them from fully participating in social practices of consumption that mark individuals as active and legitimate members of society.

People and places are gendered (e.g., McDowell 1999; Vaiou and Lykogianni 2006). However, the failure of the clothing market to cater for fat women shows how places are also sized. This failure is not benign; the structural organization of the clothing market positions fat women on the margins of society. Perhaps the greatest irony is that in order to participate in practices of consumption, the larger wearer must make her purchases from the back corner and thus inadvertently, yet unavoidably, contributes to her own marginalization. If, as Alan Warde (1994) suggests, it is through shopping that we construct identity, larger women clearly face considerable structural challenges.

The findings from this study reveal the conceptual importance of boundaries for making sense of fat women's clothed experience. These boundaries are shown to be multiple and ambiguous, weaving together material, structural, and symbolic threads. In the next section we consider the broader implications for understanding the embodied and situated practices of fat clothed women.

THE FAT CLOTHED WOMAN AS AN EMBODIED AND SITUATED PRACTICE

Bodies are, for the most part, clothed (Longhurst 2005a). Despite increased sociological interest in the body (Fox 2012) and the elevation of the body as central to identity (Shilling 1993), less attention has been paid to this social fact. Yet most people, including the dispossessed, still possess, at the very least, the clothes on their backs (Ash 1999). Importantly, clothing has communicative capacities (Kellner 1994), "embellish[ing] the body" (Entwistle 2000: 324) and providing the wearer with the "models and material for constructing identity" (Kellner 1994: 160). As such, clothing can serve as a powerful marker of social affiliation and identity, making it important for understanding the social world. But clothing is more than that because bodies and clothing have an intimate reciprocity; clothing is embodied.

This chapter has examined the relationship between *fat* women's bodies and clothing as they are located in place. And fat matters. The fat body is bound by dominant discourses that construct fat and fat people as inherently objectionable and problematic. Moreover, normative rules of dress for fat people are often underpinned by moral discourses and socially sanctioned clothing rules that limit fat women's options for clothing their bodies. Although everyday practices may begin in a particular locale, they are essentially embodied (Waskul and Vannini 2006). For larger women, the body becomes an object through which the world is experienced, and serves at the same time, as a reminder of the body's failure to align with normative constructions of feminine identity. At these times, every interaction is experienced through the body as the larger woman becomes acutely corporeally conscious, her "subjectivity . . . irrevocably corporeal" (Murray 2005: 272). The perpetual presence of the (fat) body and the concomitant visibility of size ensure that "impression management of the stigmatised body" (Goffman 1986, 1990) is unfeasible, as the fat body is "always already an 'outed body': it is always hyper visible, its flabby flesh is always irrevocably seen" (Murray 2005: 273).

Through the notion of the "absent body," Drew Leder (1990: 84) argues that people are not fully conscious of their bodies as they carry out everyday activities. The body is relegated to the background until such a time as an event, such as a specific physiological or negative social experience, causes its corporeal reappearance or, more precisely, its corporeal "dys-appearance." In other words, the body emerges suddenly and problematically into one's direct consciousness. Certainly, Leder suggests that women's bodies are more corporeally present than men's. Perhaps this is due, as Elizabeth Grosz (1994) articulates, to dichotomies of body/mind and nature/culture and the concomitant association of women with the former and men with the latter. Perhaps, too, it is because women's bodies are more commonly found to be the object of others' attention.

With regard to the *clothed* body empirical research supports the claim that for women, their bodies intrude problematically into their consciousness. Joanne Entwistle showed that women at times (such as when wearing jeans that are too tight) became conscious of the boundaries of their clothed bodies, resulting in an "epidermic self-awareness" (2000: 334). Further, Sophie Woodward found that in order for an outfit to "feel right," the aesthetics must be right; otherwise, a self-conscious "aesthetic disjuncture" occurs (2005: 25).

However, in the present study concerning not just any clothed women but *fat* clothed women, the clothed body continually intruded. For clothing to feel right, it had to fit comfortably against the body, but it also had to fit the socio-normative practices of the site in which the clothing is worn (although we focused on the shopping experience in this chapter, we could just as easily have focused on other spaces such as the beach). The way in which the materiality of the body and the materiality of cloth rubbed up against each other ensured that the body remained perpetually present. And, importantly, the social judgment faced by fat women in public spaces, continually reminds the fat woman of her body's failure to align with normative models of feminine beauty. The research presented in this chapter suggests that rather than being part of the corporeal background, the body is part of the corporeal foreground as the fat body continually returns to view. It seems there is not so much an "aesthetic disjuncture" (Woodward 2005: 25) as a spatio-corporeal disjuncture in which the clothed body is experienced as misplaced. Clothes and space reside in *dis*harmony.

This research has shown how one of the functions of clothing for larger women is to disguise or cover up rolls and folds of flesh, but the slippage of clothes into bodies and the slippage of bodies into clothes ensure that the boundaries of each remain ambiguous. These ambiguities arise from the fluidity or viscosity of flesh and the malleability of cloth, as each intrudes on the other. This problematic relationship between clothing and the body ensures a greater corporeal consciousness for fat women. The physical materiality of the (clothed) larger body refuses to be ignored.

These ambiguous boundaries of the situated fat clothed body are often keenly felt as bodies, clothing, and place come together, creating potentials for surveillance, othering, and marginalization. For fat women, being situated means being the potential object of attention. Making a spectacle of oneself is arguably a "specifically feminine danger" (Russo 1997: 318). We would add that it is, more specifically, a *fat* feminine danger. In this research, we have brought bodies, clothing, and place together to consider the clothed fat woman's body as an embodied and situated practice. In doing so, we argue that fat is a substance that is simultaneously *in* the body, *on* the body, and *of* the body and, as such, cannot be separated from fat as experience.

8 FATSPLOITATION

Disgust and the Performance of Weight Loss

Jennifer-Scott Mobley

Celebrities have been performing the materiality of weight gain and weight loss in the media for years. From Lynn Redgrave in the 1980s to Jennifer Hudson today, actors have performed weight gain and loss for the camera, frequently spinning it into self-promotion but always emphasizing the material production and reduction of body fat. In the context of advertising diet products, their performances aim to stress the materiality of fat that consumers can lose. Through performance, they attempt to represent the earthly, molecular presence of body fat after it is lost—to make material what is absent. In order to dramatize and highlight lost pounds, performers prey on spectators' fear of contamination and feelings of disgust conjured by their previously fat bodies. If indeed disgust attracts even as it repels, evoking a visceral response in the spectator, then it is a powerful marketing tool that these public figures skillfully deploy. Yet the very earthly, organic nature of body fat always "ghosts" the slim body and necessitates constant reinscribing of slenderness in performance. This circular pattern through which celebrity figures perform weight loss and gain in popular representation, as well as the commodification of the performance, results in what I call *fatsploitation*—or the process whereby celebrities exploit consumer prejudices by evoking disgust toward their (famous) fat bodies for commercial gain. In 1988 Oprah Winfrey famously wheeled a wagon full of sixty-seven pounds of animal fat onstage during her talk show to represent her weight loss in material form. The juxtaposition of the fat in the wagon with her newly slimmed body attempted a material performativity of her absent fat. Although the diet industry had a stranglehold on the United States by the 1970s, Oprah raised the bar for public performances of weight loss thereafter (Harpo Productions 2010). At that time, *Oprah* was one of the most popular daytime talk shows to date, with a huge viewership. The January episode in which she revealed her (first) weight loss received the highest ratings ever. She was an innovative pioneer in terms of attempting to make material her lost fat by dramatically externalizing it through the proxy of animal fat. Oprah's willingness to perform weight loss and her accompanying feelings of shame also endeared her to audiences as someone who struggled with her weight just as many Americans do, and it started a "personal" conversation with fans that became part of her marketing appeal for decades to come. She effectively captivated 100 percent of her (predominantly female) viewing demographic; the anxiety surrounding fat in our culture is universal, and she appealed easily to those who struggle with their weight, as well as to those who are disgusted by fat people or fear gaining weight.

What is more, Oprah tapped into a common quirk of human nature, which is that things we find disgusting may attract even as they repulse. The film and entertainment industry, including the news media, relies on this allure and goes to increasing lengths to attract viewers through this paradigm (Miller 1997: x). We see this in television programming, ranging from programs such as *Fear Factor*, which films participants eating or touching disgusting matter such as bugs or refuse of some type, to news coverage that shows bodies mangled or bleeding from trauma. Oprah capitalized on this phenomenon, not only by materializing her absent pounds with "disgusting" matter, but by evoking the response of disgust in her audience. As a theater and performance studies scholar, I am interested in the ways fat is represented and embodied in performance and popular representations as well as the impact of fat on spectators, which can include the embodied response of disgust. This chapter argues that commercial spokespeople and celebrity figures perform the materiality of fat in the context of weight loss and gain in order to commodify themselves and sell diet products, and that the emotion of disgust is central to these performances. I will demonstrate how celebrities and public figures such as Oprah Winfrey and Kirstie Alley deliberately employ tactics in performance to elicit disgust for effect in order to manipulate spectators. Moreover, I will show how celebrity performances aim to materialize fat that is lost as a means of erasing the "ghost" of fatness that haunts their public image.

THE MATERIALITY OF FAT AND DISGUST

Fat on the human body is at once frustratingly abstract and decidedly material. After all, it is a substance—adipose tissue—but, visually speaking, the notion of what constitutes a fat person can be wildly subjective. Fat is something we eat and something we become. It is both external matter that we can touch and consume as well as internal, embodied matter. As Rachel Colls (2007: 358) states, fat "is ambiguous; placed simultaneously under the skin yet materialized as a substance in and of itself . . . and can be absent and present simultaneously as in the case of weight loss and weight gain."

Moreover, fat has unique connotations in American culture and is imbricated not only in the culture's material and social conditions but also in its consumption and commodity chains. Fat people are fundamentally incriminated in consumer culture because the assumption is that they use more resources—more food, more textiles for clothes, more space in airline seats, and so on. Thanks to the "war on obesity" fat people are also implicated in our economic structures as a drain on our national health care system and taxpayer dollars because of the presumed long-term health complications that arise from fat. On the other hand, fat people, presumed to spend more on everything from food to diet products, are depicted as the ultimate consumers in a culture obsessed with acquiring material items. Their fat bodies thus materialize the abundance of our consumer culture. However, the stigma of being fat in the United States carries with it a burden of shame and guilt. In our culture, nothing is monitored more than individuals' weight loss and weight gain.

Moreover, as Elizabeth Grosz (1994) asserts, Western logic compels us to view the body as an external expression of the inner self. Mark Graham (2005: 178–79) states that "[i]n a fat-obsessed culture, we are all 'lipoliterates' who 'read' fat for what we believe it tells us as about a person. This includes not only their moral character, but their health." In her seminal text *The "Fat" Female Body*, Samantha Murray (2008: 13–14) builds on these ideas and summarizes how Americans respond to bodies identified as fat. She argues that "we have a well-developed and readily deployed literacy when it comes to reading bodies" (13). Her analysis delineates how a fat body is contrasted with the normativized body as aberrant and even deviant or perverse. More specifically, when it comes to the fat female body and, in particular, a fat white woman, people make instant assumptions about her character based on her appearance. She is presumed to be less intelligent than average, lazy, out of control, morally flawed, and is considered an affront to normative feminine standards of beauty and body size. She is a food addict incapable of managing her own desires. The excessiveness of her body is also often associated with an excessive appetite for sex and power. In much of Western culture, especially the United States, fat people, particularly women, trigger moral and social judgment from all who encounter them.

Furthermore, I assert that attitudes toward fat bodies in our culture go beyond aesthetic or medical judgment and include an experiential response. Fat may not only prompt the aforementioned prejudices but also actively evoke the sensory emotion of disgust from those who behold it. Indeed, because of the way fat has been demonized by the media in our culture, fat has the power to elicit disgust in many cases, including from the fat subjects themselves, on whose bodies the fat materializes. Certainly, fat bodies may evoke disgust from those who see or come in contact with them. They threaten to contaminate the spectator with their very presence. In his study of disgust, William Miller (1997: 12–14) not only explores what elicits this complex emotion but also notes that one of its central elements is fear of contamination through contact with the disgusting object. He asserts that disgust is both an emotion and a sensory feeling that can evoke not only fear of contamination but abject horror. Central to the larger discussion of materiality is this idea that disgust is an embodied response manifesting in physical revulsion to a subject's bodily matter. Miller also notes that disgust is intrinsically linked with the viscera of organs and fluids that are the "body's interiors" and that disgust is conceptualized differently from other emotions and is not merely an intellectual or emotional perception of something but is connected to "what it feels like" (36). Unlike other emotions, disgust, which is considered a "core" emotion, provokes an instinctual response tied in with bodily senses. Miller suggests that fear "is a response to harms threatening the body, disgust to harms threatening the soul" (26). Given all the negative moral implications associated with fat, compounded by the perceived contaminating power of fat, it is no wonder that a fat person provokes disgust. Fat threatens to contaminate the very soul. Miller also argues that disgust is fear-infused horror, the distinction being that fear implies the option of running away from the feared object, while horror (disgust plus fear) "denies flight as an option. . . . Because the threatening thing is disgusting, one does not want to strike it, touch it, or grapple with it" (26). I would add to his paradigm "become it." In American culture a fat body can evoke a visceral response from those who encounter it; not only do we recoil from touching a fat person for fear of contamination, but their fat also serves as a reminder of our own fleshiness—our vulnerable humanity—and the potential to become fat ourselves.

In trying to uncover what people find disgusting (animals, for example, do not experience disgust), Miller identifies key oppositions, many of which are central to the experiential emotion of disgust. These include human versus animal, outside (external) versus inside (internal), dry versus wet, firm versus squishy or soft, health versus disease, beauty versus ugliness, and moderation versus excess, among other binaries. Indeed, a fat body fulfills all of the criteria that potentially elicit disgust from those who see or come into contact with it. Fat people are often characterized as subhuman, more id driven, and animalized because they seemingly cannot control their appetites. Their fat is not only an exterior aesthetic but also part of their bodily makeup—their interior. Thus, exterior fat on a body indicates that the fat subject is already contaminated from within, and this contributes to the threat of contamination to those around them. Fat bodies are squishy and potentially sweaty or moist to touch; they are uncontained and grotesque and embody surfeit (Miller 1997: 38).

Moreover, fat bodies serve as an embarrassing reminder of our own embodiment/materiality. In a culture that tends to situate "the self" as immaterial, connected to the mind and spirit, a fat body is an "othered" body, an abject body reminding us that human bodies are flesh and viscera, vulnerable to illness, aging, and death (Kent 2001: 135). Therefore, disgust is fundamental to Americans' response to fat bodies. One illustration of how this disgust manifests on a daily basis is the ongoing controversy surrounding fat passengers in airline seats; consumer complaints have focused not so much on space but on the contact with someone else's fat flesh. For example, the *New York Daily News* quoted one passenger as saying, "It was disgusting to have to share my seat with someone else's fat" (Huff 2009: 181).

HAUNTED BY THE GHOST OF BODIES PAST

An average fat person in the United States may elicit disgust in his or her day-to-day activities. But the disgust evoked in a spectator becomes particularly powerful in a performance context. When a public or celebrity figure has appeared fat in popular representation—on the stage, on screen, or in the mass media—he or she has not only triggered various assumptions about a fat person's character in the minds of viewers but potentially elicited disgust in them. For obvious reasons, this is an identity formation that most celebrities do not want to be associated with. Thus, they endeavor to lose the weight and perform their weight loss in popular representation in order to remake their image. The impulse, especially by popular entertainers, to perform weight loss in an attempt to materialize the lost pounds may be inspired in part by what theater scholar Marvin Carlson calls "ghosting." Carlson (2003: 8) argues that performance—dramatic presentation—is an "attractive repository for the storage and mechanism for the continued recirculation of cultural memory." He asserts that the body of an actor is "recycled" and already imprinted in the audience's memory in a particular way from their experience of that actor in previous roles, which can lead to powerful and unexpected audience responses. I argue that this recycling includes not only previous roles but also the actor's instrument, his or her material body. If an audience has experienced the actor as having been fat, which necessarily extends to include all the aforementioned prejudices triggered by their fatness, as well as the phenomenological response evoked in the spectator, then the actor often feels obliged to somehow erase that collective memory of his or her fat self. In other words, "even when an actor strives to vary his roles, he is, especially as his reputation grows, entrapped by the memories of his public, so that each new appearance requires a renegotiation of those memories" (Carlson 2003: 9). Few would deny that once an actress has appeared as fat in any popular representation, escaping the ghost of that identity is a Sisyphean task, not only because her fatness has evoked a feeling of disgust in the spectator, but also because images of her erstwhile fat self can be circulated endlessly in mass media such as the Internet.

Prior to 1988 and Oprah's celebrity exploitation of fat to sensationalize her struggle, the diet industry employed a more generic approach to hawking its products and touting its results. Testimonials by supposedly real people were depicted in advertisements for the latest panaceas for relief from unsightly weight gain. Carlson's theory about the ghosting of bodies can explain why earlier advertising campaigns more frequently relied on nameless actors—"real people"—who would not have to renegotiate any previously disseminated images of themselves as fat. Most unknown spokespersons for diet products perform the materiality of their weight loss by appearing on the commercial emphasizing the disparity between their previously fat body and their "new" body, speaking animatedly about their success while juxtaposed with a (static) photographic image of their fat self, usually frowning, slumping, and drawing the focus to their rolls of flab, aiming to evoke disgust from the viewer. Alternatively, spokespeople may wear a garment that fit their fat body prior to weight loss and emphasize the disparity between their slender body and the implied matter that once filled their enormous garment. In most cases, these individuals remain anonymous. Their testimonials are more effective not only because they are *not* celebrity figures whose fatness has been embedded in the popular imagination of the public through previous performances but also because their new slender bodies are ghosted only by a static image of their former fat selves. The memory of their fat bodies is not inscribed in the collective memory in any deep or visceral way, and the aliveness of their slender figure in a commercial, or even juxtaposed in print against a smaller, less-animated image, easily captures the attention over the static photo of their formerly fat self.

Jared Fogle, who in 1999 became a spokesperson for the fast-food franchise Subway, is a rare case of an unknown person gaining fame and name recognition from performing weight loss on a commercial scale. Fogle, who ironically alleges that he gained weight by eating too much fast food, slimmed down by choosing the healthiest menu options at Subway. He was successful in his unique dieting endeavor, and when his story found its way to Subway advertising executives, they hired him as the company's spokesperson. Fogle, who lost about 245 pounds on "the Subway Diet," became a dieting and pop-cultural icon. Like many spokespeople before him, his signature performative gesture of weight loss was to stand inside his sixty-two-inch-waist pants and hold out the waistband to display the absence of what had been the rest of himself for the camera. In some commercials Fogle delivered a Subway pitch standing next to an image of his fat self that highlighted his immense size and his rolls of fat, again playing on viewers' disgust at his formerly massive, flabby body.

Subway sales more than doubled as a result of this marketing tactic, and Fogle was the company's primary spokesperson until about 2009 (Leung 2007).

However, in 2009 Fogle's popular commercial appeal began to wane. Perhaps his performance of weight loss (and value as a marketing tool) lost potency because, unlike most dieters, who regain their lost pounds within three to five years, he essentially maintained his weight loss for ten years, and viewers could no longer experience his absent fat as material or real; he was no longer perceived as a fat person who had lost weight. Miller (1997: 27) suggests that "the disgusting can possess us, fill us with . . . feelings of not being in control, of being *haunted*" (emphasis added). But Fogle's body no longer evoked disgust in viewers because he maintained his weight loss for so long and appeared often enough in representation as his slimmer self that he was no longer ghosted by his 400-pound body. Unlike Oprah or other celebrities I will discuss, the lingering sense of material contamination was no longer present in Fogle's viewers. Instead, he had entered the realm of a normal-weight individual, and his credibility as someone who had lost weight evaporated. In Fogle's case, this meant the end of a lucrative advertising deal. However, Fogle remains in the weight-gain panopticon in which subjects police themselves, and, within which the discipline of normative bodies in the Foucauldian sense, is dispersed and anonymous, arbitrated by cultural forces such as the media and advertising (Bartky 1990: 63–67). Fogle still appears occasionally in a Subway ad and continues to be a subject of public fascination; he receives unfavorable media attention whenever he gains any weight, which he has done to a lesser degree than most dieters, considering the total amount he lost (North 2010).

Indeed, a 2009 Subway ad campaign returned to using anonymous actors performing weight *gain* (a performative gesture that I will discuss in more detail with the example of Kirstie Alley). In this ad the nameless actors are shown in various poses eating (significantly) greasy fast food from other restaurants. In each case, this gesture of eating simultaneously results in the actors popping the buttons of their clothing, breaking the chairs on which they are sitting, and popping the tires of the automobiles in which they are riding, all of which leads to a chain reaction of calamity in their surroundings. This highlights not only the "outside of me" to "inside of me" transmission of greasy fast food from the mouth to the cellular level of fat tissue, which I will elaborate on later in my discussion, but also the implied association of fat with disorder. Fat bodies not only threaten to contaminate but also violate cultural boundaries of space and hygiene and threaten to pollute those around them with dirt and disorder. In her foundational text *Purity and Danger*, Mary Douglas (1966: 2) discusses the primal fear associated with dirt and disorder in many cultures. A fat body is a disordered body, aesthetically out of place, and the weight and size of a fat person create disorder in an environment designed for normative bodies.

Fat bodies do not fit; they disrupt, bump into, and break objects they come into contact with. In these more recent ads, Subway not only emphasizes the heft and greasiness of alternative fast foods eaten by the chubby actors but exploits the implicit association of fatness with dirt and disorder—the proverbial fat slob—for comic effect (Subway Company 2009). The chaos that ensues in the anonymous actors' surroundings in each frame as a result of their fatness underscores this. Each popped button and pratfall is punctuated by the *1812 Overture* soundtrack as the voiceover encourages viewers to "start the year off right" and "eat fresh," pointedly highlighting the freshness of Subway food in contrast to the grease-laden fast food of competitors.

"ALL OF THIS": OPRAH'S SHAME AND SELF-LOATHING

Let us return to Oprah's infamous episode, which took place in 1988, two years after the show debuted in 1986. Throughout the course of the first years on the air, Oprah had slowly gained weight. In July 1988 she reached a "maximum weight" of 212 pounds, and by the time the episode aired in November of that year she had quietly and quickly lost sixty-seven pounds through an extreme liquid diet. This episode began with Oprah speaking to her audience while wearing a pink trench coat presumably disguising her currently fat body, while showing images of herself years earlier before she had gained weight. She told her audience, "That was me, sixty pounds ago." She then performed the "big reveal," as so many dieters before and after her have done, whipping off the coat to reveal her new size-ten body. But that was not enough; the real landmark moment of that episode occurred when Oprah wheeled out a red wagon containing a clear plastic bag filled with what appeared to be the fat carved off of animal parts. The fact that Oprah used animal fat to represent her weight loss is significant. She could have opted for a sixty-seven-pound bag of flour or sugar, a block of lard, or even bricks or dumbbells. Instead, she chose not only a (potential) food item but an animal product; the slabs of fat in the plastic bag clearly retain the shapes of their bodily form. The bag of fat also plays on the aforementioned cultural fears of dirt and contamination; the animal fat is raw and juicy and threatens to break through the clear plastic bag and leak, potentially infecting innocent bystanders with salmonella or some other food-borne disease. In other words, to illustrate her absent weight Oprah decided to draw attention to the troubling matter that caused that weight, thus deploying a prop calculated to elicit disgust from her audience. Indeed, when she first attempted to pick up the bag to show what sixty-seven pounds of fat looked like, there was an audible response of disgust from the studio audience—perceptible gasps of "eww," "oh!," and so on. This tactic of evoking disgust in others is paramount to the performance of weight loss. It helps delineate Miller's binary of "outside of me" versus "inside of me," aiming to materialize lost pounds as "outside." It also provokes a visceral response in the audience that further dramatizes the absence of fat on a newly slimmed body, whether in an advertising context or celebrity reality performance.

To illustrate the abjection of lost fat, Oprah engaged in a series of gestures. Initially, she laboriously pulled the wagon onto the stage, highlighting the heft and bulk of the fat as well as the need for wheels to move it. She then proceeded to try to lift the heavy bag of fat but was unable to do so, effectively performing the weight of this object for her audience. She went on to describe the fat as "gross" and "shocking" and declared that when she was fat she had to carry it around inside of her body but was now unable to lift it. She also made a point of gesturing to the fat and saying how she worried about her "poor heart" delivering blood to "all of this" (Harpo Productions 2010).

During that episode, she also stated that she thought of life in terms of her weight. In other words, she understood her own history through her weight rather than her accomplishments or some other personalized timeline. With this statement, Oprah hinted at the shame associated with being fat. The remark also implies that her fat is her "embodied archive," an apt metaphor considering the biological function of fat as storage. In other words, the fat body is a physical archive storing fat cells, and even after the fat is lost the body carries physical marks of the absence of fat with stretch marks, for example. But some studies also suggest that that on a cellular level bodies "remember" being fat (Parker-Pope 2011). Therefore, despite the absence of the materiality of actual fat, the body remembers its presence and is prepared for its return not only psychically but physiologically. If we think of traditional archives as places of remembrance, then, in terms of fat, the body is an archive of itself. More significantly for this discussion of shame, Oprah draws on the psychic archive of embodied knowledge regardless of her actual weight at any given moment. In this particular episode, Oprah performed her physical knowledge of her absent fat. Miller (1997: 34) asserts that when directed at oneself the feeling of disgust produces shame, resulting from an inability to adhere to "communal standards that one is deeply committed to." He goes on to say that "the physical sensation of shame and disgust are indistinguishable." Certainly, cultural mandates for female slenderness are stringent, and those who fail to achieve them experience shame at their inability to fit into contemporary standards for health and beauty. Oprah, like many other Americans, is ashamed of her fat. In this episode, Oprah performed her shame for her studio audience and viewers around the country. Years later, in 2007, following a benefit concert with Tina Turner and Cher, to whom she compared herself unfavorably because of her body, she was perhaps even more open about her shame concerning her weight, declaring that "money, fame, and success don't mean anything if you can't control your own being. It doesn't mean anything if you can't fit into your clothes," she said. "It means the fat won. It means you didn't win" (Greene 2009).

Oprah now describes the "wagon of fat" television history moment with a touch of self-denigration (or shame) as my "biggest, fattest mistake" (Yogi, 2011). Having lost that weight through a dangerously low-calorie, restrictive liquid diet plan, she was not able to maintain the loss. It marked the beginning of a yo-yo dieting rollercoaster ride for Oprah that has spanned more than twenty years. For the past two decades, as her wealth, power, and humanitarian accomplishments have grown, Oprah's weight has fluctuated up and down by more than sixty pounds. When she was slim, she performed her slenderness and mastery over her body, showing off her "new" figure on the cover of magazines, sometimes juxtaposed with images of her "old" figure in order to assure her followers of her new size. The impulse to put the two images side by side—one fat, one slim—harkens back to the anonymous testimonial, but because of her international celebrity status, it also speaks directly to her attempts to exorcise the ghost of her bodies past.

Celebrity figures will always be ghosted by previous images of themselves, and this is especially salient when they have appeared fat and engendered disgust from spectators. This explains the differentiating nuances between a known celebrity performing weight loss in a commercial or sitcom setting and an anonymous spokesperson performing weight loss specifically for the commercial diet industry. In the context of marketing diet products, anonymous spokesmodels only briefly emphasize the disgust associated with their former fatness in order to highlight their new slender figure by contrast.

FATSPLOITATION: KIRSTIE ALLEY CAPITALIZES ON FAT

Oprah's "big reveal" and her wagon of fat were a watershed moment with respect to a celebrity figure performing the materiality of weight loss, as well as trying to capture the disgust associated with fat bodies by representing absent pounds with a potentially contaminating material. Frequently, as with Oprah's wagon of fat, the performances stress the materiality of the absent flesh; Fogle and Oprah were primarily concerned with making material the pounds they had shed. However, some advertising and celebrity performances endeavor to materialize weight gain through performing eating that emphasizes the fatty, greasy, or sugary qualities of the excessive food they put in their mouths.

One of the best extended examples of a celebrity performing the materiality of weight gain began in 2005 with Kirstie Alley's self-produced, short-lived Showtime series *Fat Actress*. The premise of the program was to narrate Alley's struggles as a fat actress trying to get work in body-obsessed Hollywood. In fact, the show revolved primarily around her efforts to lose weight and was in step with other so-called reality makeover shows at that time, such as the recently established *The Biggest Loser* (2004). The comedy of the show was rooted in Alley lampooning herself by performing her disgusting habits. In contrast to Oprah, who experienced shame even as she evoked disgust with the wagon of fat, Alley deliberately disgusted her audience, in part by her shamelessness. She engaged every fat stereotype of an all-consuming woman out of control and insatiable for food and attention. Miller (1997: 80) reminds us that "[a]ny action which ought to elicit shame in the doer can elicit disgust in the viewer. Any serious breach of modesty, dignity-maintenance, and self-presentability can be disgusting to behold." Alley preyed on this effect by shame-lessly engaging in acts of embarrassing fat behavior and excessive eating. Similar to the way in which Oprah's weight loss enraptured her viewers, Alley's performance of weight gain garnered media attention and strategically primed consumer interest in her eventual weight loss through Jenny Craig.

In the opening sequence of the first episode, we see Alley weigh herself and then collapse to the floor in horror at the number on the scale. This excessive horror directed at herself harkens back to the claim that fear plus disgust equals horror. She then crawls like a wounded animal to the phone. Between hyperdramatic moans of "I'm dying," she tells her agent she will not accept the Jenny Craig commercial deal. The next sequence shows Alley with disheveled hair, still in her robe, voraciously eating a double hamburger at the drive-through while "chewing out her agent" for failing to get her jobs. As she does so, food spills down her bodice, which is a sexy lace brassiere that accentuates her fleshy, jiggling breasts. The camera focuses on her mouth as she shoves the hamburger into it while talking with her mouth open, emphasizing the grotesqueness of her eating—significantly—fast food, the ultimate food contaminant in contemporary culture.

The filmic framing of Alley's mouth and the fatty, contaminating foods she eats is critical to eliciting disgust in the viewer. As I mentioned earlier, the human body's slimy, gooey, smelly interior often elicits feelings of disgust. Additionally, any place the body's seal is broken is fraught with potential for disgust because the rupture creates a conduit for the "outside of me" to "inside of me" relation. Bodily orifices, such as the nose, mouth, ears, and anus, are sites of danger—critical channels through which contaminating substances can more readily pass and thus pollute the body and the soul (Miller 1997: 59). As several scholars have noted, grease or fat as a substance is particularly troubling matter layered with multiple cultural associations of impurity, disease, immorality, and even illicit sexuality (Forth 2012). Consuming this troubling matter in the form of fast food implies automatic contamination as the grease makes its way to the body's interior.

It often disgusts us to watch people chew their food with their mouths open in our presence or onscreen. The camera work in *Fat Actress* not only accentuates the unsavory qualities of the food but focuses on how indecorously it enters Alley's mouth; we experience revulsion when we see the contaminating fatty food go from outside of Alley's body to inside of her body, where we know it will become body fat. Essentially, this is also the tactic deployed in the aforementioned "Eat Fresh" Subway ad campaign.

In these first few frames, Alley performs many of the classic fat-woman tropes that I have mentioned above: she is "out of control," unable to contain her emotions, and unable even to dress or groom herself before she goes out and eats more. Her behavior falls into what I call "fat behavior." Fat behavior relies on cultural assumptions associated with the fat female body, such as the belief that that she will behave excessively by being out of control emotionally or verbally (yelling at or harassing others) as well as physically (for example, falling, crying, or eating or drinking excessively). We frequently see actors perform fat behavior in various modes of representation. Furthermore, fat behavior and the performance of a fat identity may sometimes be independent of the appearance of the performer's body (Mobley 2012). More significantly for this discussion of materiality, throughout the course of the first episode, Alley's fat behavior explicitly includes her voraciously eating something in nearly every sequence, effectively performing the story of how she got fat.

Particularly in the first few episodes of the series, Alley performed her weight gain onscreen. Each episode featured Alley eating something "bad" for her with careless abandon. In one sequence, she discovers French fries that have been lost in the folds of her gown—or fat—and begins to eat them; in another she goes to a soul food restaurant notorious for its fattening food; in yet another, she eats potato chips by the handful, salaciously licking her fingers to bring attention to the greasiness of the food product and her prurient pleasure in consuming it. It is hardly surprising that the one sexual encounter she has during the course of the entire series provides an opportunity to perform eating; she and her lover parody the eating scene from the film *9 1/2 Weeks*. In this sequence, as sexual foreplay, Alley's lover feeds her all sorts of decadent foods from the refrigerator; he hand-feeds her strawberries and popsicles and sprays whipped cream directly into her mouth. The camera zooms in on the acts of eating, focusing on the food entering her mouth, echoing the various ubiquitous close-ups in pornography that emphasize proof of penetration or that highlight the act of objects entering bodily orifices. Although the setup for the scenario in the narrative is foreplay, the sequence is anything but erotic; rather, it is grotesque, emphasizing her mouth as a dangerous breach through which contaminating food is transmitted to become bodily matter.

However, by the time Alley began filming her series, she had indeed already accepted the offer to be Jenny Craig's spokesperson. Not only did she spin her fat into a commodity as part of the *Fat Actress* series, but she commodified her weight *loss* and her absent flesh in the commercials that earned as much or possibly more than her self-produced series, given that the average celebrity earns $33,000 per pound lost (Gowen 2012). Moreover, the commercials provided extensive publicity to get Alley's face back into the national pop-culture conversation. I suggest that the performance of weight gain in the series strategically set the stage for and enhanced spectator interest in her promised weight loss. During the course of the series and thereafter, a new commercial came out every few weeks, in which Alley showed off her figure and announced how much weight she had lost. Interestingly, in this series of commercials, Alley did not show a photo of herself at her heaviest weight. Instead, the commercials announced the amount she had lost in pounds thus far, and the camera focused on her body in the present as she danced around the screen flatteringly dressed and coifed. Unlike Fogle, for example, whose fat body eventually disappeared from his audience's sense memory, the image of Alley at her most slovenly and fat was freshly ingrained in spectator's minds; showing it alongside her slimmed-down figure would be unnecessary, if not counterproductive. Because her weight gain was performatively constituted in the series, Alley's increasingly slender performing body was more potent than a static image. Furthermore, the commercials outlasted the series *Fat Actress*, so that Alley performed her weight loss in the public eye longer than her weight gain.

Alley's self-authored performances point to another aspect of the way in which fat haunts a body. Indeed, the performance of weight loss for celebrity figures can extend beyond escaping the ghosting of a previously fat body. It can include revising a "fat identity." In addition to eating, I posit that Alley exploited fat stereotypes and deliberately performed a fat identity as part of a marketing tactic. A fat body in representation is a cultural signifier that can provoke disgust in the spectator. Thus, if the circulation of the (fat) image precedes that of the personality, fat—and all the negative stereotypes and disgust feelings associated with it—becomes an individual's public identity. As Judith Butler (1990: 134) asserts, "rhetoric can control discourse and communication-speech acts are the primary processes through which identities are negotiated and narratives are constructed." The ongoing national conversation surrounding the so-called obesity epidemic and the dangers of fat, as well as the various behavioral and emotional stereotypes associated with fat people, constitute such identity-constructing speech acts. Butler identifies the political and cultural inscriptions on the human body when she asserts that "[a]ny discourse that establishes the boundaries of the body serves the purpose of instating and naturalizing certain taboos regarding appropriate limits, postures, and modes of exchange that define what it is that constitutes bodies" (166). The pop-culture visual vocabulary relentlessly disseminated in all media forms is such a discourse. The boundaries of the appropriate American female body are limited to very particular criteria as established in our cultural texts. Butler goes on to point out that "what constitutes the limit of the body is never merely material, but . . . the surface, the skin, is systematically signified by taboos and anticipated transgressions . . . the boundaries of the body become the limits of the socially hegemonic" (166–67). She sees gender identity as performatively constituted and naturalized through existing cultural structures of power. She also reminds us that the production of identity is deeply connected to the "heterosexual matrix" and the "grid of cultural intelligibility through which bodies, genders, and desires are naturalized" (194). Like gender, the fat female body is a lived identity produced discursively and narrativized in various cultural texts. Thus, if a fat body implies a lived fat identity, the loss of that fat can conceivably establish a new identity for an individual.

EXORCISING A FAT IDENTITY: MONICA'S MAKEOVER

One example of a public personality performing weight loss in order to escape the ghosting of her previous body—and the contempt and disgust associated with it—and thereby reshape her public identity is Monica Lewinsky. Lewinsky, a former White House intern who infamously had an affair with sitting President Bill Clinton in about 1995–1997, was characterized in the media as an oversized, oversexed power grubber and home wrecker. When the incident came to light and Lewinsky's face and body became staple tabloid images, her chubby figure, perhaps even more than her adulterous behavior, was a primary target for public censure. The media focused on her size, describing her with every possible fat insult. Among other slurs, the *New York Post* called her "Portly Pepperpot." The *Enquirer* repeatedly taunted her for being fat, and Barbara Walters (Cloud 1999a) euphemistically referred to Lewinsky's "weight problem" in their interview for the news program *20/20*. She was fodder for late-night comedians, with Jay Leno joking that "I have two words for people who think that sex burns calories: Monica Lewinsky" (Shapiro 1999). In *The Obesity Myth*, Paul Campos (2004) argues that part of the public fascination with the Lewinsky/Clinton affair was that they were both perceived as overweight individuals who were unable to control their appetites and were, therefore, presumed culpable because their fatness marked them as guilty. For a time, Lewinsky was a media pariah, and her name and public identity were synonymous with Jezebel, "first bimbo," and whore, all of which were implicitly tied to her so-called fat body, which made flesh her morally reprehensible character. Lewinsky was possibly the most vilified woman in the United States, and that she was overweight by popular-culture standards only exacerbated public contempt. Unlike the aforementioned examples, Lewinsky did not deliberately set out to elicit disgust from Americans. Nonetheless, her fat and her widely broadcast sexual activities with the president resulted in public scorn. If her adultery and fleshy body were not repugnant enough, the much-publicized report that she retained her blue dress stained with semen—the ultimate contaminant—solidified her vileness in the popular imagination (see Miller 1997: 103–5).

However, in 2000, the Jenny Craig company approached Lewinsky about losing forty pounds with its product and becoming an advertising spokesperson in return for a significant paycheck. She subsequently began to lose weight and appeared in ads to show off her new, slimmer self. One ad depicts a slimmer Lewinsky in various nonthreatening domestic scenarios, watering flowers and cutting out dress patterns (although there is a shot in her bedroom as a reminder of her formerly lascivious self). She eventually tells the camera, "I think Jenny Craig is a great program for someone who not only wants to lose weight but who's looking to change their life" (Farrell 2011: 122–25). Certainly, this statement speaks to the long-held cultural belief that losing weight translates directly to a shift in an individual's social, economic, and personal circumstances, as well as his or her work ethic and basic morals. But in the case of Lewinsky, it also hints at the belief that her slimmer body had fundamentally changed her identity. Following her weight loss, she appeared on the cover of *Time Magazine* (Cloud 1999b), as well as in various other print media, to visually reinforce her new appearance and perform her weight loss, which aimed to establish a new public identity. If embodied fat signifies sexual immorality, Lewinsky's weight loss could potentially indicate a moral reform—a body purified of fat (Forth 2012). However, despite her efforts to reassure viewers that she was a reformed woman as embodied by her lost pounds, Lewinsky is still haunted by her fat identity and the public disgust provoked by her seduction of the president. This may be partially due to the fact that the media storm eventually abated, and she simply did not have enough opportunity to reinscribe the collective cultural memory. It could also be in part because Lewinsky, who had struggled with her weight all of her life prior to the Clinton incident, was not able to lose as much weight as Jenny Craig hired her to lose, and she was subsequently unable to keep it off.

ALLEY'S ONGOING EPILOGUE

Kirstie Alley, on the other hand, has possibly been the most successful at turning her weight gain, as well as her weight loss, into a commodity. She is a master at fatsploitation, and her self-authored fat narrative has yet to reach a conclusion. *Fat*

Actress successfully reinvigorated her career after she spent years exiled to the margins of Hollywood due to her fatness. She appeared several times on *Oprah* in 2005 and 2006, openly discussing her weight loss, and vowed to lose enough weight to appear again on *Oprah* in a bikini, which she did on January 6, 2006 (Harpo Productions 2006). Once again, this episode was the highest-rated *Oprah* show of 2006, spinning Alley's weight loss into capital for both women. Like Oprah's great reveal years before, Alley's new body was spectacularly staged for maximum dramatic effect. After a typical interview with Oprah (with Alley fully clothed), Alley went backstage and reappeared from behind the curtain performing her new body. She strutted out on the stage in her bikini like a model on a catwalk, accompanied by music and lights. She then engaged in a staple gesture of the newly slimmed performing body, shimmying and dancing seductively in her contained body, which did not jiggle or bounce with excess flesh (Harpo Productions 2006). She also wore nude panty hose that helped contain her lower half and ensure that the audience would not be exposed to disgust-invoking cellulite or bouncing flab.

However, she was back on *Oprah* within a year, having gained half of the weight back. She once again reverted to her self-shaming tactics and with heavy self-abasement blamed her excessive eating for her weight gain. Dressed in an unflattering garment that emphasized her large size, she described at length her excessive eating habits and unhealthy choices that had made her fat, once again enacting her weight gain. By 2008 Alley had definitively gained all of her weight back but created yet another short-lived series about herself, called *Kirstie Alley's Big Life*, which aired briefly in 2010. In the fall of 2011, she was invited to appear on *Dancing with the Stars*, during which time she lost about 100 pounds and successfully used her weight gain and loss, yet again, to promote herself as a personality. She simultaneously launched Organic Liaison Rescue Me, her own line of diet products, which she credits, along with the activity of dancing, for her newly trim figure. She has subsequently appeared on *Entertainment Tonight*, *The Tonight Show*, *The View*, *Ellen*, and *Late Night with David Letterman*, among other talk shows, hawking her diet products and performing her weight loss, once more reinscribing the images in circulation of her body, from her fat self to her thin self. As of this writing, she remains at her slimmest size in twenty years (Alley 2012), but arguably she continues to be fat in the collective memory of her public—for the time being, her fat figure still ghosts her slim one.

CONCLUSION: FROM MATTER TO COMMODITY AND BACK AGAIN, OR FATSPLOITATION

Not only do all of the individuals in these examples attempt to perform the materiality of their weight loss or gain by eliciting disgust in the spectator as a tactic to emphasize the "before and after" of weight loss, but they also in some way spin their performances into a form of economic capital, either literally, by getting paid to promote diet products, or via ratings, as with Oprah's big reveal, which not only earned her the highest ratings in her show's history but established an intimate rapport with her viewing audience that continues to this day. Indeed, Oprah's public struggle with her weight is perhaps one of the most strategic self-marketing feats in television history and her talk show, which ran for twenty-five seasons continues to be the highest-rated talk show in American history. Rather than a diet product, her product was and remains herself. Lewinsky, who did not successfully reform her public identity, at least scored a lucrative advertising deal that helped her pay her legal bills at the time. Moreover, their celebrity weight-loss exploits have solidified a place in our culture for programs such as *The Biggest Loser*, a show that capitalizes on the shame of fat people by chronicling their bodies graphically throughout the weight-loss process while simultaneously hawking consumer diet products as part of the show's reality formula. Thus, the materiality of fat spins from fat as a substance on the body to the commodification of fat in consumer culture and back again.

While live performance is the most ephemeral of media, here and gone in an instant, popular entertainment media such as film, television, and mass marketing have enabled these celebrities to use performance in an attempt to give material substance to human fat that is both subjective to the viewer when it is present on the body and abstract once it is gone. Although these celebrities have performed the materiality of their weight loss, or gain, in order to escape the haunting of their slim bodies with the ghost of their fat bodies, their performances live on in print and advertising media, on YouTube, and in their television appearances. Their respective performances of weight loss have had various degrees of success as far as erasing the memory of their fat bodies from the mind's eye of their audience. And their relative success has been heavily influenced by whether or not they gained the weight back. However, there is no denying that all of the aforementioned examples transformed their fat into economic capital, successfully exploiting the American obsession with weight gain and loss into exposure and advertising, resulting in a very material gain in their bank accounts.

NOTES

Introduction: Materializing Fat

Many thanks to Alison Leitch and Samantha Murray for their comments on early versions of this introduction.

1. Social psychologists argue that in recent years "the affective reactions to heavy-weight individuals consist of disgust and contempt" (Crandall, Nierman, and Heble 2009: 477) and that some reactions may even function as a form of "symbolic racism" (Crandall 1994).
2. Frequently invoking Mary Douglas's (1966) structuralist understanding of pollution, Julia Kristeva's (1982) psychoanalytically oriented analysis of abjection, and/or Mikhail Bakhtin's (1984) description of the bourgeois denigration of the "grotesque" body, fat studies often regards shifts in discourse and social structure as determining how bodies are perceived.
3. Yet something similar occurs when we shift our focus from dietary fats to carbohydrates, key examples of which are flour-based products like pasta, bread, cookies, and cakes, which have long been considered to be fattening. Hence, long-standing stereotypes depict fat people as "doughy" and "pasty," although the sources of such images may not be entirely reducible to foodstuffs. Contemporary research on France reveals a rich tactile lexicon in which corpulent bodies are often described as moist (*moite*), pasty (*pâteux*), and soft (*mou*), while a fat individual may be summarily referred to as "slimy" (*le visqueux/la visqueuse*) (Galiana Abal n.d.). Consider the connotations of *la pâte*, a word that, in addition to denoting dough, refers more generally to any form of indeterminate or "pasty" matter whose consistency is somewhere between solid and liquid (Bachelard 2002). Thus, French descriptions of fat people as *pâteux* gesture beyond the merely "doughy" to an arguably more fundamental form of troubling matter, the very thing that repulsed Antoine Roquentin, the squeamish protagonist of Jean-Paul Sartre's *La nausée*, when he encountered a rotting tree root that evoked for him "the very *pâte* of things" (1938: 182). In current usage, moreover, the *pâteux* is as much a matter of heaviness as it is of tactility. Being

essentially formless and yielding, *la pâte* may designate an especially good and accommodating person (*une bonne pâte*) as well as one without character (*une pâte molle*). *Le pâteux* and *le visqueux* thus seem to share a number of overlapping properties that are ready-to-hand and thus available for immediate use in the characterization of fat personhood.

4. For a discussion of the problem with such structural-functional models see Duschinsky (2011). Drawing on Sartre's (1966) phenomenological analysis of the experience of slimy and sticky things (*le visqueux*), however, Douglas concedes the power that certain substances may have on culture. Distinctions between the "anomalous" and the "ambiguous," she writes, have little practical value when it comes to sticky substances like treacle (molasses), which, being "neither liquid nor solid," could be said "to give an ambiguous sense impression" just as it may be seen as "anomalous in the classification of liquids and solids" (Douglas 1966: 39). This suggests that the properties of treacle—and, one may argue, other indeterminate substances—are therefore not completely arbitrary in relation to culture but that, by impressing themselves on the senses, they adopt an active role in forming culture. In fact, the indeterminate properties of such substances offer a material example of the very concept of ambiguity, thus suggesting that materiality motivates as well as reflects cultural categories.

5. It has more in common with Don Kulick and Anne Meneley's collection *Fat: The Anthropology of an Obsession* (2005), which explores the many uses, meanings, and practices associated with fat bodies and fatty/oily substances across the world, adopting an eclectic approach that drives home the relative distinctiveness of fat prejudice in the West.

Chapter 1: The Qualities of Palestinian Olive Oil

I would like to thank Christopher Forth and Alison Leitch for their invitation to join this volume and for their valuable feedback and patience. I also thank Paul Manning and Bruce Grant for their careful readings. An earlier version of this chapter was presented in the Speaker Series "The Anthropology of Morality and Ethics" at the Centre for Ethnography at the University of Toronto, Scarborough, in 2012. Many thanks to Girish Daswani for the invitation and the engagement of the audience members, whose comments were smart and thought-provoking. Special thanks to all the wonderful people I met in Palestine who have helped me so much with this research and impressed me with their love of the history of olive oil in Palestine and their love of their trees.

The data on which this article is based were gathered during a preliminary field trip to Palestine in April 2006 with a group affiliated with the British branch of Jews for Justice who imported Palestinian olive oil. This short trip was enormously important in formulating my project, which was subsequently funded by the Social Science and Humanities Research Council of Canada. I conducted participant observation with Palestinian families and international volunteers in the fall of 2007, 2008, 2009, 2010, and 2011 while picking olives. I made additional field trips in the spring of 2007, 2008, and 2009 to interview olive oil producers and professionals (those involved in running co-ops and nongovernmental organizations, as well as testers, tasters, and marketers) when the hectic olive-pressing season was over. For the past five years, I have conducted participant observation with volunteers involved with distributing Palestinian olive oil in Toronto, Washington, DC, and London. I have also conducted ongoing archival research, as much of the activism surrounding the distribution of Palestinian olive oil is web based. This kind of "multi-sited" (Marcus 1995) field research was necessary for this project that considers how the production, consumption, and circulation of food commodities are fundamentally connected. All the names in this paper are pseudonyms.

1. Canaan, the medical doctor, disagrees with the native interpretation of *asabi*, stepping into his Western medical role and away from his role as a sympathetic ethnographer in a rare moment.

2. Holiness can also be indicated by "the occurrence there of unnatural phenomena, as for example, hearing religious music, *seeing a light lit by itself*, or a severe punishment befalling a trespasser" (Canaan 1927: 46, emphasis added).

3. Olive trees must be pruned every second year. These trimmed branches are valued as fuel for the *taboun* oven as the olive wood imparts a delicious flavor to the bread cooked within it.

4. The tourists have been fast disappearing as well. Most of the international tours are run by Israelis. The tourists are taken into Bethlehem only for a quick visit to the Church of the Nativity and then whisked away, leaving few tourist dollars in their wake.

5. Along with dozens of other international volunteers I picked olives on Antwan's land for five years. The Israelis would allow only Antwan, his brothers, and his elderly mother onto the land, which was a far from adequate labor force to complete the harvest. As foreign passport holders with Israeli stamps in our passports, we were allowed on the land but never without delays and gruff treatment by the soldiers.

6. Olive oil is important in Judaism as well, most famously for being used to light the menorah, but for the Palestinians, the olive tree has become a sign of the inaccuracy of the Zionist claim that Palestine was uninhabited before 1948. See Habib 2004: 46 for a useful discussion of how olive trees are invoked in presenting a continuity between the ancient Israelites and the contemporary state of Israel in a move that erases Palestinian presence on the land.

7. Tamari (2009) is critical of this move, as he argues, rightly to my mind, that this is essentially mimicking what the Israelis are doing by claiming biblical stakes to the land.
8. Rachel Corrie was an American peace activist who was crushed to death by an Israeli Defense Force armored bulldozer in 2003 while protesting house demolitions in Gaza.

Chapter 2: In Tastes, Lost and Found

1. In 1987, when the campaign began, the *New York Times* reported, "Chicken lovers are the main target since the experts say that this year, for the first time, chicken will push pork out of second place in consumer hearts and threaten beef" (Dougherty 1987).
2. Shapin notes that "[c]ompared to the language pertaining to vision, we do not possess a rich vocabulary for describing tastes" (2005: 30).
3. My thanks to Margaret Weiner for encouraging me to examine this contrast between loins and bacons/bellies.

Chapter 3: Thinking through Fat

Many thanks to Anthony Corbeill and John Younger for fielding numerous queries on ancient bodies and texts, and to Alison Leitch, Pilar Galiana y Abal, and Damon Talbott for their comments on early versions of this text. Parts of this chapter have appeared in Forth 2013.

1. Thus I will not examine fat's immiscible properties, nor will we consider its buoyancy and, in certain quantities, heaviness. Nor will mouthfeel and taste be addressed, even though these are often counted among the chief pleasures of fat.
2. All subsequent in-text Bible quotations are from Coogan 2007.

Chapter 4: Joseph Beuys

I would like to thank Christopher Forth for his patience and valuable feedback on this chapter, and my colleagues Jennifer Deger and Eduardo Dela Fuente, as well as Peter Lister and Marianne Leitch, who all read various drafts. I would also like to acknowledge the comments of the Sydney Women's Anthropology Group, with whom I have shared many inspiring conversations over the last few years.

1. Ingold reminds us that even the term *material* comes from the Latin word for "mother" and has "a complex history involving feminine-gender words for wood . . . which has been alive" (2007: 11).

2. It is important to note that one difficulty in talking about the materiality of fat in Beuys's work is the fact that he used a variety of fats in his work, from animal fat in the form of tallow to margarine and butter, as well as plant oils, for example, in his 1961 piece *Lavender Filter*.

3. Beuys had a complex relationship to Duchamp's work and questioned the latter's artistic vision, once declaring that "Duchamp's silence is overrated" (quoted in Taylor 2012: 35). For a fuller discussion of this issue see Taylor 2012: 35–37.

4. For more on this lecture tour and the compilation of a series of Beuys's essays and writings, see *Energy Plan for Western Man: Joseph Beuys in America*, edited by Carin Kuoni (1990).

5. See Gandy 1997 and Strauss 1999 for an extensive discussion of this action and its critical reception.

6. According to Ulmer (1984: 21), in 1979 an international art dealer who ranked the 100 leading artists of the day ranked Beuys number one, replacing Robert Rauschenberg.

7. Apart from Taylor 2012, see Adams 1998 for an extensive discussion of Steiner's influence, as well as Beuys's interviews with Volker Harlan (2004).

8. For example, in 2012 the Moscow Museum of Contemporary Art held a major retrospective subtitled "Germany's Most Notable Artist of the Second Half of the 20th Century."

9. For example, in Papua New Guinea fat is a major metaphor for making social relationships. It is rubbed on bodies to enhance sexual attractiveness, and the phrase *to grease someone* refers to making them amenable for transactions of social reciprocity (Andrew Lattas, July 1, 2013, personal communication). See also Helen Sobo's (1994) classic analysis of the relationship between fat and fertility, as well as decline, in rural Jamaica.

10. The standard Beuys biography has the crash taking place during a snowstorm in the winter of 1943 (Stachelhaus 1987: 26). However, in their meticulous examination of the military records, Frank Gieseke and Albert Markert (1996: 71–78) pinpoint the date as March 16, 1944.

11. According to Nisbet (2001: 7), once Beuys realized the emblematic significance that the "Story" was quickly acquiring, the artist tried to distance himself from it. Nisbet's study of the "Story" also refers to Beuys's later clarification that the images he perceived of his rescue by the Tartars were not necessarily experienced in rational consciousness.

12. See Chametzky (2010: 190) for a more extended discussion of German fat politics.

13. Donald Kuspit puts this more explicitly, arguing that "Beuys consciously set himself up as Hitler's opposite in every way. Indeed his shamanistic uniform mocked the Nazi uniform, which looked sinister in comparison. His wounded appearance spoke the German historical truth giving lie to the fantasy that Hitler could make Germans primordially whole and unconquerable, restoring them to mythological barbaric greatness" (1993: 92).

14. See David Adams (1998) for a fuller discussion on Beuys's use of these materials and the way in which Steiner's anthroposophy influenced his selection of materials. Adams describes two of Beuys's most famous works using honey: *How to Explain Pictures to a Dead Hare*, which was a three-hour action first performed for the opening of his art exhibition at Galerie Schmela in Düsseldorf in 1965, and *Honey Pump at the Workplace*, an installation in 1977 at the international art show Documenta 6 in Kassel. Adams notes that Beuys also employed plants in his work and records that while Beuys was working on his famous *7000 Oaks* project, inaugurated at the Documenta 7 exhibition in Kassel, Germany, in 1982, Beuys stated "his feeling that trees are more intelligent than people. In the wind that blows their leaves he sensed the essence of suffering human beings, as trees, too, are sufferers" (Adams 1992: 30). See also Gandy 1997 for a discussion of this work and its political impact.

15. Donald Kuspit provides a compelling explanation of these ideas and the influence of both alchemical thought and Rudolf Steiner's influence on Beuys. He notes that:

> One of the key points of Steiner's mysticism is the spiritual need for "going beyond"—transcending the senses and the material world they mediate. For Beuys, recognition of the expressive physiognomy of material is the first step of transformation, and its definition as spiritual. The whole aim of alchemy, as Paracelsus notes, is to articulate "the inherency of a thing, its nature, power, virtue, and curative efficacy, without any . . . foreign admixture". Transformation as such is the spiritual revelation of substance, and alchemical art, is in Beuys's words "a 'trans-mission' or transformation—transformation is the 'spiritual-divine' element of 'earthly' material, and art is the demonstration of the spiritual-divine in the earthly, and the earthly in the spiritual-divine." (1984: 353)

16. For more on Beuys's sense of humor see the interviews with Volker Harlan (2004).

17. Taylor notes that "*Gestaltung* means formation, forming, construction, shaping, fashioning, modeling; creation and production" (2012: 197).

18. In his 1974 action *Coyote: I Like America and America Likes Me*, Beuys tackled the lack of respect for Native American people and wild nature in

the form of the coyote, a Native American symbol of cosmic and physical transformation.

19. Heather McDonald (2003) notes that in many traditional contexts only the old were ritually strong enough to eat all kinds of fat, and in Central Australia the fattiest parts of a butchered animal were commonly reserved for old men (Roheim 1974: 38). She also points to the wider ethnographic literature that suggests that in the past individuals in particular liminal states—such as menstruating and lactating women, fighting men, participants in secret ceremonies, and other individuals in seclusion—could not eat strong meat or fat. In their classic nineteenth-century account of tribal Aboriginal life, Walter Baldwin Spencer and Francis James Gillen (1899: 471–72) also report that young people who had not reached maturity were not allowed to eat the most prized and fatty parts of animals, including kangaroo tail, emu fat, female bandicoot, bush turkey, large quail, echidna, and wildcat.

20. Redmond (2007) notes that in the North Kimberley's, fat, in particular the fatty area around the kidneys, is seen as the seat of emotion in human beings. Fat, in other words, is seen here as a substance that connects people to the vital energy of life and is also linked to the emotional health of individuals and their community. McDonald (2003) also worked in this region on Aboriginal health issues, and she observes a close connection between loss of fat and worry, or depression. McDonald further reports on the very interesting use of fat in traditional funerary practices, noting that fat was commonly used in inquest ceremonies, where people in the right relationship to the dead placed the body on platforms in the fork of a tree. A number of stones imbued with the names of various murder suspects were placed around the bottom of the tree. If the spirit of the dead person wished to inform the living of his murderer so that his death could be avenged, fat fell onto the stone of the murderer. And in his classic account of Australian Aboriginal life, the anthropologist A. P. Elkin records more gruesome cases of the ways in which traditional medicine men, or sorcerers, said they extracted kidney fat from healthy men in order to sicken them. Although Elkin doubts the veracity of these accounts, he notes, for example, the following story: "After putting a halter around the neck of a sleeping victim and dragging him unnoticed out of his camp, the sorcerer makes an incision in his abdomen or side, through which he extracts his kidney—or caul fat—; then, inserting some grass or other packing, he closes up the wound so that no mark is visible, and restores the victim to consciousness. The latter returns to his camp, and is in perfect health for a day or two but generally dies on the third day" (Elkin 1974 [1938]: 308). Janice Reid (1983: 101) also reports a more contemporary case of the practice of sorcery using extracted kidney fat.

Chapter 5: Engrossing Encounters

The PhD research on which this chapter draws was undertaken in the Anthropology Department at Goldsmiths, University of London, and I thank my supervisors there, Dr. Simon Cohn and Professor Catherine Alexander. The PhD was funded by an Economic and Social Research Council studentship and a Goldsmiths Bursary. It won the 2010 Radcliffe-Brown/Sutasoma Award from the Royal Anthropological Institute. I should like to express my gratitude to the many individuals in the eating disorders unit and on pro-anorexia websites who have shared their stories with me.

1. The eating disorders inpatient unit is part of a large National Health Service psychiatric hospital in South England that provides specialist inpatient and outpatient care for a range of psychiatric conditions. I undertook a year of full-time anthropological fieldwork on the unit as part of doctoral research exploring pro-anorexia. Taking place between February 2007 and March 2008, this fieldwork was granted ethical approval by the National Health Service. The fieldwork on a variety of pro-anorexia websites also began as part of PhD research in 2005, but it is ongoing and continues to comprise participant observation and online interviews.
2. All names are pseudonyms.

Chapter 6: Fat Is the Future

1. This disavowal, as Rachel Colls (2007: 354) argues, is largely based on "medical claims about the health 'risks' of being overweight and/or obese and associated moral and aesthetic judgments that are made concerning what a fat body 'represents,' such as laziness, a lack of control, ugliness, and asexuality." In contradistinction to such a body, the ideal body—most particularly for white women—is a "tight, controlled, 'bolted down' form: in other words a body that is protected against eruption and whose internal processes are under control" (Bordo 1993: 190).
2. The breast is an inhomogeneous structure that is comprised of layers of tissue. Two kinds of tissue predominate: adipose tissue and glandular tissue.
3. In 2011, 96,277 breast reconstructions were performed in the United States, according to the American Society of Plastic Surgeons (2012). This is up 22 percent from 2000.
4. For an extensive discussion of biovalue see Waldby 2000, 2002.
5. For instance, see "Breast Reconstruction" 2011; Bump 2003; New Zealand Institute of Plastic and Cosmetic Surgery n.d.; and Smith 1995.
6. The seamless body is a body that is taken for granted, becoming what Drew Leder (1990) refers to as an "absent body." For Leder, the body has to become

present to the subject only when something goes wrong with its supposed normal functioning.

7. In my 2012 work, I argue that much of the discussion surrounding breast reconstruction, particularly in feminist scholarship, circulates around the endless question of whether or not it reinforces dominant norms of female embodiment. That the debate is imagined in these terms precludes looking at the practices that are involved in constructing embodiment, and the complex ways subjects emerge through their engagement with various reconstructive technologies.

8. In other words, as Stuart Murray (2007: 5) has suggested, "[w]e are . . . told that medicine is the cure to the problem of the self, the principal technology by which the self ought to relate to itself, through the body." The self is thus interpellated as an active agent, and medicine is generally constructed as enabling self-empowerment. On the instrumentality of medicine and the politics of life, see Nikolas Rose's work, specifically his recent book, *The Politics of Life Itself: Biomedicine, Power, and Subjectivity in the Twenty-First Century* (2007). As he has argued elsewhere, "a new ontology of ourselves constituted by medicine appears to offer us a rational, secular and corporeal solution to the problem of how we should live our lives for the best; of how we might make the best of our life by adjusting it to our truth, by letting medicine enlighten our decisions as to how to live it" (1994: 69).

9. In this chapter I am drawing mainly on plastic surgery research articles, breast reconstruction marketing on plastic surgery websites, and an ethno-critical study of breast cancer and breast reconstruction web forums, conducted over a three-year period. Though my research has spanned a number of web forums, here I focus on the materials from one particular site that currently has nearly 2,000 members. For reasons of anonymity I have not named the sites or any of the participants in the forums.

10. In making these distinctions, I am drawing heavily on the differences between tissue transfer and tissue autogenesis identified by Melinda Cooper in *Life as Surplus: Biotechnology and Capitalism in the Neoliberal Era* (2008). While Cooper's understanding of tissue transfer can be applied to fat transfer, her argument regarding tissue autogenesis must be amended when accounting for the use of fat stem cells, which I go into later. For Cooper, stem cell research is concerned with perpetual self-transformation (2008: 127). This argument does not hold for stem cell research using fat in breast reconstruction, where there is a teleological end point to self-transformation through the animation of the stem cell: perpetual transformation is not the goal but, rather, the materialization of a breast.

11. On these issues see Ehlers 2012.

12. See, for instance, *Journal of the National Cancer Institute* (2007). Also see the article "Obesity and Cancer Risk" (U.S. National Institute of Cancer 2012). A UK study estimated that around 9 percent of breast cancers in women in the United Kingdom in 2010 were linked to excess body weight (Parkin and Boyd 2011).

13. If, as Susan Sontag (1990: 14) argues, cancer is thought of as a demonic pregnancy—where one is pregnant with one's own death—fostering fat growth in this context can be seen as becoming pregnant (cancerous) with one's own fat.

14. This is done with a tool called a Celbrush that makes multiple perforations to create a biological mesh that will bond with existing tissue.

15. See "Promising Results Reported in Cell-Enriched Breast Reconstruction Trial," the press release for the Cytori Therapeutics–sponsored European clinical trial (Cytori Therapeutics, December 12, 2009).

16. Within contemporary biomedicine in general, and new stem cell therapies in particular, life is no longer confined to a singular teleological trajectory, nor is the individual body limited to one life. Instead, life is being enhanced, customized, and regenerated (or begun anew), and individual bodies can ostensibly live one form of embodiment and then (through these technologies) emerge to live another embodied life. For analyses of the modern concept of life, see the work of Nikolas Rose (2007), Georges Canguilhem (1994), Michel Foucault (1970), and Sarah Franklin (1995). On new forms of life enabled through biotechnological advancements, see the work of Joanna Zylinska (2010) and Susan Squier (2004).

Chapter 7: Bound Bodies

1. Throughout, we refer to *fat women* and *larger women*, a distinction that requires explanation. From an academic standpoint, we support Robyn Longhurst's (2005b) claim that employing euphemisms for *fat*, such as *larger*, inadvertently suggests that fat is so repugnant that it is undesirable to speak of it. However, this empirical research resides within the data generated from women who identified as larger but did not necessarily identify as fat. In fact, most (but not all) of these women found the word *fat* objectionable. Consequently, our academic stance was problematized, and we decided to use both *fat* and *larger* throughout the chapter, referring to *fat* when speaking of fat as an abstract concept and *larger* when addressing the participants' practices.

2. Although the fat male body is arguably also the object of considerable negative attention (see Longhurst 2005c; Monaghan and Atkinson forthcoming), the research focused specifically on women due to the long-standing objectification of women's bodies in contemporary society and the extent to which women are subject to the gaze of others (de Beauvoir 1997; Irigaray 1985; Mulvey 1985).

REFERENCES

Introduction: Materializing Fat

Alcoff, L.M. (2006), *Visual Identities: Race, Gender, and the Self*, New York: Oxford University Press.

Bachelard, G. (2002), *Earth and Reveries of Will: An Essay on the Imagination of Matter*, trans. K. Haltman, Dallas: Dallas Institute of Humanities and Culture.

Bakhtin, M. (1984), *Rabelais and His World*, trans. H. Iswolsky, Bloomington: Indiana University Press.

Bennett, J. (2010), *Vibrant Matter: A Political Ecology of Things*, Durham, NC: Duke University Press.

Boivin, N. (2004), "Mind over Matter? Collapsing the Mind-Matter Dichotomy in Material Culture Studies," in E. DeMarrais, C. Gosden, and C. Renfrew (eds.), *Rethinking Materiality: The Engagement of Mind with the Material World*, Cambridge, UK: McDonald Institute for Archaeological Research, pp. 63–71.

Boivin, N. (2008), *Material Cultures, Material Minds: The Impact of Things on Human Thought, Society, and Evolution*, Cambridge: Cambridge University Press.

Boltanski, L. (1971), "Les usages sociaux du corps," *Annales. Histoire, sciences sociales*, 1: 205–33.

Bourdieu, P. (1984), *Distinction: A Social Critique of the Judgement of Taste*, trans. R. Nice, Cambridge, MA: Harvard University Press.

Bourne, M.C. (2002), *Food Texture and Viscosity*, San Diego, CA: Academic Press.

Braziel, J.E., and LeBesco, K. (eds.) (2001), *Bodies out of Bounds: Fatness and Transgression*, Berkeley: University of California Press.

Butler, J. (1993), *Bodies That Matter: On the Discursive Limits of "Sex,"* New York: Routledge.

Campos, P. (2004), *The Obesity Myth: Why America's Obsession with Weight Is Hazardous to Your Health*, New York: Penguin.

Carsten, J. (2004), *After Kinship*, Cambridge: Cambridge University Press.

Carsten, J. (2011), "Substance and Relationality: Blood in Contexts," *Annual Review of Anthropology*, 40: 19–35.

Cheah, P. (1996), "Mattering," *diacritics*, 26 (1): 108–39.

Chumney, L.H., and Harkness, N. (2013), "Introduction: QUALIA," *Anthropological Theory*, 13 (3): 3–11.

Colls, R. (2002), "Review of *Bodies out of Bounds: Fatness and Transgression*," *Gender, Place and Culture*, 8 (2): 218–20.

Colls, R. (2007), "Materialising Bodily Matter: Intra-action and the Embodiment of 'Fat,'" *Geoforum*, 38: 353–65.

Cooper, C. (2010), "Fat Studies: Mapping the Field," *Sociology Compass*, 4 (12): 1020–34.

Corbin, A. (1986), *The Foul and the Fragrant: Odor and the French Social Imagination*, trans. M. Kochan, Cambridge, MA: Harvard University Press.

Cowley, N.A. (2006), "Saturated: A Study in Fat Obsession," master's thesis, University of Waikato, New Zealand.

Crandall, C.S. (1994), "Prejudice against Fat People: Ideology and Self-Interest," *Journal of Personality and Social Psychology*, 66 (5): 882–94.

Crandall, C.S., Nierman, A., and Heble, M. (2009), "Anti-fat Prejudice," in T.D. Nelson (ed.), *Handbook of Prejudice, Stereotyping, and Discrimination*, New York: Psychology Press, pp. 469–87.

Crinnion, W. (2010), *Clean, Green and Lean: Get Rid of the Toxins That Make You Fat*, Hoboken, NJ: John Wiley.

Douglas, M. (1966), *Purity and Danger: An Analysis of Concepts of Pollution and Taboo*, New York: Routledge.

Durham, D. (2011), "Disgust and the Anthropological Imagination," *Ethnos*, 76 (2): 131–56.

Durif, C. (1992), "Corps interne et physiologie profane," *Ethnologie française*, 22 (1): 71–78.

Durif-Bruckert, C. (2007), *La nourriture et nous: corps imaginaire et normes sociales*, Paris: Armand Colin.

Durif-Bruckert, C. (2008), *Une fabuleuse machine: anthropologie des savoirs ordinaires sur les fonctions physiologiques*, Paris: L'œil Neuf.

Duschinsky, R. (2011), "Ideal and Unsullied: Purity, Subjectivity and Social Power," *Subjectivity*, 4 (2): 147–67.

Forth, C.E. (2012), "Melting Moments: The Greasy Sources of Modern Perceptions of Fat," *Cultural History*, 1 (1): 83–107.

Fusco, C. (2004), "The Space That (In)Difference Makes: (Re)Producing Subjectivities in/through Abjection—a Locker Room Theoretical Study," in P. Vertinsky and J. Bale (eds.), *Sites of Sport: Space, Place, Experience*, New York: Routledge, pp. 159–76.

Galiana Abal, P. (n.d.), "An Apology for Fat? French Media Perceptions of the Fat Female Body," unpublished manuscript.

Garreta, R. (1998), "Ces plantes qui purifient: de l'herboristerie à l'aromathérapie," *Terrain*, 31: 77–88.

Gilman, S.L. (1991), *The Jew's Body*, New York: Routledge.

Graham, M. (2005), "Chaos," in D. Kulick and A. Meneley (eds.), *Fat: The Anthropology of an Obsession*, New York: Tarcher, pp. 169–84.

Hahn, H.P., and Soentgen, J. (2010), "Acknowledging Substances: Looking at the Hidden Side of the Material World," *Philosophy and Technology*, 24: 19–33.

Hardy, K.A. (2013), "The Education of Affect: Anatomical Replicas and 'Feeling Fat,'" *Body and Society*, 19 (3): 3–26.

Hodder, I. (2011), "Human-Thing Entanglement: Towards an Integrated Archaeological Perspective," *Journal of the Royal Anthropological Institute* (n.s.), 17: 154–77.

Hodder, I. (2012), *Entangled: An Archaeology of the Relationships between Humans and Things*, Oxford: Wiley-Blackwell.

Keane, W. (2005), "Signs Are Not the Garb of Meaning: On the Social Analysis of Material Things," in D. Miller (ed.), *Materiality*, Durham, NC: Duke University Press, pp. 182–205.

Kent, L. (2001), "Fighting Abjection: Representing Fat Women," in J.E. Braziel and K. LeBesco (eds.), *Bodies out of Bounds: Fatness and Transgression*, Berkeley: University of California Press, pp. 130–50.

Korsmeyer, C. (2011), *Savoring Disgust: The Foul and the Fair in Aesthetics*, New York: Oxford University Press.

Kristeva, J. (1982), *Powers of Horror: An Essay on Abjection*, trans. L.S. Roudiez, New York: Columbia University Press.

Kulick, D., and Meneley, A. (eds.) (2005), *Fat: The Anthropology of an Obsession*, London: Tarcher.

LeBesco, K. (2004), *Revolting Bodies? The Struggle to Redefine Fat Identity*, Amherst: University of Massachusetts Press.

Leder, D. (1990), *The Absent Body*, Chicago: University of Chicago Press.

Longhurst, R. (2005), "Fat Bodies: Developing Geographical Research Agendas," *Progress in Human Geography*, 29 (3): 247–59.

Lupton, D. (1996), *Food, the Body and Society*, London: Sage.

Margat, C. (2011), "Phénoménologie du dégoût : inventaire des définitions," *Ethnologiefrançaise*, 41 (1): 17–25.

Marvin, S., and Medd, W. (2006), "Metabolisms of Obe-*city*: Flows of Fat through Bodies, Sewers and Cities," *Environment and Planning A*, 38 (2): 313–24.

Meneley, A. (2007), "Like an Extra Virgin," *American Anthropologist*, 109 (4): 678–87.

Meneley, A. (2008), "Oleo-Signs and Quali-Signs: The Qualities of Olive Oil," *Ethnos*, 73 (3): 303–26.

Miller, D. (2010), *Stuff*, Cambridge, UK: Polity.

Miller, W.I. (1997), *The Anatomy of Disgust*, Cambridge, MA: Harvard University Press.

Monaghan, L.F. (2008), *Men and the War on Obesity: A Sociological Study*, London: Routledge.

Mouritsen, O.G. (2005), *Life—as a Matter of Fat: The Emerging Science of Lipidomics*, Berlin: Springer.

Murray, S. (2008), *The "Fat" Female Body*, New York: Palgrave Macmillan.

Nussbaum, M. (2004), *Hiding from Humanity: Disgust, Shame, and the Law*, Princeton, NJ: Princeton University Press.

Onians, R.B. (1951), *The Origins of European Thought about the Body, the Mind, the Soul, the World, Time, and Fate*, Cambridge: Cambridge University Press.

Oudenhove, L. van, McKie, S., Lassmanm, D., Uddin, B., Paine, P., Coen, S., Gregory, L., Tack, J., and Aziz, Q. (2011), "Fatty Acid–Induced Gut-Brain Signaling Attenuates Neural and Behavioral Effects of Sad Emotion in Humans," *Journal of Clinical Investigation*, 121 (8): 3094–99.

Pond, C.M. (1998), *The Fats of Life*, Cambridge: Cambridge University Press.

Ravenau, G. (2011), "Suer. Traitements matériels et symboliques de la transpiration," *Ethnologie française,* 41 (1): 49–57.

Saguy, A.C. (2013), *What's Wrong with Fat?*, New York: Oxford University Press.

Sartre, J.-P. (1938), *La nausée*, Paris: Gallimard.

Sartre, J.-P. (1966), *Being and Nothingness*, trans. H.E. Barnes, New York: Washington Square.

Scott-Dixon, K. (2008), "Big Girls Don't Cry: Fitness, Fatness, and the Production of Feminist Knowledge," *Sociology of Sport Journal*, 25: 22–47.

Shove, E. (2003), *Comfort, Cleanliness and Convenience: The Social Organization of Normality*, Oxford: Berg.

Smith, M.M. (2006), *How Race Is Made: Slavery, Segregation, and the Senses*, Chapel Hill: University of North Carolina Press.

Sofaer, J.R. (2006), *The Body as Material Culture: A Theoretical Osteoarchaeology*, Cambridge: Cambridge University Press.

Strang, V. (2005), "Common Sense: Water, Sensory Experience and the Generation of Meaning," *Journal of Material Culture*, 10 (1): 92–120.

Throsby, K. (2008), "Happy Re-birthday: Weight Loss Surgery and the 'New Me,'" *Body and Society*, 14 (1): 117–33.

Warin, M. (2010), *Abject Relations: Everyday Worlds of Anorexia*, New Brunswick, NJ: Rutgers University Press.

Warnier, J.-P. (2001), "A Praxeological Approach to Subjectivation in a Material World," *Journal of Material Culture*, 6 (5): 5–24.

Warnier, J.-P. (2007), *The Pot-King: The Body and Technologies of Power*, Leiden: Brill.

Chapter 1: The Qualities of Palestinian Olive Oil

Abufarha, N. (1998), "Land of Symbols: Cactus, Poppies, Orange and Olive Trees in Palestine," *Identities: Global Studies in Culture and Power*, 15: 343–68.

Canaan, T. (1927), *Mohammedan Saints and Sanctuaries in Palestine*, London: Luzac.

Coleman, S., and Elsner, J. (1995), *Pilgrimage: Past and Present in the World Religions*, London: British Museum Press.

Doumani, B. (1995), *Rediscovering Palestine: Merchants and Peasants in Jabal Nablus, 1700–1900*, Berkeley: University of California Press.

Doumani, B. (2004), "Scenes from Daily Life: The View from Nablus," *Journal of Palestine Studies*, 34: 1–14.

Frankel, R., Avitsur, S., and Ayalon, E. (1994), *History and Technology of Olive Oil in the Holy Land*, Arlington, VA: Olearius Editions; Tel Aviv: Eretz Israel Museum.

Frazer, J. (1922), *The Golden Bough*, New York: McMillan.

Gell, A. (1977), "Magic, Perfume, Dream . . .," in I.M. Lewis (ed.), *Symbols and Sentiments*, London: Academic Press.

Habib, J. (2004), *Israel, Diaspora, and the Routes of National Belonging*, Toronto: University of Toronto Press.

Heath, D., and Meneley, A. (2011), "The Naturecultures of Foie Gras: Techniques of the Body and a Contested Ethics of Care," *Food, Culture and Society*, 13 (3): 422–52.

Keane, W. (2003), "Semiotics and the Social Analysis of Material Things," *Language and Communication*, 23 (3–4): 409–25.

Marcus, G. (1995), "Ethnography in/of the World System: The Emergence of Multi-Sited Ethnography," *Annual Review of Anthropology* 24: 95–117.

Meneley, A. (2008), "Oleo-Signs and Quali-Signs: The Qualities of Olive Oil," *Ethnos*, 73 (3): 303–26.

Nusseibeh, S. (2007), *Once Upon a Country: A Palestinian Life*, New York: Farrar, Straus and Giroux.

Pappé, I. (2007), *The Ethnic Cleansing of Palestine*, London: One World/Oxford.

Peteet, J. (2008), "Stealing Time," *Middle East Report*, 248: 14–15.

Porter, J.R. (1993), "Oil in the Old Testament," in M. Dudley and G. Rowell (eds.), *The Oil of Gladness: Anointing in the Christian Tradition*, Collegeville, MN: The Liturgical Press, pp. 35–45.

Rosenblum, M. (1997), *Olives: The Life and Lore of a Noble Fruit*, New York: Farrar, Straus and Giroux.

Tamari, S. (1981), "Building Other People's Homes: The Palestinian Peasant's Household and Work in Israel," *Journal of Palestine Studies*, 11: 31–66.

Tamari, S. (2009), *Mountain against the Sea: Essays on Palestinian Society and Culture*, Berkeley: University of California Press.

Chapter 2: In Tastes, Lost and Found

Agamben, G. (2004), *The Open: Man and Animal*, Palo Alto, CA: Stanford University Press.

Appadurai, A. (1981), "Gastro-politics in Hindu South Asia," *American Ethnologist*, 8: 494–512.

Behr, E. (1999), "The Lost Taste of Pork: Finding a Place for the Iowa Family Farm," *The Art of Eating*, 51: 1–20.

Blanchette, A. (2010), "The Industrialization of Life, Capitalist Natures, and the American Factory Farm," unpublished manuscript, Department of Anthropology, University of Chicago.

Bourdieu, P. (1984), *Distinction: A Social Critique of the Judgement of Taste*, trans. R. Nice, Cambridge, MA: Harvard University Press.

Buckser, A. (1999), "Keeping Kosher: Eating and Social Identity among the Jews of Denmark," *Ethnology*, 38 (3): 191–209.

Dougherty, P.H. (1987), "Advertising; Dressing Pork for Success," *New York Times*, January 15, http://www.nytimes.com/1987/01/15/business/advertising-dressing-pork-for-success.html (accessed January 15, 2012).

Dransfield, E. (2008), "The Taste of Fat," *Meat Science*, 80: 37–42.

Edge, J.T. (2005), "Redesigning the Pig," *Gourmet Magazine*, 65 (7): 49–54.

Farquhar, J. (2002), *Appetites: Food and Sex in Postsocialist China*, Durham, NC: Duke University Press.

Fehérváry, K. (2009), "Goods and States: The Political Logic of State-Socialist Material Culture," *Comparative Studies in Society and History*, 51 (2): 426–59.

Fennema, O. (1996), *Food Chemistry*, 3rd ed., London: CRC Press.

Golden Leaf Foundation (2009), http://www.goldenleaf.org (accessed January 4, 2011).

Guardian (2010), "Taste Test: British Charcuterie," December 9, http://www.theguardian .com/lifeandstyle/2010/dec/09/taste-test-british-charcuterie (accessed January 4, 2011).

Holtzman, J. (2009), *Uncertain Tastes: Memory, Ambivalence, and the Politics of Eating in Samburu Northern Kenya*, Berkeley: University of California Press.

Kaminsky, P. (2005), *Pig Perfect: Encounters with Remarkable Swine and Some Great Ways to Cook Them*, New York: Hyperion.

Keane, W. (2003), "Semiotics and the Social Analysis of Material Things," *Language and Communication*, 23 (3–4): 409–25.

Kenner, R. (dir.) (2009), *Food Inc*, New York: Magnolia Home Entertainment, 94 min.

Korsmeyer, C. (1999), *Making Sense of Taste*, Ithaca, NY: Cornell University Press.

Marx, K. (1988), *The Economic and Philosophic Manuscripts of 1844 and the Communist Manifesto*, Amherst, NY: Prometheus Books.

Meinert, L., Christiansen, S.C., Kristensen, L., Bjergegaard, C., and Aaslyng, M.D. (2008), "Eating Quality of Pork from Pure Breeds and DLY Studied by Focus Group Research and Meat Quality Analyses," *Meat Science* 80 (2): 304–14.

Meinert, L., Tikk, K., Tikk, M., Brockhoff, P.B., Bejerholm, C., and Aaslyng, M.D. (2008), "Flavour Formation in Pork Semimembranosus: Combination of Pan-Temperature and Raw Meat Quality," *Meat Science* 80 (2): 249–58.

Meneley, A. (2008), "Oleo-Signs and Quali-Signs: The Qualities of Olive Oil," *Ethnos*, 73 (3): 303–26.

Morgan, R. (1998), "Legal and Political Injustices of Industrial Swine Production in North Carolina," in M. Kendall, E. Thuand, and P. Durrenberger (eds.), *Pigs, Profits and Rural Communities*, Albany: State University of New York Press, pp. 138–44.

Munn, N. (1986), *The Fame of Gawa: A Symbolic Study of Value Transformation in a Massim Papua New Guinea Society*, Cambridge: Cambridge University Press.

National Pork Council (2012), "Pork. Be Inspired," http://www.porkbeinspired.com/towm_ promo_heritage_page.aspx (accessed January 17, 2012).

National Pork Producers Council (2009), *Pork Quality Standards*, Des Moines, IA: National Pork Producers Council.

Niman, N. (2009), *Righteous Porkchop: Finding a Life and Good Food beyond Factory Farms*, New York: William Morrow.

O'Laughlin, M. (2010) "London's Sandwich Bars: A Tasty Slice of Culinary Life," *London Times Metro*, July 20, http://metro.co.uk/2010/07/20/londons-sandwich-bars-a-tasty-slice-of-culinary-life-453473/ (accessed January 15, 2011).

Peirce, C. (1955), *Philosophical Writings of Peirce*, J. Buchler (ed.), New York: Dover.

RAFT Alliance: Renewing America's Food Traditions, "About RAFT," http://www.albc-usa. org/RAFT/ (accessed October 15, 2012).

Robertson Smith, W.W. (1972 [1887]), *The Religion of the Semites: The Fundamental Institutions*, New York: Schocken Books.

Seremetakis, C.N. (1994), *The Senses Still: Perception and Memory as Material Culture in Modernity*, Boulder, CO: Westview.

Shapin, S. (2005), "Hedonistic Fruit Bombs," *London Review of Books*, 27 (3): 30–32.

Shapin, S. (2010), "Changing Tastes: How Foods Tasted in the Early Modern Period and How They Came to Taste Differently Later," unpublished manuscript, Harvard University, Cambridge, MA.

Søltoft-Jensen, A.J. (2007), *Organic Feed Results in Tough Pork Chops*, report of the Danish Meat Research Institute, København, Denmark: Danish Agriculture and Food Council.

Stoller, P. (1989), *The Taste of Ethnographic Things: The Senses in Anthropology*, Philadelphia: University of Pennsylvania Press.

Sutton, D.E. (2001), *Remembrance of Repasts: An Anthropology of Food and Memory*, Oxford: Berg.

Talbott, C., See, M.T., Kaminsky, P., Bixby, D., Sturek, M., Brisbin, I.L., and Kadzere, C. (2006), "Enhancing Pork Flavor and Fat Quality with Swine Raised in Sylvan Systems: Potential Niche-Market Application for the Ossabaw Hog," *Renewable Agriculture and Food Systems* 21 (3): 183–91.

Trubek, A. (2008), *The Taste of Place: A Cultural Journey into Terroir*, Berkeley: University of California Press.

Watson, L. (2004), *The Whole Hog: Exploring the Extraordinary Potential of Pigs*, Washington, DC: Smithsonian Books.

Weiss, B. (2011), "Making Pigs Local: Discerning the Sensory Character of Place," *Cultural Anthropology*, 26 (3): 440–63.

Weiss, B. (2012), "Configuring the Authentic Value of Realfood: Farm-to-Fork, Snout-to-Tail, and Local Food Movements," *American Ethnologist*, 39 (3): 615–27.

Chapter 3: Thinking through Fat

Aelian (1997), *Historical Miscellany*, trans. N.G. Wilson, Cambridge, MA: Harvard University Press.

Aristotle (1936), *Physiognomics*, in *Minor Works*, trans. W.S. Hett, Cambridge, MA: Harvard University Press, pp. 81–137.

Aristotle (1943), *Generation of Animals*, trans. A.L. Peck, Cambridge, MA: Harvard University Press.

Aristotle (1953), *Problems,* trans. W.S. Hett, Cambridge, MA: Harvard University Press.

Aristotle (2001), *On the Parts of Animals*, trans. J.G. Lennox, Oxford: Clarendon.

Artemidorus (1990), *The Interpretation of Dreams: Oneirocritica*, trans. R.J. White, Torrance, CA: Original Books.

Athenaeus (1933), *The Deipnosophists*, trans. C.B. Gulick, Cambridge, MA: Harvard University Press.

Baumgarten, J.M. (1994), "Liquids and Susceptibility to Defilement in New 4Q Texts," *Jewish Quarterly Review*, 85: 91–101.

Beaune, S. de (2000), "Les techniques d'éclairage paléolithiques: un bilan," *Paléo*, 12: 19–27.

Berquist, J.L. (2002), *Controlling Corporeality: The Body and the Household in Ancient Israel*, New Brunswick, NJ: Rutgers University Press.

Bille, M., and Sørensen, T.F. (2007), "An Anthropology of Luminosity: The Agency of Light," *Journal of Material Culture*, 12: 263–84.

Bilu, Y. (1981), "Pondering the 'Princes of Oil': New Light on an Old Phenomenon," *Journal of Anthropological Research*, 37: 269–78.

Boivin, N. (2008), *Material Cultures, Material Minds: The Impact of Things on Human Thought, Society, and Evolution*, Cambridge: Cambridge University Press.

Bowie, A. (1993), "Oil in Ancient Greece and Rome," in M. Dudley and G. Rowell (eds.), *The Oil of Gladness: Anointing in the Christian Tradition*, London: Society for Promoting Christian Knowledge, pp. 26–34.

Brown, F., Driver, S.R., and Briggs, C.A. (1974), *A Hebrew and English Lexicon of the Old Testament*, Oxford: Clarendon.

Brumley, A. (2010), "'As Horace Fat' in a Thin Land: Ben Jonson's Experience and Strategy," in E. Levy-Navarro (ed.), *Historicizing Fat in Anglo-American Culture*, Columbus: Ohio State University Press, pp. 111–28.

Bull, I.D., Simpson, I.A., van Bergen, P.F., and Evershed, R.P. (1999), "Muck 'n' Molecules: Organic Geochemical Methods for Detecting Ancient Manuring," *Antiquity*, 73: 86–96.

Bynum, C.W. (1995), *The Resurrection of the Body in Western Christianity, 200–1336*, New York: Columbia University Press.

Carsten, J. (2004), *After Kinship*, Cambridge: Cambridge University Press.

Columella (1968), *On Agriculture*, trans. H. Boyd, Cambridge, MA: Harvard University Press.

Connor, S. (2004), *The Book of Skin*, Ithaca, NY: Cornell University Press.

Coogan, M.D. (2007), *The New Oxford Annotated Bible*, Oxford: Oxford University Press.

Daiches, S. (1913), *Babylonian Oil Magic in the Talmud and in the Later Jewish Literature*, London: Jews' College Publication.

Dalby, A. (2000), *Empire of Pleasures: Luxuries and Indulgence in the Roman World*, New York: Routledge.

Dean-Jones, L. (1994), *Women's Bodies in Classical Greek Science*, Oxford: Clarendon.

Dench, E. (1998), "Austerity, Excess, Success, and Failure in Hellenistic and Early Imperial Italy," in M. Wyke (ed.), *Parchments of Gender: Deciphering the Bodies of Antiquity*, Oxford: Clarendon, pp. 121–46.

Dershowitz, I. (2010), "A Land Flowing with Fat and Honey," *Vetus Testamentum*, 60: 172–76.

Drysdall, D.L. (trans.) (2005), *Collected Works of Erasmus: Adages, III iv 1 to IV ii 100*, Toronto: University of Toronto Press.

Evershed, R.P., Mottram, H. R., and Dudd, S.N. (1997), "New Criteria for the Identification of Animal Fats Preserved in Archaeological Pottery," *Naturwissenschaften*, 84: 402–6.

Forth, C.E. (2012a), "Fat, Desire, and Disgust in the Colonial Imagination," *History Workshop Journal*, 73: 211–39.

Forth, C.E. (2012b), "Spartan Mirages: Fat, Masculinity, and 'Softness,'" *Masculinidades y cambio social / Masculinities and Social Change*, 1: 240–66.

Forth, C.E. (2013), "The Qualities of Fat: Bodies, History, and Materiality," *Journal of Material Culture*, 18: 135–54.

Foucault, M. (1990), *The Use of Pleasure*, trans. R. Hurley, New York: Vintage.

Gowers, E. (1996), *The Loaded Table: Representations of Food in Roman Literature*, Oxford: Clarendon.

Griffith, R.M. (2004), *Born Again Bodies: Flesh and Spirit in American Christianity*, Berkeley: University of California Press.

Hahn, H.P., and Soentgen, J. (2010), "Acknowledging Substances: Looking at the Hidden Side of the Material World," *Philosophy and Technology*, 24: 19–33.

Héretier-Augé, F. (1991), "Étude comparée des sociétés africaines," in *Annuaire du Collège de France: Résumé des cours et travaux 1989–1990*, Paris: Collège de France, pp. 497–518.

Herodotus (1969), *Histories*, vol. 4, trans. A.D. Godley, Cambridge, MA: Harvard University Press.

Hill, S.E. (2011), *Eating to Excess: The Meaning of Gluttony and the Fat Body in the Ancient World*, Santa Barbara, CA: Praeger.

Hippocrates (1957), *Airs, Waters, Places*, in *Hippocrates*, vol. 1, trans. W.H.S. Jones, Cambridge, MA: Harvard University Press, pp. 71–137.

Hippocrates (1959), *Aphorisms*, in *Hippocrates*, vol. 4, trans. W.H.S. Jones, Cambridge, MA: Harvard University Press, pp. 97–221.

Hodder, I. (2012), *Entangled: An Archaeology of the Relationships between Humans and Things*, Oxford: Wiley-Blackwell.

Keane, W. (2005), "Signs Are Not the Garb of Meaning: On the Social Analysis of Material Things," in D. Miller (ed.), *Materiality*, Durham, NC: Duke University Press, pp. 182–205.

Kellermann, D. (1995), "*kᵉlāyôt*," in G.J. Botterweck, H. Ringgren, and H.-J. Fabry (eds.), *Theological Dictionary of the Old Testament*, vol. 7, trans. D.E. Green, Grand Rapids, MI: Eerdmans, 175–82.

Kottek, S.S. (1996), "On Health and Obesity in Talmudic and Midrashic Lore," *Israeli Journal of Medical Sciences*, 32: 509–10.

Kronenberg, L. (2009), *Allegories of Farming from Greece and Rome*, Cambridge: Cambridge University Press.

Kuriyama, S. (1999), *The Expressiveness of the Body and the Divergence of Greek and Chinese Medicine*, New York: Zone Books.

Lee, M.M. (2009), "Body-Modification in Classical Greece," in T. Fögen and M.M. Lee (eds.), *Bodies and Boundaries in Graeco-Roman Antiquity*, New York: De Gruyter, pp. 155–80.

Martin, D. (1995), *The Corinthian Body*, New Haven, CT: Yale University Press.

Martínez, F.G., and Tigchelaar, E.J.C. (eds.) (1999), *The Dead Sea Scrolls Study Edition*, Leiden: Brill.

Marx, A. (2005), *Les systèmes sacrificiels de l'Ancien Testament*, Leiden: Brill.

Meneley, A. (2008), "Oleo-Signs and Quali-Signs: The Qualities of Olive Oil," *Ethnos*, 73 (3): 303–26.

Münderlein, G. (1980), "Chelebh," in G.J. Botterweck and H. Ringgren (eds.), *Theological Dictionary of the Old Testament*, vol. 4, trans. D.E. Green, Grand Rapids, MI: Eerdmans, pp. 396–97.

Neusner, J. (2005), "Bavli Berakhot," *The Babylonian Talmud*, Peabody, MA: Hendrickson.

Onians, R.B. (1951), *The Origins of European Thought about the Body, the Mind, the Soul, the World, Time, and Fate*, Cambridge: Cambridge University Press.

Plato (1980), *The Laws*, trans. T.L. Pangle, New York: Basic Books.

Plaza, M. (2006), *The Function of Humour in Roman Verse Satire: Laughing and Lying*, Oxford: Oxford University Press.

Pliny (1947), *Histoire naturelle, livre XI*, trans. A. Ernout, Paris: Société d'édition "Les Belles Lettres."

Pliny (1971), *Natural History*, vol. 5, trans. H. Rackham, Cambridge, MA: Harvard University Press.

Pliny (1983), *Natural History*, vol. 3, trans. H. Rackham, Cambridge, MA: Harvard University Press.

Plutarch (1914), *Plutarch's Lives*, vol. 1, trans. B. Perrin, Cambridge, MA: Harvard University Press.

Popenoe, R. (2004), *Feeding Desire: Fatness, Beauty, and Sexuality among a Saharan People*, New York: Routledge.

Ringgren, H. (2006), "Semen," in G.J. Botterweck, H. Ringgren, and H.-J. Fabry (eds.), *Theological Dictionary of the Old Testament*, vol. 15, trans. D.E. Green and D.W. Stott, Grand Rapids, MI: Eerdmans, pp. 249–53.

Sansone, D. (1992), *Greek Athletics and the Genesis of Sport*, Berkeley: University of California Press.

Schiefsky, M.J. (2005), *Hippocrates, On Ancient Medicine*, Leiden: Brill.

Seneca (1979), *Ad Lucilium Epistulae Morales*, trans. R.M. Gummere, Cambridge, MA: Harvard University Press.

Simpson, I.A., van Bergen, P.F., Perret, V., Elhmmali, M.M., Roberts, D.J., and Evershed, R.P. (1999), "Lipid Biomarkers of Manuring Practice in Relict Anthropogenic Soils," *The Holocene*, 9: 223–29.

Smith, R.R.R. (1997), "The Public Image of Licinius I: Portrait Sculpture and Imperial Ideology in the Early Fourth Century," *Journal of Roman Studies*, 87: 170–202.

Sommer, B.D. (2009), *The Bodies of God and the World of Ancient Israel*, Cambridge: Cambridge University Press.

Stanton, M.O. (1890), *A System of Practical and Scientific Physiognomy; or, How to Read Faces*, Philadelphia: F.A. Davis.

Stearns, P.N. (1997), *Fat History: Bodies and Beauty in the Modern West*, New York: New York University Press.

Stewart, A. (1990), *Greek Sculpture: An Exploration*, vol. 1, New Haven, CT: Yale University Press.

Strauss, E. (1994), *Dictionary of European Proverbs*, London: Routledge.

Tétart, G. (2004), *Le sang des fleurs: une anthropologie de l'abeille et du miel*, Paris: Odile Jacob.

Theophrastus of Eresus (1916), *An Enquiry into Plants*, vol. 2, trans. A. Hort, Cambridge, MA: Harvard University Press.

Theophrastus of Eresus (2003), *On Sweat, on Dizziness and on Fatigue*, ed. W.W. Fortenbraugh, R.W. Sharples, and M.G. Sollenberger, Leiden: Brill.

Varner, E.R. (2004), *Mutilation and Transformation: Damnatio Memoriae and Roman Imperial Portraiture*, Leiden: Brill.

Varro (1934), *De Re Rustica*, trans. W.D. Hooper and H.B. Ash, Cambridge, MA: Harvard University Press.

Varro (1978), *Économie rurale, livre I*, trans. J. Heurgon, Paris: Société d'édition "Les Belles Lettres."

Vernant, J.-P. (1991), *Mortals and Immortals: Collected Essays*, Princeton, NJ: Princeton University Press.

Vialles, N. (1994), *Animal to Edible*, trans. J.A. Underwood, Cambridge: Cambridge University Press.

Virgil (1978), *Georgics*, in *Virgil, I: Eclogues, Georgics, Aeneid I–VI*, trans. H.R. Fairclough, Cambridge, MA: Harvard University Press, 2.248–250 (pp. 132–33).

Warnier, J.-P. (2007), *The Pot-King: The Body and Technologies of Power*, Leiden: Brill.

Winiwarter, V. (2000), "Soils in Ancient Roman Agriculture: Analytical Approaches to Invisible Properties," in H. Nowotny and M. Weiss (eds.), *Shifting Boundaries of the Real: Making the Invisible Visible*, Zürich: vdf Hochschulverlag, pp. 137–56.

Chapter 4: Joseph Beuys

Adams, D. (1992), "Joseph Beuys: Pioneer of a Radical Ecology," *Art Journal*, 51 (2): 26–34.

Adams, D. (1998), "From Queen Bee to Social Sculpture: The Artistic Alchemy of Joseph Beuys," afterword in *Bees: Lectures by Rudolf Steiner*, trans. T. Braatz, n.p.: Anthroposophic Press, pp. 189–213.

Adriani, G., Konnertz, W., and Thomas, K. (1979), *Joseph Beuys: Life and Works*, trans. P. Lech, Woodbury, NY: Barron's Educational Series.

Bachelard, G. (1983), *Water and Dreams: An Essay on the Imagination of Matter*, trans. E.R. Farell, Dallas: Dallas Institute of Humanities and Culture.

Bachelard, G. (2002), *Earth and the Reveries of Will: An Essay on the Imagination of Matter*, trans. K. Haltman, Dallas: Dallas Institute of Humanities and Culture.

Bennett, J. (2010), *Vibrant Matter: A Political Ecology of Things*, Durham, NC: Duke University Press.

Beuys, J. (1986), *In Memoriam Joseph Beuys: Obituaries, Essays, Speeches*, trans. T. Nevill, Bonn, Germany: Inter Nationes.

Biddle, J. (2008), "Festering Boils and Screaming Canvases: Culture, Contagion and Why Place No Longer Matters," *Emotion, Space and Society*, 1: 97–101.

Boivin, N. (2008), *Material Cultures, Material Minds: The Impact of Things on Human Thought, Society, and Evolution*, Cambridge: Cambridge University Press.

Borer, A. (1997), *The Essential Joseph Beuys*, Cambridge, MA: MIT Press.

Buchloh, B. (2001), "Beuys: The Twilight of the Idol: Preliminary Notes for a Critique," in G. Ray (ed.), *Joseph Beuys: Mapping the Legacy*, Sarasota, FL: John and Mable Ringling Museum of Art, D.A.P., pp. 199–211.

Chametzky, P. (2010), *Objects as History in Twentieth-Century Art*, Berkeley: University of California Press.

Danto, J. (1979), "Lard, Honey, Felt: Joseph Beuys' Spiritual Art," *Columbia Daily Spectator*, November 29.

Devitt, J. (1991), "Traditional Preferences in a Changed Context: Animal Fats as Valued Foods," *Central Australian Rural Practitioners' Association Newsletter*, 13: 16–18.

Elkin, A.P. (1974 [1938]), *The Australian Aborigines*, Sydney: Angus and Robertson.

Forth, C.E. (2012), "Melting Moments: The Greasy Sources of Modern Perceptions of Fat," *Cultural History*, 1 (1): 83–107.

Foster, N. (2011), "Anthropology, Mythology and Art: Reading Beuys through Heidegger," in C.-M.L. Hayes and V. Walters (eds.), *Beuysian Legacies in Ireland and Beyond*, Münster, Germany: Litverlag, pp. 49–64.

Gandy, M. (1997), "Contradictory Modernities: Conceptions of Nature in the Art of Joseph Beuys and Gerhard Richter," *Annals of the Association of American Geographers*, 87 (4): 636–59.

Gibson, J. (1979), *The Ecological Approach to Visual Perception*, Boston: Houghton Mifflin.

Gieseke, F., and Markert, A. (1996), *Flieger, Filz and Vaterland: eine erweiterte Beuys-Biografie*, Berlin: Elefanten.

Harlan, V. (ed.) (2004), *What Is Art? Conversations with Joseph Beuys*, West Sussex: Clairview Books.

Hodder, I. (2012), *Entangled: An Archaeology of the Relationships between Humans and Things*, Oxford: Wiley-Blackwell.

Ingold, T. (2007). "Materials against Materiality," *Archeological Dialogues*, 14 (1): 1–16.

Keane, W. (2005), "Signs Are Not the Garb of Meaning: On the Social Analysis of Material Things," in D. Miller (ed.), *Materiality*, Durham, NC: Duke University Press, pp. 182–205.

Klein, R. (1996), *Eat Fat*, New York: Vintage Books.

Kuoni, C. (ed.) (1990), *Energy Plan for Western Man: Joseph Beuys in America*, New York: Four Walls Press.

Kuspit, D. (1984), *The Critic Is Artist: The Intentionality of Art*, Ann Arbor: University of Michigan Press.

Kuspit, D. (1993), *The Cult of the Avant-Garde Artist*, Cambridge: Cambridge University Press.

Kuspit, D. (1995), "Joseph Beuys: Between Showman and Shaman," in D. Thistelwood (ed.), *Joseph Beuys: Diverging Critiques*, Liverpool: Liverpool University Press, Tate Gallery Liverpool, pp. 27–49.

Leitch, A. (1996), "The Life of Marble: The Experience and Meaning of Work in the Marble Quarries of Carrara," *Australian Journal of Anthropology*, 7 (1): 235–57.

Leitch, A. (2000), "The Social Life of Lardo: Slow Food in Fast Times," *Asia Pacific Journal of Anthropology*, 1 (1): 103–18.

Leitch, A. (2003), "Slow Food and the Politics of Pork Fat: Italian Food and European Identity," *Ethnos*, 68 (4): 337–462.

Leitch, A. (2010), "The Materiality of Marble: Explorations in the Artistic Life of Stone," *Thesis Eleven*, 103 (1): 65–77.

McDonald, H. (2003), "The Fats of Life," *Australian Aboriginal Studies*, 2: 53–61.

Meneley, A. (2008), "Oleo-Signs and Quali-Signs: The Qualities of Olive Oil," *Ethnos*, 73 (3): 303–26.

Mesch, C. and Michely, V. (2007), *Joseph Beuys: The Reader*, Cambridge, MA: MIT Press.

Mintz, S. (1979), "Time, Sugar and Sweetness," *Marxist Perspectives*, 2: 56–73.

Moffit, J. (1988), *Occultism in Avant-Garde Art: The Case of Joseph Beuys*, Ann Arbor: UMI Research Press.

Nisbet, P. (2001), "Crash Course—Remarks on a Beuys Story," in G. Ray (ed.), *Joseph Beuys: Mapping the Legacy*, Sarasota, FL: John and Mable Ringling Museum of Art, D.A.P., pp. 5–17.

Novero, C. (2010), *AntiDiets of the Avant-Garde*, Minneapolis: University of Minnesota Press.

Ray, G. (2001), "Joseph Beuys and the 'After-Auschwitz' Sublime," in G. Ray (ed.), *Joseph Beuys: Mapping the Legacy*, Sarasota, FL: John and Mable Ringling Museum of Art, D.A.P., pp. 55–74.

Redmond, T. (2001), "Places That Move," in A. Rumsey and J.F. Weiner (eds.), *Emplaced Myth: Space, Narrative, and Knowledge in Aboriginal Australia and Papua New Guinea*, Honolulu: University of Hawai'i Press, pp. 120–38.

Redmond, T. (2007), *The Saturated Fat of the Land: Diamonds in the Western and Ngarinyin Imaginary*, Paper presented at the Freud Conference, Melbourne, Australia, May.

Reid, J. (1983), *Sorcerers and Healing Spirits: Community and Change in an Aboriginal Medical System*, Canberra: Australian National University Press.

Roheim, G. (1974), *Children of the Desert: The Western Tribes of Central Australia*, New York: Basic Books.

Rozin, P. (1998), "Food Is Fundamental, Fun, Frightening and Far-Reaching," *Social Research*, 66 (1): 9–30.

Sobo, E. (1994), "The Sweetness of Fat: Health, Procreation, and Sociability in Rural Jamaica," in N. Sault (ed.), *Many Mirrors: Body Image and Social Relations*, New Brunswick, NJ: Rutgers University Press, pp. 132–54.

Spencer, W.B., and Gillen, F.J. (1899), *The Native Tribes of Central Australia*, London: Macmillan.

Stachelhaus, H. (1987), *Joseph Beuys*, trans. D. Britt, New York: Abbeville.

Strauss, D.L. (1999), *Between Dog and Wolf: Essays on Art and Politics*, Brooklyn: Automedia.

Taylor, M. (2012), *Refiguring the Spiritual: Beuys, Barney, Turrell, Goldsworthy*, New York: Columbia University Press.

Thompson, C. (2011), *Felt: Fluxus, Joseph Beuys and the Dalai Lama*, Minneapolis: University of Minnesota Press.

Tisdall, C. (1979), *Joseph Beuys*, London: Thames and Hudson.

Ulmer, G. (1984), *Applied Grammatology: Post (e)-Pedagogy from Jacques Derrida to Joseph Beuys*, Baltimore: John Hopkins University Press.

Walters, V. (2010), "The Artist as Shaman: The Work of Joseph Beuys and Marcus Coates," in A. Schneider and C. Wright (eds.), *Between Art and Anthropology*, Oxford: Berg, pp. 35–47.

White, N. (2001), "In Search of the Traditional Australian Aboriginal Diet—Then and Now," in A. Anderson, I. Lilley, and S. O'Connor (eds.), *Histories of Old Ages: Essays in Honour of Rhys Jones*, Canberra, Australia: Pandanus Books, Research School of Pacific and Asian Studies, pp. 343–59.

Chapter 5: Engrossing Encounters

Allen, J.T. (2008), "The Spectacularization of the Anorexic Subject Position," *Current Sociology*, 56: 587–603.

American Psychiatric Association (APA) (1994), *Diagnostic and Statistical Manual of Mental Disorders IV*, Washington, DC: American Psychiatric Association.

Barad, K. (2003), "Posthumanist Performativity: Toward an Understanding of How Matter Comes to Matter," *Signs: Journal of Women in Culture and Society*, 28: 801–31.

Bennett, J. (2010), *Vibrant Matter: A Political Ecology of Things*, Durham, NC: Duke University Press.

Bordo, S. (1993), *Unbearable Weight: Feminism, Western Culture, and the Body*, Berkeley: University of California Press.

Braziel, J.E., and LeBesco, K. (eds.) (2001), *Bodies out of Bounds: Fatness and Transgression*, Berkeley: University of California Press.

Butler, J. (2000), "Ethical Ambivalence," in M. Garber, B. Hanssen, and R.L. Walkowitz (eds.), *The Turn to Ethics*, New York: Routledge, pp. 15–28.

Carden-Coyne, A., and Forth, C. (2005), "The Belly and Beyond: Body, Self and Culture in Ancient and Modern Times," in C. Forth and A. Carden-Coyne (eds.), *Cultures of the Abdomen: Diet, Digestion and Fat in the Modern World*, New York: Palgrave Macmillan, pp. 1–11.

Cockell, S.J., Geller, J., and Linden, W. (2002), "Decisional Balance in Anorexia Nervosa: Capitalizing on Ambivalence," *European Eating Disorders Review*, 11: 75–89.

Colls, R. (2007), "Materialising Bodily Matter: Intra-action and the Embodiment of 'Fat,'" *Geoforum*, 38: 353–65.

Colton, A., and Pistrang, N. (2004), "Adolescents' Experiences of Inpatient Treatment for Anorexia Nervosa," *European Eating Disorders Review*, 12: 307–16.

Corin, E. (2007), "The 'Other' of Culture in Psychosis: The Ex-centricity of the Subject," in J. Biehl, B. Good, and A. Kleinman (eds.), *Subjectivity: Ethnographic Investigations*, Berkeley: University of California Press, pp. 273–314.

Curtin, D.W., and Heldke, L.M. (1992), "Introduction," in D.W. Curtin and L.M. Heldke (eds.), *Cooking, Eating, Thinking: Transformative Philosophies of Food*, Bloomington: Indiana University Press, pp. x–xiii.

Delpeuch, F., Maire, B., Monnier, E., and Holdsworth, M. (2009), *Globesity: A Planet out of Control?* London: Earthscan.

Eivors, A., Button, E., Warner, S., and Turner, K. (2003), "Understanding the Experience of Drop-Out from Treatment for Anorexia Nervosa," *European Eating Disorders Review*, 11: 90–107.

Espeset, E., Gulliksen, K., Nordbø, R., Skårderud, F., and Holte, A. (2012), "The Link between Negative Emotions and Eating Disorder Behaviour in Patients with Anorexia Nervosa," *European Eating Disorders Review*, 20: 451–60.

Evans, J. (2011), *Becoming John: Anorexia's Not Just for Girls*, Bloomington, IN: Xlibris.

Farrell, A.E. (2011), *Fat Shame: Stigma and the Fat Body in American Culture*, New York: New York University Press.

Fischer, M.J. (2007), "To Live with What Would Otherwise Be Unendurable: Return(s) to Subjectivities," in J. Biehl, B. Good, and A. Kleinman (eds.), *Subjectivity: Ethnographic Investigations*, Berkeley: University of California Press, pp. 423–46.

Gilman, S. (2010), *Obesity: The Biography*, Oxford: Oxford University Press.

Gooldin, S. (2008), "Being Anorexic: Hunger, Subjectivity and Embodied Morality," *Medical Anthropology Quarterly*, 22: 274–96.

Grahame, N. (2009), *Dying to Be Thin: The True Story of My Lifelong Battle against Anorexia*, London: John Blake.

Grossberg, L. (2010), "Affect's Future: Rediscovering the Virtual in the Actual," in M. Gregg and G.J Seigworth (eds.), *The Affect Theory Reader*, Durham, NC: Duke University Press, pp. 309–38.

Grosz, E. (2001), *Architecture from the Outside: Essays on Virtual and Real Space*, Cambridge, MA: MIT Press.

Haraway, D.J. (1991), *Simians, Cyborgs, and Women: The Reinvention of Nature*, London: Free Association Books.

Haraway, D.J. (2008), "Otherwordly Conversations, Terran Topics, Local Terms," in S. Alaimo and S. Hekman (eds.), *Material Feminisms*, Bloomington: Indiana University Press, pp. 157–87.

Hayes-Conroy, J., and Hayes-Conroy, A. (2010), "Visceral Geographies: Mattering, Relating, and Defying," *Geography Compass*, 4: 1273–83.

Hornbacher, M. (1998), *Wasted: Coming Back from an Addiction to Starvation*, London: Flamingo.

Hornbacher, M. (2008), *Madness: A Bipolar Life*, London: Harper Perennial.

Jackson, M. (2002), "Familiar and Foreign Bodies: A Phenomenological Exploration of the Human-Technology Interface," *Journal of the Royal Anthropological Institute* (n.s.), 8: 333–46.

Katzman, M.A., and Lee, S. (1997), "Beyond Body Image: The Integration of Feminist and Transcultural Theories in the Understanding of Self-Starvation," *International Journal of Eating Disorders*, 22: 385–94.

Kent, L. (2001), "Fighting Abjection: Representing Fat Women," in J.E. Braziel and K. LeBesco (eds.), *Bodies out of Bounds: Fatness and Transgression*, Berkeley: University of California Press, pp. 130–50.

Klein, R. (2001), "Fat Beauty," in J.E. Braziel and K. LeBesco (eds.), *Bodies out of Bounds: Fatness and Transgression*, Berkeley: University of California Press, pp. 19–38.

Kristeva, J. (1982), *Powers of Horror: An Essay on Abjection*, trans. L.S. Roudiez. New York: Columbia University Press.

Kyriacou, O., Easter, A., and Tchanturia, K. (2009), "Comparing Views of Patients, Parents, and Clinicians on Emotions in Anorexia: A Qualitative Study," *Journal of Health Psychology*, 14: 843–54.

Lavis, A. (2011), "The Boundaries of a Good Anorexic: Exploring Pro-anorexia on the Internet and in the Clinic," PhD thesis, Goldsmiths, University of London. Available at http://eprints.gold.ac.uk/6507/ (accessed June 11, 2012).

Lavis, A. (2013), "The Substance of Absence: Exploring Eating and Anorexia," in E-J. Abbots and A. Lavis (eds.), *Why We Eat, How We Eat: Contemporary Encounters between Foods and Bodies*, Farnham, UK: Ashgate, pp. 35–52.

LeBesco, K. (2004), *Revolting Bodies?: The Struggle to Redefine Fat Identity*, Amherst: University of Massachusetts Press.

LeBesco, K., and Braziel, J.E. (2001), "Editors' Introduction," in J.E. Braziel and K. LeBesco (eds.), *Bodies out of Bounds: Fatness and Transgression*, Berkeley: University of California Press, pp. 1–15.

Marcus, G.E. (1998), *Ethnography through Thick and Thin*, Princeton, NJ: Princeton University Press.

Murray, S. (2005a), "Introduction to 'Thinking Fat,'" special issue, *Social Semiotics*, 15: 111–12.

Murray, S. (2005b), "(Un/be)coming Out? Rethinking Fat Politics," in "Thinking Fat," special issue, *Social Semiotics*, 15: 153–63.

National Collaborating Centre for Mental Health (2004), *Eating Disorders: Core Interventions in the Treatment and Management of Anorexia Nervosa, Bulimia Nervosa and Related Eating Disorders*, National Clinical Practice Guideline no. CG9, Leicester: British Psychological Society and Gaskell.

Palmer, B. (2005), "Concepts of Eating Disorders," in J. Treasure, U. Schmidt, and E. Van Furth (eds.), *The Essential Handbook of Eating Disorders*, Chichester, UK: Wiley, pp. 1–10.

Rasmussen, N. (2012), "Weight Stigma, Addiction, Science, and the Medication of Fatness in Mid-Twentieth Century America," *Sociology of Health and Illness*, 34: 880–95.

Seigworth, G.J., and Gregg, M. (2010), "An Inventory of Shimmers," in M. Gregg and G.J Seigworth (eds.), *The Affect Theory Reader*, Durham, NC: Duke University Press, pp. 1–28.

Serpell, L., Treasure, J., Teasdale, J., and Sullivan, V. (1999), "Anorexia Nervosa: Friend or Foe?," *International Journal of Eating Disorders*, 25: 177–86.

Serres, M. (2008), *The Five Senses: A Philosophy of Mingled Bodies*, trans. M. Sankey and P. Cowley, London: Continuum.

Tan, J. (2003), "The Anorexia Talking?," *The Lancet*, 362: 1246.

Tan, J., Hope, T., and Stewart, A. (2003), "Anorexia Nervosa and Personal Identity: The Accounts of Patients and Their Parents," *International Journal of Law and Psychiatry*, 26: 533–48.

Throsby, K. (2012), "Obesity Surgery and the Management of Excess: Exploring the Body Multiple," *Sociology of Health and Illness*, 34: 1–15.

Treasure, J. (2012), "Editorial: Emotion in Eating Disorders," *European Eating Disorders Review*, 20: 429–30.

Treasure, J., Smith, G., and Crane, A. (2007), *Skills-Based Learning for Caring for a Loved One with an Eating Disorder: The New Maudsley Method*, London: Routledge.

Treasure, J., and Ward, A. (1997), "A Practical Guide to the Use of Motivational Interviewing in Anorexia Nervosa," *European Eating Disorders Review*, 5: 102–14.

Tucker, I. (2010), "Everyday Spaces of Mental Distress: The Spatial Habituation of Home," *Environment and Planning D: Society and Space*, 28: 526–38.

Warin, M. (2006), "Reconfiguring Relatedness in Anorexia," *Anthropology and Medicine*, 13: 41–54.

Warin, M. (2010), *Abject Relations: Everyday Worlds of Anorexia*, New Brunswick, NJ: Rutgers University Press.

Warren, L., and Cooper, M. (2011), "Understanding Your Own and Other's Minds: The Relationship to Eating Disorder Related Symptoms," *European Eating Disorders Review*, 19: 417–25.

World Health Organization (2007), "Anorexia Nervosa and Atypical Anorexia Nervosa," in *International Statistical Classification of Diseases and Related Health Problems 10th Revision*, Geneva: World Health Organization, section F50.0–50.1.

Chapter 6: Fat Is the Future

American Society of Plastic Surgeons (2012), "2011 Reconstructive Plastic Surgery Statistics Reconstructive Procedure Trends," http://www.plasticsurgery.org/Documents/news-resources/statistics/2011-statistics/2011-reconstructive-procedures-trends-statistics.pdf (accessed March 7, 2012).

Begley, S. (2010), "All Natural: Why Breasts Are the Key to the Future of Regenerative Medicine," *Wired*, November, http://www.wired.com/magazine/2010/10/ff_futureofbreasts/all/1 (accessed September 23, 2013).

Blondeel, P.N. (1999), "The Sensate Free Superior Gluteal Artery Perforator (S-GAP) Flap: A Valuable Alternative in Autologous Breast Reconstruction," *British Journal of Plastic Surgery*, 52: 185–93.

Bordo, S. (1993), *Unbearable Weight: Feminism, Western Culture, and the Body*, Berkeley: University of California Press.

"Breast Reconstruction: Dr. Ron Israeli Offers Hope and Wholeness after Cancer Diagnosis" (2011), ABC News, November 15, http://abcnews.go.com/Health/video/breast-reconstruction-14958838 (accessed March 8, 2012).

Bump, R. (2003), "Surgeon: Breast Reconstruction after Cancer Helps Women Regain Wholeness," *The Prescott (AZ) Daily Courier*, July 13.

Canguilhem, G. (1994), *A Vital Rationalist: Selected Writings from Georges Canguilhem*, ed. François Delaporte, New York: Zone Books.

Cohen, E. (2009), *A Body Worth Defending: Immunity, Biopolitics, and the Apotheosis of the Modern Body*, Durham, NC: Duke University Press.

Coleman, S., and Saboeiro, A. (2007), "Fat Grafting to the Breast Revisited: Safety and Efficacy," *Plastic and Reconstructive Surgery*, 119 (3): 775–85.

Colls, R. (2007), "Materialising Bodily Matter: Intra-action and the Embodiment of 'Fat,'" *Geoforum*, 38: 353–65.

Cooper, M. (2008), *Life as Surplus: Biotechnology and Capitalism in the Neoliberal Era*, Seattle: University of Washington Press.

Cytori Therapeutics (2009), "Promising Results Reported in Cell-Enriched Breast Reconstruction Trial," press release, December 12, available at http://ir.cytori.com/files/doc_news/CYTX_News_2009_12_12_General.pdf (accessed March 11, 2011).

Davis-Floyd, R. (1994), "The Technocractic Body: American Childbirth as Cultural Expression," *Social Science and Medicine*, 38 (8): 1125–40.

Del Vecchio, D., and Fichadia, H. (2012), "Autologous Fat Transplantation—a Paradigm Shift in Breast Reconstruction," in Marzia Salgarello (ed.), *Breast Reconstruction: Current Techniques*, available at http://www.intechopen.com/books/breast-reconstruction-current-techniques/autologous-fat-transplantation-a-paradigm-shift-in-breast-reconstruction (accessed March 11, 2012).

Ehlers, N. (2012), "*Tekhnē* of Reconstruction: Breast Cancer, Norms, and Fleshy Rearrangements," *Social Semiotics*, 22 (1): 121–41.

Foucault, M. (1970), *The Order of Things: An Archeology of the Human Sciences*, London: Tavistock.

Franklin, S. (1995), "Life," in W. Reich (ed.), *Encyclopedia of Bioethics*, New York: Macmillan, pp. 456–62.

Fraser, J.K., Wulur, I., Alfonso, Z., and Hedrick, M.H. (2006), "Fat Tissue: An Underappreciated Source of Stem Cells for Biotechnology," *Trends in Biotechnology*, 24 (4): 150–54.

Gill, P.S., Hunt, J.P., Guerra A.B., Dellacroce, F.J., Sullivan, S.K., Boraski, J., Metzinger, S.E., Dupin, C.L., and Allen, R.J. (2004), "A 10-Year Retrospective Review of 758 DIEP Flaps for Breast Reconstruction," *Plastic and Reconstructive Surgery*, 113 (4): 1153–60.

Journal of the National Cancer Institute (2007), "Increased Breast Cancer Risk Associated with Greater Fat Intake," *ScienceDaily*, March 22, http://www.sciencedaily.com/releases/2007/03/070321161542.htm (accessed March 11, 2012).

Kent, L. (2001), "Fighting Abjection: Representing Fat Women," in J.E. Braziel and K. LeBesco (eds.), *Bodies out of Bounds: Fatness and Transgression*, Berkeley: University of California Press, pp. 130–50.

Leder, D. (1990), *The Absent Body*, Chicago: University of Chicago Press.

Liquid Gold (2013), "Liquid Gold: A New Conversation in Cosmetic Surgery," http://liquidgoldlipobank.com/ (accessed March 11, 2012).

Murray, S. (2007), "Care of the Self: Biotechnology, Reproduction, and the Good Life," *Philosophy, Ethics, and Humanities in Medicine*, 2 (6): 1–15.

Nahabedian, M.Y., Momen, B., Gladino, G., and Manson, P.N. (2002), "Breast Reconstruction with the Free TRAM or DIEP Flap: Patient Selection, Choice of Flap, and Outcome," *Plastic and Reconstructive Surgery*, 110 (2): 466–75.

Neopec (n.d.), http://www.neopec.com.au (accessed March 11, 2012).

New Zealand Institute of Plastic and Cosmetic Surgery (n.d.), "Breast Reconstruction," http://www.plasticsurgeons.co.nz/procedures/breast/breast-reconstruction.html (accessed March 8, 2012).

Novas, C., and Rose, N. (2000), "Genetic Risk and the Birth of the Somatic Individual," *Economy and Society*, 29: 485–513.

Panettiere, P., Accorsi, D., Marchetti, L., Sgro, F., and Sbarbati, A. (2011), "Large-Breast Reconstruction Using Fat Graft Only after Prosthetic Reconstruction Failure," *International Journal of Aesthetic Plastic Surgery*, 35: 703–8.

Parkin, D.M., and Boyd, L. (2011), "Cancers Attributable to Overweight and Obesity in the UK in 2010," supplement, *British Journal of Cancer*, 105 (S2): 34–37.

Rose, N. (1994), "Medicine, History, and the Present," in C. Jones and R. Porter (eds.), *Reassessing Foucault: Power, Medicine, and the Body*, London: Routledge, pp. 48–72.

Rose, N. (2007), *The Politics of Life Itself: Biomedicine, Power, and Subjectivity in the Twenty-First Century*, Princeton, NJ: Princeton University Press.

Shildrick, M. (1997), *Leaky Bodies and Boundaries: Feminism, Postmodernism, and (Bio)Ethics*, London: Routledge.

Smith, L. (1995), "Rebuilding the Self to Your Health: Breast Reconstruction Has Been Called Vain and Anti-feminist. But Women Who've Been NTC There Hail It as a Way to Restore a Sense of Wholeness," *Baltimore Sun*, October 3.

Sontag, S. (1990), *Illness as Metaphor and AIDS and Its Metaphors*, New York: Picador.

Spear, S., Wilson, H., and Lockwood, M. (2005), "Fat Injection to Correct Contour Deformaties in the Reconstructed Breast," *Plastic and Reconstructive Surgery*, 116 (5): 1300–1305.

Squier, S.M. (2004), *Liminal Lives: Imagining the Human at the Frontiers of Biomedicine*, Durham, NC: Duke University Press.

U.S. National Institute of Cancer at the National Institutes of Health (2012), "Obesity and Cancer Risk," http://www.cancer.gov/cancertopics/factsheet/Risk/obesity (accessed March 11, 2012).

Waldby, C. (2000), *The Visible Human Project: Informatics Bodies and Posthuman Medicine*, London: Routledge.

Waldby, C. (2002), "Stem Cells, Tissue Cultures and the Production of Biovalue," *Health*, 6 (3): 305–23.

Waldby, C., and Mitchell, R. (2006), *Tissue Economies: Blood, Organs, and Cell Lines in Late Capitalism*, Durham, NC: Duke University Press.

Zuk, P.A., Zhu, M., Mizuno, H., Huang, J., Futrell, W., Katz, A.J., Benhaim, P., Lorenz, H.P., and Hedrick, M.H. (2001), "Multilineage Cells from Human Adipose Tissue: Implications for Cell-Based Therapies," *Tissue Engineering*, 7 (2): 211–28.

Zylinska, J. (2010), "Playing God, Playing Adam: The Politics and Ethics of Enhancement," *Journal of Bioethical Inquiry*, 7 (2): 149–61.

Chapter 7: Bound Bodies

Adam, A. (2001), "Big Girls' Blouses: Learning to Live with Polyester," in A. Guy, E. Green, and M. Banim (eds.), *Through the Wardrobe: Women's Relationships with Their Clothes*, Oxford: Berg, pp. 39–51.

Andersson, T. (2011), "Fashion, Market and Materiality: Along the Seams of Clothing," *Culture Unbound*, 3: 13–18.

Ash, J. (1999), "The Aesthetics of Absence: Clothes without People in Paintings," in A. de la Haye and E. Wilson (eds.), *Defining Dress: Dress as Object, Meaning and Identity*, Manchester: Manchester University Press, pp. 128–42.

Attfield, J. (2000), *Wild Things: The Material Culture of Everyday Life*, Oxford: Berg.

Barnes, R., and Eicher, J.B. (1997), *Dress and Gender: Making and Meaning in Cultural Contexts*, Oxford: Berg.

Barthes, R. (2006), *The Language of Fashion*, trans. A. Stafford, Oxford: Berg.

Bauman, Z. (1990), *Thinking Sociologically*, Oxford: Blackwell.

Bedikian, S.A. (2008), "The Death of Mourning: From Victorian Crepe to the Little Black Dress," *Omega*, 57 (1): 35–52.

Bourdieu, P. (1984), *Distinction: A Social Critique of the Judgement of Taste*, trans. R. Nice, Cambridge, MA: Harvard University Press.

Breseman, B.C., Lennon, S.J., and Schulz, T.L. (1999), "Obesity and Powerlessness," in K.K.P. Johnson and S.J. Lennon (eds.), *Appearance and Power*, Oxford: Berg, pp. 173–97.

Butler, J. (1990), *Gender Trouble: Feminism and the Subversion of Identity*, New York: Routledge.

Cain, T. (2011), "Bounded Bodies: The Everyday Clothing Practices of Larger Women," PhD thesis, Massey University, Auckland, New Zealand.

Carryer, J. (2001), "Embodied Largeness: A Significant Women's Health Issue," *Nursing Inquiry*, 8 (2): 90–97.

Cavallaro, D., and Warwick, A. (1998), *Fashioning the Frame: Boundaries, Dress and Body*, Oxford: Berg.

Clarke, V., and Turner, K. (2007), "Clothes Maketh the Queer? Dress, Appearance and the Construction of Lesbian, Gay and Bisexual Identities," *Feminism and Psychology*, 17 (2): 267–76.

Colls, R. (2006), "Outsize/Outside: Bodily Bignesses and the Emotional Experiences of British Women Shopping for Clothes," *Gender, Place and Culture*, 13 (5): 529–45.

Colls, R. (2007), "Materialising Bodily Matter: Intra-action and the Embodiment of 'Fat,'" *Geoforum*, 38: 353–65.

de Beauvoir, S. (1997), *The Second Sex*, trans. H.M. Parshley, London: Vintage.

Douglas, M. (1966), *Purity and Danger: An Analysis of Concepts of Pollution and Taboo*, New York: Routledge.

Douglas, M. (1996), *Natural Symbols*, London: Routledge.

Eco, U. (2007 [1973]), "Social Life as a Sign System," in M. Barnard (ed.), *Fashion Theory: A Reader*, New York: Routledge, pp. 143–47.

Eicher, J.B. (1995), *Dress and Ethnicity: Change across Time and Space*, Oxford: Berg.

Entwistle, J. (1997), "Fashioning the Self: Women, Dress, Power and Situated Bodily Practice in the Workplace," PhD thesis, Goldsmiths College, University of London.

Entwistle, J. (2000), "Fashion and the Fleshy Body: Dress as Embodied Practice," *Fashion Theory*, 4: 323–47.

Entwistle, J. (2001), "The Dressed Body," in J. Entwistle and E. Wilson (eds.), *Body Dressing*, Oxford: Berg, pp. 33–58.

Fox, N.J. (2012), *The Body*, Cambridge, UK: Polity.

Gies, L. (2006), "What Not to Wear: Islamic Dress and School Uniforms," *Feminist Legal Studies*, 14: 377–89.

Glick, P., Larsen, S., Johnson, C., and Branstiter, H. (2005), "Evaluations of Sexy Women in Low- and High-Status Jobs," *Psychology of Women Quarterly*, 29: 389–95.

Goffman, E. (1986), *Stigma: Notes on the Management of Spoiled Identity*, New York: Simon and Schuster.

Goffman, E. (1990), *The Presentation of Self in Everyday Life*, Garden City, NY: Doubleday.

Grosz, E. (1994), *Volatile Bodies: Toward a Corporeal Feminism*, Bloomington: Indiana University Press.

Hansen, K.T. (2004), "The World in Dress: Anthropological Perspectives on Clothing, Fashion, and Culture," *Annual Review of Anthropology*, 33: 369–92.

Hartley, C. (2001), "Letting Ourselves Go: Making Room for the Fat Body in Feminist Scholarship," in J.E. Braziel and K. LeBesco (eds.), *Bodies out of Bounds: Fatness and Transgression*, Berkeley: University of California Press, pp. 60–73.

Harvey, J. (1995), *Men in Black*, Chicago: University of Chicago Press.

Huff, J.L. (2001), "A 'Horror of Corpulence': Interrogating Bantingism and Mid-Nineteenth-Century Fat-Phobia," in J.E. Braziel and K. LeBesco (eds.), *Bodies out of Bounds: Fatness and Transgression*, Los Angeles: University of California Press, pp. 39–59.

Ingraham, C. (2008), *White Weddings: Romancing Heterosexuality in Popular Culture*, 2nd ed., New York: Routledge.

Irigaray, L. (1985), *This Sex Which Is Not One*, trans. C. Burke, Ithaca, NY: Cornell University Press.

Jutel, A. (2005), "Weighing Health: The Moral Burden of Obesity," *Social Semiotics*, 15 (2): 113–25.

Jutel, A. (2006), "The Emergence of Overweight as a Disease Entity: Measuring Up Normality," *Social Science and Medicine*, 63 (9): 2268–76.

Keane, W. (2005), "Signs Are Not the Garb of Meaning: On the Social Analysis of Things," in D. Miller (ed.), *Materiality*, Durham, NC: Duke University Press, pp. 182–205.

Kellner, D. (1994), "Madonna, Fashion, and Identity," in S. Benstock and S. Ferriss (eds.), *On Fashion*, New Brunswick, NJ: Rutgers University Press, pp. 159–82.

Kent, L. (2001), "Fighting Abjection: Representing Fat Women," in J.E. Braziel and K. Le-Besco (eds.), *Bodies out of Bounds: Fatness and Transgression*, Berkeley: University of California Press, pp. 130–50.

Kristeva, J. (1982), *Powers of Horror: An Essay on Abjection*, trans. L.S. Roudiez, New York: Columbia University Press.

LeBesco, K. (2004), *Revolting Bodies?: The Struggle to Redefine Fat Identity*, Boston: University of Massachusetts Press.

LeBesco, K., and Braziel, J.E. (2001), "Editors' Introduction," in J.E. Braziel and K. LeBesco (eds.), *Bodies out of Bounds: Fatness and Transgression*, Berkeley: University of California Press, pp. 1–15.

Leder, D. (1990), *The Absent Body*, Chicago: University of Chicago Press.

Longhurst, R. (2005a), "(Ad)dressing Pregnant Bodies in New Zealand: Clothing, Fashion, Subjectivities and Spatialities," *Gender, Place and Culture*, 12 (4): 433–46.

Longhurst, R. (2005b), "Fat Bodies: Developing Geographical Research Agendas," *Progress in Human Geography*, 29 (3): 247–59.

Longhurst, R. (2005c), "Man Breasts: Spaces of Sexual Difference, Fluidity and Abjection," in B. Van Hoven and K. Hörschelmann (eds.), *Spaces of Masculinity*, London: Routledge, pp. 165–78.

Löw, M. (2006), "The Social Construction of Space and Gender," *European Journal of Women's Studies*, 13 (2): 119–33.

McDowell, L. (1999), *Gender, Identity and Place: Understanding Feminist Geographies*, Cambridge, UK: Polity.

Miller, D. (2005), "Introduction," in S. Küchler and D. Miller (eds.), *Clothing as Material Culture*, Oxford: Berg, pp. 1–19.

Monaghan, L., and Atkinson, M. (forthcoming), *Challenging Masculinity Myths: Understanding Physical Cultures*, Farnham, UK: Ashgate.

Mulvey, L. (1985), "Visual Pleasure and Narrative Cinema," in G. Mast and M. Cohen (eds.), *Film Theory and Criticism*, 3rd ed., New York: Oxford University Press, pp. 803–16.

Murray, S. (2005), "Doing Politics or Selling Out? Living the Fat Body," *Women's Studies*, 34 (3): 265–77.

Murray, S. (2008), *The "Fat" Female Body*, New York: Palgrave Macmillan.

Parkin, W. (2002), *Fashioning the Body Politic: Dress, Gender, Citizenship*, Oxford: Berg.

Pringle, R., and Alley, J. (1995), "Gender and the Funeral Industry: The Work of Citizenship," *Journal of Sociology*, 31 (2): 107–21.

Rail, G., Holmes, D., and Murray, S.J. (2010), "The Politics of Evidence on 'Domestic Terrorists': Obesity Discourses and Their Effects," *Social Theory and Health*, 8 (3): 259–79.

Russo, M. (1997), "Female Grotesques: Carnival and Theory," in K. Conboy, M. Medina, and S. Stanbury (eds.), *Writing on the Body: Female Embodiment and Feminist Theory*, New York: Columbia University Press, pp. 318–36.

Shilling, C. (1993), *The Body and Social Theory*, London: Sage.

"Skinny White Runway Models" (2007), *The Fashion eZine*, http://fashion.lilithezine.com/Skinny-White-Runway-Models.html (accessed November 11, 2010).

Stokowski, P.A. (2002), "Languages of Place and Discourses of Power: Constructing New Senses of Place," *Journal of Leisure Research*, 34 (4): 368–82.

Sweetman, P. (2001), "Shop-Window Dummies? Fashion, the Body, and Emergent Socialities," in J. Entwistle and E. Wilson (eds.), *Body Dressing*, Oxford: Berg, pp. 59–77.

Tischner, I., and Malson, H. (2012), "Deconstructing Health and the Un/healthy Fat Woman," *Journal of Community and Applied Social Psychology*, 22: 50–62.

Tulloch, J., and Lupton, D. (2003), *Risk and Everyday Life*, London: Sage.

Turner, G. (2003), *British Cultural Studies: An Introduction*, 3rd ed., London: Routledge.

Vaiou, D., and Lykogianni, R. (2006), "Women, Neighbourhoods and Everyday Life," *Urban Studies*, 43 (4): 731–43.

Warde, A. (1994), "Consumers, Identity and Belonging: Reflections on Some Theses of Zygmunt Bauman," in R. Keat, N. Whiteley, and N. Abercrombie (eds.), *The Authority of the Consumer*, London: Routledge, pp. 58–74.

Waskul, D., and Vannini, P. (2006), *Body/Embodiment: Symbolic Interaction and the Sociology of the Body*, Hampshire, UK: Ashgate.

Wilson, E. (1987), *Adorned in Dreams: Fashion and Modernity*, Berkeley: University of California Press.

Wilson, E., and de la Haye, A. (1999), "Introduction," in A. de la Haye and E. Wilson (eds.), *Defining Dress: Dress as Object, Meaning and Identity*, Manchester: Manchester University Press, pp. 1–9.

Woodward, S. (2005), "Looking Good: Feeling Right—Aesthetics of the Self," in S. Küchler and D. Miller (eds.), *Clothing as Material Culture*, Oxford: Berg, pp. 21–39.

Woodward, S. (2007), *Why Women Wear What They Wear*, Oxford: Berg.

Wray, S., and Deery, R. (2008), "The Medicalization of Body Size and Women's Healthcare," *Health Care for Women International*, 29: 227–43.

Chapter 8: Fatsploitation

Alley, K. (2012), Kirstie Alley: The Official Site, http://www.kirstiealley.com/ (accessed January 25, 2012).

Bartky, S. (1990), *Femininity and Domination: Studies in the Phenomenology of Oppression*, London: Routledge.

Butler, J. (1990), *Gender Trouble: Feminism and the Subversion of Identity*, London: Routledge.

Campos, P. (2004), *The Obesity Myth: Why America's Obsession with Weight Is Hazardous to Your Health*, New York: Penguin Books.

Carlson, M. (2003), *The Haunted Stage: Theatre as a Memory Machine*, Ann Arbor: University of Michigan Press.

Cloud, J. (1999a), "Monica's Makeover," *CNN*, March 8, http://www.cnn.com/ALLPOLITICS/time/1999/03/08/makeover.html (accessed January 15, 2012).

Cloud, J. (1999b), "Monica's Makeover," *Time Magazine*, March 15, http://www.time.com/time/magazine/article/0,9171,990427,00.html (accessed February 1, 2012).

Colls, R. (2007), "Materialising Bodily Matter: Intra-action and the Embodiment of 'Fat,'" *Geoforum*, 38: 353–65.

Douglas, M. (1966), *Purity and Danger: An Analysis of Concepts of Pollution and Taboo*, New York: Routledge.

Farrell, A.E. (2011), *Fat Shame: Stigma and the Fat Body in American Culture*, New York: New York University Press.

Forth, C.E. (2012), "Melting Moments: The Greasy Sources of Modern Perceptions of Fat," *Cultural History*, 1 (1): 83–107.

Gowen, G. (2012), "Gaining, Losing Weight Means Big Payments for Celebs," ABCNews.com, May 11, http://abcnews.go.com/entertainment/gaining-losing-weight-means-big-paydays-celebs/story?id=16314049# (accessed November 3, 2013).

Graham, M. (2005), "Chaos," in D. Kulick and A. Meneley (eds.), *Fat: The Anthropology of an Obsession*, London: Tarcher, pp. 169–84.

Greene, Bob (2009), "Oprah's Weight Loss Confession," *Oprah.com*, January 5, http://www.oprah.com/health/Oprahs-Weight-Loss-Confession/2#ixzz1kZrhu4OG (accessed January 26, 2012).

Grosz, E. (1994), *Volatile Bodies: Toward a Corporeal Feminism*, Bloomington: Indiana University Press.

Harpo Productions (2006), "Oprah Follow-Ups," *Oprah.com*, November 6, http://www.oprah.com/oprahshow/Oprah-Follow-Ups/2 (accessed February 17, 2012).

Harpo Productions (2010), "The Wagon of Fat," *Oprah.com*, December 22, http://www.oprah.com/oprahshow/Oprah-Wheels-Out-the-Wagon-of-Fat-Video (accessed January 26, 2012).

Huff, J.L. (2009), "Access to the Sky: Airplane Seats and Fat Bodies as Contested Spaces," in E. Rothblum and S. Solovay (eds.), *The Fat Studies Reader*, New York: New York University Press, pp. 176–86.

Kent, L. (2001), "Fighting Abjection: Representing Fat Women," in J.E. Braziel and K. LeBesco (eds.), *Bodies out of Bounds: Fatness and Transgression*, Berkeley: University of California Press, pp. 130–50.

Leung, R. (2007), "The Subway Diet," CBS News, December 5, http://www.cbsnews.com/stories/2004/09/01/48hours/main640067.shtml?tag=mncol;lst;1 (accessed January 26, 2012).

Miller, W.I. (1997), *The Anatomy of Disgust*, Cambridge, MA: Harvard University Press.

Mobley, J.-S. (2012), "Tennessee Williams' Ravenous Women: Fat Behavior Onstage," *Fat Studies: An Interdisciplinary Journal of Body Weight and Society*, 1: 75–90.

Murray, S. (2008), *The "Fat" Female Body*, New York: Palgrave Macmillan.

North, A. (2010), "Jared Fogle and the Plight of the Celebrity Dieter," *Jezebel*, February 15, http://jezebel.com/5472007/jared-fogle-and-the-plight-of-the-celebrity-dieter (accessed March 23, 2012).

Parker-Pope, T. (2011), "The Fat Trap," *New York Times Magazine*, December 28, http://www.nytimes.com/2012/01/01/magazine/tara-parker-pope-fat-trap.html?_r=0&pagewanted=printhttp://www.nytimes.com/2012/01/01/magazine/tara-parker-pope-fat-trap.html (accessed December 1, 2012).

Shapiro, W. (1999), "The First Bimbo," *Walter Shapiro: Pundicity*, January 30, http://www.waltershapiro.com/3542/the-first-bimbo (accessed February 16, 2012).

Subway Company (2009), "Subway Commercial 1812 Overture," YouTube, January 22, http://www.youtube.com/watch?v=QsZFsZw5jtU&feature=related (accessed June 21, 2012).

Yogi (2011), "Oprah's Most Memorable Moments," Magic 106.3: R&B and Classic Soul, May 25, http://mycolumbusmagic.com/1446771/oprahs-most-memorable-moments/ (accessed January 26, 2012).

INDEX

Using Film to Understand Childhood and Practice

ALSO AVAILABLE FROM BLOOMSBURY

Using Film to Understand Childhood and Practice

EDITED BY SUE AITKEN

Bloomsbury Academic
An imprint of Bloomsbury Publishing Plc

B L O O M S B U R Y
LONDON • OXFORD • NEW YORK • NEW DELHI • SYDNEY

Bloomsbury Academic

An imprint of Bloomsbury Publishing Plc

50 Bedford Square	1385 Broadway
London	New York
WC1B 3DP	NY 10018
UK	USA

www.bloomsbury.com

BLOOMSBURY and the Diana logo are trademarks of Bloomsbury Publishing Plc

First published 2018

British Library Cataloguing-in-Publication Data

A catalogue record for this book is available from the British Library.

ISBN: HB: 978-1-4742-7456-2
PB: 978-1-4742-7455-5
ePub: 978-1-4742-7457-9
ePDF: 978-1-4742-7458-6

Library of Congress Cataloging-in-Publication Data

A catalog record for this book is available from the Library of Congress.

Cover image © Jackie Sumerfield

Typeset by Newgen KnowledgeWorks Pvt. Ltd., Chennai, India
Printed and bound in Great Britain

To find out more about our authors and books visit www.bloomsbury.com. Here you will find extracts, author interviews, details of forthcoming events and the option to sign up for our newsletters.

For HB and NH

Contents

Acknowledgements

First and foremost, I would like to thank all the contributors to this book, not just for the chapters they have written but also for their continuous support and encouragement, and more importantly their continued belief in the project itself. I would also like to thank my publisher Bloomsbury, especially my editors Rachel Shillington and Maria Giovanna Brauzzi, whose patience I greatly appreciate.

I am very grateful to my friend Jackie Sumerfield, who very kindly allowed me to use her painting, *The Playground*, for the front cover. It conveys perfectly the connection between children and film.

Finally, I must thank my family for their understanding during the lengthy process of writing and editing this book, I couldn't have done it without you.

Foreword

Rachel Holmes

The overall ambition of this book is to illustrate how the university class-room can be and should be a critical space where film and theory together with practice can resist draining 'education of overt political content, recasting it as a predominantly technical exercise' (Fielding & Moss, 2012: 2). This edited book argues that academic tutors and students alike can use film with theory creatively so as to put a brake on and curb our taken-for-granted assumptions concerning a range of childhood issues, including attachment, knowledge, normalization, identity and participation.

The book argues that the university classroom, mindful of the political, economic, sociocultural and technological complexities that characterize mod-ern society, nevertheless should be a critically creative space for 'opening up' where ' there is always more than the actual world; there are also all the potential worlds we might see' (Colebrook, 2002: 6). In bringing the multiplici-tous and accessible worlds of popular culture together with theory to rethink issues related to childhood and practice, it is the editor's contention that to begin to contemplate these other 'potential worlds' we need theoretically informed and deeply thoughtful individuals. As such, we consider the univer-sity classroom a fertile space for a process that Fielding and Moss refer to as 'permanent provisionality' (2012: 18), where critical questions can be posed by students and tutors, resisting the rush to oversimplified understandings of issues young children face as they grow up 'in an increasingly ... bound-ary blurring, heterogeneous and ethically confronting world' (Taylor, Pacinini-Ketchabaw & Blaise, 2012: 81).

The contributors of this book are drawn from a range of university contexts, departments and research institutes, teaching in undergraduate and postgrad-uate vocational, professional and academic (early) childhood studies-related programmes. Using a different film as a stimulus in each of the chapters, the authors put film to work in the examination of HE teaching–learning pro-cesses. More specifically, they focus on the affordances of film narratives and images as they evoke postcolonial, sociocultural, psychoanalytic, feminist and other theories to, first, alert us to 'the plurality of reality' and secondly to 'the precarious nature of knowledge claims' in relation to such realities (McLaren, 2009: 2). Following Foucault, 'theory' in this text is understood as a driver where tutors and students together become *curious*, where curiosity insists on a journey that is characterized by a thoughtful toing and froing so that habitual, mechanistic and familiar ways of perceiving the world are opened up.

Following Deleuze and Guattari (1987) and Foucault (1972), it is through grappling with theory as part of the classroom assemblage that the (early) childhood studies students go on to develop mindsets that are sufficiently flexible so as to first recognize that the discursive structures in which they will be immersed are neither benign nor innocent and second to question where the spaces are so that something different could emerge. The crucial work of this book lies in its capacity to use film to evoke the university classroom as a place of tension, and a place of struggle where rather than solutions we offer forms of *uncertainty*. While 'uncertainty' carries dubious worth in a world that is seduced by 'certainties', the authors find this uncertainty 'empowering' because 'it gives a margin of manoeuvrability … It gives the feeling that there is always an opening to experiment, to try and see. This brings a sense of potential to the situation' (Massumi in Zournazi, 2002: 12).

Rachel Holmes
Manchester Metropolitan University, UK

References

Colebrook, C. (2002). *Gilles deleuze*. London: Routledge.

Deleuze, G. and Guattari, F. (1987). *A thousand plateaus: Capitalism and schizophrenia*. Brian Massumi (Trans.). Minneapolis: University of Minneapolis.

Fielding, M. and Moss, P. (2011). *Radical education and the common school: A democratic alternative (foundations and futures of education)*. London: Routledge.

Foucault, M. (1972). *The archaeology of knowledge and the discourse on language*. Routledge: London.

McLaren, H. (2009). Using 'Foucault's toolbox': The challenge with feminist post-structuralist discourse analysis.

Taylor, A., Pacinini-Ketchabaw, V. and Blaise, M. (2012). 'Children's relations to the more-than-human world.' *Contemporary Issues in Early Childhood*, 13 (2): 81–85.

Zournazi, M. (2002). 'Navigating movements: An interview with Brian Massumi'. In M. Zournazi (Ed.), *Hope: New philosophies for change*. Annadale, NSW: Pluto Press.

Contributors

Sue Aitken is Senior Lecturer in Childhood Studies at Manchester Metropolitan University, UK, and has had a successful career managing Early Years settings before becoming a lecturer. She gained her first degree in politics and sociology and later an MA in education with the Open University, UK. In addition to teaching, she has also worked as a consultant for Cheshire and Staffordshire local authorities helping to design better client-focused services and improved training for practitioners.

Jo Basford is Senior Lecturer at Manchester Metropolitan University, UK, in the School of Childhood, Youth and Education Studies. Jo's career began in primary education where she worked as a teacher and head of nursery. Before moving into higher education, she was a senior manager for a local authority early years' quality assurance team. Her research expertise is in the area of early childhood curriculum, pedagogy and professional identity, and her doctoral research investigated the interrelationship between professional habitus, assessment practice and the wider policy context.

Jackie Braithwaite is Senior Lecturer at Stockport College University Centre, UK. She teaches a range of courses and is the course leader for the Foundation Degree in Early Years. She has a masters in early education and her interests are effective pedagogy, in relation to observation and assessment in the early years. She has undertaken research using photo elicitation techniques as a reciprocal approach to assessment by enabling young children to contribute to their own Learning Journeys using digital photography. Prior to taking up her post at Stockport, she managed a successful preschool and taught at Macclesfield College of Further Education, UK.

Jim Dobson is Senior Lecturer in Early Years and Childhood Studies at Manchester Metropolitan University. Jim worked as a researcher in local authorities for a number of years, managing projects around tracking vulnerable children and youth offending. Jim's MA in Crime Law and Society led to his doctorate, looking at the impact of the imprisonment of a family member on children and families. Jim works as a volunteer for Home-Start, supporting families who are experiencing difficulties.

Nicky Hirst is Programme Leader for the undergraduate Early Childhood Studies programme at Liverpool John Moores University, Illinois. Nicky has previously worked in the Early Years sector and has spent the past ten years working and researching in higher education. Research interests include education for sustainability within Early Childhood Education and the application of theory and practice with community-based projects with children, practitioners and students. Nicky is also involved in research projects related to sustainable feedback practices with students in higher education.

Martin Needham is Associate Head of School for Childhood Youth and Education Studies at Manchester Metropolitan University, UK. He trained and worked as an early years and primary teacher in Nottinghamshire, London, and Pakistan. This was followed by development roles in education management and leadership in Pakistan and then with early education, extended schools' services and children's centre provision in England. A senior lecturer since 2003, he has frequently taught on multi-agency working in the early years at undergraduate and postgraduate levels. Martin has published work on multi-agency working, young children's learning, professionals engaging with parents and leadership in the early years and has conducted research projects in these areas funded by the DFE and NHS Scotland. He has recently been involved in early education policy contexts exploring early learning and workforce development in the UK and internationally.

Sarah Sharpe is Senior Advisor at the Open University, UK, and has spent the past eight years working in higher education, lecturing at both Manchester Metropolitan University, UK, and Staffordshire University, UK. Prior to this she worked in workforce development for Staffordshire local authority and for a number of years in further education in Lincolnshire and Nottinghamshire. Her research interests lie in student engagement and persistence, and in transitions in both early childhood and higher education.

Kurt Wicke studied social pedagogy at Freiburg, Germany. After migrating to Sweden, he added a master's in education and a teacher's qualification in German, Civics, Psychology and Social Sciences for upper secondary schools. After some of years teaching in upper secondary schools and adult education, in 2000, he was invited to teach at Gothenburg University, Sweden, and was transferred shortly thereafter to University West, Trollhättan, Sweden. Currently, he is teaching on the teachers training programme with citizenship education, intersectionality, ethnicity and identity as the main teaching areas. Citizenship education and textbook discourses are his primary research interests. He is currently studying for his doctorate.

Introduction

Sue Aitken

This book originated from my belief that engaging with complex and challenging issues within Childhood Studies could be usefully explored and better understood using the medium of filmed drama as a vehicle of both explanation and analysis. Throughout my teaching career I have used both film and images to initiate discussion and give substance to nebulous ideas that are sometimes difficult to grasp. This book is not, nor was it ever intended to be, a treatise on film technique or film theory. The dramas chosen are merely used as a useful conduit for discussion. The construction of children and childhood are notions which are typically embedded within Childhood Studies programmes. The authors of the chapters in this book have therefore carefully selected scenes that allow for discussions of the varying perspectives of these notions, and is a key theme that runs throughout the book.

The book was always intended to be aimed at a readership of undergraduates from levels 4 to 6, which is why the first and last chapters identify the reader as being at the beginning of their studies and then as a final year student who will go into practice. Consequently, the final chapter explores practice and theory drawing on previous chapters to illustrate that theory is and should be part of a compendium of skills and understandings that can inform and enhance the reader's abilities as a practitioner.

Working with children can encompass numerous contexts and cover many disciplines, not just preschool care and formal education but also within social services, health, the judiciary and law enforcement services. Graduates therefore need to engage with children and their families in situations that require both personal understanding and persistence. The aims of this book are therefore twofold: first, to provide a hook on which to hang multifaceted and sometimes contradictory ideas and theory and, second, to provide readers with a potential gateway to a paradigm shift which will allow students, practitioners and lecturers new ways of seeing, applying and understanding the lived lives of children and their experiences of childhood.

My intention was always that this book would serve not only as a core text within a unit of study on social issues and policy but also as a starting point for redefining a working relationship between theory and practice, effectively positioning and repositioning the student reader from apprentice to professional. Consequently, while covering a range of core principles that are embedded within the study of children and childhood, additionally the book covers engagement with learning at HE level and workplace issues and concepts that may occur after graduation. By using film drama to provide accessible and often familiar narratives, each chapter author has demonstrated how theoretical ideas and challenging concepts may be usefully applied to a range of contexts. Thus, theoretical explanations of attachment, identity, the social construction of children and families, political and biological narratives, children's rights and participation are moved from the abstract to the concrete. By utilizing popular culture, the aim is to expose a range of ideas to tangible situations often from more than one perspective. The book has been deliberately written to weave similar theories throughout the chapters in order to provide the reader with a sense of how a single theory may be used in differing ways and with differing interpretations.

Each chapter opens with a rationale for the choice of the film; providing a description of the film and its main story line. The theoretical ideas and the main authors that are discussed are signposted from the beginning. Within each chapter the reader is provided with short descriptors (and timings) of the scenes selected for analysis. Some of the films used in this book may be familiar to the reader, others not, and while it is not a prerequisite to know or to have the seen the film in question, some readers may be sufficiently intrigued to want to watch the whole film and to apply theory in their own way.

The chapters are organized into four sections.

- Becoming a graduate
- Early years and development
- Adolescence, perception and consequence
- Becoming a practitioner

Part One: Becoming a Graduate

Chapter 1: The Journey to Graduateness: Educating Rita

The chapter is based on the 1983 film, *Educating Rita*, and places the reader at the beginning of a learning journey that will establish the ongoing conflicts and dilemmas of undertaking study in higher education. It also establishes a parallel between the experiences of children in education and that of studying for a degree. As such it sets the 'stage' for subsequent chapters where common threads and key ideas, such as communities of practice, identity, habitus and cultural capital, reoccur and are discussed in a range of different contexts.

Part Two: Early Childhood and Child Development

Chapter 2: Using Bourdieu to Explore Identity and Assumption: Charlie and the Chocolate Factory

Through the use of Bourdieu's 'thinking tools', students are encouraged to consider notions of behaviour, habitus, power and social inequalities, and how these are reflected in and on social policy.

Students often struggle with ideas that surround the nature and impact of social position, social credit and their long-term effect on development and ultimate attainment. The choice of *Charlie and the Chocolate Factory* is in recognition of its familiarity both as a book and as a film and the ease with which it offers a clear interpretation of social and cultural understandings.

The chapter provides an interesting theoretical framework in which to examine notions of power, structure and agency from a social constructionist perspective. Such a framework allows students to challenge some of the dominant discourses apparent in social policy especially those related to disadvantage, social justice and inequality as depicted in the film. More importantly, it enables students to examine the relationship between attitudes, dispositions and behaviours of individuals and their position within the social field.

Chapter 3: State Paternalism, Postcolonial Theory and Curricula Content: Rabbit-Proof Fence

This chapter considers perceptions of freedom and choice, voice and participation, and the content and delivery of the Early Years Foundation Stage and The National Curriculum. It uses postcolonial theory and notions of assimilation to explore constructions of 'the other' and the marginalization of self-concept in the pursuit of a homogenized society.

Using the historic context of the film and its dominant ideas of race and culture (including language), this chapter explores the concept of state paternalism and social engineering. By using postcolonial theory, the chapter seeks to demonstrate how current dominant discourses can lead, often inadvertently, to discriminatory and oppressive practice. Additionally, it looks at the nature of personal freedom and personal choice and potentially, how current curricula models, while espousing uniqueness and individuality, contain assessment procedures based on a universal and age-determined matrix of skills and abilities.

Chapter 4: Attachment, Transitional Objects and Relationships: The Red Balloon

Sarah Sharpe uses both the oldest (1956) and the shortest film in this book (34 minutes). She skilfully manages to engage the reader with new ways of perceiving the familiar, while offering a deeper examination of often unchallenged theoretical ideas. Concepts such as attachment, transitional and object attachment, friendships and relationships, the role of imaginary friends and the key person are explored and understandings challenged. Using the film as a guide, elements of childhood that may be uncomfortable and far from idyllic are uncovered.

The chapter offers a broad view of attachment theory in contrast to the commonly presented two-dimensional mother–child relationship. Sarah argues that a host of diverse – often conflicting – factors affects the formation of strong bonds and friendships in early and later childhood. Indicating perhaps that there is no single way to understand the complex nature of attachment and relationships in the holistic development of children and that the formation of strong bonds and friendships are multifaceted in their complexity.

Chapter 5: Attachment, Personality and Deviant Behaviour: We Need to Talk about Kevin

In continuance of the previous chapter, this chapter uses the film *We Need to Talk about Kevin* to allow a discussion of attachment and psychological development, genetics and behaviour, socialization, criminality and morality, together with Durkheim's theory of anomie, in the context of a bleak and murderous narrative.

The film and this chapter provides further understanding of the continuing debate about nature versus nurture and, ultimately, the futility of seeing children in simple binaries. Instead, it is suggested that an appreciation of the complex interplay of social, environmental and biological factors is more helpful. While it offers no definite answers as to why children might behave uncharacteristically; seem disconnected from any form of socialization, and, in extreme cases (such as Kevin's), commit horrific acts, the chapter seeks to enhance and add to our understanding of why this might be.

High-profile media cases, notably that of the James Bulger murder in 1993 and the Newtown, Connecticut, shooting in 2012, connect with the film in as much as the debates they raise about criminality, socialization and the positioning of children in contemporary society. The chapter shows how such positioning is sociocultural, and in particular, how historical context offers an alternative window.

For readers, the chapter is a device which helps to make sense of potentially confusing, sometimes competing, explanations of childhood and child development. Although the content of the film is disturbing, offering as it does an extreme scenario, the ideas raised are transferable to those explored in the classroom. For lecturers, the film is a vehicle to help articulate and demonstrate how theory can be applied to contemporary scenarios.

Part Three: Adolescence, Perception and Consequence

Chapter 6: Future-Proofing Children and Families: Minority Report

This chapter takes a wide perspective of the theoretical and actual implications for children and childhood, in the use of legalized surveillance and power, labelling and self-fulfilling prophecies, stigma and identity.

The film *Minority Report* is based on the premise that the future might allow law enforcement officials to intervene and prevent crime from taking place and that the 'potential offender' can be punished for a criminal act they were going to (but did not) commit. It is hard to ignore the fact that there has been a social shift from a post- to a pre-crime discourse in which the possibility of prevention can take precedence over the response to wrongdoing. In the twenty-first century, this is no more evident than in the 'war against terror' where pre-emption and prevention form the basis of state policing and security. This chapter discusses ideas around early intervention in the lives of children and young people, and especially the rationale that preventing problems from escalating can be cost-effective. However, interactionist, social reaction and labelling perspectives highlight the possible counterproductive nature of early intervention in the youth justice arena where it often serves to intensify the very problems that it apparently seeks to resolve, where pre-emption may lead to both increased radicalization and criminalization.

Chapter 7: Questions of Identity: Harry Potter and the Philosopher's Stone

Kurt Wicke considers perceptions of identity in the film adaptation of Joanne K. Rowling's novel *Harry Potter and the Philosopher's Stone* and alludes to the underlying fear of the abnormal and the different. Thus, it is argued that notions of a true, or authentic identity, and successful migration from one group to another are complex and often misunderstood. Relating to the question: is identity a matter of *being* or rather a matter of *becoming?* The chapter unpacks this position to demonstrate its internal inconsistencies, thus enabling a repositioning of social identity as a constructed, contested and contingent open-ended process. The main objective is to show how and in what ways the narrative can be deconstructed and used as an illustration of transitions between different identities. As is evident from the film, these transitions are never painless, and potentially, any psychological trauma may originate not in the individual but in the reaction and treatment of children by others. Kurt usefully uses the position of migrants and the reaction of host communities, within an increasing global tide of nationalism, to explore and contrast today's experiences with those in Chapter 3.

Chapter 8: The Dystopian State and the Safeguarding of (Normalized) Childhoods: The Hunger Games

This chapter explores competing political perspectives such as neoconservatism, social democracy and liberalism in the context of the relationship between childhood and the state. By providing an accessible platform from which to discuss political philosophy, an area that some students find unfamiliar and consequently difficult, this chapter enables the current political environment to be explored and better understood. Intertwined is a discussion of identity, culture, wealth and power. Martin Needham uses the dystopian future depicted in the film to examine concepts of inequalities and injustices, culture, wealth and power. He offers a framework that invites readers to develop their own analysis of the social groups in and of the state. The second part of the chapter considers children's rights, challenging and provoking the reader to observe how injustice affects children in a range of contemporary contexts. The chapter draws attention to the need for practitioners to take responsibility for the protection of children in an adult world of violence. The final section of the chapter draws attention to a less visible political commentary, the critique of centralized state control, which romanticizes the individual and vilifies the power of state.

Chapter 9: Gender, Performativity and Society: Oranges Are Not the Only Fruit

The chapter explores wider issues of performative gender identity and orientation within notions of social concepts of normative and non-normative behaviour. It uses the three-part adaptation of Jeannette Winterson's novel, *Oranges Are Not the Only Fruit*, by the BBC in 1990. Sue Aitken uses the filmed narrative to track the historical, social and cultural shifts in the discourse surrounding the lesbian, gay, bisexual and transgendered (LGBT) community. The discussion, while tracking the important changes in legislation and policy, highlights the continuing difficulty for young people who identify themselves as non-heterosexual in a heterosexual-dominated environment. It identifies homophobia in education and social groups as a persistent and ongoing part of some young people's experiences. Thus the chapter explores discrimination and oppression in general using notions of sexual identity and social construction as its main vehicle.

Part Four: Becoming a Practitioner

Chapter 10: Becoming a Graduate: Using All the Tools in the Toolbox: Danny's Story

This chapter uniquely and deliberately does not use a specific film drama within its structure. Instead it takes each of the film narratives discussed earlier and, together with the dominate discourses and theory already analysed, deconstructs a realistic scenario (Danny's story). The chapter invites the reader to recognize that a single understanding of ideas, such as identity, attachment and notions of the state, can be inadequate and that theories need to be considered holistically and conjointly when used in practice. In so doing, it illustrates for the graduate practitioner how understandings need to be flexible and malleable to meet the changing needs of children and their families. Consequently, it asks all practitioners to shape and construct their own meanings of theory, in order that they can apply them in a variety and sometimes unexpected ways. It also highlights that practitioners need to understand and see ideas such as identity, attachment and social interactions as everyday occurrences, not just abstract theory.

PART ONE

Becoming a Graduate

1

The Journey to Graduateness: *Educating Rita*

Jackie Braithwaite and Nicky Hirst

This chapter will consider:

- Social and academic success when studying for a degree: Smale and Fowlie, (2011) and Briggs, Clark and Hall (2012).

- Communities of Speech and Self-Identity: Romaine (1994); Oyserman (2004).

- Motivation: Maslow's Hierarchy of Needs (1970).

- Self-efficacy and Self-regulation: Zimmerman (2000) and Dweck (2007).

- Community and Community of Learners: Smith (2001); Wenger, McDermott and Snyder (2002).

- Habitus and cultural capital: Bourdieu (1991) and Community of Practice: Wenger (1998).

- Feedback dialogues and learning to be reflective: Schon (1984); Bray, Lee, Smith and Yorks (2000) and Bolton (2010).

The film

Educating Rita is a dramatic comedy set in the 1980s and is based on a screen-play by Willy Russell. Rita, played by Julie Walters, has had very little schooling, and in her mid-twenties, she enrols in an Open University literature degree course, in order to 'become educated'. Although set in the 1980s, the film was selected because it resonates with contemporary learning in higher education. The social, political and cultural contexts portrayed in the film can easily be compared to the widening participation agenda within higher education, in terms of student experience, student outcomes and personal development. The journey that Rita takes is characterized by personal anxiety and moments of doubt related to her ability to fit in and to succeed. Selected scenes provide a platform to discuss the relationship between key theories and notions of social and academic success when studying at university. Importantly, the film illustrates the notion of personal resilience, as readers are signposted to significant points in Rita's journey to become a graduate, a journey that many students will recognize.

Rita works full-time as a hairdresser. Her husband (and everyone) expects her to start a family, but Rita is unhappy with this expectation; she wants to 'discover herself first'. In an early scene, it becomes apparent that Rita's real name is Susan, but she has changed it to match the name of a favourite author. As the film progresses she learns about herself as a person and she relinquishes this pretence. Rita has embarked on her degree because she believes that becoming educated will give her more opportunities in life, enabling her to 'sing a better song'.

Frank, Rita's personal tutor (Michael Caine), has grown weary of academia. Although reluctant at first to tutor Rita, he quickly finds her honesty, naivety and passion for her impending studies refreshing. The film follows their parallel journeys as Rita adapts to academic culture, develops confidence, re-visits her preconceptions around class and society while Frank regains his confidence in the value of what he has to offer. Rita/Susan's story is in essence a film about education, and how it affects lives and identity.

Using Rita's experiences, this chapter will explore the challenges and rewards for students as they endeavour to succeed both socially and academically when studying at university. As Briggs, Clark and Hall (2012) suggest, there may be many preconceptions about what being a university student actually is, and if there is a mismatch between aspiration and reality, then difficulties can occur, particularly in the first year. As Briggs et al. (2012:4) suggest, the transition to higher education 'involves learners creating for themselves a new identity as higher education students.' Notions of self-identity (Oyserman, 2004), communities of speech (Romaine, 1994), communities of practice (Smith, 2001) and a community of learners (Wenger, McDermott & Snyder, 2002) will be examined through the context of the film while using Bourdieu's (1991) concepts of habitus and social/cultural capital to explain how students may learn to 'fit in' as HE learners. Maslow's (1970) humanism theory will be used to explore student motivation and their evolution into reflective learners (Schon, 1984; Bolton, 2010; Brookfield, 2011).

Rita is studying with the Open University, which largely offers part-time courses often for 'mature' students. Additionally, admission to an Open University undergraduate programme is not dependent on prior academic success such as 'A' levels or level 3 vocational qualifications. While most students enter traditional universities at eighteen years, having successfully achieved the necessary grades for entry, Rita is atypical as she is twenty-six and has no formal qualifications. However, as Marr (2006) points out, the 'mature student' label is, of itself, a social construct encompassing a broad age range. Consequently, this chapter encourages reflection on the experiences of all students regardless of their age and/or academic qualifications. Thus, it begins at the beginning, first-day nerves, the challenges of beginning a degree course and the ultimate concern, that of being able to achieve a successful outcome.

Social and academic success when studying for a degree

Rita meets Frank for the first time (00:01:00–00:09:53)

The opening scene is set in an idealized academic world of green spaces and traditional brown stone buildings. University students are strolling around the campus; others are depicted as chatting nonchalantly in the grounds. Rita is clutching the written details of her appointment to meet her personal tutor, Frank. As she negotiates the paved path in her high heels, she looks around the campus trying to locate the building where Frank's room might be. Despite needing to ask for directions, Rita lacks the confidence to approach any of the students. Instead, she chooses to ask someone wearing a uniform, who looks like he is a non-academic staff member.

Once inside the building, Rita walks upstairs and looks daunted as a group of established and animated students pass her on the stairs. Not noticing her, they share banter about a lecture or class, one student commenting, 'he actually said what is assonance.' The other replying, 'really!'. Rita appears apprehensive, but she continues to Frank's room.

> Once in the room it does not take long before Rita asks Frank what asson-ance means. In his attempt to explain, he asks Rita whether she is familiar with Yeats (00:09:53), whereby she answers 'The Wine Lodge?' Frank continues to explain, giving her the example of stone and swan as rhyming words, to which Rita replies, 'so it means getting the rhyme wrong!' Frank replies that he sup-poses that it does, although he had never thought of it in that way.
>
> Before the end of the meeting, Rita asks Frank whether he thinks she will be able to learn.

This first scene depicts the start of Rita's journey and exposes her insecur-ities from the beginning. It represents how students can be plunged into a different cultural world with new language from the outset. The scene articu-lates a common experience for most new students who can feel daunted or insecure as they venture into the unknown and the unfamiliar. Smale and Fowlie (2011:10) describe this as a form of 'culture shock', suggesting that this is 'experienced when people are first exposed to a new and alien culture.' They conclude that 'it is generally true to say that the greater the difference between where you came from and where you are now, the more likely you are to feel the effects of culture shock.'

The fictional Rita lives and was probably born in Liverpool, a major city in the northwest of England, and comes from a working-class background. Abbott (2003) highlights that during the period of Thatcherism and the Conservative government from 1979 to 1990, unemployment in Liverpool was high, and jobs for school leavers were hard to find. In 1981, rioting lasted for several weeks in Liverpool and other industrial areas because, despite government interven-tion and investment in the city, unemployment remained high, and there was a continuing sense of declining opportunities (Benyon & Solomos, 1987). In this context, Rita's arrival on the campus would have provided her a clear sense of difference between her own background and the university campus, what Creme and Lea (2005) suggested could be compared to visiting a foreign coun-try. Similarly, Briggs et al. (2012:4) take the view that a move to university can be

> a significant social displacement, which may be intensified where the stu-dent is mature; is the first in their family to attend university, or is from an ethnic group under-represented in the university population.

Moreover, as students make the 'academic shift' to undergraduate study, regardless of whether they have or have not had recent academic experience of studying at school or college, studying at university level can still create 'academic culture shock' (Quinn et al., 2005, cited in Thomas, 2012:25).

Rita is worried from the start about not only gaining academic success, but also 'fitting in', which is a feeling likely to resonate with most students particularly as the interplay of social and academic success quite quickly begins. This feeling may also re-emerge as students make the transition into their second and third years of study. Burke and Jackson (2007), cited in Jackson (2012:111), note that 'there are complex ways in which people come to understand themselves' as 'learners' or 'non-learners'; however, as Jackson (2012) points out, learning is lifelong, and it incorporates cultural, social, personal and professional development.

Students can and do reflect upon their previous learning experiences and will bring notions of success and failure to university study. For instance, they may have achieved good marks in their previous educational life and may worry about sustaining that position in HE. Bourdieu's notion of habitus, which is further discussed in Chapter 2, can provide a useful analysis of the processes that influence how and why a person feels, behaves and thinks the way he or she does. Habitus is an unconscious identity, borne out of personal experience. Literally, derived from the Latin word *Habito*, it refers to where we psychologically dwell, live or inhabit (Di Giorgio, 2009). Depending on their individual habitus, students may feel different pressures to succeed, because they come from a family with a history of going to university or, conversely, they may be the first to enter HE. These insecurities are not limited to the beginning of the degree, they may reoccur during the transition to level 5 (year 2) and then to level 6 (year 3).

In addition to academic workload and intellectual challenge, pressure can also be felt to achieve socially. Students may have friendships, which may have held longevity throughout their schooling, and making new friendships may seem harder, particularly in the first year. Briggs et al. (2012) discuss Freshers' and induction weeks to point out that although students do value this time to meet people, alcohol-related events in Fresher's Week do not suit everyone. However, student union events can provide students an opportunity to discover their own personal niches through a wide range of familiar and unfamiliar activities. However, it is not unusual for students to feel 'like a fish out of water'; often a long way away from home and family, it is important therefore that students know where to seek, both academic and personal, support via campus-based counselling and advisory services.

As a consequence of high fees and rising living costs, Thomas (2012) suggests that more students may consider the option of living at home and may choose to combine part-time study with work or may choose to postpone HE study until later. Rita, as a mature student, was working full-time and therefore had to face the challenges of balancing part-time study with work and home life. Many contemporary full-time students also have had to work in order to meet their living costs and so face similar challenges in their attempt to balance a variety of competing commitments, having to prioritize demands on their time.

Creme and Lea (2005) note that students can adjust and they do settle into a different way of speaking, thinking and writing, accommodating new and different uses of words. In this early scene, Rita hears the other students use a word she has not encountered before ('he asked what assonance meant'); in her keenness to learn and to fit in, she asks Frank what 'assonance' means. The scene clearly illustrates a two-way teacher/learner dynamic as her response ('it means getting the rhyme wrong then') prompts Frank to consider alternative ways of looking at things. This shared dialogue is important, as within the context of education and indeed most other disciplines, dialogue is considered central to learning; indeed, 'much learning is an activity that occurs in and through dialogue' (Walsh 2002:15). Rita's openness to dialogue with Frank and Frank's capacity to learn from Rita is a key feature of the relationship portrayed in the film.

Communities of speech and self-identity

The meeting with Frank continues
(00:06:39–00:08:39)

Frank asks Rita why her initial is S on his paperwork if her name is Rita. Rita explains that her real name is Susan, but she is not a Susan anymore. She tells him that she has chosen Rita as it is the name of her favourite author whose book she has in her handbag. She deflects the conversation by asking Frank what people call him 'round here', and he replies, 'Sir, but you may call me Frank.'

As Frank continues to read her application, Rita notices a painting in his room, which she comments on, referring to it as 'erotic' because you can see her 'tits.' Frank does not respond, and Rita asks him whether he minds her using that word, Frank replies that he doesn't. Rita tells Frank that she uses 'shock language' particularly at work, to gain a reaction from people, which usually causes a fuss. She tells Frank that she is not surprised that he isn't shocked about bad language because 'educated people, they don't worry, do they ... it's the aristocracy that swear more than anyone'.

In an attempt to gain some understanding of Rita as a learner, Frank asks her why she wants to do a degree. She tells Frank that she has always felt 'slightly out of step' explaining that at twenty-six, it is expected that she should have a baby but she wants to discover herself first. She discloses to Frank that she does not have the support of her husband because he does not like her reading or doing anything that makes him feel she doesn't embrace the same interests as him and their friends.

The scene above highlights Rita's use of language and provides a glimpse of how she uses it as a mechanism to construct her self-identity. Oyserman (2004:5) states that '*self-concept* and *identity* provide answers to the basic questions "Who am I?", "Where do I belong?" and "How do I fit in?"' This scene shines a spotlight on Rita's insecurities; about her identity and concept of self in terms of her class, educational stance and gender role; and feelings that Rita seems to have been grappling with before joining her Open University course.

Rita's admits that she uses language as a shock tactic with those around her, implying that she is looking for social approval or perhaps disapproval as she tests people's responses. Romaine (1994:106) discusses communities of speech, these she describes as groups of people who share the 'same norms and rules for the use of language', which includes the types of language that is accepted and expected of gender. According to Romaine (1994:106), language is 'a human creation' and offering a feminist view of language she suggests that it is made '*by* men *for* men in order to represent their point of view and perpetuate it' (authors italics). By commenting that the aristocracy are always swearing and nobody minds, Rita demonstrates her awareness that while language use positions her in terms of gender, class and education, equally it can be disapplied to others.

It could be argued that Rita's decision to study is viewed by her husband and family as a rejection of her gender role and what is expected of her in terms of her cultural habitus (position) and what emerges through the film is a discomfort with her home social and cultural circle, their values and their expectations in life.

The following scene highlights the notion of widening participation and some of the dilemmas which can ensue from the changing of identities and new ways of thinking.

Rita's house (00:31:44–00:32:44)

Rita's husband is carrying out some building work in their home and finds Rita's contraceptive pills hidden under the floorboards. He angrily confronts Rita who is studying at the kitchen table. Rita calmly tells him, 'I don't want a baby. Not until I have discovered myself' (00:32:11). Her husband scoops up her books and heads to the back garden where a small fire is burning. A physical scuffle ensues as Rita tries to reclaim her books from her husband, but he continues to the back garden and puts her books onto the bonfire. Rita watches tearfully from the kitchen window as her books burn.

According to Abbott (2003:162), by the end of the 1980s (Rita's era), women had come to 'value themselves as much or more, for their achievements outside the home as in their traditional domestic sphere.' Abbott highlights that despite widening participation through Access Courses and part-time study, many women did not have the full support from their families for continuing studies. She uses the term 'sabotage' where partners intentionally disturbed study time or flushed work down the toilet. This powerful scene in Rita's home demonstrates this view explicitly. This scene highlights how, for many mature students, starting a degree can set in motion the first steps in the fracturing of the accepted habitus, sometimes introducing disharmony and dissatisfaction with their existing circumstances and relationships. Jackson (2004) cited in Jackson (2012:116) notes, 'empowerment whilst often exciting, can lead to changing identities and new ways of thinking can damage current relationships' and while Rita is highly engaged with her course and intent on achieving her personal goals, her husband is still intent on her having a baby. His rejection of her studies and personal goals culminates in a disturbing scene that finally leads to an ultimatum to choose between her study and their marriage (00:52:24). By this point in her journey, Rita sees personal fulfilment as having primacy over her marriage and her cultural anchors.

Motivation, self-regulation and self-efficacy

The following scene shows Rita, unconsciously, identifying with her clients; they want to look different and she wants to be different. It provides a useful stage from which to discuss student's motivation and student's mindsets when studying at university and makes links to children's learning in the Early Years Foundation Stage (EYFS).

Tutorial in Frank's office (00:10:40–00:10:56)

Frank asks Rita whether she is a good ladies hairdresser (00:10:40) and she replies that she is, but her clients expect too much from her, claiming that they want to walk out of the salon as a different person. Rita stresses 'but if you want to change you have to do it from the inside, like I'm trying to do'.

Armitage et al. (2007:65) state 'motivation is a key factor in learning and is linked very closely to attitude … [it is about] desire for participation in a learning process'. Motivation is often viewed as needs related (Crawley, 2005;

Armitage et al., 2007) and Maslow's (1970) Hierarchy of Needs is 'perhaps the most well-known theory of motivation' (Armitage et al., 2007:66). The five needs represent different levels of motivation, with the highest level labelled as self-actualization and the lowest labelled as physiological needs. Accordingly, when needs are satisfied at one level, progression can be made to the next. Many authors offer different perspectives on the value of this theory; for example, Crawley (2005) suggests that this is useful in helping tutors to understand their students as learners. A humanist perspective on adult education is usually interpreted as one that emphasizes respect for each adult learner's individuality and one that seeks to help the student to realize his or her potential to the fullest extent possible. However, Brookfield (2011:152) offers a more critical lens where he considers how 'many contemporary adult educators see humanism is a benign, friendly word associated with notions of self-actualisation or the fully functioning adult'. He asserts that there is less attention paid to the political underpinnings of adult education practice and to the way 'political economy makes self-actualisation a luxury for a certain social class' (2011:152). Reviewing the idea of self-actualization in this way helps to remind us that students come to university with disparate experiences and aspirations and, as noted earlier, for many students the need to work alongside studying can be a financial necessity. Rita enrols with the intention of becoming a different person and is still unsettled by the choices she faces; some students are less certain about change.

The reason(s) why students have enrolled on their degree will undoubtedly influence the level of motivation they begin and/or end up with. Motivation is often described as extrinsic or intrinsic. According to Entwistle (1998:16), extrinsic motivation is described as being 'strongly influenced by external rewards and pressures.' He suggests that this 'leads to a surface approach to learning' that is coupled with a fear of failing. Conversely, intrinsic motivation 'reflects a personal goal, derives from interest in the subject area and leads to a deep approach and conceptual understanding' (1998:16). Brown, Armstrong and Thompson (1998) suggest that there seems to be the assumption that somehow intrinsic motivation is superior, arguing that motivation is a personal construct because what is intrinsic for one person may be extrinsic for another. However, is motivation a simple either/or? Perhaps motivation should be seen as an amalgam of internal and external influences, while extended academic study may reflect internal interests, without the promise of future reward, few would be able, or want to commit to the personal and financial demands of a degree. As in the scene earlier, Rita recognizes the value of internal motivation in affecting change and while she tells Frank she is a good hairdresser, she is no longer satisfied with her life and wants more.

In order to understand the learning experiences of children, students need to reflect upon their own learning journey. Students, through their own employment or placement, may notice how behaviourist incentives and sanctions are often used in everyday practice to motivate children and young people. Examples may include the use of stickers, reward charts, or golden time, all of which are used as extrinsic rewards. However, the value of supporting children's intrinsic motivation is a key feature of the early years' framework. The Early Years Foundation Stage (DfE, 2014b), with its discourse around the Characteristics of Effective Learning, highlights *how* children learn, rather than *what* children learn. This principle also relates to learning in higher education, where emphasis is on the development of the self, as the architect of personal learning and not just the delivery of the curriculum. Within this notion of self-motivation is the concept of self-regulation. Zimmerman (2000) suggests that within the concept of self-regulation lie several components, including self-efficacy, metacognition, emotion and, most significantly, motivation, but it is important to note that none of these components acts discretely. Thus, motivation often helps students to commit to a degree course and the juxtaposition of motivation and self-belief in one's ability, often referred to as 'self-efficacy', also reflects confidence in the ability to exert control over one's own motivation, behaviour, and social environment (Zimmerman, Bandura, & Martinez-Pons, 1992). While Dweck's (2007) research was primarily with children, her research, around mindsets or learning dispositions, considers how learners can have a fixed or growth mindset, which can be just as useful when applied to motivation in higher education. In a fixed mindset, learners believe that basic qualities, such as intelligence, are simply fixed traits. According to Dweck (2007), learners with this mindset spend their time simply documenting their intelligence or talent rather than developing them. In a growth mindset, learners believe that their abilities can be developed through an evolutionary process. Dweck (2007) asserts that this mindset facilitates a love of learning and a resilience that is essential for success. Importantly, as Thomas, Jones and Ottaway (2015) point out, students need support to study in *different* ways as opposed to simply studying *harder.*

Community and community of learners

Frank's office Rita's tutorials (00:17:57–00:18:00 and 01:09:48–01:10:30)

Rita has arrived at Frank's office to discuss her first essay. She walks into the room and goes to the window. She tells Frank she likes looking through the window at the 'proper students' on the lawn.

One year later Rita is walking to Frank's office to discuss another piece of writing. She passes a group of students sitting on the same lawn that she has admired through Frank's window a year earlier. The students call her over and ask her to 'settle a literary argument.' With newfound confidence, Rita (now called Susan) joins them and engages in discussion.

Rita breezes into Frank's office for feedback on her latest essay apologising for being late but explains that she had been talking to students outside on the grass. Franks reminds her that she used to be 'so wary' of talking to other students. Rita tells Frank that the students have invited her to the south of France for a summer school after her final exam.

These two contrasting scenes provide a useful example of the notion of a community of learners and draw attention to the importance of students recognizing the process of becoming a graduate. They illustrate Rita's journey from being an outsider looking in, to being seen, and seeing herself as a member of the student community. According to Wenger, McDermott and Snyder (2002:31), 'whatever creates [a] common ground, the domain of a community is its *raison d'être*'. They suggest that 'the identity of the community depends in good part on the importance of its domain in the world, which in turn makes the domain important to the members' (2002:31). Smith (2001) notes three different ways a community can be described: place, interest and communion. Therefore, in terms of this discussion, a university can be considered as 'place', an even smaller community could be Student Halls. Community members (students) have something in common with each other. 'Interest' is concerned with a shared characteristic for example being away from home, studying the same course, whereas 'communion' is the 'spirit of the community' and in the HE context this includes motivation, supporting and sharing. However, as Smith points out, members, in this case students, have to interact with others who share the commonality. He notes that we are social animals who interact and make connections with others, which 'both widen[s] and deepen[s] what we can achieve' (2001:8). It also generates a sense of belonging.

When Rita looks out of the window at the 'proper students' she demonstrates her sense of ambiguity in terms of her role as a student because she places herself outside that community. Yet during a later tutorial when Rita has been studying for a year, she is recognized by others as a member of 'their' community when they call her over to settle their 'literary argument.' Rita subsequently views herself as an integral part of that community as she accepts their invitation and sits down with them on the lawn assuming the mantle of 'a proper student'. Her acceptance into the community of learners is again demonstrated when she is invited to France in the summer after her final exam. As her confidence grew, her barriers to learning came down. This once more illustrates that students should recognize the process and the journey to graduateness, rather than concentrate merely on the student journey.

Habitus and cultural capital

The dinner party (00:40:30–00:44:41)

Frank has invited Rita and her husband to his home for a dinner party. We see Rita trying on different outfits and 'performing' what she perceives to be different cultural roles appropriate for a dinner party. Finally, dispensing with trying to find the right persona, she wears her jeans. Her attempts to encourage her husband to join her are futile as he is adamant that he won't go, preferring to meet the family in the pub and making it clear that he feels that's where Rita's 'place' should be. On arrival at Frank's house, she can see a clear view of Frank and his guests through the window. However, she does not have the courage to go inside, instead she leaves a note on his car windscreen apologizing and joins her family in the pub.

Frank's office (00:45:05–00:49:05)

When Rita next meets Frank, she attempts to explain why she did not go to his dinner party using the reasons of bringing the right type of wine and worrying about what to wear. While Frank wants her to be herself, Rita wants to be taken seriously and wants to be 'like the rest of you', she wants to migrate to his community of practice. She informs Frank that she doesn't belong anywhere as she can't talk to her family anymore or Frank's guests.

Rita recounts the scene in the pub where the whole family, including herself, sang along with the jukebox. During the singing, Rita noticed that her mother was crying. She asked her what was wrong and her mother replied 'there must be better songs to sing than this'. Rita turns to Frank and says, 'well that's what I'm trying to do, sing a better song'.

As the above scene identifies, Rita has become aware that her current community of practice, her family, can no longer meet her aspirations. Wilson and Pickett (2010) point out that family background affects educational attainment both in school and later when studying in higher education. They suggest that if parents have higher incomes, are university educated and have homes that reflect a knowledge-based environment, it is subliminally presenting a culture where education is valued. Thus, all students bring with them, or have banked on, an amount of social and cultural capital. In terms of the dinner party scene, Rita believes she has little cultural capital, as she feels that others at Frank's party, who she sees as sharing the same cultural understandings, will have known which wine to bring and understood the dress code.

Cultural capital is a term Bourdieu (1991) used in order to explain how knowledge is used and exploited, this he believed was generated from a person's habitus, as discussed earlier; ways of behaving and ways of knowing; ways of seeing the world, all learned and absorbed from family and cultural surroundings. Language itself is one such tool and can initially be alienating and frightening (Brookfield, 2011), but adaptability in language is also the passport to membership of a range of Communities of Practice (Wenger, 1998). Rita writes to Frank from summer school to proudly inform him that she has stood up in a lecture theatre and phrased a question to the professor asking him, 'Do you think Chekhov was showing the aristocracy as a decaying class?' (00.59:42), and that she subsequently engaged in the debate. Rita's letter clearly alludes to her membership of the academic community of practice demonstrating as it does her linguistic shift from a hairdresser to a motivated student. However, while Rita's linguistic journey takes her nearer to the other students and academic engagement, its trajectory continues to take her further away from her family.

Bray, Lee, Smith and Yorks (2000:85) discuss the centrality of questioning to participation in a learning culture and that by not seeking 'definitive closure' or answers, members 'pursue new paths and seek new perspectives'. The central remit of education in HE is to expand the world of the student, creating an opening up and not a closing down of perception and experience.

The following scene depicts this notion as Rita discovers, through dialogue, new ways of 'seeing'.

Frank's classroom (00:38:54–00:40:00)

Frank has invited Rita into one of his literary classes where he begins to compare the 'tragedy of the drama' with 'the merely tragic', comparing this notion using Shakespeare's *Macbeth* and a newspaper article. The students begin to engage in debate, and when Rita leaves the class, she is motivated by this collaborative learning experience. She tells Frank enthusiastically that she wishes she could see things like 'they do' because she had only seen Macbeth 'as exciting', she had not noticed the other points that students in Frank's class had made.

For students who are making the transition to HE, dialogue allows for a co-construction of meaning, which, it could be argued, is central to the acquisition of new and important knowledge. Students often comment that the language associated with HE and their specific subject discipline can be both complex and too often de-contextualized. However, both formal and informal dialogue can permit an exploration of language within a safe environment with members of an emerging and increasingly cohesive community of practice (Wenger, 1998). The scene described earlier shows that Rita found new depth and meaning in Macbeth and was motivated by this experience. Through exploring ideas with her peers, Rita's academic thinking is developing, from merely finding the play 'exciting' to a position where alternative and challenging ideas can exit.

The content of any degree programme demands the ability to question and acknowledge different theoretical and ideological perspectives, therefore while acknowledging what a powerful catalyst social interaction can be in the development of cognitive processes, Oates and Grayson (2004) warn of the 'risk of supporting a form of ethnocentrism'. This term is an interesting one as it refers to the idea that an ethnocentric approach – when a person looks at and evaluates the experience of others against their own experience – is potentially dangerous as it has the 'the tendency to view one's own culture as best and to judge the behaviour and beliefs of culturally different people by one's own standards' (Kottak, 1994: 48). For a more detailed discussion of cultural and ethnic dominance see Chapter 3. Frank is concerned that study will compromise Rita's originality and make her conform to standardized ideas. Rita's ability to change but retain herself helps to renew Frank's faith in humanity and himself.

Feedback dialogues and reflective practice

The following scene is used as to facilitate a discussion of the importance of feedback and how students must take responsibility for their learning. It also explores the importance of reflexivity.

Frank's office (00:18:00–00:20:00)

Rita is receiving her first piece of feedback from her first piece of writing. Frank has asked her why she has based her essay on E. M. Forster using mostly Harold Robbins (a bestselling fiction author of 1980s). Rita looks puzzled and explains she did this because she was asked to bring in the works of other authors. When Frank says it would fail an exam, she defends her essay, insisting she is well read. Frank informs her that she must be selective in what she reads and what she references in her work and also she must not write in a subjective or sentimental way.

Feedback is associated with the disruption of existing knowledge, and perhaps this is an emotional and challenging concept. Feedback, both formative and summative, can also provide many formative learning opportunities, for instance, during class discussions, group work and tutorials and assignment feedback. Consequently, students are encouraged to take ownership and responsibility for their learning, to self-regulate but just as importantly recognize feedback as a part of the process of learning, not merely a product. Students are encouraged to focus on the journey to graduateness, not merely the destination. Feedback comes in many guises but perhaps the most recognizable method is feedback in the written form following submission of a summative (or final) assessment. In higher education, this feedback often marks the final stage of a segment of learning. It may be the culmination of several formative feedback opportunities to help students to move forward, to 'be' a learner (Molesworth, Nixon and Scullion, 2009) and to develop and improve their work. Many courses anticipate formal and informal dialogues between students and tutors during the course and it is seen as an important mechanism within the feedback process, but its success relies on both parties being ready and able to engage with each other in honest and productive discussions.

The earlier scene shows Rita engaging in her first feedback dialogue with Frank, where she is struggling to understand 'the rules of the game'. In her written work she has referenced books from popular culture; however, Frank tells her she must be selective in what she reads, suggesting that future essays must provide well-balanced arguments and be devoid of emotional language and subjectivity. In Rita's case, she has based her essay on texts she knows and is familiar with. This links with the notion of intertextuality which explores how we base meaning(s) and personal interpretation on ideas and experiences that we have already engaged with, making connections (consciously and subconsciously) to other texts (written or visual) and community experiences (Lemke, 1997, cited in Daniels, 2006). Therefore, there is an expectation that HE studies move beyond personal experiences and previous learning as without reflection it may foster assumption and limit engagement with alternative ideas. Instead, students must learn to question ideas, aided by wider reading, in order that presumptions and dominant discourses may be challenged and rebuked.

Reflection is a state of mind, an ongoing constituent of practice, not a technique, or curriculum element. Rather, reflective practice can enable practitioners to 'learn from experience about themselves, their work, and the way they relate to home and work, significant others and wider society and culture' (Bolton, 2010:3). Reflective thinking is not an add-on to any degree however, where graduates will be advocates for children and their families; it is an essential element. As stated in the QAA's benchmarking document for Early Childhood Studies degrees, all graduates should possess 'a highly developed ability to produce critical arguments for improvements to multi-agency, multiprofessional and interprofessional practices for babies and young children' (QAA, 2014:18).

Thus, critical reflection requires not only a reflective exploration of personal subjectivities but also to acknowledge the discourses that may have dominated personal understandings in the pre-university world. As courses progress, students with practical experiences will reflect 'in action' (Schon, 1984), but often it is the conversations, discussions and interactions that form part of group inquiry that produce the criticality that helps to disrupt one's own 'knowledge'. Indeed, as Bray et al. (2000) assert, 'action inquiry methods celebrate a basic truism about much human learning – that it is a social activity'. Students may have strong beliefs about the way to do something, for example, many practitioners working with young children 'know' what the Early Years Framework states. They may be able to cite the rhetoric around 'learning through play', but the realities of a playful pedagogy are often intercepted by the need to evidence learning and 'readiness for school'. Students who grapple with the complexities of a childhood studies–related degree find that the journey towards critical reflection is, simultaneously, liberating and frightening. Bolton (2010:21) notes that reflexivity is about reviewing oneself through another lens, 'focusing close attention upon one's own actions, thoughts, feelings, values, identity, and their effect upon others, situations, and professional and social structures'. In practice, the reflexive thinker has to stand back and review themselves and their work and, in so doing, construct mechanisms of change and avenues of improvement.

Conclusion

Educating Rita is a film about change and transformation, but it is a fictional story. What this chapter has attempted to show is how lives change through studying for a degree. As noted early in this chapter, learning is lifelong, and *Educating Rita* shows Rita's personal and academic growth. It is hoped that through the discussion of her journey, it has become clear that personal growth at university is not necessarily concerned with just grades, but the events that led up to them.

From the beginning, Rita showed that she was able to challenge ideas both in the dialogue that she shared with Frank and in her early written work. In the beginning these ideas were raw and undisciplined; however, over time, Rita managed to adopt a more articulate and disciplined approach, to express her ideas both linguistically and in written form in an academic manner. She quickly became hungry to learn more and to 'see' using different perspectives, which meant that there was no going back to her life before university. Indeed, tutors often consider that entry to university is a one-way valve, with no way back.

Rita began her journey seeking support from Frank and expecting him to teach her. However, she soon learnt that his role was not to 'teach.' Instead, his role was to provide her with the tools to teach herself by building her self-confidence and helping her to recognize her abilities as a student and eventual graduate.

However, as *Educating Rita* demonstrates, the road to graduateness is rarely simple or linear. Rita came across adversity in many guises. On an emotional level, she lacked support from her husband and she worried about her social class and not fitting in or belonging anywhere other than in her traditional habitus. She felt academically 'othered' at university – unable to see herself or feel like 'a proper student.' But over time, Rita begins to review and view herself as a learner and as a 'proper student' managing to propel herself forward to achieve success, partly because she was a resilient person but mostly because she was intrinsically motivated to learn. Early in her studies, Rita challenged herself 'to sing a better song' (00:49:05), a vision that lends her resilience and motivation; what raises the story up is that this vision leads her back to Susan.

With regard to the discussions in this chapter you may wish to reflect upon your own responses to the following questions:

- What do you hope to achieve during your time at university?

- On reading this chapter, is there anything in Rita's story that resonates with you?

- Can you identify any areas for personal and professional development?

- Can you define a growth mindset to others?

PART TWO

Early Childhood and Child Development

2

Using Bourdieu to Explore Identity and Assumption: *Charlie and the Chocolate Factory*

Jo Basford

This chapter will consider perceptions of:

- Power, structure and agency: Bourdieu (1986, 2010), Wacquant (1989).

- Social status and its relationship with parenting: Gillies (2005), Hartas (2014), Lareau (2003).

- Poverty, educational achievement and life chances: Henderson (2012), Reay (2000).

The film

Roald Dahl's book *Charlie and the Chocolate Factory* has been adapted in film twice in the past forty years, first in 1971 and then in 2005. The screenplay of the 2005 adaptation of the film is more accurately aligned with Dahl's book. Therefore, for the purpose of this chapter the scenes referred to are based on this version of the story. Put simply, the storyline of this book could be explained as an account of how different players in a game (or to be more precise, a competition) drew on the resources that they had at hand to position themselves advantageously to win an ultimate prize. This notion of game playing is a term that Bourdieu used to illustrate notions of social positioning and its reproducing effects. The film therefore provides a novel context in which to explore and understand how his conceptual ideas can be applied to practice based on social advantage and disadvantage.

The film provides a cautionary tale of capitalist greed and consumerism for both children and their families. The five children in the story are the lucky winners of a 'Golden Ticket' who have gained unprecedented access into Willy Wonka's Chocolate Factory for just one day. The secret recipes of Wonka's chocolate bars and candy have long been the subject of speculation and interest throughout the world, since for many years there have been no known human beings working in the factory. The desire, therefore, to win a Golden Ticket that allows for entry into the factory to discover the secrets of Wonka's world of chocolate, as well as the temptation of a special prize for one lucky winner, is a phenomenon that captures the interest of the world.

The opening scenes of the film introduce the five lucky ticket winners and provide an initial insight into their lifestyles and personalities. The first four characters (Augustus Gloop, Veruca Salt, Violet Beauregard, Mike Teavee) are all children who have some form of advantage in society due to either their economic or their knowledge and skills-based capital that is embodied by their family circumstances. This is in stark contrast to the final winner of the Golden Ticket: Charlie Bucket. He is the son of a toothpaste factory worker living with his parents and four grandparents in a small, dilapidated house. As the day of the grand opening and entrance into the factory arrives, the characters and their family members meet each other for the first time. It becomes clear to all of the children that they are competing against each other, and (other than Charlie) they are intent on using whatever strategies they have at hand to win the coveted prize. However, on entering Wonka's world of chocolate and candy, the children find themselves unable to resist the temptations that the factory offers (Honeyman, 2007), and one by one the children suffer the consequences of their own embodied greed and self-importance. Charlie is the only remaining child at the end of the day and receives the ultimate prize of becoming the owner of Willy Wonka's Chocolate Factory.

Bourdieu: Power, structure and agency

This chapter draws on Bourdieu's 'thinking tools' (Wacquant, 1989) of habitus/practice and capital/social fields to help interpret notions of consumption, assumption and identity. They provide both an interesting and useful theoretical framework in which to examine ideas related to power, structure and agency from a social constructionist perspective. Bourdieu was very clear that there was an interrelationship between his conceptual tools, and that they should not be viewed in isolation. In his text *Distinction* (2010:95), he provides a formula to illustrate their interrelationship:

[(habitus) (capital)] + field = practice.

Bourdieu referred to the world as a field or 'site of an ongoing struggle to tell the truth of this world' (Wacquant, 1989:35). He used a game analogy, in which he argued that in order to provide a sociological understanding and explanation of social practices, it is necessary to expose the 'very logic of the field's functioning' (Vuorisalo and Alanen, 2015:80). The world that Dahl presents is based on Westernized society with all of the neo-liberal traits in which it is constituted (see Chapters 3 and 8 for further explanations of this term). Under the conditions of globalization, there is an increased move towards individualism in which people are required to actively construct their own identities (Giddens, 2006:68) to be successful players. In the context of this film, we can view the field as the social world in which the characters exist, and explore how the characters' capital and associated habitus places them in a position of either advantage or disadvantage in the Chocolate Factory Game. Bourdieu's framework allows students to challenge some of the dominant discourses apparent in social policy related to disadvantage, social justice and inequality that are depicted in the film. More importantly, it enables students to examine the relationship between attitudes, dispositions and behaviours of individuals and their position within the social field. This chapter will explore notions of identity, consumption and assumption by utilizing Bourdieu's conceptual tools to form the basis of three key themes as a foundation for exploration. The themes are concerned with parenting, poverty and game playing; and the discussion will be intersected with a critical consideration of how reading social policy through a social constructionist perspective can situate different social groups in positions of both power and disadvantage.

Social status and parenting

The five Golden Ticket winners (00:16:03–00:26:29).

The world's media are following the stories of the lucky Golden Ticket winners. One by one, each of the winners is revealed. The children and their parents give interviews as to how they came to win their ticket. Charlie's family watches each story with interest, commenting on the moral integrity of the children and their parents. The first winner, Augustus Gloop, is the son of a butcher. The family's physical appearance is suggestive of an excessive and indulgent diet. His mother proudly explains that 'he eats so many candy bars a day, that it was not possible for him **not** to find one.' The second winner, Veruca Salt, is pictured with her parents in their stately home. Her father acknowledged how he 'just hated to see my little girl feeling unhappy … so I vowed I would not give up the search until I could give her what she wanted.' Not satisfied with the coveted Golden Ticket, Veruca quickly moves on to her next demand for another pony to add to her already excessive collection of pets. Charlie watched the TV coverage, noting how it 'wasn't really fair, as she hadn't found the ticket herself'. Violet Beauregard and Mike Teavee are the third and fourth winners of the tickets. Violet, a junior world champion gum chewer, had shifted her attention from chewing gum to eating chocolate bars in the quest to get her hands on a winning ticket. The fourth winner, Mike Teavee, is the son of a geography teacher. During the interview, he spends the entire time aggressively playing a video game. He explains that he devised a mathematical formula to determine the time and place of distribution of the winning chocolate bar that he needed to purchase which, by his own admission; he hates. By the end of the scene, the final ticket holder has been announced. Unbeknown to Charlie, it was a fraudulent claim. Following a chance discovery of a ten-dollar bill on the pavement, Charlie decides to purchase a single Wonka Chocolate bar, before returning home with the rest of the money for his family. To his surprise – as he opens his 'Wonka Whipple-Scrumptious Fudgemallow Delight' – he reveals the final, genuine Golden Ticket.

Bourdieu (1998) referred to habitus as having a 'feel for the game'. This analogy fits well with the overall theme of the film. By looking more closely at how the children were socialized by their parents, Bourdieu's ideas help to provide an explanation as to how the strategies the children brought to the Chocolate Factory competition were influenced by their family's parenting habitus. Habitus can be defined as a collection of dispositions that allow individuals, or groups of agents, to engage with and make meaningful contributions to practice (Rawolle and Lingard, 2013:123). Such dispositions are situated in individual and collective histories that are representative of a person's social and economic status, or using Bourdieu's terms, their cultural and economic capital. Through the act of socialization, dispositions become internalized and they create broad parameters and boundaries of what is possible or unlikely for a particular group in a stratified social world. Therefore, habitus sets structural limits to what is possible for a particular social group and it generates perceptions, aspirations and practices that correspond to the structuring properties of earlier socialization (Swartz, 1997:103). From this perspective, parents can be understood to play a significant role in generating perceptions, aspirations and practices that fit with the social group in which the family belongs. The aforementioned scene serves as a useful starting point to begin to explore the relationship between habitus and capital, and how this creates a particular 'taste' in parenting styles.

There is a growing field of research related to how specific parental models of behaviours and attitudes that are used to influence children tend to fit with parents' own beliefs and interpretations of social norms (Rhee, 2008; Gillies, 2005). Bourdieu would define this as having a particular 'taste' or manifested preference (Bourdieu, 2010:49) that forms part of a parenting habitus. Yet, Bourdieu (2010) was quite clear that habitus functions below the level of consciousness. This is an interesting contention when we examine the consequences of what could be argued as unconscious parenting as the story unfolds.

Looking particularly at the types of parenting practices observed by the characters in the film provides a helpful context in which to apply Bourdieu's conceptual ideas. Our first encounters with Augustus and Veruca portray them as children who have been indulged by their parents. Their parents have utilized their economic and cultural capital as strategies to give their children an advantage in the competition. Sweet treats and material possessions form part of the habitus for those who have economic capital. For Augustus, eating chocolate was an everyday occurrence, and Veruca was seen readily making demands regarding the purchase of her next pet or other material possession. Despite his ability to distinguish different flavours, Augustus showed little interest or pleasure in the sensitized aspects of eating chocolate. He had no regard for the qualities of the chocolate, which, we could assume, were as a result of the sheer quantities he consumed on a daily basis. Likewise, Veruca had no regard for the value of material possessions. Her adoption of the role of 'Daddy's little girl' enabled her to demand a new pet whenever she wanted. For both of these children, the possession of cultural capital is a form of 'cultural signalling' (Henderson, 2012) that provides them with an increased likelihood of gaining a Golden Ticket. Indeed, this was acknowledged by one of Charlie's grandparents, who noted 'the kids who are going to find the golden tickets are the ones who can afford to buy candy bars every day' [15.49]. This form of tacit acceptance of the Bucket family's disadvantage in the social field is what Bourdieu referred to as 'doxa'. Such comments were gentle reminders to Charlie that winning a Golden Ticket was always going to be out of his reach. Yet, as addressed later in this chapter, such indulgent strategies were not necessarily the appropriate ones to win the ultimate prize.

In an American study by Lareau (2003), she argued that middle- and working-class families follow different 'cultural logics' of parenting (Irwin and Elley, 2011), resulting in two contrasting parenting typologies. These typologies have since been used by other commentators in the field (see. e.g. Hartas,

2014; Henderson, 2012; Gillies, 2005). The practices associated with the differ-ent typologies are referred to as 'concerted cultivation' and 'accomplishment of natural growth'. The term 'concerted cultivation' is used to describe typi-cally middle-class parental practices where parents on the one hand invest in services and resources that are intended to accumulate intellectual and social capital for their children's social advancement. Parents of working-class fami-lies on the other hand tend to adopt a 'natural growth' approach where there is much less parental involvement in children's daily social life, recreational activities and talk.

The middle-class parents in Lareau's (2003) study were seen to be typically proactive and were willing and able to 'play with the rules' as and when required (Hartas, 2014:55). Similarly, Gillies's UK study (2005) also revealed how parents with access to 'middle-class resources', such as money and legitimated cultural knowledge, were able to draw on these in order to consolidate their power and advantage. In relation to Augustus and Veruca, their parent's concerted use of capital to purchase large quantities of chocolate bars was seen as a worthy and worthwhile investment, as it enabled them to bend the rules of the game to their advantage. Concerted cultivation behaviours can also be found to manifest themselves in how parents actively teach their children to assert themselves to adults in authority (Henderson, 2012). This was a strategy that many of the children used when they were visiting the factory. It will be explored further in the section related to Game Playing, but for now, we can examine this in the context of assertion when we look particularly at Violet's parenting.

Violet Beauregard (00:21:20–00:22:38).

In Violet's first TV appearance, she is filmed alongside her mother – wear-ing matching tracksuits. In the background are display cabinets that host her medals and trophies for numerous sporting and gum chewing achieve-ments. Her mother is keen to reveal her own sporting achievements for 'the baton', which serves as a subtle hint of her parental influence on Violet's suc-cess ... 'she's such a driven young woman. I don't know where she gets it.' As the scene concludes, Violet's mother encourages her to tell the audience why she is going to win the prize. Staring determinedly into the camera, she proclaims,'I'm the winner.'

Violet and her mother's matching 'taste' in dress code are symbolic of a particular lifestyle choice that was representative of their social positioning and their dispositions towards competitive sporting activities. The awards and trophies formed part of their symbolic capital that were recognizable and tangible signifiers of their success in the competitive sporting field. Violet's mother's active encouragement and role modelling provide examples of her concerted parenting role. It seems at this point that Violet's own successes in her social field had given her specific strategies that she expected to utilize in the remainder of the competition. Violet had effectively been empowered through gaining a competitive and self-affirming disposition that had become embodied as a result of her mother's parenting strategies.

Mike Teavee had an equally self-affirming and confident disposition, but unlike the other children, it was not as a result of his parents adopting concerted cultivation parenting strategies. Bourdieu would argue that cultural capital is primarily transmitted through the family and that children typically derive modes of thinking, types of dispositions, sets of meaning and qualities of style from their parents (Reay, 2000:570). However, this explanation does not necessarily fit for Mike. His father's occupation may serve as a useful starting point for unpicking this tension. Mike's father is a Geography teacher. He possessed cultural capital in relation to qualifications and subject knowledge within his field (and this did not include digital literacy capital). Yet this form of capital does not hold the same value or status as the economic capital that was possessed by the parents of Augustus and Veruca. It seems, as well, that Mike did not value his father's modes of thinking, qualities and styles either – their 'tastes' were effectively incompatible. Mike's life revolved around computer technology, and this had allowed him to gain additional capital in the form of knowledge about the world that was alien to his parents. His father acknowledged: 'Most of time I don't know what he's talking about ... Kids these days, what with all the technology ... doesn't seem like they stay kids for very long.' Dr. Tanya Byron, in her report Safer children in a digital world (2008), outlined the increasing 'generational digital divide' where parents do not necessarily feel equipped to engage with children in this space, resulting in fear and sense of helplessness and this is discussed in more detail in Chapter 6 of this book. Byron's research findings seem applicable for the Teavee family. Technology was a feature of Mike's life that gave him agency, where he could feel powerful in an environment where children often have little power or control (Kehily, 2003). Technology, and the information derived from it, was a resource that Mike was using to define himself. The knowledge that would typically be imparted by parents had been replaced by knowledge from an alternative source that his parents were unable to arbitrate. Consequently, his parents found themselves relinquishing the traditional parental role of carer and rule enforcer, and instead adopted a submissive parenting role, where the power now sat with Mike.

Shifting the focus towards Charlie Bucket and his family allows us to consider Lareau's (2003) claims that parents in working-class families tend to work towards an accomplishment of children's 'natural growth'. In her study,

Lareau (2003) found that due to their lack of financial resources and cultural preferences (or economic and symbolic capital from a Bourdieuan perspective), working-class families were less likely to pursue organized leisure and cultural activities for their children. Indeed, for Charlie, it seems that much of his time was spent within the confines of his own home engaging in activities that were of minimal financial cost to the family. Charlie's parents were all too aware of how their lack of economic capital was a structural constraint that would maintain his position in the field. Their concern was therefore synonymous with the working-class families in Gillies's study (2005:842), who, in order to preserve their limited stock of capital, would actively inculcate their children with the necessary 'survival skills' that would help to emotionally and practically deal with the disadvantages and challenges that would most likely characterize their lives. Rhee (2008:23) refers to this type of parenting as a 'positive parenting style', which is exemplified by sensitivity, emotional warmth and involvement by the parent as well as high expectations and demands for maturity and self-control from the child. This is in stark contrast to Augustus and Veruca in particular, who received a 'permissive parenting' style, characterized by indulgence without discipline. This style of parenting, according to Rhee (2008), can result in lower levels of self-control – something which is illustrated in later scenes in the film where the two children's lack of self-control in the factory leads to their own demise.

Bourdieu noted that 'taste' can result in an aversion to other lifestyles. There are a number of scenes throughout the film that effectively illustrate how the Bucket family's parenting habitus is concerned with a taste towards modelling dispositions associated with fairness and resilience. Charlie seemed particularly concerned with notions of fairness, commenting for example on the strategy Veruca's father employed for gaining her a Golden Ticket. Charlie's grandparents in particular were vocal in showing their aversion to spoiling children. Augustus Gloop was referred to as a 'repulsive boy', and they warned Charlie of the consequences for Veruca, that 'no good ever comes of spoiling a child like that.'

Charlie's birthday (00:19:03–00:20:35)

It is the evening before Charlie's birthday, and his parents excitedly return home with his birthday present, asking whether he would like to open it that evening. Holding the gift (wrapped in a page from a magazine), he suggests that 'maybe I should wait till morning.' As he opens the wrapper, his parents remind him not to be too disappointed if there is no Golden Ticket, as he will still have the chocolate to enjoy. Following the initial disappointment of not finding a Golden Ticket in his chocolate bar, Charlie shares the chocolate bar between all seven family members. They relish the taste, texture and smell of the chocolate, slowly enjoying the full sensory experience of eating their small chocolate square.

The impact of the positive parenting style that Charlie received is evident in this scene. Charlie's developing dispositions of moral integrity and self-control were exemplified through his suggestion to wait until the morning before opening his present. While his parents were all too aware of his dream of winning a Golden Ticket, they were also mindful of the necessity of ensuring he had a resilient disposition to deal with the disappointment of not finding a ticket in his chocolate bar. This is an example of how Charlie's family had modified their aspirations to fit with the norm of their own social grouping (Podesta, 2014). As Charlie unwrapped his chocolate bar to find there was no Golden Ticket, Grandpa Joe replied, 'ah well, that's that'. The birthday scene also provides an additional insight to notions of taste, which can be exemplified by comparing how Augustus and Charlie responded to eating chocolate bars. While Augustus seemed to have become desensitized to the taste of chocolate through his excessive consumption, we see Charlie and his family consuming the chocolate in a very different way.

The ideas that have been presented in the first part of this chapter are intended to encourage the reader to begin to question some of the taken-for-granted assumptions that underpin sociological and political discourses related to parenting. While there is an assumption that social class is a determiner of parenting style within contemporary society, it seems that for many parents, what matters mostly is who they are, rather than what they do (Hartas, 2014:3). Hartas (2014) argues that placing the most value on 'capital' reduces parenting to an economic construct that is seen as a financial asset or commodity, where 'economic activity and profit are the ultimate arbiter of a successful family life' (p. 4). Yet more recently, a greater emphasis is being placed on the fact that positive parenting can mediate the effects of poverty and disadvantage (Kiernan and Menash, 2011). Indeed, as the Allen Report (2011) acknowledges, 'the right kind of parenting is a bigger influence on their [children's] future than wealth, class, education or any other social common factor' (p. xiv). Family policy has seen a shift in trend towards focusing on individual parent's capacity to support their children's learning and character development – such as self-control and resilience. These are the characteristics that are embodied within Charlie's own habitus, and in the final section of this chapter, we explore how alternative forms of capital can serve to change the conditions of the field and place him in a position of power.

Poverty, educational achievement and life chances

Opening scene of Charlie's family life (00:00:09–00:05:50)

The opening scenes of the film provide both a visual and narrative depiction of Charlie's contrasting lifestyle to that of the other competitors. He is described as an 'ordinary little boy', whose family were 'not rich, or powerful, or well connected'. Charlie is dressed in threadbare clothes that barely fit him, and he lives in a dilapidated house that appears to consist of just one bedroom. Charlie's four elderly grandparents live with his family. They share a double bed, and this serves as the focal point for all family activity. Charlie's father works in the local toothpaste factory and his mother takes in washing. Later in the film, Charlie's father is made redundant, as he is replaced by a robot. The family struggles to make ends meet, and they have minimal material possessions. In the opening scene Charlie is sitting at the table completing his homework. Mrs Bucket is in the kitchen making the regular family meal of cabbage soup, awaiting her husband's return from work, in anticipation that he has been able to bring something 'extra' to add to the soup. The family happily greet Mr Bucket, waiting to see whether he has been able to bring any 'unexpected surprises' from the factory that day. He presents Charlie with a handful of misshaped toothpaste lids, which to his delight are just what he needs to complete his ongoing construction of his impressive Wonka Factory (made entirely out of toothpaste lids).

> Poverty blights the life chances of children from low income families, putting them at higher risk of a range of poor outcomes when compared to their more affluent peers. (Field Report, 2010:27)

Poverty in contemporary society can be typically determined by a lack of resources to obtain the type of diet, participate in activities and have living conditions and amenities which are customary, or at least widely encouraged in the societies to which we belong (Townsend, 1979:31). Dominant sociological and political discourses have served to inform certain assumptions, or a 'doxa' about the lives and habitus of families living in poverty. Doxa refers to the 'apparently natural beliefs or opinions which are in fact intimately linked to field and habitus' (Deer, 2012:115) and result in 'natural' and unquestioned practices. Such practices can be commonly characterized by assumptions that family members will have low educational attainment, ill health and many will be lone parents (and will indeed be poor parents). This view also serves to provide the explanation for the 'culture of dependency' that has led to intergenerational worklessness (Harkness, Gregg & Macmillan, 2012). Such assumptions also extend to families who are in employment. Despite their endeavours to increase their symbolic and economic capital through employment, policy discourse serves to reinforce the doxa of disadvantage. This is exemplified in the Field Report, where it was suggested that there is a correlation between a father's employment status and their children's behaviour.

> Children whose fathers have routine or manual professions have a higher than average risk of infant mortality ... the poorest 20% of children are more likely to display conduct problems at age five. (Field, 2010:28)

The social environment and its structure is both the medium and the outcome of social action (La Placa & Corlyon, 2016), and individuals have to negotiate this terrain in their endeavour to transform their social positioning and status. The film allows us to contest some of the views related to the assumed correlation between deprivation in cultural and economic capital and roles in society. For example, while the Field report implies that children whose parents possess greater economic and cultural capital are able to regulate their own behaviours, it was only Charlie who was able to conduct himself appropriately once placed in the game-playing situation. Indeed, research indicates that there is evidence of improvements in aspects of parenting in disadvantaged families related to involvement with home learning, which is a key contributor to supporting children's self-regulatory habitus. Hartas (2012:9) argues that it is a 'mistaken belief' that parents in poverty are less involved with their children's learning, and that they lack the aspirations and other middle-class values thought to promote social mobility (Note, e.g. in the film, how Mr Bucket is seen sitting at the kitchen table reading books while Charlie is building his toothpaste factory model). Yet widening income inequalities are still very much a reality for many families, and therefore the opportunities to increase their own social mobility remains very much an aspiration.

In the opening scene of the film, we are first introduced to Charlie and his family. His ill-fitting clothing and poor living conditions are signifiers that reinforce the doxa of family life for those living in poverty. The family tradition of paid employment as a factory worker is indicative of an accepting habitus; that the structure in which they exist could only ever mean there would be limited opportunities to gain further assets (capital), assets that could transform their family's life chances. Thus their position in the field is preserved. However, there are a number of scenes in the film that help us to challenge some of the taken-for-granted assumptions associated with disadvantage and poverty. The scenes of Charlie's family home life provide an insight into the family's resourcefulness and emotional capital that, while not always typically associated with a disadvantage, form strategies which Charlie was able to draw upon as the game unfolded.

The Bucket family's social positioning created a particular 'class unconsciousness' (Crossley, 2012), or class habitus, which was based on a virtue of necessity. A key disposition in the class habitus is resourcefulness. The necessity to be resourceful is a direct consequence of the lack of resources available, and something that is shaped by interactions with other class members who possess the same volume and composition of capital. In the film, we see how Mrs Bucket seeks to find ways of embellishing the daily cabbage soup meal. She is accepting that if Mr Bucket is unable to produce anything "extra" through his contacts in the factory, then she will just need to take in more washing. While the film doesn't directly show the practice of bartering and exchanging goods between fellow factory workers, it is easy to imagine the type of dealings that may occur in the workplace that would enable Mr Bucket to obtain such "extras' to supplement the family resources. Bourdieu noted that "social identity is defined and asserted through difference" (Bourdieu, 2010:167), and while for this social group, this form of game playing was seen as a necessary act, it may well be viewed as distasteful and unnecessary for the other characters in the film.

Material possessions were deemed as luxuries within the Bucket family. Charlie did not have access to technology, extracurricular activities or the sweet treats that the other children in the film took for granted, and this consumerist style of parenting did not form part of Mr and Mrs Bucket's parenting habitus. There was therefore a necessity, instead, for the family to utilize the limited resources available to them in order to enhance the Home Learning Environment (HLE). For example, in the birthday scene, Charlie's chocolate bar is wrapped in a page from a magazine. The ritual of receiving and sharing a birthday gift with the family had much greater value than the actual gift and its wrapping. The other most noteworthy example of resourcefulness was the creation of a scaled model of the Wonka factory made from misshaped toothpaste lids. The model of the factory was a long-term project that had taken up much of Charlie's spare time. It required self-regulatory skills and attitudes most commonly associated with a creative disposition. This type of resourcefulness is a trait that teachers seek to encourage in children when planning problem-solving and project-based work. Yet, for many children, the opportunities to develop these types of dispositions outside of the confines of school life are limited to digital technologies and 'safe' play that does not encourage risk, emotional resilience or collaboration. Charlie in this situation would arguably be in a more advantageous position to deal with such teaching and learning experiences while in school.

The emphasis placed by Charlie's family on encouraging dispositions such as resilience, motivation and problem solving serve as a form of emotional capital that is characteristic of working-class families, and one of the positive parenting strategies that was discussed earlier in the chapter. Emotional capital is a term most commonly associated with the mother in the family, and it is associated with the stock of emotional resources built upon over time within families which children are able to draw upon (Reay, 2000). A study by Reay (2000) explored emotional capital and mother's involvement in education. She noted a distinction between how middle- and working-class mother's prioritized the enhancement of cultural capital and emotional capital. Working-class mothers placed much greater emphasis on emotional capital, whereas cultural capital and educational success were of greater priority to middle-class families. Yet what was significant for all of the mothers in the study was the cost to their own emotional well-being in supporting their children to achieve success. For Mrs Bucket, unlike the other mother's in the film, she was unable to draw upon her own educational capital, material resources and social capital to support her mothering role. This is an important consideration for professionals working with families, and something which policy has sought to address. The New Labour vision, for example, was based on the belief that by enhancing community life and promoting social cohesion, it would help to build social capital for all members of society (Bagley, 2011). In the early days of Sure Start Local Programmes, and the expansion into Children's Centres, it was not uncommon to see parental support programmes that took account of the well-being of mothers and fathers.

One of the key aspects of the Sure Start programme was the offer of universal, informal activities that encouraged participation from the widest possible in a non-stigmatizing way (Eisenstaedt, 2012; 4Children, 2015). However, the shift in governmental leadership to the right, alongside sweeping welfare cuts, raised concerns about middle-class parents 'colonizing' children's centres (Jupp, 2013), resulting in a paradigm shift of interventions concerned only with 'problem' and 'troubled' families. Children's centres have now effectively become an isolated space, occupied only by actors who have limited social and cultural capital, and professionals and policy makers. Bourdieu argued that social norms and hierarchies govern people's capacity to negotiate their way in the world. Viewing the ideological shift of the purpose of Children's centres thus provides an ironic tension. While the nature of early, targeted intervention is intended to empower and transform the lives of those who are disadvantaged, the strategies employed by professionals serve to preserve social order and status.

Playing the game

Waiting to enter the factory (00:31:43–00:39:40)

The day of the competition has arrived, and the world watches eagerly as the five lucky winners of the Golden Tickets are waiting at the gates of the factory to meet Mr Wonka. The children and parents glance warily at each other, clearly trying to gain a sense of who will be their key competition. Violet's mother reminds her daughter of the need to keep her 'eyes on the prize'. As the children enter the factory, their game-playing strategies begin in earnest with three of the children endeavouring to position themselves as the favourite by making themselves known to Mr Wonka. Violet initiates the game by introducing herself with a hug, claiming 'I'm the girl who's going to win the special prize at the end'. Next, Veruca greets Mr Wonka with a curtsey, politely telling him 'it's very nice to meet you Sir'. Augustus follows, informing Mr Wonka, with a mouth full of Wonka chocolate that … 'I love your chocolate'. Mike's approach is more aloof, choosing not to introduce himself. Instead Wonka seeks him out, noting that he was 'the little devil who cracked the system'. Charlie is the remaining player; who, Wonka acknowledges, is 'just lucky to be here'. The game playing continues throughout the film; the children reveal the less pleasant aspects of their game-playing strategies that consume them when faced with the temptations of the chocolate factory world.

One by one, the children reach their demise, until at the end of the day, Charlie is the last remaining participant. He is rewarded with being given ownership of the factory, with the condition that he leaves his family behind. Charlie chooses not to accept the offer, making it clear to Mr Wonka that he wouldn't give up his family for anything, 'not for all the chocolate in the world' [01.35.05].

Having the feel for the game is having the game under the skin; it is to master in a practical way the future of the game; it is to have a sense of the history of the game+…. the good player is the one who anticipates, who is ahead of the game…she has immanent tendencies of the game in her body, in an incorporated state: she embodies the game. (Bourdieu, 1998:80–81)

The initial encounter with the first four winners of the Golden Ticket leads us to assume that their symbolic and economic capital, their parenting practices and associated habitus will provide them with an advantage in the chocolate factory game. The features of their habitus are associated with being a 'winner', synonymous with many contemporary reality TV programmes and documentaries where contestants become ruthless and inconsiderate of their actions on others (see Chapter 8 for further discussion). Once in the factory we see the game-playing dispositions in action. Such dispositions range from a tokenistic interest in the heritage that underpins Wonka's factory and faux friendliness towards each other (note, e.g. how Violet and Veruca cautiously eye each other up, and agree to be 'Best Friends' while linking arms [38.34]). The strategies all formed part of the 'illusio', which is the view that there is worth in playing the game. They were conforming to social expectations of how to conduct themselves in order to make the right impression. For these children, the emphasis was on material gain, with no sense of interest or understanding of the whole ethos that underpinned Wonka's chocolate world.

Strategy is seen as an unconscious calculation of profit when playing a game (Grenfell, 2012:152) where players draw on both their capital and associated habitus in order to improve their advantage in the game. With the exception of Charlie, the children were acting in particular and predictable ways that they believed would increase their chances of winning the prize. Charlie was the only contestant who took a keen interest in the factory, asking genuine questions about how the factory evolved and Wonka's childhood. Bourdieu notes that habitus is an unconscious aspect of our own disposition, and this is an interesting idea to explore. For Charlie, the emotional capital that he possessed seemed to form a part of his habitus that was genuine and caring. This served as a mechanism for forging an authentic relationship with Wonka, which to begin with seemed to be unnoticed. Indeed, Wonka's perception of Charlie in the first instance was one of pity. It was not until the end of the film that Charlie's emotional capital was fully legitimized, when he teaches Wonka the importance of family values.

Bourdieu argued that the root of educational inequality lies in the unequal distribution of the skills and abilities needed to succeed in education (Henderson, 2012:543). This view assumes that cultural capital inherited from the family environment is a key indicator of success and achievement. When this is combined with a concerted cultivation approach to parenting, children from middle-class families are more likely to have the right disposition to deal with the performative ethos of schooling that is synonymous with neo-liberal educational policy, and Bourdieu's analogy of game playing. We can use the analogy of the chocolate factory game to serve as an illustration of how children from varying social, cultural and economic backgrounds will predictably perform and succeed in their schooling. Schools reward those who come to school with the appropriate amount and type of economic and cultural capital – and those with the right type are deemed as school ready, presumably leading to 'employment ready' (Bowles & Gintis, 1976) in later life. In the factory, the other competitors were deemed to be more 'game ready', from experience they had developed the dispositions and strategies that had hitherto served them well. Children who know how to conform and respond to the learning expectations are placed in a position of advantage in an educational context. Assumptions are made that they have been exposed to the appropriate cultural experiences that will ensure that they are school ready. The discourses associated with school readiness are embodied in policy discourse, such as the Allen Report (2011):

> School ready – having the social and emotional foundation skills to progress in speech, perception, ability to understand numbers and quantities, motor skills, attitude to work, concentration, memory and social conduct; having the ability to engage positively and without aggression with other children and the ability to respond appropriately to requests from teachers. (Allen, 2011:3)

As alluded to in the previous section, assumptions are made that children living in poverty are less likely to do well in school. Policy discourse concerned with narrowing the gap, or a term now more commonly used, 'diminishing disadvantage' is an indicator of the doxa that assumes that disadvantaged children will never be as successful as their more affluent peers. The gap in the social space will remain, and the best that they can expect is to make some improvements to their life chances. Wonka was guilty of this taken-for-granted assumption himself in his earliest encounters with Charlie. He noted that Charlie was 'just lucky' to have made it to the competition, and mindful of his malnourished demeanor later offered him a ladle of chocolate. We can possibly recognize such responses in our own practice with children, where, for example, student teachers talk of how they have looked for ways of giving certain children extra portions of snack to make up for the deficits in their diet. Current education policy reinforces the doxa that children and young people who are disadvantaged need to be encouraged to develop strategies that build resilience and character in order to improve their aspirations and educational attainment. Policies such as Pupil Premium have been introduced as a form of intervention to address the perceived attainment deficits of those in receipt of Free School meals. Interestingly, Charlie would not have been eligible for such benefits as his father was employed – even though their family income was not sufficient enough to be provide wholesome and nutritious food. This is part of the discourse that Raffo, Forbes and Thomson (2015:1127) claim serves as a strategy for assisting those students most at risk of having the 'wrong' type of educational beliefs and behaviours for educational success.

The Bucket family had neither the practical knowledge, capital nor arguably the desire to know how to play the game. Instead, they took on the role of spectator, taking an active interest in watching from the sidelines the strategies that the other competitors were utilizing to establish their positions within the field. Throughout the film, different family members were seen to provide moral commentaries regarding what they perceived as distasteful behaviours and dispositions that seemed to be an embodiment of the habitus of wealth and advantage. Their commentaries provided a moral compass for Charlie who later saw first-hand the effect of greed and consumption and the inability to resist temptation as each of the other players met with their demise. The scene where the children first enter the chocolate world provides a number of powerful signifiers regarding the relationship between capital, habitus and consequential actions.

In the opening factory scene, Wonka invites the children to explore the candy-filled heaven and 'enjoy'. While Charlie is in awe of the setting, the other children are seen to greedily and mindlessly devour the treats that are on offer. The negative portrayal of obesity (Latner, Rosewell & Simmonds, 2007) comes into play for Augustus and his mother, as they are both unable to restrain themselves from overindulging in the candy that is on offer to them. Mike Teevea's violent disposition plays out as, despite his father's protests, he takes delight in destroying a candy pumpkin (without actually eating any). Violet and Veruca on the other hand are more intent on gaining the ultimate prize as neither of them seem to understand or seem to be interested in Wonka's passion and creativity that underpinned the chocolate and candy that the factory produced. Charlie was the only child who marvelled in the chocolate world, and he understood the ethos that embodied Wonka's approach to chocolate production. Effectively, while the other four characters had the capital to pass the test to gain entry into the factory, their selfish and greedy habitus meant that they never learned how to have an interest in the subject matter. Therefore, the strategies that they were able to draw upon were insufficient to win the game.

A useful consideration of Bourdieu's conceptual tools is his idea that they are interlinked, and change in one aspect can lead to change in another. This is an interesting position to consider in relation to how some of the taken-for-granted assumptions related to the construction of social status and its associated dispositions were transformed as the story unfolded. Our initial encounter with Charlie and his family would lead us to believe that his chances in winning the prize at the end of the competition were as limited as his life chances in gaining employment that would provide him with material wealth and well-being. However, as the film progressed, Charlie's positon within the field shifted from one of disadvantage to advantage. The extent of the power of his emotional capital was evident when he initially declined Wonka's offer of living in the factory. He was unwilling to sacrifice his family for the factory and was willing to let that go. The depth of his emotional capital and associated habitus provided him with the necessary agency in which he was able to change the conditions of the field. He challenged the taken-for-granted assumptions that business is cut-throat, harsh and individualistic and instead helped Wonka appreciate family values, collaboration and respect for each other. Winning competitions that result in life-changing amounts of money are commonly associated with significant lifestyle changes and a shift in social status. Yet, for Charlie, he remained in his family home. The features of his home life were maintained, but he was able to use his capital to ensure his family's health and well-being was transformed through improved living conditions and good food.

Conclusion

In all three themes of this chapter, the interrelationship between capital, habitus, field and practice are very evident. It is not possible to talk about one, without the other. Reay (2004) states that choice lies at the heart of habitus. Such choices form part of what Bourdieu referred to as strategy, or a 'feel for the game' (Grenfell, 2012), and are bound by both opportunities and constraints that are determined by external circumstances – namely, the state of the field. Choice is also determined by internal frameworks (i.e. individual dispositions) that make 'some possibilities inconceivable, others probable and a limited range acceptable' (Reay, 2004:435). Applying these conceptual ideas to the film allows us to disrupt and challenge some of the taken-for-granted assumptions related particularly to how social positioning can be a key determiner for life chances. The emotional and cultural capital that Charlie possessed alongside his habitus that was cultivated by his family served to strengthen his advantage in the chocolate factory game. These provided him with choices that would normally be inconceivable in the social world outside. For children living in contemporary society, emotional capital and creativity are only attainable for those who have the economic capital to accompany it.

Mayall (2015:13) reminds us that institutional and ideological structures shape childhoods and adult–child relationships, and long-established traditions, policies and beliefs structure how childhood is understood. Mayall (2015) refers to such aspects as being 'absorbed' into our understanding of the characteristics and status of different social groups in society. Our own professional habitus should be shaped by a disposition towards critical and reflexive thinking that seek to challenge the taken-for-granted assumptions related to poverty and disadvantage that pervade social policy. Engaging in academic study and providing spaces for critical and reflexive thinking provide professionals with valuable capital, which can have agentic powers. It has been argued by numerous authors that habitus is not inevitably an unconscious feature (Reay, 2004), and that insufficient attention is paid to the reflexive 'inner conversations' that occur in everyday practice. The most likely environment for habitus to remain unconscious is where there are no opportunities to bring these to the forefront of discussion about the inequalities that social policy produces. Bourdieu (2008) argued, 'It is by knowing the laws of reproduction that we can have a chance, however small, on minimizing the reproductive effect of the educational institution' (p. 53).

The world and characters portrayed in the film are larger than life, but it is their very exaggeration which provides a useful mechanism for constructing an alternative reading of the world we inhabit. This chapter therefore serves to help open up and encourage the exploration of those discursive and critical spaces that practitioners need in order to recognize and consider issues related to identification, consumption and assumption.

Having considered the ideas discussed in this chapter, you may wish to reflect on the following questions in terms of policy, practice and application of theory.

- Identify a policy text related to parenting.
  - What discourses are apparent in the text that reinforce the 'doxa' (taken-for-granted assumptions) about the relationship between capital/habitus and parenting capacity?
  - How could you offer an alternative perspective that would enable you to challenge the doxa?
- In your own professional context, how could you work with children to develop their dispositions that encourage them to take risks, build emotional resilience and collaborate with others (emotional capital)?

- Think of an example in everyday life where institutional and ideological structures have shaped our professional relationship with children and their families. In what ways could you draw on Bourdieu's conceptual tools to explain how the identified structures could shape your own practices?

3

State Paternalism, Postcolonial Theory and Curricula Content: *Rabbit-Proof Fence*

Sue Aitken

This chapter will consider perceptions of the following:

- State paternalism versus individual freedom and choice: Dworkins (2014); Le Grand and New (2015).

- Postcolonial theory and notions of assimilation Fanon (1952); Young (2001); and Spivak (1990).

- How the content and delivery of the Early Years Foundation Stage and The National Curriculum may be read using alternative theory.

The film

Rabbit-Proof Fence was chosen as the basis of the discussion in this chapter as it offers an opportunity to explore, discuss and reflect on both the role of the state and the use of state power. However, it also offers an opportunity to engage with theories such as postcolonialism through the lens of a colonial past, thus providing a useful platform from which to engage with potential contemporary applications. The film was released in 2002 and was based on the book *Follow the Rabbit-Proof Fence* by Doris Pilkington Garimara. Set in

Australia in 1931, the film tells the story of Doris's mother, Molly, who together with her sister Daisy and her cousin Gracie, were forcibly removed from their Aboriginal mothers and grandmother under the Western Australia Aborigines Act (1905). All the children had white fathers and Aboriginal mothers. The Act provided for the post of chief protector who became the legal guardian of every Aboriginal and 'half–caste' (*sic*) child under the age of sixteen. A. O Neville held that post from 1915 until 1936; from 1936 until his retirement in 1940, he was Western Australia's Commissioner of Native Affairs. In the film, Neville is seen presenting a slideshow explaining the need to remove children from Aboriginal homelands, in order to facilitate a diluted (even eradicated) indigenous population in Australia. A policy that Tatz (2006) has referred to as genocide.

Having been removed from their family and homeland, the children are taken 1200 miles southwest to the Moore River Native Settlement for education and training. Housed in locked dormitories and subjected to a rigorous and harsh regime, they are told that that they must only speak English now. The children subsequently 'escape' and walk the 1200 miles home; following the rabbit-proof fence, a 1500-mile structure built ostensibly to keep the rabbit population separate from productive farm land. Regularly repaired and maintained, the fence represented not only the protection of farmland from damaging wildlife but also the loss of the nomadic Aboriginal freedom to roam and hunt for food. In an early scene when the children are still living in the settlement, Molly looks out onto the other side of the fence and says, 'You can't go there …. you get big trouble.' Neville however is determined to recapture the children and the film follows them as they walk home through the harsh and dangerous outback using their cultural knowledge to outwit the police and Moore River's native tracker. Towards the end of the film when the chief protector finally accepts he is unable to recapture the children and remarks, 'if only they would understand what we are trying to do for them', reflecting his justification for the treatment of children who later became known as the 'Stolen Generation'.

This chapter explores notions of state power, governance and paternalism and its influence on social policy and its impact on individual freedom. Finally, by using postcolonial theory (Fanon, 1952; Said, 2003), it seeks to demonstrate how current dominant discourses can lead, often inadvertently, to discriminatory and oppressive behaviour and practice. Easton (1985) stated that political power is 'the authoritative allocation of values', indicating that states can, and do, have the authority to determine societal behaviours and their value in order to maintain governance. Consequently, this chapter explores the nature of personal freedom and personal choice in the wake of state interference and how this might impact on personal identity. It examines how an individual's language use may be subverted in order to meet policy-driven criteria. Additionally, it investigates how current curricula guidance which, while espousing uniqueness and individuality, decrees that assessments are set against a singular matrix of age-related skills and abilities.

State paternalism

Arrival at Moore River (00:14:43–00:29:34)

The children arrive at the Moore River Native Settlement; the location is remote and isolated. The children sleep in large single-storey huts, which are locked at night. In the morning, the children are exposed to the rituals and routines of the settlement, undertaking the domestic tasks of making their beds, empting the toilet bucket and sweeping up. After a Christian church service, Neville inspects the children; he examines their skin in order to decide if they are 'light' enough to warrant additional education. Molly is told by another child that Neville is checking for the 'fairer ones'; when Molly asks why, she is told it is because they are 'more clever than us' so they can go to 'proper school' (00:20:58).

Towards the end of the scene (00:23:14), a child who has run away is returned to the settlement by the native tracker. Her punishment is to be beaten, have her hair cut short and to be imprisoned in a corrugated iron 'cell'. At which point Molly decides that she and her sister and cousin have to run away and go home.

As the scene earlier illustrates, the children are subject to the power of the state in terms of where and how they live. Part of any discussion around social and economic policy must initially have regard to the nature of governance and political theory. Politics and the nature of the state are complex and deeply debated. At its most basic level, the activities of the state are often defined by reference to its size and functional purpose. From the perspective of liberalism (Locke, 1689; Hume, 1742; Mill, 1865) and later neo-liberalism (Hayek, 2006; Friedman, 2002; Nozick, 1974), the size and reach of government should be limited as state interference is contradictory to personal freedom and choice. Both liberalism and its later development, neo-liberalism, regard ensuring personal freedom and personal choice as the state's primary function; therefore, they champion small state governance, which interferes as little as possible in the personal lives of its citizens. Conversely, its binary opposite, socialism, sees extensive state intervention as the only way through which equal freedom can be delivered, thus ensuring parity of experience and opportunity. These positions are variously referred to as representing the right and left of politics, liberalism or socialism or merely small state, big state theories. However, as with many theories, such definitions are too simplistic to acknowledge the complexity of political thinking. Consequently, this chapter uses *Rabbit-Proof Fence* to illustrate how seemingly benign and well-intentioned state actions and motivations can be reassessed with a view to illustrating how the state may justify and validate their actions as a general good, while discriminating against a minority.

The relationship between state paternalism and colonial subjugation is well known (Spivak, 1990; Said, 1993; Hall, 1993) and in many ways paternalism is the articulation of colonization, where culture and beliefs are imposed on indigenous populations in order to make 'them' more like 'us'. In the case of Australia, paternalistic legislation with regard to its Aboriginal population remained a statutory mechanism until 1970. By its very nature, state paternalism involves the notion that governments have the right and power to make decisions that affect the lifestyle and choices of individuals. Le Grand and New (2015:7) suggest that paternalism can be simply defined as 'the interference by some outside agent in a person's freedom for the latter's own good'. Thus, the state in the form of paternalistic policy is that 'outside agent'.

Theoretical discussion around paternalism however often bifurcates into two polarities, defining state intervention as either benign or harmful. Dworkins (2014) suggests that state activity is often represented in terms of either moral or welfare paternalism where the justification is the improvement of the individual's moral, physical and psychological condition. In this context, the state acts as would a protective parent who seeks to prevent a child from making potentially harmful or irrational decisions. The question remains, however, as to whether that intervention is welcomed or accepted by the subject and whether the intervention is motivated by reasons other than purely the protection of the individual. In the case of the children in *Rabbit-Proof Fence*, state paternalism was enacted in the role of chief protector who was deemed to know what was best for the children, to know better than the children or their carers.

Foucault (1977b) discusses how society may subjectivize and imprison individuals in order to normalize behaviour. The Moore River Native settlement represents one example of a form of a prison, it is tightly managed and regulated; the children's clothing and rituals such as mealtimes are clearly institutionalized. The children are made very aware of the consequences of transgressions as highlighted in the earlier scene when a runaway is recaptured and punished. However, the rabbit-proof fence itself also functions as another, if less perceptible, reference to personal imprisonment. While overtly fulfilling the function of preventing rabbits from damaging farmland, implicitly it acts as a deterrent to the free movement of Aboriginal communities.

Foucault (1977b) refers to Bentham's notion of the Panopticon, the structure of surveillance, which ensures compliance. Thus the mere presence of the fence induces a knowledge in the Aborigines that crossing over the fence is forbidden; that their ancestral homelands were no longer accessible; no longer theirs to use as they wish or need.

While it might be tempting to confine these views to the prevailing beliefs of the 1930s, it is worth considering how subtler views may still exist today and to what extent seemingly benign or beneficial state interventions may obscure a loss of personal freedom and equality of choice. Can the justification that the state is serving the best interests of everyone by addressing the needs of the most vulnerable and disadvantaged be re-examined? The Aboriginal Act (1905) stated that its purpose was 'the better protection and care of Aboriginal inhabitants' yet removed children from their homes against their will. For the state, the wording 'the better protection and care' meant the state's perception of what was better. As we shall see in the remainder of this chapter, the state has the power to dictate and maintain dominant discourses, thus establishing a position of impeachability, where state and citizenry seemingly agree. van Dijke (1996:85) suggests that 'state power in democratic societies is persuasive and manipulative rather than coercive' and cites Herman and Chomsky (1988) in referring to the crucial role of discourse in manufacturing consent.

The slideshow (00:11:31–00:14:30)

The chief protector, Neville, is shown giving a slide presentation to a small group of white women, who Neville indicates are supporters of the Moore River Native Settlement.

In a darkened room, he explains the rationale behind his belief that only by intervening in the lives of these Aboriginal children would the dominant European society be able to help them. He refers to the children of a white and an Aboriginal parent as creating an 'unwanted third race' that is neither white nor black. He is seen stating that the solution is progressive racial assimilation to 'stamp out the black colour'; by ensuring that 'half caste' children are prevented from marrying full-blood Aborigines. His slides show how, within three generations, it would be possible to 'breed out' any trace of visual Aboriginal characteristics. He uses scientific and mathematical language such as Quadroon and Octoroon to describe the dilution of the indigenous race. Neville states that he wants the children to 'advance' to white status and be absorbed into the white population. He sees this as a benefit to both the children and the wider society of Australia.

In this scene, it is possible to see how the Australian state's interventions in the lives of these children will have had repercussions not only for them but also for Australian society for decades to come. Democratically elected governments are, by definition, charged with shaping the present and future of its population in terms of economic activity, health, social policy and social behaviour. Few would argue with the state's right and duty to police and protect the state from internal and external threats to maintain order and promote prosperity. However, in order to critique this dominant discourse, it is necessary to understand the extent to which individual freedom maybe compromised by meeting the perceived needs of the majority, and this is discussed further in Chapter 6. The narrative of *Rabbit-Proof Fence* reflects a powerful discourse of the time, that of eugenics; based on Darwinism and selected breeding, it illustrates how state power may undermine individual choices and freedom. As well as having the power to remove children from their homeland, the chief protector also had the power to deny native Australians and white Australians the right to marry. John Stuart Mill arguing from a Liberal perspective in 1869 wrote, 'The only purpose for which power can be rightfully exercised over any member of a civilized community, against his will is to prevent harm to others.' Thus, within this argument, the exertion of power for 'his own good, either physical or moral, is not a sufficient warrant' (1869:6). In the context of the film the children are removed from their home, family and culture, against both their own will and the will of those who care for them; but whose interests are being served? Arguable the state would say the children's, and the abducted children would say the state's.

All governments espouse their dedication to improving the lives of their citizenry, especially children; equally however debates will always arise with regard to how that pledge is to be achieved. The practice of politics and political theory forms part of any study of children and childhood, as children and families are often situated as the focus of state legislation. In 1930s' Western Australia, power over the Aborigines population was enacted through the Aborigines Act (1905), whose remit as described earlier was 'an Act to make provision for the better protection and care of the Aboriginal inhabitants of Western Australia'. Yet the Act goes on to restrict the free movement of Aborigines from their designated 'reserve' (reserved homeland), remove children from families and deny couples the right to marry. An example perhaps where legislative rhetoric and governmental policy may be mismatched. The state believed that the welfare of Aboriginal children and therefore the safety of the dominant European society could not be entrusted to their parents or carers as they could neither protect nor provide for these children in line with a Western understanding of what was 'best' for them.

Intervention versus freedom

While the explicit events depicted in *Rabbit-Proof Fence* may seem a long way from the political and social landscape of a twenty-first century Western culture such as the United Kingdom, it provides a useful mechanism through which to examine how legislation may operate within an understanding of state paternalism. Using examples of the Early Years Foundation Stage (EYFS) and the National Curriculum, the following discussions explore how the state has legislated to provide what it considers better outcomes for children in terms of education and achievement. Reminiscent perhaps of the foreword to the Aboriginal Act (1905): 'to make provision for the better protection and care of the Aboriginal inhabitants of Western Australia'.

The first incarnation of the EYFS was contained in the Childcare Act (2006) and prescribed for the first time a set of learning and development requirements for children aged three and four. All early years' providers were required to register under the Act and continued registration was based on the setting's ability to meet the requirement of both the welfare and the learning and development elements of the Statutory Framework for the EYFS. While exemptions to registration existed, these were few, and generally referred to settings that undertook care for two hours or less per day; for less than six days per year or provided a singular activity such as sport, performing arts or cultural and religious study (DFCS, 2008). On a prima facie basis, the intent of the Act would seem benign and in the best interests of child and parent. It provided for universal standards, regulatory inspection by the Office of Standards in Education (OFSTED) and was intended to promote a smooth transition to compulsory education at age five. However, many early years' academics and practitioners challenged both the need and the content of the framework. House (2011:20) questions 'the legitimate role of central government in intervening in early childhood experience, and the many dangers that such intrusions may entail'. Leach (2011:21) suggests that while increased government focus on early childhood care and education is welcomed, 'it is principally motivated by economics'. Both House and Leach argue that statutory regulation and state-funded provision has less to do with enhancing the experience for individual children but more to do with an ultimate aim of replacing dependence on state benefits with remunerative work. A stated aim of the Children Act (Department for Education, 2004) was that children should be supported to 'achieve economic well-being', which could be translated as aiming to promote self rather than state reliance when these children become adults. While of itself this is a positive ambition, it perhaps leads to questioning whether the motivation is for the benefit of children or the state. Much of the criticism of the EYFS has been in the form of whether holistic development or educational preparation is the primary motive. Leach (2011) points out that by emphasizing cognitive development and education throughout the EYFS, the 'school readiness' agenda is set not only for preschoolers but for babies and toddlers as well; consequently, running the risk of creating a 'tunnel vision' approach to the learning and development of children.

Another theoretical position, which endeavours to challenge the model of universalized state education, is that of 'de-schooling'. This position is thoughtfully articulated by Illich (1971), who maintains that it is not education that is problematic, but the 'institutionalization of education' which has created state dependency on organizations, a paternalistic overview that dictates rather than enables. Where to be included means to be the same. As he suggests:

> The pupil is thereby 'schooled', to confuse teaching with learning, grade advancement with education, a diploma with competence, and fluency with the ability to say something new. (1971:3)

The notion of social control is particularly disconcerting in any society where 'freedom' is celebrated as an intrinsic right. The United Nations Convention on the Rights of a Child (1989) states that:

> In those States in which ethnic, religious or linguistic minorities or persons of indigenous origin exist, a child belonging to such a minority or who is indigenous shall not be denied the right, in community with other members of his or her group, to enjoy his or her own culture, to profess and practise his or her own religion, or to use his or her own language. (UNCRC 1989: Article 30).

While the experiences of the children at Moore River predated the ratification of the Convention by half a century, it is perhaps questionable that this fundamental right to speak in a way that reflects personal cultural values can be upheld when 'state institutions' demand otherwise.

Politically, the EYFS and publicly funded provision for three- and four-year-olds was an initiative of the centrist Labour government of 1997–2010 and formed part of its 'ending childhood poverty strategy' which was enshrined in the Child Poverty Act (2010). However, in terms of state paternalism, does this represent state interference in the care and education of children at the expense of personal choice? While the uptake of free places is not compulsory, are parents coerced by persuasion? If acceptance implies benefit, does rejection imply potential educational damage? Laing (2011:68) suggests that:

> No parent wishes to be seen to 'hold their children back', 'to restrict their education' or 'to deny them opportunities' – therefore many hold back from

criticizing the Early Years Foundation Stage. Some parents are afraid that *their* child will 'fail' at school.

Laing goes on to suggest that the Early Years Foundation Stage policy was sold to the general public in England on the basis of 'moral blackmail' and 'the exploitation of parental fears' (2011:81). What Laing refers to as 'moral black-mail' and 'exploitation', Le Grand and New (2015:26) refer to as 'soft paternal-ism', where coercion is achieved not by force, as in the *Rabbit-Proof Fence*, but by an assumption of individual ignorance or lack of information, thus the state may be justified in overriding parental preference and choice, as parents are deemed to have insufficient knowledge of the educational needs of their children.

This is perhaps particularly relevant to the enrolment of children at the age of four into school reception classes. The statutory school-starting age in the United Kingdom is five, as set out in Section 8 of the Education Act (Department for Education, 1996, 1998). A parent is only statutorily required to enrol their child into formal education in the term following their fifth birth-day. However, it is now common practice for children to be offered a place in reception classes within a school in the term following their fourth birthday. The Department for Education (2014) provides advice with regard to exemp-tion for four-year-old children whose birthday falls between 1 April and 31 August. The advice states that these 'summer born' children are not required to start school 'until a full school year after the point at which they could first have been admitted'. This advice refers to children who are below the statu-tory school-starting age. However, this exemption also advises that this may mean that the child at age five will be admitted into reception rather than a year-one class and 'will involve taking account of the potential impact on the child of being admitted to year 1 without first completing the reception year'. Though, regardless of whether a child is in a reception class or a non-school setting, both are required to follow the EYFS and will be expected to achieve the same goals and develop the same skills. The Department for Education (2014) advice would seem to imply that the non-school model might be a defi-cient one. The vast majority of children enter reception classes in the autumn term following their fourth birthday. This may be because parents believe that this is the right decision for their child, it may be because currently a four-year-old in an EYFS setting other than a school will attract only fifteen hours of free funding rather than the thirty hours when enrolled in school (DFE, 2014). From September 2017, this was increased to thirty hours per week; however, this increase would only apply to only working parent(s). The same restriction does not apply to children who enter a reception class at four years. However, it could be that parents are unaware that they have the option not to send their child to school at age four or if they are aware they may feel that by exercising this option they will somehow, as Laing describes, have 'failed' their child educationally. The tone and language of the Departmental advice would seem to suggest that it is advisable that children should be in a school environment from the age of four.

Postcolonialism

The first day at Moore River (00:18:34–00:18:48)

The children at Moore River go for breakfast; they stand in front of rough wooden tables and recite Grace before eating. Daisy has one mouthful, spits it out and utters a word in her own language. She is immediately shouted at by an Aboriginal male member of staff who bangs the table with a heavy stick telling her she can only speak English.

As the scene earlier indicates, the children find themselves at odds with a new set of cultural rules, rules which are harshly enforced. If childhoods of the past may be seen as a period of colonization, where adults dictated outcomes and where children were seen and not heard, then the more recent cultural shift that advocates listening to children, child-centred learning and respect for individual needs and identities may also be seen as operating within a postcolonial identity. Postcolonial theory according to Young (2001) addresses the enduring legacy of colonialism long after supposed self-determination is achieved. Both Derrida (1974) and Spivak (1988) refer to 'catachresis'. Spivak uses the term as part of her examination of the colonial and postcolonial legacy where language is misused, misappropriated and abused. She refers to a cultural continuum where the colonizer and the colonized 'share 'a language that serves both to underpin and to validate a discourse of supremacy. Thus at Moore River the lingua franca is English and the language of the colonizer becomes the language of the colonized, seamlessly and without question. This presentation of shared, rather than imposed beliefs holds fast as the decolonized seek to resurrect their precolonial language and culture; only to find it no longer has currency, and instead is regarded as a curiosity and of little value in the globalized and largely capitalized world (Ashcroft, Griffiths & Tiffin, 2002). As Nettle and Romaine (2000: ix) suggest:

Few people seem to know or care that most of Australia's 250 languages have already vanished and few are likely to survive over the long term.

Using postcolonial theory in the context of language presents two tasks. The first is to disengage perceptions of colonialism and postcolonialism as a discourse that encompasses and articulates political and military imperialism located within a distant geography. The second task is to realign the theory so that while recognizing that there remains a political imperative, there is an acknowledgement that military power has been replaced by the imperatives of economic power. Additionally, there is the need to reconstitute postcolonial theory as less-defined and binary and more nebulous and as relevant to 'here' as 'there'. Postcolonial theorists endeavour to challenge the notion of 'universalism' and explore the 'oppressive regimes and practises that they delineate' (Young 2001:58). In this context, we can begin to tease out how postcolonial theory may be applied to childhood and education and the development of literacy.

In this context, it may be perceived that some children do not 'fit in' to the dominant cultural norm of 'using appropriate language', and consequently may slip into the deficit model, potentially leading to marginalization, isolation and exclusion. The dominance of cultural perceptions of what is 'correct English' can lead to perceptions that its lack will result in reduced levels of power and status and have become common drivers within education. At Moore River, success could only be achieved by using the 'right 'language. Frantz Fanon's *Black Skin White Masks* (1967) places great emphasis on language being at the heart of marginalization, within his own context; a black person, in a 'white' society. 'A man who has a language,' Fanon suggests, 'consequently possesses the world expressed and implied by that language,' (Fanon, 1967:14). Fanon argues that language becomes an index of social/cultural difference and power imbalance. His work, although based on the black/white dichotomy, can also be applied to the educational context, in the sense that one's culture and status situates a particular code of speech. If this speech is classed as 'incorrect' or 'inappropriate' by more powerful groups in society, the child may become powerless.

> What we are getting at becomes plain: Mastery of language affords remarkable power. (Fanon, 1967:18)

Consequently, linguistic success in the early years can mean mastery, not *of* language but mastery of *the* language, in the belief that there exists a shared and good way of speaking, as the curriculum 'is organised in such a way that certain dispositions are invalidated and denied' (Skeggs, 1997:68).

Schools have the power to decide what constitutes language competency; therefore, to avoid being assessed as incompetent, some children may be forced to accept that their language use falls short of speaking in the 'correct' way and therefore needs to be 'corrected'. Thus 'the correct way' becomes an 'undeniable truth'. However, what if that truth is culturally determined rather

scientifically proven? The 'truth' of educational policies such as phonics, legitimized by scientific research, maybe only one truth among many. If every child
is unique, what is the value of a one-size-fits-all education system, where culture has little or no part to play, save for tokenistic acknowledgement?

Having explored the nature of state provision for children before the compulsory school age in terms of access, it is necessary to examine the content
of the EYFS and the National Curriculum. Katz (2013) identifies four principles
that should inform curriculum design. These she states as follows:

- What should be learned?

- When should it be learned?

- How is it best learned?

- How can we assess and evaluate the implementation of the first
  three questions?

In terms of content (what should be learned), the DFE (2014) identifies
seven areas of learning within the EYFS. Communication and language; physical development; and personal, social and emotional development, the DFE
describes as the three prime areas of learning. Additionally, the areas of literacy; mathematics; understanding the world; and expressive arts and design
are designated specific areas, through which the prime areas are strength-
ened and applied. In terms of practice, the DFE provides that all of the above
should reflect the EYFS's overarching principles, which are that every child
is unique; that children learn to be strong and independent through positive
relationships and enabling environments that respond to individual needs; and
that every child will learn and develop in different ways and at different rates.

The remainder of this chapter will look at one specific area of learning, that
of communication and language and how the overarching principles may be
compromised. It explores the relationship of this prime area of learning to the
specific areas of literacy and particularly the use of phonics. In *Rabbit-Proof
Fence*, language is also a fundamental demonstration of power. The children
at Moore River are made to communicate only in English and the children are
admonished for using their own language. Thus establishing a hierarchy of culture where their own language has no value. In Australia, the language of the
colonizer became the *de facto* language of the state. If paternalistic activities of
the state can, in part, be viewed as a consequence of colonialism, it is important to see colonialism in its widest sense, not merely with regard to notions of
empire and global relationships but also in the domestic sense of a state and
its citizenry. Postcolonial theory is an attempt to explore how freedom *from*
subjection (decolonization) may not result in freedom *to* make free choices. By
using dominant notions of language, in terms of its use and validity this final
section explores how contradictions may arise within the curriculum in terms

of respecting the uniqueness of every child and providing environments that respond to the needs of all children. The children featured in *Rabbit-Proof Fence* are told by the staff that they cannot use their own language, reflecting a clear position that English is not only preferred but also essential. Within early years' settings, while practitioners may wish to encourage a child's home language, the phonic and literacy drivers of the EYFS and the National Curriculum make it difficult not to construct a child's nonstandard home language as unhelpful and distracting. However, this is not restricted to children for whom English is not their first language but may also include children with a strong accent or who use a local dialect.

The DFE (2014) describes communication and language as 'giving children opportunities to experience a rich language environment; to develop their confidence and skills in expressing themselves; and to speak and listen in a range of situations' (2014:8). Literacy is referred to as 'encouraging children to link sounds and letters and to begin to read and write. Children must be given access to a wide range of reading materials (books, poems, and other written materials) to ignite their interest' (2014:8), while recommending that 'practitioners must consider the individual needs, interests, and stage of development of each child in their care' (2014:8).

The process of learning to read in the United Kingdom is largely based on the acquisition of phonological awareness and knowledge. Thus, a child begins the process by allocating sounds to letters, by sounding out individual letters and blends of sounds using phonics. The use of synthetic phonics became the dominant strategy for the teaching of reading in the UK, following the publication of the Rose (2006) report.

However, even without accent and dialectic variance, reading and spelling in English can be a complex activity, requiring the early reader to negotiate differing pronunciations where words have similar spelling such as 'most' and 'lost'; 'river' and 'driver'. Honeybone and Watson (2006) refer to teaching phonics to children with Liverpool English accents, as the correlation between sound (phonemes) and letters (graphemes), as envisaged by commonly used phonics programmes, do not fit perfectly to Liverpool English or many other localized accents.

Honeybone and Watson clearly identify that irregular applications of phonics, when added to a distinctive accent can present challenges. However, guidance on the teaching and assessment of phonics is based on a 'shared understanding' of how words should be pronounced.

Honeybone and Watson (2006:1) highlight that,

In England, most phonics schemes are designed on the basis of the phoneme to grapheme correspondences that work for the closest thing that there is to a neutral, 'standard' accent. There isn't really a standard accent in England, but the closest thing is the accent often called 'RP' (or 'Received Pronunciation').

Logically, therefore, there is a need to privilege a universality of pronunciation. A child who pronounces 'book', as 'boowk', may encounter difficulties in decoding and applying phonological knowledge. Therefore, children need not only to recognize but also to acquire the 'acceptable' accent and pronunciation, which is close to but not quite what has become known as Received Pronunciation (RP). It is the acquisition of this acceptable 'voice' that is seen as the natural precursor to successful reading, spelling and writing; and implicitly, future learning leading to social and economic success. With regard to future life chances, McMahon et al. (1994) suggests that we draw both 'geographical and social' conclusions from accent and dialect, potentially leading to subconscious stereotyping and allocation of traits such as personality and intelligence. In research undertaken by Giles and Powesland (1975), a university lecturer gave two identical lectures to two different groups of 'A' level students: one was delivered using Received Pronunciation (RP), the other using a Birmingham accent. The student's assessment of the content and the lecturer's intelligence gave greater academic credibility to the lecture delivered in RP. Luke (1986) also discusses that children from backgrounds that are perceived as 'disadvantaged' may be perceived as suffering 'linguistic deficit', but goes onto declare that this deficit may be 'an imposition of schools and teachers' rather than an inevitable consequence of inherent traits and poor acquisition of language at home. At Moore River, language becomes one of the mechanisms by which these children will be elevated to a position that is judged to be closer to the dominant white culture. Arguably some English children are also required to suppress a first or home language in order to reach acceptable standards. More overtly, in the early scene where Neville is shown selecting children to receive enhanced education and training purely on the basis of skin colour, because these children were seen as 'the clever ones'.

Since June 2012, children at the end of year 1 are required to undergo statutory phonics screening (Standards and Testing Agency, 2012) and should be able to:

- apply phonic knowledge and skill as the prime approach to reading unfamiliar words that are not completely decodable;

- read many frequently encountered words automatically;

- read phonically decodable three-syllable words;

- read a range of age-appropriate texts fluently;

- demonstrate understanding of age-appropriate texts.

(Standards and Testing Agency, 2012:8)

The Standards and Testing Agency (2012:12) goes on to advise that,

> A child's accent should be taken into account when deciding whether a response is acceptable. There should be no bias in favour of children with a particular accent.

By the time of the screening, some children will have already self-regulated their accent or dialect in order to 'fit in'. In essence, they have identified and accommodated the requirements of the phonics to reading process and have renegotiated their accent and, in part, their identity, to fulfil the institutional expectations of how reading is accomplished. In effect, children have facilitated their own inclusion and accepted their linguistic assimilation.

It would seem therefore that while both the EYFS and National Curriculum allow for uniqueness in terms of accent and dialogue, there is little space for individuality if it cannot deliver phoneme to grapheme understanding.

Language plays a key function in shaping not only the people we are, and the society that we are part of, but also on the way that others view us. The appropriateness of a child's speech is initially determined by culture, which will vary from place to place, and from time to time. Neither the Aboriginal children nor their families considered their cultural language as incorrect or problematic. But the dominant state discourses believed there was a singular 'correct way' of speaking and any child who used language outside of that determination would be designated as having what Bourdieu and Passeron (1977) described as poor 'cultural capital'. Consequently, every child will either have to *earn* additional cultural capital or be demonized by its lack. Payne (2000) suggested society will categorize or pigeonhole these children who failed the cultural capital test. He contends that, 'social divisions result in social inequalities. Those in the "better" categories have more control over their own lives, usually more money, and can be generally seen to have happier lives' (Payne, 2000:4). Certain forms of speech are therefore favoured, but at the expense of others, and their users become quite literally the 'othered' or less powerful group. From this perspective, schools and policy makers set the level of acceptable cultural capital usually on par with the standards and morals of the middle class or as in *Rabbit-Proof Fence* the dominant racial group. When employed in a classroom situation it can set some children apart, those who share the same cultural capital and those who do not. Bourdieu's concept of the *cultural arbitrary* states that the cultural values taught in schools are not intrinsically better than any other set of values, but are simply the dominant ones. What is selected and taught in the curriculum, including how to 'talk', is merely one selection of knowledge among many (Lambirth, 1997). In terms of language, on entering school, some children will have to earn additional cultural capital, by modifying their accent and vocabulary, in order to fit into an imposed external model of attainment. By gaining inclusion in the classroom, these children may have had to exclude (or deny) their home voice, the voice used with family and friends. Thus, inclusion can be both partial and fragmented across life experiences. Had they stayed at Moore River, Molly, Daisy and Gracie, the children portrayed in the film, may have ceased openly using their own language and would have been employed away from their homeland. As already noted, indigenous languages in Australia and across the world have gradually been lost as the colonial languages, such as English, Spanish, Portuguese and French, have become dominant. In the same way the number of local languages, dialects and localized accents within the UK have diminished. Only in Wales where many schools teach through the medium of Welsh has public policy recognized cultural pressure; however, in Scotland, Scottish Gaelic is taught largely as a second optional language. Perhaps a recognition that English language proficiency is the gatekeeper to success.

In terms of language and reading proficiency, therefore, policy makers and subsequently practitioners and teachers support children to increase their 'cultural capital' by means of correcting a child's unwanted speech, in a bid to meet statutory norms and measurements. What is not addressed, however, is the effect that this may have on a child and their family if an important part of their lives; is deemed to deviate from the perceived norm. As at Moore River these children may learn to believe that their language is not important or good enough. Wood (1988) stated that, 'no one dialect of English, in any linguistic sense, is superior as a means of communication to another' and O'Connor (2011:120) suggests that practitioners unknowingly reaffirm the cultural power of one social group over another.

> Children's home life and parental attitudes, beliefs and traditions, if not fully integrated into the pedagogic and social practises of the setting, can disadvantage a child and lead to a failure to learn.

To extend O'Connor's ideas it may also mean that children may 'learn to fail'.

Conclusion

By exploring dominant discourses and hierarchical positioning, this chapter has examined how state paternalism, notions of freedom and choice and colonializing constructions may permeate understandings of identity and culture. The aim of this chapter was to disturb ideas of 'norms' and acceptability. By looking at state provision in terms of the school-starting age, notions of parental choice, curriculum and language, state dictate has been explored. At the time of writing (2017), the position of 'summer born' children and their admission into schools remains under discussion. However, the curricula content with regard to language use and the acquisition of phonic understanding is still in place. The stark and severe treatment of the children in *Rabbit-Proof Fence* can be used as a powerful tool, not merely to expose a callous and insensitive period of Australian history but also as an insight into how governments may, in the guise of a benign but authoritative parent, deplete uniqueness in favour of universality. This provides the reader with ways of thinking in contrast to conventional, traditional and dominant ideas, which informs the understanding of many parents and the practice of many practitioners. Questions have been asked regarding the potential for conflict between concepts of the 'unique child' and 'school readiness,' and phonic screening, which could, in turn, affect identity and induce identity migration.

Fanon (1967) suggests that the powerless may achieve a modicum of acceptance and a promise of self-determination only by replicating the cultural nuances and characteristics of the powerful. As described earlier, in linguistic terms, this could result in the removal and/or suppression of those dialects (languages) which might be seen as a hindrance to social mobility and social acceptance. The three children taken to Moore River had yet to acquire competency in the singular and preferred language of the dominant culture. Throughout the film when talking among themselves or to others, they will use either their own language or Pidgin English, neither of which was regarded as acceptable. When words and accent can become social passports, who becomes the border guards? Who regulates or denies entry? Language reinforces notions of acceptability, notions that implicitly suggest that not possessing the *lingua franca* may become a barrier to success or, in the postcolonial sense, assimilation. Thus in the past, dominant colonial powers imposed the 'mother tongue' within its colonies and its mastery was the personification of being acceptable and assimilated. Within schools perhaps, the accepted and assimilated are those who can demonstrate the use of the prescribed language of the curriculum and where accent or non-English language use becomes a barrier and a hindrance. Where being one of us is better than being one of them.

Finally, in terms of the ideas used in this chapter you may wish to consider the following questions.

- How might accent and language use that impact on a child's sense of self, cultural inheritance and identity?

- How does the EYFS and the National Curriculum construct children and their education?

- Can dominant state discourses with regard to children be challenged and if so how?

4

Attachment, Transitional Objects and Relationships: *The Red Balloon*

Sarah Sharpe

This chapter seeks to encourage students to engage with and explore complex theoretical ideas with regard to attachment, relationships and transition. It will consider the following:

- Attachment: Bowlby (1951); Ainsworth (1989).

- Transitional phenomena and object attachment: Winnicott (1953).

- Friendships and relationships: Dowling (2010); Dunn (2004).

- Imaginary friends and paracosms: Taylor (1999); Gopnik (2013).

- Transitions and the key person role: Elfer, Goldschmied and Selleck (2012).

The film *The Red Balloon* was chosen for this chapter because it depicts a timeless tale of love and loss, friendship and rejection, that is as relevant today as it was over 60 years ago when the film was produced. It is set in Paris and thus brings an international flavour to the book, yet its message is one which is universal and pertinent the world over. It is virtually voiceless, yet through its imagery the voice of the child is clearly heard. It tells a tale of what might be, allowing us to consider how the red balloon might be interpreted in the life of a young child. Students are encouraged to consider the issues that are explored in the light of theoretical concepts and their own emerging professional identity and practice.

The film

The Red Balloon is a short Oscar-winning fantasy film released in 1956 and directed by French filmmaker Albert Lamorisse. It is a tale of friendship, loyalty, envy, bullying, grief and triumph – compelling in its simplicity. It conveys a poignant symbolic story, rich in metaphor and allegory; yet it contains virtually no dialogue, and thus leaves much to the viewer's interpretation.

Its setting is the Parisian quarter of Ménilmontant. A young boy (played by the director's own son, Pascal) finds a shiny red balloon as he wanders alone to school one day – the only vivid colour in a backwash of hazy drizzle and watery shades of grey. The balloon is mute, yet endowed with a mischievous and endearing persona; somehow it expresses emotion and conveys human-like characteristics and responses. The boy and the balloon seem to connect magically and soon become firm companions. The attachment that Pascal forms with this inanimate object is as intimate and as real as any.

Despite the best efforts of various authoritarian figures to separate them (bus conductor, parent, headmaster, priest), Pascal and his new friend remain inseparable, until they are hounded by a mob of jealous street thugs who conspire to hunt down the balloon and destroy it. Pascal is left bereft without his only friend, but the final twist to the story brings hope out of despair and shows Pascal's magical transition into a world free of repression.

Attachment

The opening scene (00:01:54–00:07:33)

The film opens with Pascal winding his way to school alone as the morning light breaks over the city. Halfway down a steep flight of steps leading to the main street below, he finds a red balloon caught high up in a lamp post. He climbs up to retrieve it and descends with its string held firmly between his teeth. The balloon is half his size, huge and bright! He appears entranced with his new toy as he wanders on through the streets towards the bus stop, oblivious of everyone and everything as he waits for the bus at the roadside. People file onto the bus, but as Pascal's turn comes, the conductor refuses to allow the balloon on board, shaking his finger to indicate 'No entry!' The boy will not part with his new balloon, and as the bus pulls away he is left stranded at the roadside.

On arriving late at school, the balloon is again denied access, and Pascal is dismissed from the classroom. He approaches the janitor and asks, 'Could you hold my balloon while I'm in school? Don't let it go!' As he runs back to his classroom, the headmaster watches him disapprovingly from a window high above.

Later as the school closes, Pascal emerges with his treasured balloon into the pouring rain. Unable to ride on the bus, he begins his long walk home. Although he is wearing no coat himself, he is more concerned about protecting his friend from the weather. He joins one pedestrian after another, seeking shelter for his balloon under their umbrellas.

As the rain stops, Pascal runs with his balloon through the streets and up the steep flight of steps leading to his home – a tall tenement block, grey and shabby. His disapproving mother is watching from the balcony high above. Pascal enters a narrow passageway, checking carefully to ensure his balloon can squeeze through safely. His mother turns sharply from the balcony as she hears the door open; and then, a moment later, the balloon is thrust firmly out of the open window, high over the street.

These scenes depict the beginning of an enduring, affectionate bond between the boy and the balloon, and will be used to discuss the notions of attachment. They portray the 'othering' of the boy and the balloon as they are barred from entry and dismissed by figures in authority; together they become unwanted, ostracized from society. The balloon represents freedom, vivaciousness, joy and colour to Pascal, whose own world is dull and repressive.

During this opening scene, we see two key aspects of attachment. The first is an unmet attachment need evident in Pascal in terms of any positive relationship with the significant adults in his life – either his own mother or other adults in authority – or even his own contemporaries. Pascal appears isolated, detached and friendless. His mother seems harsh and severe and demonstrates no emotional warmth towards her son. A later scene shows an equally indifferent father. His schoolteachers and headmaster, who might offer some warmth and understanding, are cold and dismissive, and treat him (and his balloon) as a nuisance. The headmaster shouts at him, 'Hurry up, get out of here! Get lost, you little pest!' Pascal is later hauled out of class and locked in detention by his irate headmaster when, on the second day, his balloon disrupts the lesson. Even the church has no place for him; the balloon threatens to disturb the service, and he and his new friend are cast out by an angry priest.

The second aspect depicted is the increasing attachment that develops between Pascal and his newfound 'friend'; as the story unfolds, they become inseparable. When his balloon is refused entry onto the bus, Pascal also refuses to board, making himself late for school. When his balloon is barred from the classroom, he seeks out another to take care of it in his absence. In the rain, he shelters it under the umbrellas of passers-by. And later, when it is pushed out of the tenement window by his disapproving mother, he secretly retrieves it and smuggles it back inside.

The film allows us to consider aspects of attachment theory that extend beyond the accepted view of shared relationships with caregivers and presents a helpful model for explaining how the development of our feelings and behaviour from early childhood through to adulthood may be affected by our earliest relationships.

John Bowlby, and subsequently Mary Ainsworth's work in developing attachment theory, provides a useful framework and context from which to explore how children thrive within secure, warm relationships. Bowlby (1969) believed that babies are born with instinctive predispositions to remain close to their mothers, or primary caregivers, as an innate form of self-preservation; separation can be emotionally and psychologically damaging. Research has shown that, among other factors, 'the forming of strong attachments and the demonstration of love, care and affection from the earliest days of a child's life ... can be crucial to the child developing emotional strength and resilience' (Field, 2010:87). This was initially believed to be through a secure relationship with the principal attachment figure or mother figure (Bowlby, 1951), leading to the view that mothers offered their children the best chance in life if they stayed at home with them in their earliest years. The idea that maternal deprivation could cause a child emotional and behavioural difficulties in later life and that day-care provision for young children could be detrimental became widely accepted (Harding, 1996; Burman, 2008).

Aldgate and Jones (2006) point out, however, that Bowlby, from his earliest writings, emphasized the importance of the caregiver's behaviour and nature, rather than their status, and that children could develop multiple attachment figures. The view has gradually morphed into one that recognizes that not only the primary caregiver but also other secure adults or settings such as nurseries and schools can provide a strong, secure base for the child; but a secure attachment bond is still recognized as a key attribute in a child's social and emotional development.

What does seem vital is that 'children need to feel others are positive towards them, and to experience realistic expectations in order to become competent, assertive and self-assured' (David, Goouch, Powell, & Abbott, 2003:61). Securely attached children tend to be more confident and self-assured with their peers and be comfortable with interacting socially with others (Rubin et al., 2015). Children who have an initial physical and emotional bond with a significant person – whether mother or other – grow to become independent and resilient and be able to tolerate later separation. They may be confident enough to explore beyond the circle of attachment, secure in the knowledge that their primary caregiver will be there for them as a secure base (Malekpour, 2007).

If attachment can be defined as 'an affectional bond' (Ainsworth, 1989:711), it would be difficult to imagine that young Pascal had a positive attachment to his mother. She appears indifferent to his wishes and to the significance of his newfound companion. We could surmise that a lack of secure attachment in his earliest years could have led to an inability to adjust in later years to forming relationships with his peers or other key figures in his life.

The Early Years Foundation Stage (EYFS) (DfE, 2014b) recognizes that the social context of a child's upbringing is important for their social and emotional development, and that children thrive when there are secure and loving relationships within the home and other settings. What if that secure attachment is missing, as appears in Pascal's case, or has been eroded? According to statistics, about 40 per cent of children in the UK do not have a secure attachment with their parents (Moullin, Waldfogel and Washbrook 2014). Does this mean that children in these situations are unable to develop socially and emotionally? If so, what are the implications for practice?

Bowlby proposed that a newborn baby moves and responds in tune to his/her mother's voice, and that the function of a baby's instinctive gestures such as crying and smiling is to draw forth favourable parental responses (Klaus & Kennel, 1982). Bowlby termed this pattern of responses to a baby's needs as social releasers, where a baby learns how to elicit pleasurable responses from its caregiver (Jarvis & Chandler, 2001). It is this interplay between social releasers and reciprocal responses that builds up an attachment between a baby and a carer.

However, not all parental responses are positive and not all children respond in expected ways. Some children learn from an early age to suppress emotions and natural responses because they are suffering abuse, neglect or other forms of trauma. Children who have experienced trauma – defined by Gerhardt (2014:158) as 'a confrontation with damage to body or mind' – may retreat into disengagement as a form of self-protection, and this is further discussed in Chapter 10. Practitioners need to be alert to 'the quiet child', the child who slips into the background unnoticed, who presents no trouble and poses no threat, yet who may be internalizing powerful and potentially harmful emotions.

Bowlby (1969) suggested that a young child forms a mental representation of its first attachment relationship, and once internalized, it becomes a pattern for the development of subsequent personal relationships. He termed this an internal working model. If the earliest/primary attachment was of a warm, responsive and caring nature, similar relationships would tend to follow; conversely, if abuse or neglect were to take place, then the child would more than likely reproduce this abusive pattern in the future. According to Jarvis (2004), Bowlby believed each generation carries forward their internal working model to the next, so a pattern of future relationships is forged in the past.

It is recognized that attachments formed in infancy play a significant and influential role in a child's social and emotional development (Malekpour, 2007). As Field (2010) points out, by the age of three, a child's brain is already 80 per cent developed; it is the child's earliest experiences that affect the way the brain grows and develops in these crucial formative years. As he reiterates, 'We imperil the country's future if we forget that it is the aspirations and actions of parents which are critical to how well their children prosper' (Field, 2010:11). The Strange Situation Procedure developed by Mary Ainsworth was designed to measure the security of mother–child attachments and patterns that they formed (Ainsworth et al., 1978). Van Rosmalen, van der Veer and van der Horst (2015) suggest that virtually all children experience attachment in one form or another, but it is the quality of that attachment relationship that is important. Malekpour (2007:86) acknowledges the 'array of developmental deficits that may endure over time' in children who lack a positive, trusting relationship with at least one emotionally responsive caregiver.

Additionally, there appears to be a direct correlation between insecure attachment in the early years with subsequent low academic achievement and behavioural issues in school. Cairns (2006) draws attention to the disorders that can result from trauma brought on through insecure attachment, including inability to self-regulate and manage behaviour, feelings of worthlessness and difficulty in making sense of feelings. These in turn may have an adverse effect on a child's ability to learn and cope with the pressures of school life. Read (2014:20) reminds us that 'each child has a story so far and to respect this fact each time we greet a new baby or child'. Practitioners need to be able to recognize the extent to which insecure attachment and early childhood experiences may have significant effects for the child within a setting, school and beyond, thus demonstrating clearly the important role that teachers and other practitioners play in providing secure, nurturing relationships, which may help children repair the effects of insecure attachment (Rose, Parker, Gilbert, Gorman, & McDonald, 2014).

Both Bowlby's and Ainsworth's work has come under scrutiny for a number of reasons, not least because of scepticism over the validity and reliability of the research studies (Brain and Mukherji, 2005) and their culture-specific nature (Smidt, 2006). Although Bowlby's findings were hugely influential at the time and had a significant impact on women's working patterns, it has been felt that they were too narrowly focused on attachment with one primary caregiver (Tizard, 1991).

The critical challenges to some of the research surrounding attachment does not focus on the mother/child bond alone; David et al. (2003) note that attachments can be both shifting and variable, influenced by a number of factors, such as the family's situation at a given time, or the changing nature of the mother's relationship with her developing child. Nonetheless, much lasting value has been drawn from Bowlby's and Ainsworth's early studies. Thinking has changed and is still evolving, but their work has made a significant impact on thinking and practice. According to Van Rosmalen et al. (2015:261), attachment theory 'has now reached textbook status and its adherents have published thousands of studies inspired by this theoretical framework'. Ainsworth's findings around attachment types have extended into the classroom as experts look at the ways early attachment issues are echoed in later relationships (Geddes & Hanko, 2006; Bergin & Bergin, 2009; Riley, 2010; Bombèr, 2011). Ideas around primary caregivers, a secure base and the need for secure attachments have had a profound influence on early years' practice, and are evident in the introduction of the 'key person approach', initiated by Elinor Goldschmied and promoted by Peter Elfer and colleagues (Elfer, Goldschmied & Selleck, 2003). This approach will be discussed in more detail later in the chapter.

Transitional phenomena and object attachment

The balloon becomes a friend (00:08:04–00:12:17)

Having thrust the balloon out of the window, Pascal's mother turns inside and closes the balcony doors firmly behind her. The balloon wafts in the air but keeps returning to the window, nudging against the glass as if to gain attention. Pascal spreads his hands on the window and peers out wistfully. He looks back to check his mother is not watching, opens the balcony door, reaches out to grab the string and sneaks the balloon back inside, closing the door behind him.

The next morning Pascal takes the balloon onto the balcony and addresses it for the first time: 'Balloon, you must obey me, and be good!' He releases it as he goes down to the pavement below; looking up and he calls the balloon down. Obediently the balloon descends, but as Pascal tries to catch it, it playfully evades him, staying just out of reach, dancing in his path. As he starts walking, the balloon follows. Every few steps Pascal looks back to check it is still behind him. Back and forth the balloon bobs, always staying just out of reach. Pascal hides around a street corner, waits for the balloon to come along, and at last manages to catch it! He appears to talk to it sternly, wagging his finger, then lets it go and walks on, checking behind him regularly. Gradually trust builds up between the boy and the balloon as they test each other out. The balloon hides in a doorway, Pascal turns round and it is gone! He walks back past the doorway, it pops out mischievously and follows just behind him; the boy turns suddenly, catches it again and runs on towards school.

This scene leads us to explore the concept of attachment further while raising a number of questions. Can a young child be said to have attachment to an inanimate – or even imaginary – object, which nonetheless in his or her imagination possesses human-like traits? Must attachment be to a prescribed entity or can it exist entirely in the imagination of the individual and still have validity?

'Transitional objects' and 'transitional phenomena' are concepts developed by Donald Winnicott, so termed because they support a child through the stages of transition from one experience to another. Winnicott (1953) describes transitional objects as the child's first 'not-me' possession that takes the place of the mother–child bond, as the child comes to terms with the discovery of its 'true self' as a separate entity. As a child begins to recognize its mother as distinct and separate (thought of at first as 'both self and not-self'), so a transitional space opens between them that may be filled by a toy or a blanket (Farrell, 2004:188). In this way, the transitional object symbolizes the mother–child union, but now as two separate but close entities, in the dawning realization that the mother is a separate being who is not and cannot always be present in times of need (Fritz, 2015). The object in itself, of course, is not transitional, but symbolizes the transition from a state of being one with the mother to a state of being in a distinct and separate relationship with her (Winnicott, 1971).

Inanimate, transitional objects can play an important part in alleviating attachment distress, as 'a concrete representation of an external source of comfort such as the mother' (Gleason, Sebanc & Hartup, 2000:420). Playing with such objects, or holding them close, tests the capacity for separation (Farrell, 2004). According to Fritz (2015:8), the child's attachment to a specific object reflects 'an imaginary transfer of the mother's soothing power onto the object', bringing relief from anxiety or separation. Emotional ties to transitional, inanimate objects such as a soft toy or a blanket (often referred to as a 'security blanket' or 'comfort object') are common in young children and appear to reduce anxiety, particularly when a primary caregiver is absent

(Passman, 1977). Lehman, Arnold and Reeves (1995:458) consider it to be 'a normal and important developmental phenomenon'. Use of these objects is more frequent when children become tired, anxious, ill, lonely or frightened. The treasured objects then become a source of comfort and consolation to children in lieu of their parents or primary caregiver, helping to reduce anxiety (Fortuna, Baor, Israel, Abadi & Knafo, 2014).

As Datler, Ereky-Stevens, Hover-Reisner and Malmberg (2012) point out, studies such as Ainsworth's Strange Situation Procedure, which measured secure and insecure attachments between mother and child, have proved that very young children experience feelings of loss and insecurity – even threat – in the presence of strangers and the absence of parents or primary caregivers. Children who regularly spend time in day care may develop an attachment to an inanimate object as a coping mechanism, as a means of securing comfort (Passman, 1977; Fortuna et al., 2014). In the film, we see Pascal's attachment to an inanimate object and his determination not to be parted from it, despite the best attempts of adults in authority. The balloon had become part of his life; it provided him with much-needed companionship, interacting with him in the absence of other close relationships. It became his comforter, a buffer to protect him from reality. That being the case, questions must be raised about when it is appropriate to confiscate or withhold such transitional objects from children who may rely on them to provide comfort from anxiety and separation. Indeed, do we as adults have the right to decide? Studies conducted by Lehman et al. (1995) indicate that children believe it is their prerogative, rather than an adult's, to make important decisions as to when to give them up. Jalango (1987) notes that young children can become frantic if their treasured object is removed or misplaced. She suggests that an attitude of tolerance and welcoming acceptance on behalf of teachers is more appropriate than insensitively insisting that a child should abandon its special object. Transition can, for some children, be traumatic; consequently, it should be managed at the natural pace of the child rather than the speed of the setting.

Friendships and relationships, imaginary friends and paracosms

Relationships (00:18:54–00:22:00)

Pascal is seen wandering through a flea market and encounters an antique painting as large as himself, leaning up against a wall; it features a life-size girl standing alone under a tree, holding a wooden hoop and stick.

Pascal seems entranced, held by her gaze. It is a poignant moment: does he recognize himself in this little girl – solitary and self-sufficient – or perhaps even imagine her as his friend?

At the same time, the balloon wafts through the market, coming to a halt in front of a large mirror. It hovers, turning this way and that, as if admiring its own reflection for the first time.

As they leave the flea market and enter the street, a little girl walks towards Pascal holding a large bright blue balloon. They ignore each other, but as they pass, Pascal's balloon turns around and follows the little girl. She tries to reach it, but it dodges her grasp, and Pascal runs back to claim his errant friend. Boy and girl seem to notice each other for the first time, in a scene reminiscent of those in the market earlier. There is a momentary pause as they stare at one another, and then Pascal walks off with his balloon. In a comic repetition of events, the blue balloon then takes its turn to follow Pascal, as if both are determined to bring the boy and girl together; but again, after a brief encounter, they turn and walk their separate ways.

As Pascal climbs the steps to his home, a group of boys are lying in wait for him, hiding behind a building. They let him pass, and then creep after him. He turns and sees them following, and as he begins to run, so do they. Another group is waiting to ambush him at the top of the next flight of steps, and as he begins to ascend, they climb down and trap him. He lets go of his treasured balloon and manages to escape, running fast, hotly followed by the baying gang. His balloon comes within reach and he catches it again, racing on home with the boys still in swift pursuit. Once more, he releases his balloon and runs inside. The boys watch as the balloon ascends to the fourth floor of the tenement block; Pascal opens his balcony door, reaches out and draws his friend inside to safety.

Having a friend is considered a positive influence in helping children to adjust to new transitions. Friends can offer reassurance and companionship, closeness and shared experiences, and help a child adjust during stressful times (Berndt & Keefe, 1995; Dowling, 2010). The transition to school or an early childhood setting is an uncertain time for young children. According to Dunn (2004), the development of friendships and positive interactions is a strong factor in providing social support and protection against the difficulties that some children experience. But while new transitions offer opportunities for the formation of new friendships and positive relationships, there is also the possibility of being rejected by one's peers.

There may be a host of diverse – and often conflicting – factors that affect the formation of strong bonds and friendships in early childhood. We have seen earlier that children suffer emotionally and socially when there is a lack of an established secure caregiver base, and that the consequences can be far-reaching. According to Smidt (1998), by the time most children are four years of age they will have established relationships with a significant number of other people, including parents, family relations, siblings, carers and friends. Establishing and maintaining these close childhood friendships, however, can be challenging as well as rewarding (Ruben et al., 2005).

Rose (2006) considers the difficulty of forming friendships for children whose sense of trust in others is already impaired through various adverse circumstances. This may be due in part to a lack of opportunity to develop relevant skills or build resilience and self-confidence. The effects of parental conflict or neglect can also be a factor in forming friendships, although the presence of siblings can serve as companionship and support in such circumstances, and sometimes help to ameliorate the effects (Cleaver, 2006).

However, a lack of friendships can cause developmental issues in children in terms of settling in at school, attainment and emotional resilience. Ironically, perhaps, it is that those children with the greatest need who are the ones most likely to find forming close friendships difficult. Daniel and Wassell (2002) suggest that the development of positive peer relationships, and particularly a close friend, is linked to the development of emotional resilience which can afford protection to vulnerable children. Quite simply, children who have experienced positive attachment experiences tend to be able to form positive relationships with their peers, whereas children who have suffered emotional neglect or have insecure attachment issues find the most difficulty in making and sustaining friendships (Aldgate and Jones, 2006; Dowling, Gupta & Aldgate, 2006).

Pascal seems to lead a solitary existence, unable to relate to his peers. He gazes wistfully at the little girl in the painting. Perhaps he recognized his own isolation in hers, perhaps he wondered if the toy she held was her only friend, as the balloon was his. Yet if he longed for friendship, he seemed unable to reach out and connect with it, even when he met a real girl, moments later, with a shiny balloon just like his.

The meeting and facilitating of the two balloons could, of course, be seen as representative of the mechanism of extending friendships. Practitioners should consider creating such opportunities to facilitate friendships where none exists; they need to develop strategies to support children who appear isolated and vulnerable – the 'emotionless' child in the nursery who resists affection, the solitary child in the playground, the socially isolated child who seems to find it difficult to relate to other peers, the child who appears to exist in 'another world', who daydreams or talks to an imaginary friend. Sunwolf and Leete (2004), in their extensive research into peer group experiences of children and adolescents, suggest a range of interventions to encourage social inclusion in schools, including involving pupils in the co-construction of new classroom rules; sharing stories of rejection and inclusion; and, crucially,

avoiding any insidious actions on the part of adults that reinforce marginalization, such as choosing teams for PE sessions with the inevitable consequence
of peer rejection.

Pascal seems to find establishing traditional attachments elusive, but he
is able to find friendship and companionship in the development of 'other'
strong emotional relationships. Pascal did not have what his contemporaries had – strength in friendship – yet he is suddenly in possession of something they want. The closing scene is an ugly depiction of the bullying culture
that can develop when peers become envious, or when one child stands out
from the crowd as different. Berndt (2004:210) identifies conflict and rivalry as
characteristic of the 'dark side of friendship', driven by self-interest. Sunwolf
and Leets (2004:196) acknowledge that a 'hidden culture of social cruelty'
can exist in peer groups. According to Rose (2006), bullying is extensive and
always has a negative impact on children, whatever their age. She points out
that it is often those who are already experiencing adverse circumstances
or negative experiences who suffer in this way. Bullying behaviour, as with
Pascal's peers, invariably shows 'an imbalance of power or strength between
the bully and the victim' (Levine & Tamburrino, 2014:271). Rubin et al. (2005)
identify the value of having a close mutual friend, particularly in situations
where a child is disliked, isolated or victimized by the majority of peers; they
suggest that the negative effects of peer rejection can be alleviated by the
benefits of a single best friend. Being without such a friend can exacerbate
feelings of negative self-worth in later life.

A variety of other factors, of course, may be influential in the development
of friendships and peer relationships, such as gender, appearance, disability,
social standing and family income, race and culture – or an intermingling of
these. Barron's (2011:668) ethnographic study on ethnicity and young children's
friendships in a UK kindergarten illustrates the 'shadows of difference' that
are cast by the practices and experiences offered by the setting, as children
negotiate their place in the group and their relationships with each other. In
his study, while friendships appeared at first sight to be established on the
grounds of skin colour or cultural groupings, the reality was more complex as
other less visible factors came to the fore, such as staff or family attitudes,
or the provision of culturally specific activities that reinforced the sense of
belongingness – or otherwise – to a specific group (Barron, 2011). Friendships
can therefore be shaped by the internalization of what children see, hear and
experience everyday, as much as by the individuals themselves and the choices
they make. Often the challenge for young children is to negotiate transition and
integration into a nursery or school system whose dominant values and culture – even language – are at odds with their own. The 'culture shock' may be
as real for children brought up, for example, in devout religious families or from
remote, isolated communities as for those from ethnic minority backgrounds.

The experience of being 'different' among peers, for whatever reason, and the way others react to that difference, will have an impact on a child's identity and self-esteem (Smidt, 2006). In turn, this will affect a child's ability to integrate with and belong to a peer group that sets the rules as to who should be admitted or excluded. In order to become members of a particular cultural group, Smidt (2006) suggests that children sometimes learn to assess their own cultural capital and adjust their own set of beliefs and values accordingly. The fear of exclusion and its concomitant sense of isolation can, in extreme cases, lead to disguising one's own identity in the quest to 'fit in', and this is further discussed in Chapter 3. Sunwolf and Leets (2004:197) describe group rejection as 'a silent social stress of childhood'. It can manifest itself negatively in the victim in low self-esteem, poor social skills, low academic achievement and later in aggressive behaviour. For children who are frequently rejected by their peers, school can become a lonely, anxiety-ridden experience.

Imaginary friends and paracosms

The film offers the possibility, of course, that the magical balloon is a creation solely in the mind of young Pascal. Imaginary companions in research literature generally incorporate personified objects, impersonated characters and invisible friends (Gleason et al., 2000). Imaginary friends dwell in the minds of many children as they are developing, ostensibly left behind as they enter adolescence. The ability to leave reality behind and enter the world of pretence and imagination is a remarkable human trait, which, according to Weisberg and Gopnik (2013), engages children's cognitive reasoning skills and helps them to solve problems in the real world.

Fritz (2015) recognizes the interplay between the imagination of children and the real world in which they live. He suggests that the developing imagination is one of the most wonderful aspects of childhood, and that imaginary friendships are a remarkable example of this development in action. It may be that for some children an imaginary companion may originate as a transitional object. A child's first stuffed toy is almost invariably given a name and may become animated in the child's imagination and treated as a living thing. But as the child matures so its need for a transitional or comfort object lessens, and instead a more personified, distinct character may emerge; although why this phenomenon occurs in some and not others remains unclear (Gleason et al., 2000). Fritz (2015) views the two as distinct. The transitional object may be the young child's first foray into the world of the imagination, but imaginary friendships represent 'a quantum leap beyond transitional objects in terms of childhood creativity', much like characters created within a novel (Fritz, 2015:8).

Taylor (1999) suggests that due to the influence of movies and novels, as well as related psychological research, parents tend to worry about the implications of their children having imaginary friends, concerned that they may be indicators of psychological problems. However, Taylor and Mottweiler (2008) consider their creation to be a healthy and normal – if intriguing – part of pretend play. Imaginary companions may well be created by children in response to trauma or troubling situations; however, far from being a cause for concern, Taylor (1999) believes that this demonstrates the child's resilience in the face of difficulty to continue to play freely and happily. While it appears conclusive from research that imaginary friends are created as a source of general companionship, some believe that children with imaginary friends tend to have particularly sociable natures despite seeking companionship in the invisible (Gleason et al., 2000).

Some children may use their imaginary friends as scapegoats for offences, deflecting blame and potential punishments (Emanuel, 2005; Fritz, 2015); they may be created in order to help children overcome feelings of isolation and loneliness, or as a useful vehicle through which to transfer hidden emotions, such as fear of the dark. If Pascal's companion is imagined and he 'conjured up' the balloon's existence as he wandered to school, we may suppose that his friend provided his unmet needs in terms of attachment and friendship to counterbalance his lonely existence, or as a form of escapism from a crueller, more brutal world.

According to Cohen and MacKeith (1992), children's spontaneous imaginings can take a variety of forms, ranging from pretence and daydreaming to the creation of imaginary characters; but a much more unusual form is 'worldplay', the invention of private imaginary worlds or 'paracosms'. Imaginary companions may form part of these wider invented worlds, particularly in children with intensely creative imaginations. Cohen and MacKeith (1992) suggest that children frequently return in their imaginations to their 'other world', and as they do, it becomes more and more elaborately designed and structured. Engagement in worldplay of this nature is often highly complex and may be indicative of creative giftedness, as well as providing opportunities to become creators within their own safe world (Root-Bernstein, 2009).

The final scene (00:29:28–00:34:23)

As the group of street thugs continue to give chase through the city's alleyways, Pascal and his balloon are eventually trapped on a hillside with no escape. His prized possession is downed by a single slingshot and viciously stamped into the dust. Pascal sits bereft and grieving on the waste ground overlooking the city, watching the life ebbing away from the only friend he possessed.

The balloon's lingering 'death' is a poignant scene that richly conveys the pain of separation and loss. But there follows an unexpected twist to the tale. Suddenly, vibrant balloons of every colour magically fly up from children's hands and from doorways and windows across the city, floating together in their hundreds up to the hillside where Pascal sits alone. He reaches out to catch them as they descend, and as he gathers the strings together, the balloons swing his feet off the ground and he is lifted high up into the air and over the rooftops. The film draws to a close with Pascal soaring free over the grey city under a canopy of colour – a final transition, perhaps, into freedom from those ugly scenes of brutality and the confinement of his childhood

Transition and the key person role

Developmental psychologist Urie Bronfenbrenner (1979:26) has described transitions as when the position of an individual 'is altered as the result of a change in role, setting, or both'. He explains the nature of transitions from an ecological systems perspective in terms of changing identities and expectations, influenced by people and contexts (Bronfenbrenner, 2005). His theoretical model offers a helpful approach for studying transitions. It allows us to consider the child's position in society as never in isolation, affected by the interrelationships between different influences on the child and family experience (Vogler, Crivello & Woodhead, 2008).

Transitions occur on many levels through multiple interrelating influences on the child. During their earliest years, children are likely to experience more 'handovers' than at any other stage in their lives (Dowling, 2010); by the time they reach school age, they may have experienced a transition from home to childcare provider, from one provider to another within the same day or week, between room bases within the setting, and from the setting to reception class. Once in mainstream school, they will experience further transitions as they move from reception into year 1, and subsequently into different year groups; there will also be changes in key staff or other attachment figures.

There are social and external factors, too, that may bring about change such as moving house, loss and bereavement, or birth of a sibling. For babies and young children, transitions are clearly an inevitable part of development and maturation. It is vital for children's well-being that practitioners consider ways to support transitions. Children will respond differently to transitional experiences; some with anticipation and excitement, others with nervousness or concern. The way they cope will depend on a number of factors, including their prior home-life experiences and the kind of response or support they receive in preparation for the process.

Brooker (2008:75) gives us a glimpse into the anxiety felt by a young child 'graduating' to primary school for the first time:

> I felt scared because I did not know my teacher. I did not see any sand area, or a carpentry corner, not even a see-saw or a swing … My teacher gave orders to us and we had to move quickly or else.

Such transitional changes can present challenges that are stressful for children. Datler et al. (2012) suggest that the quality of interactions provided by professionals during these periods is of key importance. Communication and consultation between parents and other professionals – and the children themselves – are crucial in tuning in to individual children's needs in order to provide positive, happy experiences. Noddings (2012) emphasizes the importance of attentive listening and engagement in dialogue on both an intellectual and emotional level in order for teachers to build caring, trusting relationships with their pupils and meet individual needs effectively.

This practice is exemplified in the 'key person' approach introduced under one of the four underlying principles of the EYFS: 'Children learn to be strong and independent through positive relationships' (DfE, 2014b:6). The approach, initiated by Elinor Goldschmied and promoted by Peter Elfer and colleagues (Elfer et al., 2003), is now a statutory part of the EYFS framework. It is linked to attachment theory and the ideas around primary caregivers and a secure base. It is an aspect of practice which encourages a reciprocal relationship between a practitioner and a child, and the parent or carer – a nurturing attachment-like relationship which provides a safe haven and secure base.

As each key person in a setting develops a close relationship with the children in their care, so each child will feel secure, cherished and cared for in the absence of the primary caregiver. Gerhardt (2004) emphasizes the need for carers not to simply follow a caring routine, even in the case of young babies, but to show sensitive responsiveness and to be highly attuned to their individual needs.

For some children, regrettably, transition is a 'painful and constant factor of their lives' as they move in and out of the care system, or from one family to another (Fisher, 2010:43). It is challenging for children in these situations to form any close or lasting attachments; as a result, they may find it difficult to socialize with peers or trust other adults, and so become anxious, fearful, withdrawn, isolated, angry, disruptive, even destructive. Further transitions may trigger painful memories of rejection and loss in an already unstable situation (Rose, Parker, Gilbert, Gorman & McDonald, 2014). Fisher (2010:42) notes the struggle for children whose home life is chaotic and uncertain; the resilience required as they have to constantly readjust to new situations can become 'a thin veil between coping and collapsing' and this is discussed further in Chapter 10.

Consequently, if the transitions in the lives of vulnerable children are not managed properly, they may result in significant setbacks or trauma (Bombèr, 2007; 2011 Rose, Parker, Gilbert, Gorman & McDonald 2014). Conversely, changes that are managed well may provide a positive experience that can aid recovery from trauma and lead to valuable learning experiences. Nagel (2009) suggests that school may act like a buffer against the impact of stress and help to build resilience. Bergin and Bergin (2014) believe that teachers need to understand the role of attachment in the classroom in order to provide for children more effectively, particularly those children who may be challenging and disruptive. Where children have struggled with secure attachments, the effects can be far-reaching (Rubin et al., 2015). As practitioners, teachers and significant others in children's lives, we need to be alert to children with attachment issues who, like Pascal, appear disengaged, isolated, in a world of their own. It is imperative that practitioners recognize their role in providing those all-important attachments and transform our settings, our classrooms, our schools into secure bases that become places of effective learning (Bergin & Bergin, 2009; Riley, 2010).

Studies have shown that important attachment-like relationships can be provided beyond the home environment by teachers, youth workers and other key adults in a child's life (Bergin & Bergin, 2009; Riley, 2010; Granot, 2014). According to Granot (2014), the establishment of nurturing relationships between teacher and child produced higher academic achievement and lower levels of behaviour problems than insecure teacher–child attachment groups. Bergin and Bergin (2009:141) likewise concluded that secure attachments – to teachers as well as parents – influence academic success, and that 'enhancing teacher-student relationships is not merely an add-on, but rather is fundamental to raising achievement'. In a culture where priority is given to children becoming school-ready and academically competent, schools need to become welcoming havens of safety, made ready for our children.

In the film, Pascal's final transition is one that represents triumph over adversity, and escape from all that confined him. And so this chapter must end with the acknowledgement that not all transitions are traumatic for children or detrimental to their well-being. For some children there will be no happy endings; but for others – even for those whose lives have already been blighted by adverse situations – change and transition can be positive and result in outcomes that transform lives.

Concluding thoughts

At one level, the film is an enchanting narrative depicting the innocence of childhood; but a closer examination exposes themes of loneliness, rejection, hatred and violence, which throw into sharp contrast discourses of childhood innocence and the joy of youth. It highlights complexities and offers a stimulus for enquiry. It poses difficult questions, for which there are no easy answers. Elements of childhood are uncovered that may be uncomfortable and far from idyllic. Students need to consider these issues in the light of their own emerging professional identity and practice.

The chapter has considered what the red balloon might mean to Pascal: an attachment-like figure meeting an unmet attachment need; a transitional object affording relief from anxiety and isolation; an imaginary friend in lieu of positive peer relationships; and a key person, sharing intuitive moments and providing a secure base. In the film, society conspired to separate the child and the balloon through a series of rejection experiences where they were refused entry, thrust out or forced apart (from the bus, the school, his home, the church and finally from each other). A useful allegory perhaps of how society and its apparatus may conspire to separate children from their safe place or treasured possession, however that may be represented.

This chapter offers a broader view of attachment theory than a commonly accepted two-dimensional mother–child relationship and argues that a host of diverse – often conflicting – factors affect the formation of strong bonds and friendships in early and later childhood, indicating perhaps that there is no single way to understand the complex nature of attachment and relationships in the holistic development of children; and that the formation of strong bonds and friendships is multifaceted in its complexity.

In relation to the discussions earlier, you might want to reflect on the following questions:

- If, as Van Rosmalen et al. (2015) suggest, the quality of attachment relationships is important, what may happen to the child who lacks a positive, trusting relationship with at least one caregiver?

- Transitional objects can be important elements in the social and emotional development of children, how are they understood within settings?

- Should a child's imaginary friend be a cause for concern? How might we respond positively if we notice a child interacting with an invisible 'friend'?

5

Attachment, Personality and Deviant Behaviour:
We Need to Talk about Kevin

Jim Dobson

T*hat children are capable of violence, of rape, muggings and even murder, is an idea that clearly falls outside traditional formulations of childhood.*
— (Jenks, 1996:127).

This chapter will consider:

- Attachment theories: Bowlby (1988).

- The interconnectedness of nature and nurture: Watson (1924), Skinner (1969).

- Genetics, psychology and criminal profiling: Hare (1998).

- Sociological theories of motherhood: Badinter (2013), Butler (1990).

- Psychotherapy: Schwab (2010).

- Philosophy: Sartre (2003).

This chapter examines the 2011 film *We Need to Talk about Kevin* (*WNTTAK*) to explore ideas about attachment, social conditioning, philosophy, psychology and sociology. What is crucial are the ideas, concepts and theories which connect to the story, rather than the story itself. Of course, much like the other chapters in this book, by watching the film, students will develop a greater appreciation of the applied concepts. The film is particularly useful for enhancing our knowledge of children's learning and development and allowing us to question long-held assumptions about why children exhibit certain behaviours. The film also helps us to explore ideas on attachment, child psychology and motherhood, helping to show that children are open to many influences which interact in complex and sometimes unexpected ways.

The film is based on Lionel Shriver's 2003 novel of the same name. Set largely in an anonymous American suburb, the film depicts the difficult and often harrowing relationship between Eva and her son, Kevin. Eva enjoys a hugely successful career in the travel business. She appears to have a happy, fulfilling relationship with her partner, Franklin. However, Eva's life changes radically from the moment she discovers she is pregnant. Eva finds herself disliking Kevin from the moment she falls pregnant, resenting his invasive, unplanned and unwelcome presence. The absence of any type of early attachment exacerbates Eva's hostility towards Kevin. As Kevin's difficult and tortuous passage through childhood is presented through a series of flashbacks (and in the form of letters in the book), the relationship between mother and child becomes increasingly bitter, adversarial and hostile. Eva begins to record Kevin's developmental milestones, not by conventional, established means, such as learning to walk and talk, play and communicate, but through his stubborn, hostile and sometimes violent interactions with her. *WNTTAK* follows a grim, increasingly desolate chronological trajectory, culminating in Kevin, aged fifteen, carrying out a high school massacre after coldly and calculatingly executing his father, Franklin, and his younger sister, Celia, before leaving the family home that same morning.

Directed by Lynne Ramsey, the film carefully exposes and emphasizes the distance between Kevin (as a teenager played by Ezra Miller) and the social world he inhabits. The film, and Ezra Miller's performance, manages to emphasize the deep contempt Kevin appears to hold for his immediate family. Tilda Swinton plays the central role, Eva, sensitively and convincingly. Although Eva's character seems cold, detached and distant and, therefore, difficult to like, there is, nonetheless, sympathy for her dreadful predicament.

Depictions of children as evil

The idea that children can inflict severe violence upon and kill others is, as Jenks (1996) suggests, difficult for many of us to conceptualize. Although tragic incidents of this nature (in which children are perpetrators) thankfully fall outside of what most of us have, or are likely to encounter, they serve a valuable purpose in provoking us into critically exploring the reasons why they sometimes happen. This chapter deals with such an extreme and disturbing scenario, and thankfully one that remains extremely rare, albeit highly publicized globally, notably the Columbine High School Massacre in America in 1999 and the murder of James Bulger in Merseyside, England, in 1993. Fictionalized accounts, often turned into popular horror movies such as *Village of the Damned* (1960), *The Omen* (1976), *Children of the Corn* (1984) and *Them* (2006), symbolize a sustained appetite and fascination with the concept that children have a propensity towards evil. Interestingly, this is a notion of childhood that is nothing new, and has maintained a presence in European countries for many hundreds of years:

> There is a vast literature which suggests that the child is at birth intrinsically evil, or at least in need of improvement, and that it is the duty of parents and adults to school the child, to get rid of unfortunate characteristics and behaviours and, in brief, to redeem it so that it can become an effective adult. This view is, of course, underpinned by much Christian literature which stresses the need for redemption and the extent to which humankind is innately evil. The idea that humankind is innately wicked is an enduring and pervasive one and it has underpinned much of the thinking about childhood during the last two millennia. (Lowe, 2004:67)

WNTTAK defies genre, and certainly does not sit comfortably with the sensational, far-fetched horror/science fiction films identified earlier. By contrast, what distinguishes this film is its proximity to the real world; the events portrayed might easily transform from pure fiction to a modern-day news story. Lynne Ramsey's film captures the fragility and uncertainty of modern life and contains painful echoes of contemporary tragedies involving children (such as those identified earlier), which leave an indelible mark on our living history. *WNTTAK*, made in 2011, seems fitting in terms of how we regard childhood today, through a more sophisticated, cautious and questioning lens (James & Prout, 1997; Rogers & Rogers, 1992).

WNTTAK, as the reader will discover, offers no answers or convenient explanations for Kevin's monstrous behaviour. Despite the setting and its trans-Atlantic distance, the ideas and possibilities raised in *WNTTAK* can be transposed to familiar, local contexts, most notably through the haunting legacy of the James Bulger case. An event which produced a significant effect on the psyche of the British public and its resultant hostile, unforgiving attitudes towards 'deviant' children (Haydon & Scraton, 2000).

The opening scene (00:02:00–00:06:30)

Eva is being held aloft and carried by a group of crimson-coated revellers at a tomato festival in Bunol, Spain. Eva's entire body is covered in thick red, pulpy juice as she is carried, dream-like, through the heaving, 'bloody' masses. The film quickly cuts to the present day. Upon awakening and opening her front door, Eva discovers that the front of her small residence has been maliciously smeared with thick red paint (the colour, red, appears a great deal in the film, offering a visceral backdrop).

This striking scene of the film clearly makes reference to Eva's attempts to reconcile the past with the present, using sudden flashbacks, often lurching with violent jolts between the pivotal episodes and events leading up to the massacre and Eva's forlorn, desperate and lonely existence, where the film begins. This rather unsettling cinematic effect serves to remind the viewer that our perceptions of children and families can be challenged: the shocking and perplexing issues the film raises are only heightened by these uncomfortable flashbacks.

Links to theory and literature

As discussed in the previous chapter, the relationship between a mother and child can wildly deviate from traditional sociological and behaviourist models based on the importance of family and the influence of our immediate environment (Watson, 1924; Skinner, 1969) and established ideas around attachment (Bowlby, 1988). The film is stark, brutal, and ultimately leads us to question conventional, established assumptions about the nature of childhood, hence its inclusion in this book.

Students can sometimes experience a profound sense of confusion and frustration in attempting to make sense of the many sociocultural and psychological theories they encounter as part of undergraduate study. Specifically, theories about children's socialization, learning, behaviour and development can (and should!) compete, overlap and transcend each other, allowing the student to consider their relative merit or limitations. This chapter, and the film it uses as a backdrop, offers some solace for those attempting to understand these shifting sands, raising the possibility that this flux of competing, contradictory and sometimes disarmingly persuasive explanations for children's behaviour might be more helpfully understood as part of a fluid, organically evolving landscape.

This chapter, the reader will appreciate, cannot account for every theory the student is likely to encounter as part of their undergraduate study, but instead contains a careful selection of perspectives drawn from a number of academic fields. Furthermore, readers are encouraged to avoid seeking simplistic explanations in relation to interpreting and explaining children's behaviour, and in doing so, be open to the possibility that the social world children (and adults) inhabit is multifaceted, ever-changing and therefore complex.

The following sections detail some of these important connections between *WNTTAK* and theories and concepts likely to be of interest to the student.

Nature versus nurture

There are a number of scenes in the film which suggest Kevin's nature has been formed wholly independently from those around him. This is often characterized by Kevin's complete detachment and disinterest in his surroundings and in his relationships with others.

Eva visits Kevin in prison (00:24:34–00:27:00)

Throughout the scene there is no warmth, physical contact or body language – signs which would normally denote a human connection. Kevin stares blankly ahead, carefully chewing off each of his fingernails and placing them on the table between himself and his mother. Kevin shows no emotion, connectedness and a striking absence of any awareness of events, objects and people around him.

Family relationships (01:02:02–01:02:46)

In contrast to Kevin, his younger sister, Celia, appears to be a happy, responsive, loving child. Celia communicates with others and shows affection towards her immediate family. In one scene, which depicts a rare moment of happiness, Franklin and Celia waltz together, Celia's feet placed on top of her father's. This affectionate scene contrasts sharply with the emotional abyss which exists between Eva and Kevin – a relationship without warmth or connection. Kevin appears to exist and act as if he is entirely independent of events and the people around him. Nurture does not appear to play any part in Kevin's life – he is clearly very different from other children.

In reviewing the earlier scenes, one might conclude that Kevin's nature and character are so innately corrupted and irretrievably damaged that nothing could possibly have prevented him from behaving the way he did. In essence, you might surmise that he is clearly a monster, devoid of all humanity, conscience and morality. What is not so clear is what creates and motivates such an individual to act so abhorrently. Can our upbringing influence our moral development and be held responsible for the actions we commit later in life or do we simply respond and act upon a series of predetermined, biological influences, beyond our comprehension and control? The picture is perhaps more complicated than we might initially assume.

A logical point to begin searching for an explanation for Kevin's crimes might be through considering the possibility that genetics and/or the environment in which a child develops play a crucial role. In the absence of a nuanced approach, the nature versus nurture debate can be presented as an overly simplistic dichotomy (Plomin, DeFries & Fulker, 2006), with little consideration of the variations in the lives of individual children. In Kevin's case, if we assume that Kevin is someone who is wholly governed by nature and his genetic predisposition, there is nothing his parents can do to alter the unfortunate and unavoidable fact that Kevin is irreducibly evil. The tranche of national media coverage, particularly from the tabloid press, surrounding the murder of James Bulger in 1993, presented similar dangerous ideas to a general public who were struggling to find a reason to explain such a tragic and unusual event. Newspaper headlines from 1993, along with readers' letters, cast a disturbing shadow over the belief that children were innocent beings, oblivious to concepts of evil. Instead, headlines referred to Venables and Thompson as 'evil freaks', 'the spawn of Satan' and 'little devils'. Jenks (1996) suggests the two perpetrators were no longer viewed as children, but instead as monsters, capable of inhuman savagery. Eva gradually begins to see Kevin as a monster, believing herself to be helpless in distracting him from his diabolical trajectory. Eva is powerless to rescue Kevin, or exert any positive parental influence; his fate irretrievably bound up with his corrupted genetic make-up.

Clearly, such primitive and simplistic explanations, while possibly satisfying a base desire for retribution for some, offer nothing in terms of identifying the underlying reasons for such atrocious deeds. It is worth taking a brief look at current research in genetics and psychology, especially in relation to criminal and deviant behaviour. These fields of enquiry seek to offer a degree of certainty, helped along by virtue of their endorsement by the scientific community.

Robert Hare's work in the field of criminal psychology, recently popularized by Jon Ronson's *The Psychopath Test: A Journey through the Madness Industry* (2011), is based on Hare's 'Psychopathy Checklist Revised' (PCL-R) test, which, according to some, is a reliable indication of psychopathy. Worryingly, Hare and many who work in the criminal psychology field are convinced that psychopaths are perhaps more commonplace than we might assume, forming part of our everyday lives. Hare describes psychopaths as 'people who are so emotionally disconnected that they can function as if other people are objects to be manipulated and destroyed without any concern' (Chivers, 2014).

Interestingly, Hare's checklist includes, among other nefarious qualities, a lack of remorse, emotional shallowness, callousness and a lack of empathy, an unwillingness to accept responsibility for actions, behavioural problems in early childhood and criminal versatility. Worryingly, Kevin's profile appears to closely match these and the other defined traits which form the PCL-R test. At first glance, using such a checklist, it is easily conceivable that one might label Kevin a psychopath.

Psychopathy, like autism, is defined and measured using a spectrum. There are individuals, maybe those familiar to us, who have certain traits that feature in the make-up of a psychopath, for example, narcissistic tendencies or a lack of empathy or compassion. These traits, in isolation, are relatively harmless, but when combined with the others on Hare's checklist, and where they all score consistently high (as perhaps in Kevin's case), there is a heightened degree of risk to others. Not all psychopaths are criminals and, according to Ronson (2011), can lead successful careers in politics, business and other lucrative, high-profile fields. It appears that being labelled a psychopath is no guarantee that you will be violent towards others or commit criminal acts.

However, Kevin's atrocities are perhaps better understood, and more easily accounted for; if we are confident that he is a psychopath. Advances in psychology and neuroscience have helped to deliver more certainty in these areas, although such developments are always contested and open to fresh challenges. What is still unclear are the root causes of psychopathy, although when Hare's checklist is scrutinized, it appears to be a mixture of emotional, behavioural, environmental and cognitive factors that are all important. While it is possible to allocate somebody a score for such conditions, we are no nearer to identifying the underlying dominant influences. Again, this suggests that what propels us to act in a certain way is complicated, changing and almost impossible to predict. Even in scientific fields such as criminal psychology, elements of uncertainty conspire against those who seek clear explanations. Research into genetics is increasingly willing to incorporate and allow for the importance of environmental influences, while maintaining the argument that aggressive behaviour is partly a consequence of variations in genetic composition and patterns of neurotransmission (Reif et al., 2007).

Perhaps Kevin's parents, life experiences and his surroundings are largely responsible for his violent behaviour and ultimately the execution of his family and school peers. The idea that a child's parents and carers are pivotal in terms of how a person develops in relation to their behaviour, morality and personality is an enduring one. Heywood, when describing such notions and their popularity through the Middle Ages and beyond (2001:35), suggests that people

> were familiar with the notion of the child as soft as wax, which could be moulded in various ways, or as a tender branch which needed to be trained in the right direction ... [while] from the Renaissance onwards ... [t]he idea that 'the hand that rocks the cradle shapes the destiny of society' became received wisdom.

James and James (2012:77) refer to traits such as altruism and aggression, noting that such qualities,

> exhibit themselves with disconcerting unevenness in people's behaviour. Therefore, the fact that we are not all equally aggressive, selfish, self-sacrificing, hardworking and so on requires us to try to identify what processes might modify our natural tendencies or help us to learn to behave differently from how our nature might otherwise dictate.

In other words, arguments which seem to favour nature over nurture or vice versa are fraught with uncertainty. We are dealing with complexity and difference and so it might be better to think in terms of likelihood rather than seeking the comfort of conclusiveness and absolute certainty in relation to explaining children's behaviour. This lack of certainty can cause students anxiety in instances where, for example through prior learning, complex phenomena are reduced to simplistic, one-dimensional explanations which lack the sophistication needed to embrace the sophistication of children's worlds. Such discomfort is helpful in recognizing alternative possibilities we might not have been aware of previously.

Valdre (2014:152) helpfully suggests that when taking account of various competing theoretical models, it is helpful to remember that 'each one of us emerges from an intricate, specific and extremely personal interrelation between nature and environment; one or the other component will prevail, sometimes mysteriously'. The suggestion here is that it is almost impossible to predict outcomes in relation to children's development and future behaviour with any degree of accuracy.

Harris (1998) rejected traditional and established theories around attachment and child development, contesting that parents should not be endowed with the credit for their children's development and progress. Harris's unpopular suggestion was that traits, instead of being predominantly forged through interactions with parents and other close family and friends, might instead be shaped through genetic patterns passed down through generations. In other words, the parents and immediate family are relatively powerless in being able to shape the child's personality and behaviour.

We are beginning to appreciate, when thinking about Kevin, that ideas around nature–nurture help to join some of the dots together, but alone are quite limited in developing a holistic understanding of his behaviour and development.

Nurture and motherhood

A quest for certainty and the demand for definitive answers can also be a concern for parents, especially those who might be seeking a diagnosis for their children's troubling behaviour. The suggestion that professionals, such as paediatricians and psychologists, may not have a ready answer can be unwelcome and unsettling, especially in cases where a child's behaviour is erratic, unpredictable or, as in Kevin's case, violent. The way parents perceive themselves as either coping or chaotic, good or bad, can also be tangled up in the quest for such answers.

Eva takes Kevin to see a doctor (00:36:06–00:36:55)

Eva seeks reassurance when she takes Kevin (aged two) to the doctors because she is worried that his development is impaired. Eva decides there must be something wrong with Kevin and she explains to the doctor that Kevin is not yet speaking and is worried that he may be autistic. The doctor checks Kevin's hearing and suggests to Eva that there is nothing wrong with him. Eva appears disappointed in the doctor for not attaching a condition or a label to Kevin and fears that his behaviour might be a manifestation of her (self-perceived) failure and spiralling incompetence as a mother.

Eva appears to lack instinctive, nurturing feelings; she is alone, lost and frightened. As a wealthy, educated, middle-class mother, the idea of asking for help might be seen as an admittance of failure and a dereliction of duty. Eva has excelled in life, as a bright, successful, self-made, independent woman: she is an icon of meritocracy, hard work and material success, a testament to Western capitalist ideology. She has grown a business empire from scratch, is the main wage earner and has achieved a status many can only dream of. Failure, for Eva, is something new, and something alien and frightening.

An underlying assumption here is that mothers instinctively know what is best for their children. Motherhood, Eva assumes, is about playing a particular role. The role involves nurture, love, the formation of strong, everlasting bonds. Despite knowing what motherhood looks like, Eva struggles to perform the role convincingly. Eva quickly begins to realize she does not conform to the familiar model of motherhood as a gendered talent; as something that comes with the territory of being a woman (Cowdery and Knudson-Martin, 2005). Perhaps this is a consequence of Eva's strong independence and her unwillingness to conform to traditional expectations of what constitutes the ideal mother. Kevin is perhaps aware of Eva's discomfort in playing the role of a mother and, in his own way, is simply reacting in kind.

The extent to which motherhood has become more open to scrutiny and comment tends to have grown alongside the values, aspirations and general welfare directed towards children in recent decades:

> As children have gained in cultural and emotional significance in affluent societies in the past century, so parenting, and in particular mothering, has become more keenly interwoven, in both practical and symbolic ways, with responsibility towards children and the problematic of risk, anxiety, and uncertainty (Coutant et al., 2011: online).

Today, the concentrated focus around, and the idealization of, motherhood is continually present. Badinter (2013) argues that mothers, in recent times, are expected to achieve on a number of levels; through the pursuit of successful careers, through the domestic sphere and as an embodiment of love and nurture – there is little scope for imperfection. Inevitably, feelings of guilt and inadequacy result in women who feel pressurized in colluding with the ideal of the perfect mother–child relationship. As Badinter (2013:14) asserts, 'The specter of the bad mother imposes itself on her even more cruelly insofar as she has unconsciously internalized the ideal of the good mother.'

Eva is acutely aware of her shortcomings as a mother. Instead of taking on this gender role with willingness and grace, Eva is repulsed by her physiological reaction to becoming a mother and is hugely disappointed that she cannot meet the social expectations that are part of this role, which only succeeds in exacerbating the difficulties she stubbornly attempts to overcome.

Eva struggles with motherhood (00:24:15–00:30:10)

The film shows Eva struggling with motherhood from the outset. Her attempts to pacify Kevin as he screams and cries meet with stubborn and sustained indifference. Eva is desperately attempting to subdue an angry Kevin who, at this point, is still a baby. Eva uses a calm, soothing voice to no avail, and so decides to take Kevin out in his pram. She pushes Kevin, still screaming loudly, around the busy sidewalks of New York, attracting disapproving looks from pedestrians. Eva finds solace by positioning Kevin's pram next to some roadworks, the pneumatic drill almost drowning Kevin's persistent and harsh cries. Eva's face is a grimace, set with futility, frustration and helplessness as she struggles through each endless day until Franklin returns from work typically upbeat and seemingly oblivious to the mental and emotional turmoil that has prevailed throughout Eva's day.

WNTTAK skilfully balances the possibility of a mother who is disconnected, impatient and lost, against the idea that Kevin is simply an exceptionally demanding child, subtly suggesting that it may be Eva who is at fault. When Franklin returns home, all is peaceful, almost as if the day and its traumas had been imagined, or at least exaggerated by Eva, given her vulnerable state of mind. The idea that Kevin might have been so unreasonable and remonstrative appears an unlikely scenario to Franklin as he greets his smiling son. The tension between Eva and Kevin intensifies throughout the film as does the distance between Eva and Franklin. It is largely unspoken, but implied through the passage of Kevin's early years that Franklin perceives Eva to be deficient and lacking in her role as a mother. Eva, of course, is acutely aware of this, adding additional pressure to her increasingly stressful and fragile situation.

Butler (1990) suggests that women undertake a series of performative acts and in doing so create and reaffirm their gender. Women are compelled to conform to and perform a particular role in relation to motherhood; good mothers are unfailingly caring, loving and protective towards their children. Eva's attempts to meet this socially constructed ideal of motherhood fail as she lacks the self-belief and conviction needed to succeed in the role and she becomes increasingly aware of her own limitations.

Such divergent and subversive performative acts might, according to Butler's ideas, attract disapproval and, in some cases, punishment. In Eva's case, such masquerading causes personal suffering in the form of self-doubt and denial.

Eva's repugnance and disgust towards Kevin are deeply felt during her pregnancy. Shiloh's (2009:3) description of Eva's feelings reveal the extent of her resentment of Kevin:

She [Eva] feels appropriated, invaded by a hostile parasite, a nine-month voracious freeloader. Rather than experiencing the elation of creating a new life, she bleakly identifies with the horrors of childbirth projected in *Rosemary's Baby* or *Alien,* in which pregnancy is portrayed as infestation, as the colonization of the female body by some nightmarish creature.

Increasing hostility and frustration
(00:43:22–01:00:00)

Eva's hostility towards Kevin, combined with her self-styled imprison-ment imposed through motherhood, gain momentum during his early years, becoming strikingly evident when manifested in episodes of uncon-tainable frustration. She explains to Kevin one day, when he is about two years old, that, 'Mummy was happy before Kevin came along. Now she wakes up every morning and wishes she was in France [Eva travelled exten-sively as part of her work before Kevin was born].' Unfortunately, Franklin hears Eva saying this and shakes his head, quietly despairing at Eva's cruel and tactless admonishment. It is increasingly clear that, as parents, Eva and Franklin do not subscribe to the same parenting style.

Eva is increasingly and uncomfortably aware of her failings as a mother, but at the same time, she is unable to suppress her emotions that some-times manifest themselves in violent and sudden ways. Eva and Franklin row about leaving New York, Kevin, now aged four, listens in, mimicking the argument through a series of 'Na, Na, Na, Na' repetitions. Eventually, Eva snaps at Kevin, smacking his hand sharply.

Eva's ability to cope with Kevin's behaviour is severely tested when Kevin, aged between four and five years old, decides to defecate in his nappy (Kevin's developmental milestones are markedly delayed despite his evident intelligence and guile). This happens while Eva is attempting to test him on his mathematical ability (00:57:10). Kevin at first refuses to answer Eva's questions, instead offering incorrect answers with the sole intent of aggravating Eva. His tactics appear, as usual, to be working, but instead of continuing to torment his mother, Kevin begins to nonchalantly count upwards from one to fifty exceptionally quickly. Eva, rather than praising Kevin, instead offers him a piece of paper with some difficult additions she has written for him to complete. Kevin screws the paper up, throws it behind him, and stares intently at Eva while filling his nappy, much to the disgust and horror of his mother. After changing Kevin, who appears to like the con-trol he crudely exerts through such tactics, he looks over his shoulder at Eva, wryly smiling as he defecates again with demonstrable audible effect. This time Eva responds badly, throwing Kevin against a wall with unnecessary, violent force. Kevin stares up at Eva, with what appears to be a look of smug satisfaction etched on his face, his arm clearly broken.

Motherhood, at least in its romanticized, wholesome form, seems unattain-able for Eva. She appears to be biologically and psychologically unsuited for the role expected of her. Motherhood, as a natural and instinctive way of being, is a powerful notion and attracts continued credibility. Motherhood, according to some, is a natural extension of womanhood, involving the same self-sacrificing, caring and nurturing ideals:

> A view that holds women to be caring to the point of self-sacrifice is propagated at all levels of thought and action; it figures in art and literature, it is the prop of official social welfare policies and it is the currency in which the social exchanges within marriage and the domestic sphere are transacted. It means that women accept the validity of this view as readily as men do. (Dalley, 1996:21)

Established, but perhaps less entrenched, Western models of fatherhood, by contrast, often confer roles of providing, guiding, protecting and sometimes nurturing upon men. Routinely negotiated, these roles depend on the economic and work imperatives within the family unit. Eva, through choice and expectation, becomes the main carer, while Franklin continues to work, a constant source of angst and regret for Eva. In contrast to Eva's relationship with her son, Franklin appears to enjoy time spent with Kevin, seemingly able to play with his son without having to resort to bribery or through putting on an act. Father and son happily sit together on the sofa playing a 'shoot 'em up' video game, Kevin excitedly shouting 'Die, die, die!!' as his father is temporarily immersed in the game, oblivious to the terrible foreshadowing of what lies ahead.

The Importance of attachment

Eva giving birth (00:27:16–00:27:40)

The birth appears to be traumatic. The camera cuts to show Eva sitting upright in bed, looking forlorn and unhappy as Kevin's father, Franklin happily bounces Kevin on his knee, cheerfully oblivious to the distressed appearance of Eva who stares blankly ahead. The film skilfully and quickly exposes the lack of emotional bond or warmth between Kevin and Eva; lack of attachment is clearly significant from the beginning of their relationship.

Bowlby's definition of attachment has particular resonance with Eva and Kevin's relationship. Bowlby (1977:127) viewed attachment as:

> A way of conceptualising the propensity of human beings to make strong affectionate bonds to particular others and of explaining particular others and of explaining the many forms of emotional distress and personality

disturbances including anxiety, anger, depression, and emotional detachment, to which unwilling separation and loss give rise.

Anger and detachment appear to be part of Kevin's habitual behaviour. Strangely, these traits become more pronounced in Kevin when he is spending time with Eva. Further investigation into Bowlby's ideas around attachment reveals that there are different types of attachment. Despite the affluence, education and social position Eva's family occupy, what is crucially significant here is the bond (or lack of it) formed between mother and child. Insecure attachment, according to Bowlby, would occur in cases where a parent might be emotionally detached. Eva's reflections on parenthood reveal a worrying lack of emotional warmth, and instead suggest that she is feeling fragile, fearful and fundamentally insecure as a parent.

The lack of attachment between Eva and Kevin, when examined by applying Bowlby's ideas, might be described as lurching between avoidant and disorganized. Kevin's indifference to his mother and to others, for example, his dislike and detachment towards the children in the kindergarten he attends, are classic manifestations of avoidant attachment. This type of attachment is disorganized in the sense that Kevin's behaviour appears to alternate unpredictably and surprisingly. For most of his childhood, Kevin is withdrawn, displays no affection to others, and is often aggressive.

Children who exhibit symptoms of disorganized attachment may, according to Bowlby, self-harm, commit cruel and violent acts on animals, and display any lack of conscience. These traits can be observed in Kevin, specifically in his deliberate targeting of Celia, his little sister.

Kevin and Celia (01:23:02–01:29:30)

Celia's pet hamster suddenly disappears one day. Celia is convinced this is her own fault, 'Kevin says I'm stupid', she later confesses to her mother. The following day, Eva discovers the kitchen sink is blocked. As the sinister realization as to what is causing the blockage is prompted by the red-stained leakage emanating from the plug hole of the kitchen sink, Kevin stares chillingly from the garden through to Eva. The effect is made more disturbing as Kevin is innocently playing swing ball with his father at the time. Kevin's pursuit of his sister intensifies. Although the film does not show how Celia (Kevin's little sister) later loses one of her eyes, the suggestion is that Kevin is responsible. A later scene set in a hospital corridor, where Eva and Franklin wait for news of Celia, contains another argument between Kevin's parents. Eva maintains that Kevin must have deliberately harmed Celia. Franklin is again horrified at this suggestion, and believes that the blame lies with Eva for leaving the 'drain stuff' out. Precisely what happened does not become apparent; viewers must make their own inferences, although there is a strong suggestion that Kevin was ultimately responsible for this terrible 'accident'.

If, as Bowlby believed, children are capable of such extreme acts, especially in instances where they suffer from disorganized attachment, it is entirely possible that Kevin falls into this category. Rutter (1972, 1981) describes the absence of any attachment as 'privation'. Children who have not formed any attachments, according to Rutter, show little or no distress when separated from somebody who is familiar. As these children get older, and specifically in cases such as Kevin's, there is more of a tendency to break rules, avoid relationships and not feel guilty.

After defacing Eva's meticulously decorated home-office by spraying the walls (00:53:17–00:55:00), in a style reminiscent of Jackson Pollack, with dark red paint (through the inventive use of a water pistol), a seven-year-old Kevin simply stares balefully and challengingly at Eva, who is clearly upset and shocked upon discovering the state of her room. It is as though Kevin is either completely unaware of the feelings of others, detached and distant from his close family, with any sense of attachment hopelessly absent.

Similarly, Fahlberg (1985) demonstrated that children who had not formed significant attachments were more likely to not have any sense of emotional awareness or sensitivity. Additionally, poor interpersonal skills and a lack of conscience exacerbate the difficulties they are likely to encounter. Fahlberg also refers to a reduced cognitive ability. What is particularly striking about Kevin, and removes him from Fahlberg's profile, is his seemingly heightened intelligence; there is no suggestion he is anything other than cunning and coldly determined in his resolve to harm those closest to him. His meticulous and strategically precise plans, which culminate in the massacre of his close family and peers, suggest that Kevin is capable, thorough and dangerously intelligent.

Eva and Kevin (00:35:02–00:35:52)

When Kevin is about two years old, Eva attempts to play with him, attempting a form of communication through rolling a ball to him, coaxing Kevin to respond by rolling it back. After a time, Kevin responds by rolling the ball back to Eva, but interestingly this only happens once. Immediately after this breakthrough, and despite Eva's newfound enthusiasm and encouragement, Kevin simply stares dispassionately at Eva, with an air of profound disinterest, bordering on contempt. This episode suggests that Kevin is intelligent, and frighteningly so, given his age. He clearly knows his mother wants a specific response, a level of engagement, which will help foster communication. By only rolling the ball back once, he seems to instinctively grasp that this will upset Eva. Eva's efforts to communicate and connect with Kevin are systematically thwarted and so she becomes increasingly stressed and impatient. It is as though Kevin understands there is a desire on Eva's part to make an attachment, but for whatever reason, he appears to reject any attempt to form a meaningful emotional connection.

Alternative Explanations

So far, this chapter has considered some familiar territories, namely, theories and ideas about nature–nurture, genetics and psychology. It is worth exploring some less obvious, but nonetheless, worthy concepts drawn from the fields of psychotherapy, and philosophy.

Valdre (2014) explores the idea and possibility of unconscious transgenerational trauma, which, in the case of the film, is passed from mother to son. Eva is of Armenian descent and has fled her native country because of war and genocide (her father and close friends having died in the conflict which, from when it began in 1915, had claimed the lives of over a million Armenian citizens). This family history is explicitly referred to in the novel (Shriver, 2003) but is absent from the film. It deserves mention here because such a theory suggests that Kevin unconsciously inherits some deep, monstrous trauma from his mother, which ultimately manifests itself in Kevin conducting the massacre of his fellow classmates.

Schwab (2010:2) describes the force and reach of such 'violent legacies' which can

far exceed the passing on of historical knowledge or even of stories with thick descriptions of personal involvement. What I call 'haunting legacies' are things hard to recount or even remember, the results of a violence that holds an unrelenting grip on memory yet is deemed unspeakable. The psychic core of violent histories includes what has been repressed or buried in unreachable psychic recesses. The legacies of violence not only haunt the actual victims but are also passed on through the generations.

Ideas and research about 'social hauntings' (Gordon, 2008) suggest that powerful legacies and personal histories, although often unseen, unspoken or repressed, have gained increasing recognition and can be seen as a valuable way of making sense of complex and confusing human interactions.

If we accept the idea of unconscious transgenerational trauma, the possibility is that a hidden, violent trauma has been passed down through generations, felt and experienced unconsciously by Kevin, powerfully enough for him to translate these dark emotions into tragic outcomes.

Terrorism and the threat of indoctrination

Although it appears that Kevin was acting independently when he murdered his family members and fellow students, there is an increasing concern that similar atrocities, played out in the real world, are the consequence of a deliberate and sustained attempt to align the actions of young people with terrorist causes. These ideas are worth briefly exploring, if only to accentuate contemporary fears about the perceived vulnerability of children and young people and their potential seduction by 'evil'.

The threat of terrorism in recent years has intensified international efforts to prevent children and young people becoming 'indoctrinated' by those groups such as Islamic State. Such fears, which happen to be increasingly commonplace, are based on certain assumptions; namely, that children and young people are 'psychologically vulnerable' to 'radicalization' (often portrayed in the media as a kind of 'brainwashing'). Such fears and beliefs, as we will read in the next chapter, can be damaging as they arguably legitimize the increase in security, child protection and prevention measures directed towards particular groups, most noticeably young British Muslims (Coppock & McGovern, 2014).

Recent cases have seen such heightened fears take precedence in attempts to explain violent mass killings, for example, in the case of Ali Sonboly (aged eighteen) in Munich, who shot and killed nine people, seven of them teenagers. Sonboly was allegedly inspired by another mass killer and fanatic of far-right beliefs, the Swedish terrorist, Anders Breivik, who murdered seventy-seven people in 2011. Crucially, in both cases, the perpetrators had a documented history of mental ill health and expressed acute disaffection to the societies in which they belonged. What is difficult to untangle, in these complex, but forensically reported cases are the precise reasons behind the attacks being committed. The extent to which 'terrorism' can be presented as the main factor is debatable. What is less contestable is the extent to which children and young people are becoming involved in what are reported as undisputed acts of terrorism. Globally, children as young as ten have been implicated in executions and suicide bombings, most recently in Nigeria (involving a group of young girls carrying explosives strapped to their backs) and Afghanistan (where a nine-year-old girl admitted having a suicide belt on her person as she was checked at a border patrol) and Kazakhstan (where a ten-year-old boy appeared to execute two Russian spies as identified by the Islamic State of Iraq and al-Sham (ISIS)) (Bloom and Horgan, 2015).

Globally, efforts to indoctrinate children into committing acts of violence tend to be most evident in nations with a history of conflict, for example, in Palestine, where children might be encouraged to attack and sometimes kill members of the Israeli army (Burdman, 2003). Child soldiers, as appropriated in recent conflicts such as Syria and Darfur, are reportedly desensitized to the mass killings they witness and tragically participate in (Grover, 2012). Perhaps, rather than focusing too much attention on the random and still, exceptionally rare instances of mass killings in America and across western Europe, there is a need to understand more about the fate of children who are effectively forced into committing murder in the name of religion or faith. By adopting such a broader view, we are reminded that children who are involved in such violence (both legitimate and illegitimate) can be regarded as the victims rather than the perpetrators of these acts.

Lessons from philosophy

Existentialism presents an alternative window in which to view and help explain Kevin's atrocious deeds. Questions of existence and the purpose of living are reflected in both Kevin's and Eva's narratives. Fundamentally, existentialism suggests that we are born without a purpose or any sense of morality. Such a lack of meaning and direction appears to afflict Kevin, particularly in the immediate period leading up to the massacre.

In contrast to psychological models, such as the transmission of transgenerational trauma, existentialism suggests that rather than inheriting or subconsciously transmitting future traits, we begin our lives as essentially empty. The world, from an existentialist point of view, is meaningless (Sartre, 2003). Kevin's actions reflect this meaninglessness, the lack of any value or feelings, his failure to attach to others, particularly his immediate family. His gratuitous thirst for causing pain and misery through violence are symbolic of a life without purpose. Despite the seeming simplicity of such an argument, existentialism does point towards a futility and emptiness felt and experienced by many, but rarely offered as a possible explanation for horrific acts such as those portrayed on the film.

Eva looks for answers (01:18:34–01:21:15)

In an effort to find out something about her son's existence, Eva one day goes through his room. She looks everywhere for a sign or an object that might help her better understand Kevin. All she manages to find is a CD labelled 'I Love You'. Without hesitating, and with a nervous urgency, Eva loads the CD into her laptop. The results are catastrophic; the CD contains a virus wiping out the contents of Eva's computer along with the entire network at her workplace. Eva later confronts Kevin, who appears, as usual, completely disinterested. 'I collect them [computer viruses]', he explains. 'What's the point?' Eva asks. 'There's no point; that's the point!' Kevin responds.

Kevin's existence appears, to him at least, to lack meaning or any sense of connection to others.

Conclusion

The various theoretical perspectives outlined in this chapter add to our understanding and appreciation of the complex issues they attempt to deal with. In seeking explanations for children's behaviour, our attention is directed towards the importance of differing personal circumstances: every child grows up in a unique environment and so theoretical models are implicitly limited through their focus on the general rather than the specifics of child psychology and development. The temptation to accept binary models and theoretical explanations, for example, in relation to the nature–nurture debate, oversimplify and detract from the importance of seeing the subtle and multiple factors which impact upon children's worlds. The chapter, through exploring a range of theoretical perspectives, encourages students to connect with and be open to a range of potential explanations for complex and sometimes disturbing behaviours.

Towards the end of the film (01:20:52–01:21:00), during a prison visit, which happens two years after the massacre (Kevin is almost eighteen years old at this point), Eva asks him 'why'? Kevin responds, 'I used to think I knew; now I'm not so sure.'

Having considered notions of nature versus nurture, parental/maternal attachment and the psychological development of children. You might like to reflect on the following questions:

- Are some children inherently 'bad'?

- Which theoretical model/s do you find plausible in relation to Kevin? Why?

- What do you understand by the term, 'a good mother', and do you think there is an expectation for mothers to conform to this model?

- Do the media portray stories which involve children and violence in an accurate/responsible way?

PART THREE

Adolescence, Perception and Consequence

6

Future-Proofing Children and Families: *Minority Report*

Jim Dobson and Sue Aitken

This chapter will consider theories and ideas relating to:

- Power and surveillance: Bentham (1791), Foucault (1977a).

- Privacy and children's rights: Harbisher (2015), Lippert (2015), Dowty (2008).

- Pre-emption and profiling individuals and populations: Lyon (2013).

- Youth Culture and Moral Panics: McLuhan (1964), Lewis (1978), Hebdige (1979) and Cohen (2002).

- Anomie: Durkheim (1951).

The film

The chapter links to the film *Minority Report* (*MR*), directed by Steven Spielberg in 2002. *MR* is based on the science-fiction novel of the same name, written by Philip K. Dick (1956). The film depicts a dystopian future in which unchecked power is wielded by an authoritarian, powerful police apparatus, seemingly unfettered by any obligations relating to human rights, privacy or legal safeguards which help to protect individuals. Spielberg's film encourages viewers to question the morality and extent of state control and unlimited surveillance and exposes the inherent danger in placing too much faith in such regimes.

The ideas which appear in *MR* have huge relevance to the lives of children, families and young people in the UK today. The rise of surveillance, risk management, assessment and future proofing within schools, through political imperatives (PREVENT, The Troubled Families Initiative), and through health, social care and criminal justice apparatus suggest some worrying parallels between the science fiction depicted in *MR* and contemporary society. This chapter, in exploring these connections, helps students and future practitioners to gain a sense of moral perspective, and perhaps to question some of the more draconian measures which have been routinely adopted to make our lives supposedly safer.

MR tells the story of a prototype 'Precrime unit', based in Washington DC, which is able to predict future offending, predominantly in the form of murders, that have not yet been committed. The year is 2054, and homicide, it appears, is a thing of the past. The crimes are accurately visualized and thus identified before they occur, by three 'mutant' beings (precogs) with the ability to predict future events with seemingly faultless accuracy. The visions generated by the precogs allow the Precrime division's police officials to intervene, make arrests and thereby prevent the predicted murders from taking place. The 'potential offender' is then punished for the act they were going to commit through a regime of cryogenic incarceration: they are essentially entombed in sealed units, oblivious to the outside world and powerless to do anything other than merely exist. This system of justice has widespread public and political approval, paving the way for the Washington project to become a national scheme.

Dick's novel (1956) briefly refers to other, less important criminal activities, such as thefts and assaults, which, although not an immediate priority, are nonetheless siphoned off to other, private policing agencies to process and clear up. This chapter begins to explore how such privatization agendas can feed into other policy domains, for example, family intervention programmes and child protection systems.

The Precrime unit's work is built around prevention and involves forcefully intervening before serious problems occur. Of course, *MR* presents an extreme example of managing risk, but as this chapter unfolds, the reader will discover how current policies and systems affecting children and families in the UK have been influenced by similar, evidence-based approaches.

The film's main character, the chief of Precrime, John Anderton, played in the film by Tom Cruise, becomes suspicious of a system he had previously had complete faith in. Anderton discovers that, despite the measurable success rates (no homicides since the pilot system started) and its flawless scientific credentials, the system appears to be a victim of corruption and human manipulation. Anderton discovers this to his cost when the precogs identify him as a future killer. Anderton's suspicions are ultimately confirmed after he discovers he has been set up by his ambitious and ruthless boss, Lamar Burgess. Burgess, it later transpires, has committed a murder himself and manipulated the system to cover up his actions, while diverting attention towards the apprehension and arrest of Anderton.

Anderton's escape and quest for the truth form the main elements of this thriller. Anderton's actions symbolize the need to question, scrutinize and resist intrusive and potentially flawed state measures to monitor and control populations. Anderton's subsequent surveillance and technology-enabled pursuit by the Precrime unit exposes the disturbing extent to which the state is able to control, manipulate and monitor the movements and actions of citizens and populations.

Making sense of the film

Although *MR* is set in the future (2054), there are worrying similarities between aspects of the science-fiction world depicted in the film and today's society, namely, in the guise of heightened levels of surveillance, a growing policy agenda involving managing risk, the perceived need to maintaining high levels of security. The debate around the extent of state control, a central theme of *MR*, is particularly apt in today's global society, where anxieties about terrorism (Mythen, Walklate & Khan, 2009), crime, social stratification (O'Neill & Loftus, 2013) and privacy (Harbisher, 2015; Lippert, 2015) ferment in political and public circles (Monahan, ibid). The resultant threats posed to individual and collective freedoms and rights are also discussed in this chapter.

Additionally, the chapter explores the rapid emergence of targeted and intelligence-led policing, where 'spying' and surveillance technology in recent years has been used by the public and private sectors to demonstrate the worrying, and arguably disproportionate extent that children and young people's rights have been systematically and steadily eroded as a consequence of such measures. This erosion has happened through the cumulative dependence on closed circuit television cameras (CCTVs) in nurseries, schools, public places and residential areas since the 1990s (Dowty, 2008); a tranche of legislation aimed at combating youth crime and the threat of antisocial behaviour (e.g. the 1998 Crime and Disorder Act, which introduced Antisocial Behaviour Orders); a growing intolerance and mistrust of children and young people (largely fuelled by the national media) and an ever-increasing fear of terrorism coupled with a desire to strengthen the national boundaries and identity (Mythen, Walklate & Khan, 2009).

Furthermore, the chapter exposes the challenges children and their representatives face in resisting such measures. Despite the international ratification of the United Nations Convention on the Rights of the Child (1991):

There is no domestic law requiring all public bodies, such as schools, hospitals and the police, to comply with children's human rights and allowing children to challenge laws and decisions which breach their rights. (Children's Rights Alliance for England, 2014:4)

If such measures remain unchecked, there is a real risk to children and families, who are gradually becoming part of a landscape that threatens their rights, liberties and, ultimately, their freedom. In order to locate the themes in a context which fits with children and families, some discussion of contemporary social welfare, criminal justice and health policies in the UK is helpful.

The following sections explore the ideas outlined earlier in more detail, allowing the reader to appreciate the sophistication and reach of modern-day institutional powers, and how they can be executed with seeming impunity against individual citizens, children and families. This chapter shows how the authoritarian nature of the world portrayed in *MR* increasingly resembles our contemporary society, particularly in inner-city areas, where risk, security, monitoring and prevention measures are more noticeable and hence heighten their impact upon the populations who live there.

Monitoring, closed circuit television and surveillance

2054: Surveillance and monitoring (00:35:48–00:48:00)

Having been identified as the perpetrator of the murder of a man he does not know, Anderton escapes the Precrime building and uses a futuristic high-speed automated car, but within a few minutes the car is 'locked down' and the destination rerouted to Precrime headquarters. Following a spectacular escape from the car, Anderton finds himself in a shopping mall, where video billboards address him by name and offer him products from holidays to Guinness.

Anderton makes his way to an underground metro system. As he enters a carriage, cameras adjacent to the train's doors flash as they scan his eyes, along with those of other passengers using the public transport system. In the following scene at Precrime headquarters, Anderton's exact location is identified, as is the route and potential exit points. While on board the train, Anderton is identified by a fellow passenger, who is reading a constantly updated electronic newspaper.

MR depicts a world in which surveillance is so fully embedded into the fabric of society that citizens are routinely scanned via the digital recognition of their irises as they go about their daily business. Furthermore, these citizens are willingly subjected to personalized, subliminal (and coercive) advertising, merging public and private interests.

As these short scenes demonstrate, detailed movements are monitored by security services with an alarming degree of accuracy. The Precrime police are able to record and follow Anderton's exact movements as he attempts to evade capture while utilizing immediate news feeds to identify him to the public. Ordinary citizens, it appears, have no anonymity; everybody's movements can be scrutinized and judged; everyone is a potential suspect.

Today, in the UK, the Civil Rights Movement estimate that there are 4.5 million CCTV cameras, capturing our daily movements on average 300 times a day. Additionally, the UK has the highest level of CCTV cameras in Europe, despite conflicting evidence as to its overall impact on reducing crime (Civil Rights Movement, 2016). Police vehicles routinely carry vehicle number plate recognition software, which will identify stolen, uninsured and untaxed vehicles as well as the personal details of the registered keeper in seconds.

Recent developments in the UK herald 'event detection technologies' as an effective means of predicting human behaviour. Such systems utilize existing camera technology, but enhance the data captured, using sophisticated programs, to predict likely outcomes from the images picked up. For example, a city centre congregation of young people at a specific time in the evening or a large public demonstration may signify a potential 'hot spot' in which police involvement is desirable (Gad and Hansen, 2013).

Globally, high street and Internet outlets have been eager to exploit these new technologies, allowing businesses not only to detect and deter crime but also to monitor human movements, traffic and facial expressions around particular displays and buying behaviour, thereby ensuring they can maximize profit by arranging and displaying merchandise to maximum affect (Frey, 2016).

Jeremy Bentham's 1791 treatise on the panopticon is widely regarded as a precursor to the modern-day, all-encompassing surveillance systems we are accustomed to, and helps us to understand and appreciate the significance of what is now a taken-for-granted part of our contemporary infrastructure – the CCTV camera. As discussed in Chapter 3 Bentham's ideas involved a prison in which the inmates are continually watched and monitored from a central tower located in the centre of the prison. Such measures, Bentham reasoned, would ensure the cooperation and good behaviour of the convicts housed within the prison who were under the impression they were being continually observed. In reality, Bentham's idea did not necessitate that the prison guards would constantly observe everything from the watchtower (this was, in fact, impossible for a solitary guard); it was enough to simply give the impression that the inmates were being constantly watched. Bentham's ideas were taken up by philosophers such as Foucault (1977a), who also considered how surveillance can have powerful and far-reaching effects on the individuals observed. Foucault noted that whereas dungeons and cells relied on placing captives in conditions of isolation and darkness, the panopticon design relied upon light and visibility through placing prisoners in backlit cells which were forward facing (so to be more easily observed by the central watchtower). In terms of applying Foucault's ideas to contemporary society, while one might argue that CCTV exerts a panoptic gaze, it is also reasonable to suggest that such systems are unable to monitor everything we do (as in the case of the prisoners in the panopticon). Crucially, it is the psychology of the panopticon which can be translated into the modern context; the idea that you are being monitored is what is important – the oppressive sense of having no freedom or escape from constant observation is a challenge to basic human rights. It is worth remembering that privacy is a universal human right entrenched in Article 12 of the United Nations Declaration of Human Rights (1948) and for children in Article 16 of the United Nations Convention on the Rights of the Child (1989).

Surveillance and controls in schools

Schools today are not simply educational institutions, but could also be regarded as instruments of policing and surveillance; perhaps as propagators for a shared morality, ensuring that future citizens are respectful, obedient and law abiding. Children's lives are increasingly subject to surveillance today, particularly within schools, where cameras have become an integral design feature. The justification for the expansion of such technology is often supported by arguments which seek to prioritize safeguarding and children's welfare (Dowty, 2008). Recent high-profile cases, in which teachers and other professionals have been assaulted in the classroom, have helped to justify the increase in surveillance technology (Hope, 2009). Although such arguments are difficult to counter, there appears to be a strong argument which suggests that the balance between individual rights and privacy has tilted too far in favour of more control and surveillance within school environments (Norris, 2003; Simon, 2005).

In American schools, technology appears to have become so entrenched that pupils are routinely watched, monitored and scrutinized inside and outside of school. Such extensive use of technology, Fuentes (2011) argues, is not conducive to learning or building healthy communities. Instead, an atmosphere of distrust builds; in which children are constantly aware they are being monitored, with the ever-present threat of punishment hanging over them, even for relatively minor indiscretions. Fuentes suggests that children in such establishments become part of a school-to-prison pipeline, with the emphasis on zero tolerance pushing the most vulnerable children out of education and into criminal career pathways.

Schools in England, although not as fully engaged as their American counterparts, are beginning to emulate the push towards fully developed, all-enveloping systems:

> The proliferation of artefacts such as closed circuit television (CCTV) cameras, webcams, automated fingerprint identification systems (AFIS), iris/vein scanners, facial recognition software, networked databases, radio-frequency identification (RFID) microchips and metal detectors inside schools has been staggering, prompting questions regarding the impetus behind this rapid expansion. (Hope, 2015:1)

To an extent, one might argue that we are all subject to the normative gaze of the panopticon in today's increasingly technological world. Richard Thomas, once the UK's information commissioner, raised concerns as far back as 2004 over the use and extent of surveillance and information held on individuals, and how, over time, there has been a steady erosion of individual privacy and the freedom of individuals (Booth, 2004; Mitchener-Nissen, 2013). In America, Edward Snowden's revelations about the amount and extent of information held about individuals by the state's National Security Agency demonstrated how technology has an immense and dangerous potential to strip away individual liberties and rights to privacy (Lyon, 2015).

Recent controversies have arisen in situations where private enterprise has taken a role in security, law enforcement and surveillance, leading to questions of morality and the regulation of such developments (Loader, 1997). Clearly, in the world of *MR*, private law enforcement agencies wield great power and have immense political and public trust placed in them. Increasingly, we see the justifications for such developments based around not only public safety, but also, interestingly, as a means to save money and improve efficiency.

The idea of 'smart' cities backed up by intelligent control systems, whereby transport, energy, weather systems and population movements are tracked, holds an increasing appeal to governments and city planners (Hancke, de Carvalho e Silva & Hancke, 2012). The quest for sterile, efficient, quantifiable crime-free zones also appeal to the respectable classes, the portion of the population who want to feel safe and secure, encased within increasingly popular, American-inspired gated communities. In this sense, one might argue that the surveillance apparatus already in place is disproportionally targeted towards those perceived as dangerous, marginal and unknown. It is those who live within and beyond the margins of society who attract the attention of the police, welfare agencies and health professionals; a population whose difficulties and stresses can now be measured, predicted and controlled through a series of rigorously tested, evidence-based interventions. In the same way that technology-enhanced systems such as CCTV are increasingly part of the private sector, the idea that family intervention, child protection and welfare services can be effectively delivered outside local authority control is gaining credibility. Foucault recognized that power and control were not purely centred around the visual aspects of policing offenders and inmates:

> The procedures of power resorted to in modern societies are far too numerous and diverse and rich. It would be false to say that the principle of visibility has dominated the whole technology of power since the 19th century. (Foucault, 1996:227)

The following section examines these other, sometimes covert, but legitimized manifestations of power and how they are distributed across disciplines and organizations. This section also discusses how the drive towards empiricism and quantifiable evidence in social policymaking has marginalized particular groups, namely, Muslims, teenagers, homeless people and vulnerable families.

Risk and prediction: Profiling individuals and populations

Ideas about quantifying risk and profiling resonate with contemporary ideas around preventive practice in the UK, for example, in the identification and subsequent interventions with 'troubled' families, the attempts to identify, track and monitor vulnerable children, and through the scientific measurement of risk via various assessment tools, such as the 'ASSET', 'ONSET', and 'Common Assessment' forms used across and within agencies. These developments point towards the blurring of traditional boundaries between social welfare, child protection and crime prevention and a deliberate, sustained move towards a world of 'responsibilization', cost–benefit analysis and managing risk (Goddard, 2012). These policy developments raise uncomfortable questions about the morality and ethics of such powerful state and institutional control and the corresponding reliance upon technologies, profiling techniques and risk management. What appears to be most worrying about such shifts is the potential erosion of human rights, freedoms and liberties and the lack of any sustained or deliberate resistance to such measures, with the exception of lobbying from Green organizations and some union activities (Lyon, 2013).

The introduction of the Children Act 2004 raised expectations of IT as an essential tool in enabling the early identification of vulnerable children and the management of subsequent interventions needed across a number of agencies. Victoria Climbie's death, it was argued, could have been prevented if certain key information had been shared between the various services who encountered her.

A number of local authority trailblazers were established to ascertain the viability of a national system. Initially, this project was rather sinisterly called 'Identification, Referral and Tracking' (IRT), but subsequently changed its name to 'ContactPoint', as a response to concerns from human rights organizations. Despite the original intention of protecting children, the project quickly became consumed with concerns and arguments about privacy, children's rights and the security such a national system could offer. Potential information sharing at this time included access to more than basic identifiers such as name, date of birth and address, and included children's sexual and mental health records, recorded criminal convictions of family members, domestic violence incidents, along with parental substance misuse and mental health episodes. Understandably, plans had to be modified, and ultimately, what was seen as a potential national system ended up as a fragmented, watered-down system, available only to a select few professions in some areas. In reality, however, the failure to implement a national framework was as much to do with financially resourcing such an ambitious, far-reaching project as it was with any concerns expressed about individual privacy.

Despite this setback, the Scottish parliament passed the Children and Young People (Scotland) Act in 2014. Contained within this legislation was a provision that every child born in Scotland would be appointed a "named person." This 'named person' would be a state-appointed professional whose role would be to ensure that the child's interests in terms of health, safety and general well-being were being met. The Act also provided that the 'named person' would have and could share relevant data about the child. The rationale for the legislation being that only when concerns about a child's well-being is shared can a full picture of the child's welfare be established (Walton, 2013). The legislation was due to come into force on 31 August 2016, but on 28 July 2016, the United Kingdom Supreme Court ruled that some of the proposals around information sharing breached the right to privacy and a family life under the European Convention on Human Rights (ECHR). Interestingly, the ECHR is formulated into British law by the Human Rights Act (1998), which the Conservative Party pledged to repeal in their 2010 General Election mani-festo. However, following the result of the UK referendum in June 2016 with regard to leaving the European Union, plans to repeal the Human Rights Act were put on hold, in recognition that following 'Brexit', the UK would no longer be subject to the ECHR (*The Independent*, 2016).

As seen before, the idea that risk could be identified early and acted upon with the aid of information technology is a persistent one, but it has also increasingly become perceived as more of a threat than a useful means of promoting children's welfare.

Managing and monitoring 'dangerous' populations

It is clear that the scale and scope of surveillance and associated information technology has grown exponentially in recent decades, along with a growing increase in private sector provision (Gad & Hansen, 2013). Upon further exam-ination, however, it appears that certain populations are disproportionately affected by such surveillance measures:

> It is the poorest and most marginalized citizens in society who are becom-ing ever more policed and problematized by the very state which Loader and others present as their best protector. Moreover, this targeting is occurring in an age where many scholars claim that the state is moving towards a system of managing deviant populations. (Feeley & Simon, 1992; Garland, 2001; Simon & Feeley, 2003; Young, 1999)

This disadvantage is manifested through, for example, an increased likeli-hood to be regarded with suspicion, to be stopped and searched/questioned by the police if you are a particular ethnicity (Waddington, Stenson & Don, 2004) or to be the subject of some kind of family-based intervention if you have a history of mental health (Social Exclusion Task Force, 2007).

It makes sense to begin by considering why such groups are perceived as a threat by the state and the wider population, as well as discussing the measures put in place to control, monitor and influence their behaviour of these groups.

Children as a dangerous population

Children have been perceived as a threat for hundreds of years and there have been various attempts to monitor, measure and control their activities over this period. The industrial revolution, as a period of social, economic and political change, posed questions about children's place and role in society. There was growing concern, particularly in newly, and heavily populated towns and cities that unless productively engaged in work or education, children may become feral and dangerous. A report from the Committee for Investigating the Causes of the Alarming Increase of Juvenile Delinquency in the Metropolis (1815) is an early example of attempting to measure and quantify the behaviour of children who were perceived as such a threat. There was a real concern that children who were not engaged in employment or education would become involved in criminal activity; involved in gangs in and around populated areas. As today, the factors seen as influential were parenting and family circumstances, and access to employment or education. Society was motivated by a desire to see children actively engaged, respecting laws and ultimately aspiring to become good citizens. Today, it is interesting to see how children not engaged in employment, education or training (NEET) continue to be a priority and their numbers and composition are actively tracked and measured by current governments. There are, according to government figures, around 856,000 sixteen- to twenty-four-year-olds who currently fall within this category, which equates to 12 per cent of the overall population for this age group (Delebarre, 2016).

Throughout the past 200 years, attempts to combat and control the threat of youth, juvenile delinquency and criminality have appeared regularly in the form of policy directives and legislation. This ongoing concern has been driven throughout this period by sentiments and beliefs which might sound strikingly familiar today. Pearson (1983:48) describes a report written by the Howard Association in 1898, which attempted to provide an explanation for the perceived increase in youth offending. The report echoes some of the concerns raised eighty-three years earlier:

> The general impression running through its pages was a riot of impunity, irresponsible parents, working mothers and lax discipline in schools, with magistrates and police believing themselves to be impotent before a rising tide of mischief and violence – particularly 'the recent serious increase in ruffianism among city youths'. (1983:48)

Similar concerns about children and young people remain today, sometimes in the form of policy directives aimed at 'deficient', 'feckless' parenting (Casey, 2013) and criminal gangs of young people in inner cities (Goldson, 2011). Measures such as dispersal orders and antisocial behaviour orders (ASBOs) find their roots in early attempts to control and curb unacceptable behaviour. Measures intended to combat youth crime today tend to be localized, and there is an onus on community-based interventions and multi-agency approaches. Consequently, there has been an increase in restorative justice projects, family intervention and outreach work, and diversionary schemes such as Positive Activities for Young People (PAYP). In this changing landscape, there is a broadening of traditional crime prevention and policing roles (primarily undertaken by the police). Increasingly, children, young people and families who are perceived as a potential risk are engaging with professionals from a range of agencies spanning social care, health and criminal justice. While one might argue this is desirable in terms of maximizing the support available to the individuals concerned, there is a strong case which suggests the invasive, coercive nature of such interventions, along with the increased likelihood of being noticed and apprehended by one of the many agencies, leads to stigma and labelling (Gregg, 2010). Youth subculture, and the theories which underpin it, offers a useful window into how children and young people can be positioned as a threat to the established social order.

A theoretical analysis of youth subculture(s) is potentially best understood from Durkheim's (1897) reference to the concept of anomie, which he categorizes as a situation where individuals and groups are judged by wider society to have rejected social norms and values. McLuhan (1967) and Cohen (2002) extend this idea to discuss notions of moral panic; a societal fear that this demonstrable social disaffection is a threat to the well-being and prosperity of society as a whole. Both McLuhan and Cohen explored the role that news media can play in the creation of moral panics and the demonization of individuals and groups. In effect, highly visible and powerful media campaigns can result in an already marginalized group becoming designated as the 'other', which as described in Chapter 3 can legitimize actions that might otherwise be seen as unlawful.

It is perhaps useful at this point to examine examples of how youth culture and moral panics can become entwined and to explore whether youth culture and movements still have a place in the twenty-first century. Lewis (1978) and Hebdige (1979) both suggest that youth and its subsequent social development was a cultural creation in the mid-1950s, borne out of the post–war era. From the 1950s, youth subgroups have been the focus of moral panic, from Teddy boys, to Mods and Rockers and groups of football supporters. The moral panic has developed into a perceived but clear connection between youth subculture and violent, deviant behaviour.

Modern-day youth culture and moral panics

Establishing the veracity of both the prevalence and identifiability of twenty-first-century youth cultures, or more correctly youth subcultures, and their resultant moral panics has become increasingly difficult. In the past, allegiance to specific youth groups was both visible and audible, often connecting a dress code with a particular form of music. Frith (1985) defines youth culture as 'the particular pattern of beliefs, values, symbols and activities that a group of young people are seen to share'. Thus the way you look, the music you listen to and the way you behave contribute to how identity is constructed both internally (self) and externally (society). The potential divergence of these identities can often be the foundations for moral panic. Hebdige (1979) referred to youth culture as an ambiguous concept as it encompasses conflicting notions of fun and trouble. At the same time, the young are the focus of lucrative commercial targeting and the site of potential danger.

It is clear that youth subcultures are continually shifting in scope and shape. Despite this continually evolving nature, law enforcement agencies will go to extreme lengths in order to purge the perceived threat children and young people carry. Such measures aimed at tackling these unruly aspects of youth culture, for example, swearing and loitering, have included powers granted to local authorities which allow them to effectively ban certain groups (often children and young people) from geographically defined areas. In the UK, Salford City Council's Public Space Protection Order (O'Connor, 2016) received ridicule and hostility in its attempt to curb swearing within a defined geographical area. Anyone in breach of the order could theoretically receive a fixed penalty notice of £90. Similar measures, elsewhere in England, which seek to impose bans on rough sleeping, busking and gathering in groups have also attracted a steady flow of criticism from civil liberties campaigners (Barnett, 2016). It appears Public Protection Orders are being used to specifically target the activities of children and young people; for example, some councils have introduced bans on anyone under the age of eighteen going outdoors alone between 11:00 p.m. and 6:00 a.m. (Barnett, 2016).

Throughout the academic analysis of youth subcultures, there has always been an acknowledgement that they occupy multiple spaces with multiple meanings. In the digital world, this multiplicity of youth subcultures is even more fragmented as young people are more likely to engage with each other via social media than in social gatherings. Consequently, location has become almost irrelevant, as young people communicate via a vast array of platforms such as Facebook, WhatsApp, Snapchat and Facetime, sharing personal experiences via YouTube and blogs. However, policing such activity both by parents and by society in general has generated a concern and perceivably a moral panic about the safety of children and the Internet. In September 2007, Tania Byron, a British psychologist and child therapist, was commissioned by the then British prime minister Gordon Brown to review children's use of video games, the Internet and social networking. The report, Safer Children in a Digital World (2008) outlined not only how games content should be classified but also the role of parents in identifying and policing children's access to potentially inappropriate and harmful digital media. The report identified that there was an increasing digital divide between children and parents, where children had now become the experts and parental lack of knowledge made them ironically either overprotective or inert.

Livingstone, Haddon, Görzig and Ólafsson's research in 2011 surveyed 25,142 children aged nine to sixteen across twenty-five European countries plus one of their parents. The key findings included that 93 per cent of nine- to sixteen-year-old users go online at least once a week and 60 per cent going online every day or almost every day. The survey discovered that 49 per cent access the Internet in their bedroom and 33 per cent via a mobile phone or handheld device. In Norway, the United Kingdom, Ireland and Sweden, more than 20 per cent of children access the Internet via a handheld device. However, 40 per cent of parents of children who had experienced risks such as sexual images were unaware of this and 56 per cent of parents were unaware that their child had received nasty or harmful messages (cyberbullying). As the report concludes, while these instances are minimal, parental underestimation is substantial.

The relationship between privacy and security is complex but no more so than in the case of children. As Taylor and Rooney (2016) suggest, despite the UNHCR, children in policy and legal contexts are often deemed too young to be 'afforded a sense of privacy in their own right'. Thus the ratio of security to freedom becomes unbalanced. While no one would or could argue that unfettered access to the Internet is in the best interests of children, there is also an argument that the trajectory from childhood to adulthood is part of a wider learning journey. Learning to be safe comes from having a deep understanding of potential risks. Children need to be able to work with parents, rather than be controlled by them. In *MR*, the risk of homicide has been removed, which might suggest that society has become safer. However, it could also be argued that the absence of a recognizable threat may lead to an inability to manage risk, resulting in potentially dangerous behaviour.

'Troubled' and 'dysfunctional' families

'Troubled families' as a distinct population do not constitute a new phenomenon, as we have already noted. Instead, we might regard them as a group who have been rebranded (Cameron, 2011). The recent political and economic motivation to tackle and help such families' challenging behaviour has its roots in the riots which took place in the UK during the summer of 2011. The footage, reporting and subsequent arrests following the riots appeared to suggest that a distinct subpopulation was emerging throughout England (London

School of Economics, 2011). Disaffection with mainstream society, mistrust of the police and the belief that they were discriminated against were some of the reasons given by the young people interviewed as part of the London School of Economics. It was clear they belonged to families and communities who no longer thought they had a stake in mainstream society (London School of Economics, 2011).

Initially, following the 2011 riots, local authorities were expected to identify and subsequently engage with and support 120,000 families who had some defining characteristics, such as truancy, crime and unemployment. In order to tackle the difficulties these families faced, local authorities engaged local partners, including the police, health and housing in identifying families they believed were in need of additional support. Guidance to local authorities suggested factors such as teenage pregnancy, domestic violence or instances of mental health were also useful indicators. Implicitly, the use of such criteria might also incorporate those at risk of future offending; in other words, predictive profiling, much like in the world of *MR*, was a serious consideration in identifying such families. Unlike *MR*, the efforts to identify families did not just involve one agency, but relied on a wider partnership, featuring locally led initiatives which routinely involved the police, social services, housing, education, health and other providers in capturing this new population. In 2015, after the scheme was heralded as a success by the government, the number of families targeted rose to 400,000 (Crossley, 2015).

Much like the dystopian future depicted in *MR* where the predictive capacities of the authorities are actively encouraged, recent governments have stressed the importance of intervening early, before problems escalate. Blair's New Labour government claimed to be tough on crime and disorder, or at least wanted to be perceived as such:

> There is no point pussyfooting ... if we are not prepared to predict and intervene more early ... pre-birth even ... these kids a few years down the line are going to be a menace to society. (Blair, 2006)

Earlier manifestations of the Troubled Families Programme have been notable if only for their short lifespan. The precursor to Troubled Families, the Family Intervention Programme (FIP) were heralded as a success by the then Labour administration (1997–2010), claiming that families who took part were able to turn their lives around and become part of the 'law-abiding majority'. Critics of such claims, such as Gregg (2010), encourage caution and suggest that these alleged successes were constructed around small clusters of families, who did not pose any serious threat, but in which there may have been a history of antisocial behaviour, often linked to mental health problems in the family. Furthermore, Gregg claimed that interventions carried out by the FIP were not appropriate for the needs of many families who were targeted. In essence, the evidence used to support such programmes, it could be argued, is manipulated and manufactured to ensure their continued success and political/public approval. The FIPs appeared to be especially damaging to some families who were targeted:

> By targeting the wrong people for the wrong reasons while failing to tackle the real underlying causes in those targeted or delivering support in key areas like mental health the FIP remains at root enforcement-led and sanctions-oriented, where someone must be blamed and punished for bad behaviour. This ethos justifies forcing very vulnerable families with mental health problems into projects under threat of eviction, loss of benefits and removal of children into care. (Gregg, 2010:5)

Family Intervention Programmes were viewed as a key strand of Labour's antisocial behaviour strategy and emphasized the importance of working with those families who had been identified as future potential problems (the emphasis, as with MR, being on the future):

> The FIP is said to apply 'assertive and non-negotiable interventions' and provide 'intensive support' for 'chaotic families', thereby eliminating antisocial behaviour (ASB) in communities and stabilising family status, reducing homelessness and improving the 'outcomes' for children. These 'interventions' are supplied by councils or by agencies hired by them. Families may be reprogrammed in their own homes, in temporary dispersed tenancies or in controlled core residential units, the ASB sin bins of the media. (Gregg, 2010:5)

Troubled families were initially identified by applying a series of broad characteristics which included looking at families who were involved in crime and antisocial behaviour, had children who were not in school, had an adult on out-of-work benefits and (even more quantifiably challenging) causing 'high costs to the public purse'.

More recently, evidence from the Department of Communities and Local Government, has shown that the work of the Troubled Families Unit has been nothing more than an expensive failure (Portes, 2016). The families singled out and targeted by the scheme who were initially labelled as dysfunctional and antisocial in the vast majority of cases have shown no discernible improvement in terms of measures such as coming off benefits, committing crime and antisocial behaviour or fundamentally in their aspirations. Much like the Precrime unit, with their emphasis on populist, political sound bites, the Conservative government elected in 2010, championed the Troubled Families

Programme but failed in their attempts to convince the public that tackling problem families by means of early intervention would improve the lives of not only these families but also those who came into contact with them.

Muslims, terrorism, ethnicity and difference

Since the terrorist attacks of 11 September 2001 (New York) and 7 July 2005 (London), and more recently in Paris (13 November 2015), Brussels (22 March 2016) and Manchester and London in 2017, there has been an increase in surveillance and security across the world, driven by a desire to monitor and control 'extremism'. Such practices have meant that some groups have been disproportionately targeted, specifically Muslim populations (Coppock & McGovern, 2014). This surveillance has been far-reaching; an unfortunate consequence has been the impact of such operations upon children. Pal Sian (2015) suggests efforts to identify and address extremism in schools are ultimately damaging, leading to increased levels of intolerance, and in particular, provoking greater incidences of islamophobia. Pal Sian (2015) maintains that there has been an ongoing shift in schools over the past two decades, which have seen a move away from celebrating and raising the profile of multiculturalism to a more determined drive towards assimilationist policies and directives. The emphasis on 'community cohesion, integration and security' in schools today (Pal Sian, 2015:184) is largely a product of mistrust, fear and ignorance. Various initiatives have been supported by the Labour, Coalition, and Conservative administrations since the London terrorist attack in 2005, for example, the Preventing Violent Extremism (PVE) initiative, aimed at monitoring and preventing the spread of extremism across local authorities, police forces along with primary, secondary schools and Further and Higher Education Institutions (Thomas, 2009). Children, it appeared, perhaps because of their perceived vulnerability and naivety, were seen as prime targets for being recruited into terrorist activities.

From 1 July 2015, all UK schools, registered early years' childcare providers and later years' childcare providers have been subject to a duty, under section 26 of the Counter-Terrorism and Security Act 2015, to have 'due regard to the need to prevent people from being drawn into terrorism' (Department for Education, 2015a). The 'Prevent' duty requires that staff working with children should be able to identify 'children who may be vulnerable to radicalization'; as in *MR* to identify the potential criminal before the crime has taken place. The statutory guidance expects that staff should assess the risk of a child 'being drawn into terrorism, including support for extremist ideas'. As a footnote, extremism is described as 'vocal and active opposition to fundamental

British values, such as democracy, the rule of law, individual liberty and mutual respect and tolerance of different faiths and beliefs'. As discussed earlier, in the dystopian context of *MR*, panoptical practices, when wrapped up in concepts of protection and safeguarding can easily cloak the loss of the very concepts that they are designed to 'protect', such as freedom of speech, the presumption of innocence before proven guilty, individual liberty and the respect and tolerance for other faiths and beliefs.

Conclusion

Franz Kafka depicted a world of powerful, unquestioned and politically driven bureaucracies that are able to exert complete control over subjects who fall within its power. In the short story, 'In the Penal Colony' (1919), Kafka's horrific descriptions of future law enforcement manifest themselves as torture, justice without trial and the physical mutilation of the accused so that others can easily identify them. There are chilling echoes here of Guantanamo Bay, which has come to be internationally regarded, in its fifteen-year existence, as an extreme example of injustice and oppression. Amnesty International (2012) points out that rendition, torture and detention without trial are the key operating principles of the American-sponsored Guantanamo. It is important to recognize the similarities in the premise behind Kafka's ideas and current thinking behind terrorism, criminal justice and social welfare policies and practice: governments seek to justify brutal and far-reaching measures as a means of promoting national security, welfare and public protection. Unfortunately, there is little evidence to show that any of this is working, but strong evidence to demonstrate the steady and deliberate erosion of human rights.

Minority Report makes reference to the political and economic imperatives which underlie the Precrime unit's work. In addition to reducing crime, cost-savings and less labour-intensive working, become politically and publicly attractive forms of criminal justice and a key part of the Precrime project's appeal. The privatization of security, prisons and social care in England (including child protection services) is actively encouraged by the Conservative government elected in 2015 and its predecessor the Coalition government between 2010 and 2015. The Department of Education's 'Children's Social Care Innovation Programme' (2014) sought innovative and creative solutions from private and other providers who could offer affordable, effective and creative new ways of delivering frontline social care. The danger in pursuing such neo-liberal, market-driven ventures is that that there will be further erosion of children's rights, less accountability and, ultimately, damaging consequences for those affected.

The Precrime unit depicted in *MR* will always remain a fictional world in terms of the mechanics used to identify future criminals. If, however, we strip away the precogs and their predictive cognitive functions, and instead look at current profiling models used by the police, youth offending teams, social services departments, DNA gathering and storage, the retrieval of Internet browsing histories and CCTV surveillance, it becomes apparent that in many ways we have already reached a similar juncture.

Following are some questions you might like to consider with reference to surveillance, monitoring, children's rights and personal liberty:

- Under what circumstances do you believe it is necessary to utilize CCTV around children and young people?

- Are there conflicts between individual freedoms, human rights and liberty when balanced against the levels of surveillance we experience on a daily basis?

- Can you think of circumstances where the push towards managing risk and promoting increased surveillance might harm children, young people and families?

- If you were to construct a database which included all children in the UK and which could be accessed by professionals who work with children, what information do you think should be included on the database and why?

7

Questions of Identity:
Harry Potter and the Philosopher's Stone

Kurt Wicke

This chapter considers the following perceptions of *identity* in the film adaptation of Joanne K. Rowling's novel *Harry Potter and the Philosopher's Stone*.

- Theories of identity: de Fina (2011).

- Identity changes as crisis due to traumatic loss: Cullberg (2008).

- Identity changes as rites of passage: van Gennep (2010).

- Identity as socialization into a community of practice: Lave and Wenger (2005).

- Concepts of identity and their importance for stabilizing social and political systems: Hall (1992).

The film

The choice of film rests on the assumption that most young people are familiar with the narrative and can identify themselves with a young Harry Potter coming of age, leaving his childhood and entering into a new world. The particular scene that has been chosen – from 12:30:00 to 00:20:40 at the beginning of the film – deals with this transition. It is pictured as a rift in Harry's knowledge and beliefs about his world, his family and himself. By and by Harry experiences loss and gain, and discovers a new narrative about the world and himself. In order to deal with this transition, he has to come to terms with two different cultures and his place in them. The chosen scene describes the conflicts emerging from this juxtaposition.

The film adaptation of *Harry Potter and the Philosopher's Stone* is based on the first novel in a series of seven books by Joanne K. Rowling and was released in 2001. Both the film and the novel tell the story of an ordinary eleven-year-old boy, Harry, who has lost both his parents, and now suffers outrageous neglect at the hands of his adopted family, which consists of his aunt Petunia Dursley, his uncle Vernon Dursley and their son Dudley. However, on his eleventh birthday, Harry learns that he is actually a wizard and is offered a place at a boarding school for wizards and witches known as Hogwarts. The film describes his journey from a stereotypical life in a white middle-class home in an English middle-class suburb (the world of Muggles) to a parallel but hidden society where magic is the norm. At Hogwarts, Harry experiences both friendship and animosity, forms alliances with like-minded individuals and battles against enemies.

This chapter follows Harry Potter's journey from being "just Harry" living in a cupboard under the stairs of number 4 Privet Drive to becoming Harry Potter: wizard and member of the Wizarding World.

Harry meets Hagrid for the first time
(00:12:30–00:19:30)

The Dursley family, plus Harry, is spending the night in a shack on an isolated island. At midnight, a giant breaks down the door, apologizes and wishes Harry a happy birthday.

The giant Hagrid assumes Harry knows about his identity as a wizard, while Harry takes for granted his identity as a plain 11-year-old who is 'just Harry'. It becomes clear that Harry's identity as a wizard has been deliberately concealed, in order to root out any possible connection between the Dursleys and the Wizarding World, which, from the Dursley's perspective, is a threat to their 'normality'. Mr. Dursley attempts to take control of the situation by threatening Hagrid and demanding that he leaves.

Mrs. Dursley explains what she felt when her sister – Harry's mother – was revealed to be a witch. Describing her as a freak, strange, abnormal. Hagrid rejects this description and informs the Dursleys that a place at Hogwarts has been reserved for Harry since he was born.

Even though Mr. Dursley states that Harry will not start school at Hogwarts. Harry leaves with Hagrid to enter the world of wizarding, a journey where Harry is recognized, even famous, although the reason for that fame is not explained, yet.

Theories of identity

Identity as a concept has been a subject of debate for quite some time, and from quite disparate positions. A close inspection of the scene above suggests an interplay between several conceptual models. Hall (1992:275) describes three historically different concepts of identity. The first concerns *the subject* of the Enlightenment:

The Enlightenment subject was based on a conception of the human person as a fully centred, unified individual, endowed with the capacities of reason, consciousness, and action, whose 'centre' consisted of an inner core which first emerged when the subject was born and unfolded with it, while remaining essentially the same – continuous or 'identical' with itself – throughout the individual's existence. This essential centre of the self-defined a person's identity.

Later a classic sociological conception of identity was developed, which, while maintaining the idea of an inner core, also assumed this core to be formed and transformed in dialogue with the cultures the individual inhabits, and the identities that they offer. Hall (1992:276) defines this sociological perspective as bridging the gap between the 'inside' and the 'outside', between personal and private worlds. He writes,

The fact that we project 'ourselves' into these cultural identities, at the same time as internalizing their meanings and values, making them 'part of us, ' helps to align our subjective feelings with the objective places we occupy in the social and cultural world.

Hall describes this as subjects investing in the positions in which they are 'hailed', with responses that accord to existing social schemes, and by adopting their systems of knowledge and beliefs (Hall & Du Gay, 2011). The concept of hailing, proposed by Althusser, Balibar and Bidet (2014), strives to explain how an individual interacts with his or her social environment by accepting an ascribed or proposed position and identity. The Althusser et al. model offers an alternative to deterministic conceptions of identity, questioning whether identity is socially forced upon the individual, or is created as a quasi-mechanistic result of internal forces. Harry's simple 'I am' (00:13.27), when asked if he is Harry Potter, means that he takes a step towards Hagrid's alternative narrative of 'being Harry the wizard'. Both structural and institutional change has made it more complicated to stabilize the interplay between the individual and culture, hence, the postmodern subject cannot simply be conceived of as having an essential, permanent identity. Instead, identity is continuously formed, reformed and transformed according to the different ways in which subjects are addressed or represented. Needless to say, subjects confront this instability by constructing comforting and stabilizing narratives about themselves and others (Amiot, de la Sablonniere, Smith & Smith, 2015; McAdams, 2001; McAdams & McLean, 2013; Usborne & de la Sablonniere, 2014).

As highlighted in the scene before, some notions of a 'true identity' are not just a matter of concern for an individual, rather it is also the external perception of the interaction of self and the culture(s) to which they belong. Identity, in this context, is not just a matter of a personally defined linear development, or an enfolding, but rather a constant interplay and assessment between culture(s) and individuals.

Thus, Harry has not really unearthed facts about his identity as a Muggle, but rather is telling and retelling a story that – from a Muggle perspective – has made sense. It has made sense because it is consistent with the culture he was living in, where car crashes occur, but deadly spells do not. However, it is not until alternative narratives come into play that the hegemonic nature of society is destabilized. Hence, the arena of conflict and struggle (antagonism) isn't within identity itself but between different societies offering different identities and how individuals make 'sense' of them.

Alternative narratives therefore make it possible to address and (re)present individuals in a new way, not as freaks or deviants, but as a different. As Hall suggests, identity is a matter of 'becoming' as well as of 'being'. It belongs to the future as much as to the past. It is not purely something that already exists; it can transcend place, time, history and culture. Cultural identities come from somewhere, they have histories, but like everything that is historical, they undergo constant transformation (Hall, 1994).

This would suggest an element of instability, especially when it comes to identification, but, despite being unstable, identities can at least, temporarily, be stabilized 'by social practice and regular, predictable behaviour' (Barker & Galasinski, 2001:31). According to Butler and Salih (2004), identities are stabilized by performance, by thinking, acting, and being treated 'in character'. Therefore, a central component of social practice and predictable behaviour is the preservation of stability through the maintenance of a clear line of difference between self and others. Thus, individuals can be made to see himself as 'the other', as an antagonistic threat that could destabilize the host society and its culture. Hence, stability can only be achieved if the anomaly is hidden or eradicated, and overpowered by an acceptance of a collective past and the promise of a collective future (Fanon, 2008; Hall, 1994; Said, 1979).

Any theory of identity has to address the questions of change and transition, as well as the relationship between individuals within the social groups they belong to. According to Burr (2002), the traditional conception of identity was seen as being the result of an individual's actions which were guided by rational decision making while striving to attain moral integrity. This conception assumed a clear demarcation between groups and individuals. Changes in a sense of identity were mostly perceived of as resulting from maturation and natural development. More recently, social scientists such as Giddens (1991) and Bauman (2005) have described the construction of identity in contemporary society as being fragmented, uncertain and unpredictable, while feminist intellectuals such as Judith Butler (Butler & Salih, 2004) have developed non-essentialist theories of identity (de Fina, 2011). Identities are actually something that people *do* or perform (See Chapter 9 for further discussion.). This performance, viewed through Butler's theoretical lens, is coordinated within society through the groups that one is part of, or expelled from, and functions to create a sense of stability despite the fact that identities are actually in flux.

Consequently, in the aforementioned sequence, Harry is confronted with a re-conceptualization of his identity, due to a clash between different concepts of 'being Harry'. From Harry's point of view, he is 'just Harry', a normal boy in a normal suburb, albeit with unusual behaviour. In this 'normal' world, Harry is seen as deviant and a threat to normalcy and decency, which threatens his aunt's and uncle's status as a 'normal' suburban family. Thus, Harry has to struggle in order to fit in, and is dealt the lowest place in the social pecking order. In terms of practice, as illustrated in Chapter 3, 'fitting in' can be become a battle between a self-constructed identity and one that is imposed.

Petunia Dursley holds two different narratives of Harry's identity. One is the overt version that concurs with Harry's perception of himself: a normal boy with deviant tendencies, who has to be treated strictly and kept in place. The other narrative, forced into the open by Hagrid's revelations, makes it plain why she is treating Harry so harshly: She perceives Harry as innately strange and different, just like his mother. In her view, Harry's alternative identity, being a wizard, means being 'a freak', and has to be weeded out, or at least suppressed by all available means. To her, the difference between being born a freak and being a freak is merely a matter of training. Petunia mocks her parents' acceptance of wizardry in the family and tries to rectify this by frantically pruning Harry's deviant tendencies. As suggested by Foucault (1995), surveillance and punishment can constitute an opportunity to impose and maintain perceptions of normality. The suppression of Harry's perceived abnormality is validated by the Dursleys' commitment to middle-class suburban values and patterns. In many ways, this replicates the experiences of migrant diasporas, where choices are between assimilation, what Gordon (1964) referred to as acculturalization, and cultural separatism. Hence, Harry's change of identity from a "troublesome boy" to "Harry the apprenticed wizard" implicitly implies losses as well as gains.

From this perspective, where identity emanates from innate traits, they are socially evaluated, disciplined and can ultimately be controlled by sheer willpower. Often parents and carers combine traditional conservative conceptions of identity as a biological inheritance of genes and breeding with the liberal notion that success can be achieved merely by adopting certain personality traits: traits such as self-control, self-discipline and the internalization of social norms and demands. Identity and society are thus closely interwoven, not just by adjustment, refinement and cultivation of one's inner self according to social demands but also by performing identity to a socially acceptable level. When Hagrid bursts in, he presents Harry with two competing social positions, being a Muggle or being a wizard. Being abnormal in a 'normal' world or normal in an abnormal world. Therefore, in both the Muggle and the Wizarding Worlds, behaviour is treated according to the identity that is ascribed to it.

The invitation letter (00:15:15)

Hagrid delivers the invitation letter, which informs Harry that he is accepted to Hogwarts and required to 'report to the Chamber of Reception upon arrival' and urges him 'to ensure that the utmost attention be made to the list of requirements attached herewith'.

Vernon Dursley states that Harry 'will not be going', because 'we swore when we took him in we would put a stop to all this rubbish'.

Harry asks incredulously, 'You knew? You knew all along and you never told me?!'

Petunia scornfully acknowledges they knew: 'How could you not be, my perfect sister being who she was'? She resentfully mentions her parents pride the day her sister got the invitation to Hogwarts, claiming she herself being the only one to understand what her sister 'really was: a freak'.

Vernon Dudley's intervention above highlights two factors that impinge on identity formation, a hidden identity narrative and the need by an external force to control how the visible narrative is performed. The scene could just as easily describe an exchange between a young adolescent and her/ his parents. The child's perception of oneself may be at odds with parental expectations and social demands. Thus, there may be two social spheres that lay claim to the child, both offering different identities, the obedient and submissive child and the independent, proactive young adult. Identity formation is thus a simultaneous matter of inclusion and exclusion – by being included into one sphere, means, by default, potentially being excluded from another. Harry's wizarding identity has been suppressed and labelled as deviant and unacceptable and just as Harry is subjected to a form of benevolent violence in order to normalize his behaviour and identity, some children are made to see himself through the eyes of those in power – out of line, out of step and potentially outcast.

Transition in many cases can mean a traumatic loss of identity, *gemeinschaft*, competence and connectivity, which has been described in the work of Swedish psychiatrist Johan Cullberg (Cullberg, 2008).

In the earlier scene, Mrs. Dursley is afraid of social exclusion and being found guilty of social infringement by association with the 'strange'. The suburban community – like any other group – expects its members to remain loyal to the group's common values and practices, threatening them with loss of status by exposure to gossip and reduced contact or even with expulsion (see Chapter 9). In order to retain status and membership every member has to construct his or her identity according to the norms and values of the group and to practice and defend those norms and values, in turn, reproducing the narrative and structure of that group. Thus, groups and individual identities are entwined and reinforce each other.

In order to reproduce and stabilize the hegemony, or the unchallenged power of the suburban narrative of orderliness, self-discipline and control of deviant tendencies, Harry has had to accept his subordination. Controlling deviancy means not only controlling the deviant, but its ultimate success is that the 'deviant' begins to control and chastise themselves.

The dialogue between Hagrid and Petunia reveals a concept of identity that they both agree upon. In this, they draw upon the same essentialist notion of identity, that is, each believe that Harry's identity is based on a fixed and fundamental attribute (Gellman, 2005). Mrs Dursley assumes that magical powers are hereditary transferable traits, which reinforces Hagrid's claim that Harry has been part of the Wizarding community since birth. This idea rests on the assumption that identities are formed by some kind of essence or intrinsic trait. As discussed in other chapters in this book, language and 'naming' form a major part of identity, often creating categories: male/female, heterosexual/ homosexual, child/adult, citizen/immigrant, them/us.

The simple procedure of naming challenges Mrs Dursley's dichotomy of normality versus deviation and offers instead a coexistence of two separate, but interconnected, versions of reality. Usually only the deviant groups are named, while the 'normal' majority is not; quite literally the social practice of 'naming and shaming' the deviant. Thus, naming implies at least partial recognition of different forms of existence, and potentially makes it easier to deal with the transition from one social identity to another.

However, without this naming process, a deviation from normality would have no place in language and would therefore seem not to exist, making it impossible to migrate to an alternative identity. This does not apply to Harry alone, as anyone who has ever felt attracted to somebody of the same sex can confirm, it can be difficult to identify with a group that is described in derogatory terms by significant others. It is generally far easier to identify oneself as part of a group that is held in high esteem.

The political implications of recognition within discourses have been explored by Mouffe (2005) who describes two different views of the political struggle. She describes political struggle as striving for control of the public discourse, that is, what can be said and thought and what is regarded as normal and reasonable. This control does not necessarily translate into violence and open suppression, instead, as Lukes's (2005) concept of power implies, there are far more powerful means of domination, such as ideas, ideologies, meaning-making processes and identities. Persuading people to regard one particular world view as natural and self-evident is a far more effective use of power than forcing people to act in certain ways. Once most people have accepted certain ideas as normal, those ideas have a hegemonic position: they are dominating, without open coercion.

This antagonistic view tries to maintain hegemony and harmony by excluding all positions but one, by marking alternatives as non-feasible, unthinkable, mentally unstable or as being harmful to the well-being of the shared and acknowledged community (Laclau & Mouffe, 2001). Alternatively, the agonistic view concedes that there might be victorious positions, but assumes they cannot win once and for all, and accepts conflict rather than perpetual stability and harmony. Thus, the agonistic view acknowledges diverging interests and ideologies and regards conflict as being part and parcel of the political sphere.

It is Mrs Dursley who initiates the downfall of the antagonistic model of suburban hegemony as she admits, albeit grudgingly, the legitimate existence of an alternative explanation for Harry's behaviour. She admits to the conflict between the parallel worlds of Wizards and Muggles, implicitly conceding that there are at least two different positions (or worlds) for Harry to inhabit. This acknowledgement of viable alternative views of society makes transition possible.

When Hagrid defines Harry as being part of his world, a paradigm shift will inevitably be the result. In practice, this is consistent with many other identity changes, like coming of age, or coming out with a different sexual identification; once the old identity is shaken off there is seldom a possibility of going back. As discussed in Chapter 4, *The Red Balloon*, transition for whatever reason and at whatever age can be discomforting, even painful.

Power, communities and identity

While there are many different conceptions of how identity construction may occur (Du Gay, Evans & Redman, 2000), some are more useful than others. A suitable starting point is the conception of identity as self-identity, this being a collection of beliefs and ideas about oneself. Until his eleventh birthday, how Harry imagines himself has been carefully edited and managed by the Dursleys and it is from this narrative that Harry initially constructs his self-identity. From the onset, children are embedded in a social world that pre-dates them. This social world consists mainly of family and carers as well as the social and educational settings a child may attend, thus creating a localized framework of social hierarchy, which can be seen replicated in wider society. Together they exert different types of power. According to Lukes (2005), power can be exerted by making somebody do, or not do, something. However, power can also be exerted by hindering or prohibiting somebody from doing something, as in the earlier scene, but most importantly power can be exerted by making others feel, wish and assume things, which in turn makes them behave and think in certain ways.

This power is often subtly exerted by way of a social milieu, as groups or even lifeworlds are structured in particular ways that can shape the way people think. Children can be subordinated within a lifeworld that conveys the information, knowledge and meaning they need to construct self-identity and from which they can see no alternative reading of the world. According to Mannheim (1928), the struggle for hegemony is exerted by competing social groups fighting for dominance by attempting to make their interpretation of the world the universal one.

Just as Harry is assumed to know about the Wizarding World, but does not, so refugee children are often expected to understand the culture they have migrated to. However, this knowledge is not merely tacit, but is often taken for granted. Lave and Wenger (2005) refer to communities of practice, as a concept that can be useful in explaining the connection between social and cultural group membership, knowledge and identity. Lave and Wenger describe how membership of the group is conferred only once the rules, practices and dispositions are learned. In terms of migrant children and notions of assimilation as discussed earlier, becoming a member of the dominant group may mean adopting the appearance, habits and language of those around them. For Harry it was a very simple choice, membership of the world of Muggles or the world of wizards.

Children who see themselves as 'not fitting in', for whatever reason, can experience the internal conflict of trying to meet external expectations, which may not match internal understandings, attempting to be a person who fits in and conducts oneself according to other people's rules. This situation can be easily compared to not only the children of immigrant workers and refugee children, but also children who consider themselves transgendered or children who are indigenous to countries that have been colonized (see chapters 3 and 9).

In other words, our social world consistently informs us about our social position and our social identity, and we use this information to constantly construct and reconstruct who we think we are. Since this information is seemingly coherent, there is neither possibility nor reason for most children to question this status quo. Where there are no clear alternatives, a child's world is narrowly constructed by all-embracing and dominant discourses. While alternative narratives make it *possible* to contemplate other identities and other means of action, access to these alternative stories may be difficult. Challenging dominant discourses surrounding ethnicity, culture, sexuality, disability and even appearance are often suppressed. Thus, it is only Hagrid's intervention that allows Harry to reinterpret and challenge the dominant discourses that have both shaped Harry's self-identity and the social identity his family have ascribed him to. Hagrid has become the catalyst and metaphor for the need to confront dominant discourses. Practitioners too can play a crucial role in helping children and young people to step back from a singular version of reality and look afresh at the world, to stimulate reflexivity by revisualizing social norms and assumptions, thereby making it possible for them to rearrange and re-engineer their lives.

There are parts of some children's lives which exist outside of the family and settings despite endeavours to establish and maintain control. One possible explanation for a child's resistance to subordination to an ascribed social identity might be seen as the exertion of counterpower. Children may seek to exert the power to resist by reference to competing narratives, or even from rejecting mainstream narratives altogether. The latter often leading to them being labelled as social problems, subversives or even as a threat to an orderly society, and this is discussed in further detail in Chapter 6.

Identity challenge and change

For many displaced children, migration to another country and another culture can mean difficult choices and rarely ones that are a simple matter of binary options. Internal conflict can arise when a dominant discourse is challenged, as Althusser et al. (2014) point out, we are all born into a social position and hailed in this position, be it gender, class, ethnicity; being a Muggle or being a wizard. Where children have hitherto only experienced a single sociocultural context with regard to understanding their position, identity and cultural history, alternatives can be both confusing and disturbing. An alternative discourse that can redefine normality and abnormality can make being different a difficult option.

With regard to refugees and migrants, especially those escaping to Europe from the war-torn Middle East, citizens of some host countries have perceived difference as an identity which encompasses threat. Across Europe, political parties whose ideological platform is nationalistic and anti-immigration have increasingly gained electoral success. In Denmark, in 2015, the Danish Peoples Party registered over 20 per cent of the popular vote, with similar results recorded in Austria in 2013. In Finland, Sweden and Norway, between 2013 and 2015, anti-immigration parties gained between 13 per cent and 18 per cent of the votes cast (Parties and Election in Europe online). In the UK, in 2016, a referendum was held with regard to membership of the European Union, while ostensibly the question asked was whether the UK should stay in or leave the EU, embedded in the 'leave' campaign were ideologies based on an anti-immigration platform. In the three months following referendum, hate crimes against migrants rose by 41 per cent (Home Office, 2016). Thus, an identity based on membership of a coherent pan-national community has come into conflict with increasingly nationalistic positions with regard to who has the right to 'belong'.

A sense of 'belonging', therefore, cannot be understood as an essentialist notion of a true and stable identity, but rather as an identity that is compatible with a generally confirmed, but a flexible account of who you are.

Just as Harry's new identity as a wizard is still subject to change, and to different narratives about present and past affairs, so too is that of the migrant. Often transplanted into a society of agonistic narratives that define citizenship as a result of ancestry, or as a result of performativity. As seen in the film, Harry and Hermione, as young wizards with Muggle heritage experience similar challenges, as they struggle to solidify their sense of identity.

In practice, competing narratives, such as those around race, ethnicity and religion, can seem mutually exclusive, containing different positions and understandings. At first encounter, many children can deny the existence of these competing and conflicting positions, seeking safety within a dominant and known narrative. However, when offered a different perspective, children can learn to accept an alternative reading about themselves and others. In accepting the existence of several narratives a contingency emerges, and the previously accepted narrative is transformed from being *the* narrative into being *a* narrative. As Woodhead (2006:19) noted,

> Respecting diversities between and within societies, and recognising the challenges of social change, migration and multiculturalism is a core issues for ECCE [Early Childhood Care and Education] policy and practice.

Thus, a previously internal conflict can be seen as an external conflict between two different social spheres both laying claim to a child's identity. The struggle is no longer taking place internally but is a struggle between the social perceptions of normality and acceptability and alternative presentations, in order to provide different identities with different meanings.

Adolescents on the cusp of adulthood often feel they have one foot in each camp and may experience similar conflicts. For example, while peers may see a petty theft as courageous and demonstrable commitment to a group, adults may define it as criminal activity, ascribing different identities to the same action. However, these identities are not based on the deed itself, but on an attribution, which, in turn, might be heavily influenced by assumptions, whether tacit or explicit, that are based on class, gender, sexuality, appearance and race.

Transition and re-evaluation of identity may cause many children to seek out alliances with like-minded individuals, no longer wishing to be 'one of them' but now one of 'us'.

Rites of passage

Transformations of identity aren't necessarily painless. Most people spend their lives in several different groups and, therefore, are represented and addressed in several different ways, which makes it necessary to permanently reconstruct their identities in everyday actions (Butler & Salih, 2004).

However, every now and then, a major shift occurs, which affects several parts of a person's identity at the same time. These shifts often imply the rearrangement of interactions, recognition, status, and so on. Examples of such shifts might be entering school, debutante balls, religious confirmation, coming of age, leaving home, coming out as a homosexual, losing one's virginity, pregnancy and childbirth, entering university, or retirement. In almost every society there are ceremonies concerning major life events, often quite elaborate. Weddings for example imply shifts in the partners' legal status, economic and social relationships. The inclusion of family and friends, as well as officials, in these rituals confirm, by their presence, the acknowledgement of these shifts.

van Gennep (2010) explained ceremonies, rituals and identity changes in traditional societies as 'passages', that is, movements from one age or occupation to another, and coined the expression rites of passage (van Gennep, 2010). He recognized three different stages in these rituals: separation, liminality and incorporation. Thus, children starting school partially leave home, and an identity where they are predominately their parents' children enters a phase where things are in flux, and eventually they become members of a school class, or a peer group with different rules and patterns of behaviour, in turn, forming an identity as pupils. This model can be used in order to understand social transitions during professional education (Holland, 1999; Barton, 2007; Draper, Sparrow & Gallagher, 2009) and even earlier childhood transitions (Vogler, Crivello & Woodhead, 2008). Drawing upon this research, one might scrutinize Hogwarts's organization and its relation to student's transitions from childhood to adolescence and from novice to trained professional.

Harry's separation from his family and his transition to the Wizarding World can be a useful tool to explore the transitional years of childhood. In separation, the person may withdraw from his or her previous identity. In Harry's case, this means challenging the familial narrative about his identity coupled with an increasing degree of rejection of their authority, as many adolescents do. He challenges the truth of their single narrative, choosing instead to explore an alternative.

Here it might be useful to briefly discuss the question of teenage identity by drawing upon the classical theories of Erikson (1965, 1971) and Marcia (1980). Both conceived adolescence as difficult years, being a part of an ongoing search for identity, an endeavour to establish a stable sense of who one is, which may create role confusion, especially when there are different expectations from all parties involved. Cognitive, biological and social development means earlier relations between a young person and his or her environment tend to become unstable and cannot form the basis of one's perception of oneself anymore. Thus, earlier relations and conceptions of one's identity are at least partially rejected and re-evaluated instead of simply being relied upon. Instead, young people increasingly 'try on' different roles at home, at school and in other social groups, and navigate between ideal selves and feared selves (Markus & Nurius, 1986). During these trials, they explore other's reactions to these roles, and work on integrating them into a functioning whole. A young person's upbringing and family background is an important platform for the exploration of new identities, as well as self-awareness, self-esteem and trustworthy reliable relations with others. Furthermore, the extent of the adolescent's economic, social and cultural capital (Bourdieu, 1984) can make this exploration of different ways of life and personal identification either easier or more difficult.

Arguably, experimentation with socially accepted and favoured identities is easier than experimenting with social identities that are less usual or even stigmatized. Class, ethnicity, sexuality and other social identities play an important role in this testing of new identities and the ongoing endeavour of forging them into a coherent identity in relation to an unstable environment. Marcia (1980) emphasized the importance of this exploration, talking about foreclosure in those cases when young people are made to embrace new identities without exploration of other possibilities, foreboding an identity crisis later on. Thus, it could be argued that creating a distance from families as the sole source of their identity is a necessary prerequisite for the exploration of the possibilities of a new sense of self. This distancing is often a disruptive process, including abrupt mood swings, changing affiliations to families, peer groups and changing identifications with groups and/ or individuals. This is significant for the next step in van Gennep's transitional scheme, the liminal phase. This phase, van Gennep says, is the phase between the different identities and groups, not clearly defined or easily categorized, it is both and neither at one and the same time. Harry doesn't completely leave the Muggle World and still hasn't completely entered the Wizarding World, like most adolescents he is standing on the bridge between two identities, that of child and adult. During this phase, identities and actions are usually ambiguous and previous certainty is replaced by unfamiliar obstacles and doubts. The young wizards are seen throughout the film 'experimenting' with being a wizard, but they are only allowed to draw on their new wizarding tools within the confines of Hogwarts. Outside of the confines of Hogwarts, the use of wizardry is forbidden; disobeying this rule runs the risk of expulsion.

For most children this is a slow transition, gradually performing and confirming options in small steps, defined through things like appearance, tastes and demeanour. However, within most societies, this gradual process is often punctuated by major 'coming of age' events such as a Bar Mitzvah or confirmation, transfer to secondary school or the arrival of a sibling. The confirmation that one has left one's old group and joined a new one, each in turn ascribing a new status and identity.

According to van Gennep, rituals can be said to be symbolic actions, expressing and confirming status and marking one's membership in a new group. As such, they fulfil an important social and psychological function by increasing group attraction and feelings of affiliation and conformity within the group (Wen, Herrmann & Legare, 2016; Keating et al., 2005). As for the group, rituals contribute to stability by symbolically cutting off remnants of previous affiliations and identifications (Kamau, 2013; Tajfel, 2010; Aronson & Mills, 1959; Klerk, 2013).

Culture clash and identity

Leaving the Muggle World for Hogwarts
(00:30:08–00:39:36)

Hagrid accompanies Harry to the railway station to catch the train to Hogwarts. He gives him his ticket and then disappears. Harry notices that the ticket says the train to Hogwarts leaves from Platform 9 ¾. Harry searches for the railway station for the correct platform but is unable to find it. He decides to ask a member of the railway staff where it might be. However, his polite question is met with a refusal to understand, and he receives a sharp response, when the official replies, 'Think you're being funny, do you?' It is only when he encounters the Weasley family that he is shown how to get to the platform, through a solid brick wall.

On arrival at the school, Harry is told he will be allocated to one of the houses of Hogwarts, and while he was there, the House would be 'like your family' (00:38:00). Just before the 'sorting ceremony', Harry encounters Draco Malfoy, who warns Harry that he will soon 'find out that some wizarding families are better than others, you don't want to go making friends with the wrong sort'.

The scene above provides a glimpse of another clash of cultures as while Harry realizes that his frames of reference might work perfectly in the Muggle World, but they don't gain him entry into the Wizarding World. His arrival at Hogwarts provides both place and position, and safety, thus further facilitating transition into a new identity. For most children and young people, this is a slow and evolutionary process but equally it may result from a crisis which requires a reorientation into a new and unfamiliar life.

Cullberg (2008), a Swedish psychologist, described a four-phase model of traumatic crisis and outlined recommendations for professionals and others who are dealing with individuals experiencing these phases. The model is meant to be a framework for understanding and dealing with patients, not as a clear-cut diagnostic model. The first phase Cullberg termed as 'shock'. During this stage, emotions are in turmoil, and reality does not feel real. During the second phase, termed as the 'reaction phase', the patient realizes the traumatic event has really happened. The reactions might be grief or despair, and reactions are not particularly reasonable. In this phase, patients might want to negotiate with their fate or demand explanations, even denial is a coping strategy subconsciously employed. In this phase, rapid and unpredictable mood shifts might occur. During the third, or coping phase, patients slowly get accustomed to their new situation. After-images of the traumatic event might occur, and emotions like anxiety and fragility are quite common. The fourth, reorientation phase, implies an orientation towards the future. People start to accept and structure their new lives and are mostly able to talk about the traumatic event without great emotional upheaval. Life finds its balance again, and the traumatic event is now part of one's new life as it is woven into past experiences. These phases, or stages, always occur in that order, even though not everybody reaches stage three or four. Thus, children who have experienced abuse or neglect may suffer from post-traumatic stress disorder (PTSD) and may be stuck in limbo somewhere between phases two and three. For practitioners this can present difficult situations where a child's behaviour may be erratic, violent and irrational. Practitioners need to understand that this is a child's reaction to past events or traumas and a subconscious attempt to retake control of their life and their future. Children who have suffered neglect or abuse are in effect reshaping and reordering their identity, and while this process may be challenging, as Cullberg suggests, the transition from shock to reorientation may be stalled or even halted without the sensitive support of those around them. This is further discussed in Chapter 10.

In the context of Harry's narrative, Harry is a migrant leaving familiarity, albeit an unpleasant one, for a new and different life. Harry leaves his native environment, which includes most of his knowledge of the world, as well as his identity and his position. Harry has lost his frames of reference. For many migrants, the narrative of one's previous life can become irrelevant in the new environment. Like any other migrant, Harry has a reasonable working knowledge of the world he is leaving, and knows how to deal with everyday situations, but in the world he is entering, he knows almost nothing. From being a more or less competent adolescent, he is thrown back to being a child, having to learn how he should function in his new society. Mirroring perhaps the experiences of many migrant children.

Social competence and the ability to cope with the world are important factors to be considered. In the real world, migrants are often traumatized by sights, sounds and loss. Cullberg (2008) explains that children who have experienced trauma may develop attachment issues, not daring to enter into new relationships, unable to talk about emotions and experiences and unable to deal with challenges and changes.

Unlike Harry, language, manners and many familiar social practices from his past are also valid in his new life, which obviously puts him into a better position than many migrants, or other people dealing with severe emotional changes. Thus, both Harry and migrants find themselves between two communities of practice (Lave & Wenger, 2005).

Hogwarts as a community of practice

As discussed here and in earlier chapters, a community of practice (Wenger, 1998) is a group that shares common positions, information and experiences with each other, developing practices through communication. These groups do not just focus on learning a new skill but on the process of socialization by which new members are initiated into common ways of thinking, acting, executing tasks and the practices of action and behaviour.

Membership of the community thus results in shared understanding of norms and the construction of supportive stable relationships. These relationships tie the community together. Casting Harry in the role of a migrant reveals that Hogwarts is such a community where relationships and mutual recognition play a crucial role. However, further events in the series of Harry Potter books reveal that there are several distinct communities with divergent practices, strong bonds and consequentially distinct ideologies, such as the four Hogwarts Houses of Gryffindor, Hufflepuff, Ravenclaw and Slytherin. Using the migrant context, this might well translate to the reality that migrants will often seek out the familiar, and quite unintentionally create themselves, as both joined and separate within their new environment, a culture and society within a larger culture and society.

The terms 'joint enterprise' and 'shared repertoire' are used to describe both the shared understanding of the community's domain and the symbolic and practical resources that identify the community (Wenger, 1998:72). Wenger underlined the role of the individual as a participant in the practices of social communities and the importance of these communities for the construction and shaping of identities. Thus, participation makes it possible to experience, create, and re-create shared identity.

As a migrant child, this means overtly taking part in the activities of the new community. It is not simply a matter of education and socialization, but it is also the process of becoming accepted as part of the community, learning its ways, participating in the community's tacit knowledge. This not only underlines important aspects of identity: identity as a matter of performativity (Butler, Laclau & Zizek, 2000), of recognition and of being recognized, but also it is about accepting and sharing a body of knowledge. A migrant must, therefore, 'perform an identity', continuously reconfirming their right to be considered a member of the community.

Lave and Wenger's (2005) theory of 'communities of practices' can thus be used in deepening our understanding of what moving from one community to another may entail, especially underlining the importance of social and cultural practices. How the 'doing' of identities and the identification of new ways of understanding the world informs oneself and others. It could even point to the importance of regarding the receiving communities as *shared* enterprise, not just as unchangeable entities demanding new apprentices to subordinate and to be subjected.

Concluding remarks

It might be reasonable to look at *Harry Potter and the Philosopher's Stone* from a contemporary Muggle perspective. To do this, it is necessary to go back to Stuart Hall's perspectives, which can also be found in the writings of Edward Said (1979) and Frantz Fanon (2008). This perspective views the construction of the 'Other' as someone who sees himself through the eyes of the observer.

Harry has had, in the past, experiences that do not fit into the narrative of the world within which he has been raised. He had come to regard this narrative as synchronized with the world around him, or at least as the only available description and explanation for the status quo. In other words, Harry is immersed in a discourse, explaining who he is, what counts as normal behaviour and how the world is to be understood. In Harry's case and for many children, the hegemonic narrative explains that maintaining normality must involve a suppression of the 'abnormal'. Within this discourse, 'normality' has to be protected from being overthrown by 'abnormality' or threatened by deviance or delinquency, thus sub- and countercultures are often constructed as threats. Consequently, if a shared understanding of normality is abandoned, notions of stability, the status quo, order and discipline, at least in this idealized social world, is lost. In this scenario, only a dystopia can prevail. The position Harry is offered is that of a loyal member of the established order, in which he must govern himself and control his own dangerous tendencies and by doing so submit to the communities of practice within the Muggle World.

Hence, in order to maintain a status quo, Harry (and anyone else labelled as deviant or subversive) is required to sacrifice the experiences and knowledge that constitute part of their identity and to see themselves as a potential threat. This requirement is typical for antagonistic societies where positions described as being anomalies, deviant or alternative have to be excluded. They cannot be accepted in political terms. There is, as Bauman (2005) puts it, no agora for the transformation of private experiences into political reasoning, and therefore these private experiences have to be treated as individual deviance from perpetual normality and harmony.

Harry has Hagrid to help him to re-evaluate his experiences thus far, and makes 'what if' considerations possible as a facilitator and enabler. What if Harry isn't a freak? What if Harry's experiences are real, reasonable and consistent with some other rationality? What if the Muggle World is abnormal?

What if denial of experiences is abnormal? What if there actually *is* an alternative after all? Hagrid, the facilitator, not only offers a way out for Harry, but he offers utopia as well.

Hogwarts: an organized community of practice, with alternative identities and alternative ways to deal with experiences. A different world is therefore indeed possible when people to work together; people who are ready to understand rites of passage and the traumatic experiences that change might bring; people who are prepared to abandon the antagonistic hegemony of an orderly status quo, and to embrace agonism, conflict and change.

In light of the discussion of ideas and theory in this chapter, you might like to reflect on the following questions.

- What emotions might Harry experience when the door between the Muggles World and the Wizarding World is literally knocked down?

- Consider the transitions between the social spheres you or others you know have experienced, and how they dealt with them.

- How has your own identity been shaped by an interplay between different narratives?

8

The Dystopian State and the Safeguarding of (Normalized) Childhoods:
The Hunger Games

Martin Needham

This chapter considers the following:

- The continuing relevance of the social class divide in the twenty-first century: Bourdieu (1997), Jones (2014), Walkerdine (2014).

- Children's right to a protected childhood; United Nations Convention on the Rights of the Child (UNCRC, 1989), Ensalaco and Majka (2005).

- Why individuals should care about neo-liberal politics and the outsourcing of responsibility for safeguarding children (Apple, 2011; Jones, 2014).

The film

The Hunger Games was chosen as the basis for this chapter because the exaggerated, simplified, fantasy context of the film makes the viewers feel shocked and upset by the actions of the state in violating children's rights. This helps us gain insights into the application of concepts of social class and political ideology liberated from the personal politics of twenty-first-century society. The chapter explores the state's role in safeguarding and protecting children, a theme that is explored through an analysis of the tense relationship between Katniss and the state of Panem.

Following the success of *The Hunger Games* book trilogy by Suzanne Collins, the first of *The Hunger Games* films, released in 2012, also proved a huge international success. The film is set in Panem, a nation state located in a dystopian future world apparently created by a rise in global sea levels submerging some of the lowland geography of the continent. Panem is divided into subjugated 'districts', political power is centralized in the Capitol and the nation is socially stratified in the service of the Capitol's elite. While Panem is clearly not the contemporary United States, it does perhaps present an exaggerated caricature of contemporary divisions in US society, where decaying industrial areas such as Detroit are contrasted with high-tech media-savvy centres such as Washington, DC. In the film, District 12 and the 'Capitol' represent these contrasts. The Capitol asserts power over citizens by staging an annual reality TV show called the *The Hunger Games*. This pitches twenty-four young district champions against each other in a protracted gladiatorial survival contest, a barbaric fight to the death between the twelve male and twelve female tributes.

In the early scenes, Katniss Everdene, the central character of the film, is depicted as the key carer for her younger sister and mentally fragile mother. To make ends meet she skilfully, but illegally, hunts game in the forests surrounding her mining community home. Early in the film, she is dramatically uprooted from her family when she takes her sister's place as one of the two randomly chosen District 12 tributes to *The Hunger Games*. The film charts her journey, as she prepares for and then participates in the 'games'.

The first part of the chapter guides readers through an analysis of social class archetypes linked to Katniss's home in District 12 and the social values of the Capitol. The film illustrates how a controlling social elite can exist out of phase with sectors of society; this resonates with Jones's (2014) analysis of the upper-class elite in British society occupying key roles in media as well as law, business and politics. The analysis draws attention to the need to challenge deterministic stereotypes of a disadvantaged underclass and promote mutual understanding across social boundaries (Walkerdine, 2014).

The second part of the chapter examines children's rights to protection by the state from extreme poverty and participation in combat. The film highlights how childhood is not respected or recognized by Panem. The Hunger Games tournament section of the film is particularly challenging, because it provokes a strong sense of injustice on behalf of the children forced into mortal combat. Readers are encouraged to reflect on the depth of feeling the film evokes about the need to protect children from a violent adult world. The chapter invites readers to consider what the protective duties of the state towards children.

The concluding section of the chapter draws attention to the underlying political commentary of the film as a critique of centralized state control. It argues that the film romanticizes the individual pioneer spirit and vilifies the state. Readers are encouraged to reflect on the rights and responsibilities of the citizen and the state.

Growing up in District 12.

The first scenes of the film introduce us to District 12, a community dependent on coal mining. The buildings and inhabitants are rundown, uniform, plainly dressed, shabby and functional. This is a disadvantaged neighbourhood living in poverty, where the children go hungry.

Choosing the tributes (00:09:45–00:17:13)

The downtrodden children of District 12 file into a guarded compound and line up in rows, corralled by heavily armed guards. The location is a rundown bleak late industrial landscape. The people of District 12 wear garments reminiscent of 1930s and 1940s American workwear: dungarees, caps, homemade dresses. By contrast, the police guards from out of the district wear futuristic white Stormtrooper suits and helmets. The landscape and retro clothing of District 12 evokes periods of depression and hardship.

The children are assembled in an unnatural silence and compelled to watch a giant video screen that reminds them that they are assembled to select a male and a female tribute for the seventy-fourth annual Hunger Games. Everyone is reminded that this is done as an assertion of power by the Capitol who defeated the rebelling districts seventy years previously. The Hunger Games demands the sacrifice of the lives of two young people from each district. A piece of paper bearing Primrose Everdene's name is drawn from a glass bowl. When the name is read out, the children part around a terrified young girl, yielding her up to the waiting guards. A few silent seconds later, her elder sister Katniss screams out that she will volunteer. Everyone is surprised because, as the MC announces, this is the first volunteer from District 12 in seventy years. Guards move in to surround and escort Katniss up to the stage. She is clearly terrified and in shock at what she is doing. The crowd remains silent. The ridiculously dressed MC calls for applause, but the children remain silent and then unsettle the MC further by all kissing three fingers and raising them in a silent salute. Peeta Mellark, a baker's son, is then chosen as the male tribute; he walks resignedly up to the stage.

The scenes in District 12 summon up cultural archetypes not just of the hard masculine cultures and grinding poverty of industrial towns in the United States, but also of family hardships connected with disaffected or absent father figures with undercurrents of alcohol abuse, domestic violence and neglect. The film uses these archetypes to portray working-class societies as so difficult that there is little space for activity outside the bounds of work and where survival is the daily focus.

The so-called American dream was created by migrants escaping the class-ridden societies of old Europe where one's station in life was fixed by the social position of the family you were born into and essential to one's character. While twentieth-century Europe saw a change from a rigid class-based division of labour to a more meritocratic system, many sociologists suggest that education systems still favour certain social groups (Bernstein, 2000; Bourdieu, 1997; Giddens & Sutton, 2013). The once clearly defined boundaries between a labouring working class, the merchant/trading middle class and the property-owning upper class are now much more blurred in societies where nearly everyone attends school (Savage, 2015). At the beginning of the twenty-first century, even established educational sociologists acknowledged that the traditional labels of working, middle and upper class were dissolving. Bernstein (2000) acknowledges that social class groups were less clearly marked in contemporary society because the nature of work was shifting from one dominated by industrial, factory-based labour to an information and service-based economy. Though class might be less visible in contemporary society, Jones (2014) offers a helpful and persuasive analysis of how those from the former upper classes with wealth and power remain in control of politics, business, media and law. Jones argues that money still buys advantage in a meritocracy where attending particular private schools offers increased chances to access particular universities and then to progress into top jobs in politics, business, media and law. While only 7 per cent of people attend fee-paying private schools in Britain they are disproportionately represented in top jobs; 35 per cent of MPs, 55 per cent of senior civil servants and 54 per cent of the top 100 media jobs and 22 per cent of pop stars (Social Mobility and Child Poverty Commission, 2014). In contemporary British society, few jobs require no qualifications. As technology takes over mundane heavy-labour tasks, many jobs require more technical or more sophisticated communication skills.

In contemporary British society, communities with a shared working-class lifestyle, based on a single industry such as mining, are rare and decreasing, but many communities in today's society are still haunted by their industrial past, which can make it hard for some families to adjust to find work in the modern labour market (Walkerdine, 2014). However, this idea of a working class fixed to a geographic area and a specific industry aligns with the population of District 12.

New accounts of social groups in society identify vulnerable low-income groups sometimes called the 'precariat' at the bottom of a social order and then more complex middle layers varying by wealth and income; tastes, interests and activities; social networks friendships and associations (Savage, 2015). The precariat has become a new archetype of disaffected families living on social housing estates divorced from more affluent communities and is becoming a common part of the narrative of contemporary news, politics and fiction in Britain (Walkerdine, 2015). In this archetype, class is marked not only by type of work but also by a limited engagement with social rules, conventions and the institutions of society. An underclass is identified, within the media, as poor, lacking in education, social manners and wider cultural awareness (Walkerdine, 2015; Jones, 2012). There are clear parallels to Katniss Everdene's situation.

This is a dangerous stereotype that casts people in a deterministic or self-perpetuating cycle where limited family social and cultural capital mean that children are likely to continue in a life of low-paid work or worklessnenss (Vandenbroeck et al., 2009; Walkerdine, 2014).

Studies of working class areas noted not only poverty and poor living conditions, but also a kind of moral economy which has been increasingly pathologized in the present, such that all opprobrium about chavs (a derogatory English word for working class youth; Jones, 2012), for example, is directed towards poor parenting styles and the need for their correction. (Walkerdine, 2014:186)

Walkerdine gives examples of how archetypes in the minds of society haunt communities creating self-fulfilling prophecies by those interacting with them who expect, see and reinforce certain behaviours. It is essential as childhood practitioners that we avoid a deterministic view of childhoods. To see children as trapped by the sociocultural conditions may fail to safeguard and encourage alternative futures, by setting low and limiting aspirations, judging their communities as failing and inadequate. Vandenbroeck et al. (2009) illustrate the importance of a sensitivity and respectful approach, demonstrated through practitioners entering into genuine open non-judgemental dialogues with migrant families in order to facilitate their inclusion.

In *The Hunger Games*, we see Katniss is clever and resourceful in terms of hunting, tracking, archery and her knowledge of plants. She is very caring towards her sister but tough, self-reliant and independent. She is comfortable in her own company, natural, unaffected and plain speaking. She embodies strength and dignity in facing the difficulties and challenges of her district. As the film progresses, we see that Katniss is not well educated by the state, she knows very little about culture, politics and life beyond her immediate circumstances.

The fantasy context of *The Hunger Games* film legitimates Katniss's law breaking because the state is so clearly unjust, and because she acts to save her sister. If Katniss lived in an urban British disadvantaged neighbourhood, her transgression of the law would probably be vilified in the press as showing her to be 'out of control'. In the film, we see her from her community's viewpoint as something of a local hero for supporting her family and providing fresh meat to the local community. Another factor in her acceptability as a hero is that the values she displays do not conform to an underclass stereotype of being uncouth, with a crass disregard for others and for social rules. She is presented as shy and awkward, aloof and unapproachable rather than sassy and antagonistic.

The focus of this chapter is on the state's role in safeguarding children however, safeguarding is not just immediate protection from harm, it is about looking to the longer-term well-being of children's futures. It has been argued that in contemporary society the problem of breaking the cycle that reproduces poverty in successive generations is a cultural expectation, supported by media and politicians that frequently reinforces stereotypes that demonize an underclass and in doing so increase the alienation and social exclusion of already disadvantaged children. For some children in contemporary societies, the processes of education can demand a conformity to rules that fail to value the talents they have, so that they are ascribed labels of failure that mark their futures. This is a challenge for professionals to resist cultural stereotypes in their day-to-day practice.

The Capitol, cultural capital and the state's role in supporting social mobility

As Katniss and Peeta are taken to the Capitol for training, we are introduced to three more social groups: the politicians, the media workers and the slaves. The media workers have employment but they live in a palpably different social world from the workers in District 12. They are well fed, elaborately, individually and expensively dressed; they wear elaborate make-up and hairstyles. Their clothes are diverse fashion items, worn as much as a personal statement as for practicality. This is a consumerist society; it uses food, clothing, power and human resources to heighten experiences in the moment with little concern for future sustainability. The population of the Capitol talk in an elaborate way and expect outsiders to conform to their elaborate customs. The Capitolists are ill informed about what life is like in the distant districts, but, in their world, it does not matter. *The Hunger Games* alludes to the detached power of the political and media elite in contemporary Washington, DC, and their distance from the production of the products, energy and food they consume. The slaves are those found guilty of crimes in the districts whose punishment is to have their tongues removed, rendering them voiceless, kept under constant surveillance as menial servants. The role of Katniss and Peeta's mentors, Haymitch and Effie, is to introduce them to complicated social expectations, behaviours and knowledge of the Capitol. They are introduced to the language, artefacts and materials that are endorsed as valuable by the state, for example, the transport systems, technology, clothes, culture, food and rituals. In their first TV interview, they are presented as amusingly naïve, as an entertainment to be laughed at for their inept country manners.

In the Capitol (00:49:33–00:56:56)

Katniss and Peeta are about to be interviewed in front of a live studio audience for the first time by *The Hunger Games*' TV master of ceremonies. We have already been introduced to extravagantly dressed, exotically made-up characters, but here we see over the scale of this extravagance. Katniss is initially stage-struck; when she misses the first interview question, the audience roar with laughter when she says simply, 'what?' The crowd are won over by her beautiful dress that shimmers with flames and her touching self-sacrifice for her sister, but she is still something to be pitied not respected. Similarly, in scene 11, Peeta is laughed at in his interview for saying the showers in the Capitol are different and that he now smells of roses. He invites the MC to smell him. When the MC does this, he asks in return how he smells. Peeta says, 'You smell better than me'. The MC replies that because I have been here longer, the audience continues to laugh at Peeta as a country clown. Peeta, unlike Katniss, is comfortable to play to the crowd.

As seen earlier, Peeta, in particular, rises to the challenge of adapting to the social rules and expectations of the Capitol, demonstrating greater social adaptability than Katniss. Peeta is learning the rules of playing the game, but Katniss wants to reject them.

Sociologists Bernstein (2000) and Bourdieu (1997) pointed to the role of language, social cultural awareness and social connections as implicit but important markers of difference that permit or deny access to different social spheres. Bernstein describes the restricted and elaborated codes of language and culture existing in educational discourses that make it harder for working-class children to fit into, largely due to the middle-class discourse of schools. Bourdieu (1997) argued that the process of education is bound up with the transmission of cultural capital. He identified three forms of cultural capital: embodied cultural capital relating to the knowledge and skills located in the person and habitus of the individual; objectified cultural capital acquired through books, artefacts, and so on; institutionalized cultural capital, the grouping of people by the processes of education they have undertaken that are marked by qualifications (Bourdieu, 1997).

Bourdieu (1997) argued that the process of education, while seeming to offer families a route to increased cultural, social, and economic capital, conceals the propensity of education to reproduce existing societal stratifications because it rewards those who are already comfortable with the modes of communication endorsed by those in power, which are in turn valued in education. The concept of habitus as developed by Bourdieu and discussed in Chapter 2 can also be helpful in moving beyond broad class labels towards a more refined analysis of individual values and dispositions.

> The habitus, as the word implies, is that which one has acquired, but which has become durably incorporated in the body in the form of permanent dispositions. So the term constantly reminds us that it refers to something historical, linked to individual history, and that it belongs to a genetic mode of thought, as opposed to essentialist modes of thought. (Bourdieu et al., 1993:86)

Bernstein's and Bourdieu's models of the demarcations of participation in social groups are also helpful because they are not essentialist or deterministic (Connolly, 2004). This means that peoples' fates are not fixed at birth or even through their childhood as unchanging aspects of their identity. People always have the potential to revise their habitus although they may lack the opportunities to do so. The emphasis that individuals and groups place on particular aspects of life and human activity can be more helpful in distinguishing them than the outward appearance of the objects they use in activity. A criticism of some multicultural comparisons is that they focus too much on clothes and food (samosas and saris) rather than significant values and beliefs. For example, while the food in two countries might be very different and lead to differences in cooking and eating utensils, attitudes to food, cooking and eating might be more similar than different. The following table offers a summary of the contrasting values exhibited in District 12 against those exhibited in the Capitol. You are invited to compare these values to those of communities that you know.

Values	District 12	The Capitol
Eating	Food is simple, uncomplicated, people eat to live, eat what there is, there are no elaborate eating rituals	Food is extravagant, people eat to excess, taking pills to induce vomiting so they can eat more
Speech	Communication of facts is more important than expression of ideas	Spoken and visual messages are elaborated, carefully chosen and nuanced to demonstrate status and power
Education	Practical skills are more important than educational qualifications	Knowledge of customs, practice, language, social codes is essential to maintaining and progressing one's position in society
Community	Collective survival is more important than individual survival	People are less concerned about maintaining the society than maintaining their own position within cultural cliques
Dress	Clothes are practical and facilitate dirty work. They demonstrate conformity and community belonging	Clothing is extravagant to demonstrate individuality, status and fashion awareness
Work	Working is essential for survival	Working is also pastime and a game that brings an overabundance of rewards
Personal appearance	Make-up and hair styling is minimal, plain and practical	Make-up, hair style and body augmentation is important to status and to standing out as an individual

In the film, it is not just being trapped in the District 12 community that denies any possibility of social mobility. Even for those gaining admission to the Capitol, the state's systems continue to disadvantage those from other cultural backgrounds from breaking into and controlling the corridors of power.

The educational market is strictly dominated by the linguistic products of the dominant class and tend to sanction the pre-existing differences in capital. (Bourdieu, 1990:62)

In Panem the districts are haunted by the ghosts of defeat and subjugation, that is the function of The Hunger Games; they are intended to remind the districts they have been defeated by the Capitol and therefore subject to humiliation. Panem does not seem to offer any way to improve one's life circumstances, other than through the long odds and horror of The Hunger Games. The increasing sense of injustice provoked by Katniss's performance in The Hunger Games troubles the president. He is keen to avoid Katniss providing others with any hope of beating the state; thereby challenging its power. He recognizes that every time she survives unbowed, her power to inspire rebellion grows.

In many contemporary societies, the apparently equitable offer of opportunity to pass from one class to another through the process of education gives enough hope to maintain the status quo. However, in reality, the journey from growing up in a disadvantaged district to gaining high-paid work is more challenging. Hopelessness may lead to alienation if not revolution. We need to be able to see the potential in the children that we support, to understand the challenges they face, to help make societies' codes more visible and accessible, to offer extra support when it is needed.

The Hunger Games and the Convention on the Rights of the Child

As early as 1924 Egalntyne Jebb, the founder of the Save the Children Fund, set out a declaration of the rights of the child (Ensalaco and Majka, 2005). However, it was not until 1989 that this was formally adopted by the United Nations in the Convention on the Rights of the Child (UNCRC, 1989). Every nation has now fully accepted the convention as a legal framework except for the United States. The CRC asserts that children under the age of eighteen should have additional rights beyond the declared Universal Human Rights (UHR) (1948). I focus on five of the fifty-four articles that are at the heart of resistance to the United States fully ratifying the CRC.

Material welfare

The fictional state of Panem fails in its responsibilities in relation to article 6, that all children have the right to life. Governments should ensure that children survive and develop healthily. Governments should also ensure that children are properly cared for, and protect children from violence, abuse and neglect by their parents, or anyone else who looks after them (CRC, Article 19). Governments should provide extra money for the children of families and need (CRC, Article 26) and children have a right to a standard of living that is good enough to meet their physical and mental needs. The government should help families who cannot afford to provide this (CRC, Article 27). In the United States, members of the Republican party have voiced concerns that by ratifying the treaty, a door will be opened that could allow lawsuits on behalf of those families let down by a lack of state provision and protection.

From the first scene, we are introduced to the hard life that Katniss has led; in order to care for her sister, she has had to learn to be resilient and self-sufficient. Katniss Everdene's family is so poor that she has been forced by hunger to break the law by leaving the fenced borders of District 12 to hunt game in the surrounding forests. The backstory we are given for Katniss explains her family circumstances. Three flashback memory sequences appear at different points in the film that offer us important insights into her circumstances.

Hallucinations of the past (01:25:21–01:26:25)

Katniss has been stung by venomous wasps and is hallucinating, we see a group of miners in a lift, the door closes and seconds later the doors explode. The explosion then rips through Katniss's home, which shatters to fragments and then reassembles itself. We see a photograph of the some of the miners who were in the lift and then Katniss silently mouthing at her mother to snap out of it, Katniss is as she is now but we see a much younger girl through refracted glass. Katniss's voice comes into focus imploring her mother to snap out of it.

From the earlier sequence, we realize that this was Katniss's father being killed in a mining disaster and that her mother, who has not recovered from this personal tragedy, was completely incapacitated by the loss of her husband and still struggles to meet the physical needs of her two daughters. Two other memory flashbacks feature the same encounter with Peeta prior to The Hunger Games; Katniss is sitting in the pouring rain propped against a tree too tired and weak to carry on. Peeta appears on the porch of the bakery with a basket of stale loaves. His mother, presumably for spoiling the bread, chastises him. He tosses the loaves of bread into a pigpen. He catches sight of Katniss and tosses the final loaf into the giant puddle that is the main street for her to scavenge. This scene from their shared past, which plays through both Peeta and Katniss's minds, is not discussed until Peeta is gravely ill. Katniss says, 'you fed me once', and he immediately knows what she means and replies that he is sorry that he tossed the bread into the street. 'I should have gone to you!' he says. She is acknowledging that she owes him a debt, but he asserts that this does not mean that she owes him her life.

In District 12 the community struggles to survive with limited resources; there is little support for Katniss's mother following the death of her husband. Ideally, the state would have the resources to support lone parents and thus reducing the need for young carers such as Katniss. In an ideal world, Katniss would be encouraged and helped to maintain her studies potentially providing opportunities to achieve key qualifications and engage productively in society. Within the film, Panem first leaves Katniss to fend for herself and her family, then takes her away, leaving her sister and mother at even more risk. This is clearly a fictional caricature and the injustice of this situation is tangible. Sadly, many children around the world in positions of care receive no support. While in many countries the state may not have the resources to support every family in crisis, the CRC acknowledges that they should be striving to do this. Panem's policy seems to be deliberate in terms of not providing adequate food to the districts, contemporary states do not deliberately deny children resources, but, sadly, many nations do not have the resources to meet articles 6, 19, 26 and 27 effectively. In the real world, many nations are also reluctant to intervene in family matters to ensure good-quality health care and food. The Chinese government, for example, which has demonstrated considerable power over the family through its one child policy is only just beginning to consider whether it has not just the resources, but also the social will to intervene in family-based abuse. The idea that children are not the property of parents (or the state) and have their own rights is a relatively recent concept. As citizens, we can support initiatives to hold governments to account on developing and addressing these issues. We can actively follow and support campaigns. We can inform ourselves about important issues and voice objections to our political representatives. We can protest our disagreement as policy changes are introduced.

Protection from violence: Children and combat

The final countdown to the games (01:04:16–01:07:45)

The twenty-four participants are on circular plinths arranged in a wide arc around the cornucopia of weapons and survival packs. Haymitch has warned them not to enter the circle, so when the countdown ends Peeta runs away to hide. Katniss waits to see what she can grab, the taller, fitter, stronger combat-trained tributes from the military districts quickly set to work with the first weapons that come to hand, reducing the competitors by half; there is no hesitation or mercy as they cut down the younger, weaker tributes. Katniss grabs a survival backpack, but she is pushed to the ground. She is about to be struck with an axe when a knife instantly fells her assailant from behind. Nevertheless, this is not the help of an ally. A second knife thrown straight at Katniss is stopped only by the pack that she holds up as shield. She runs and does not stop running except for a collision with a girl similar to herself, they a pause for a moment and then run on. In the last moments of the scene, the camera shows us, one by one, the lifeless faces of the child corpses strewn over the field.

This is a shocking scene, where the faster, stronger, more aggressively trained volunteer tributes from District 1 and 2 kill as many of the weaker participants as they can in just a few minutes. The injustice of the state's neglect of Katniss, followed by the removal of her liberty by the Capitol, are magnified in these few moments of screen time, offering a further insight into this state's callous disregard for human rights and how power can be gained and maintained.

We have become used to the deaths of children being reported as shocking incidents in high-profile child abuse cases such as Maria Colwell and Victoria Climbié (Collins & Foley, 2008). The murders of innocent children provoke public outcries that can change state institutions. In the summer of 2015, the image of a young dead child washed up on a Mediterranean beach featured in the newspaper and TV headlines around the world (The Guardian, 2015). This image created a shock wave that (at least temporarily) shifted European perceptions of the Syrian refugee crisis in a way that weeks of earlier reporting had not. The instinct to nurture, care and protect children is ingrained in our epigenetic nature. There are social rules or taboos against displaying the body of a child. There is an instinctive physical revulsion to certain acts; eating excrement, eating human flesh and incest (Goleman, 1995). The word epigenetic implies that there is an inherited genetic response as well as a conditioned response to some events. While killing another person is a taboo, there are some circumstances where soldiers, executioners, people defending themselves are permitted to kill others, this is not taken lightly and is increasingly recognized as potentially linked to future psychological trauma. Killing a child is not permitted in any circumstances. Society is repulsed and outraged by crimes against children. What is shocking about The Hunger Games is that the government and society make children kill other children. Panem has done this for seventy-four years. Watching the broadcasts is compulsory; this is accepted as entertainment, but it is also a visual and explicit demonstration of ultimate power. The climax of the film, it might be argued, is not end of The Hunger Games but the death of the youngest competitor, Rue, who has become Katniss's ally in the games,.

Rue's death (01:34:40–01:40:16)

Rue has not arrived at an agreed rendezvous and Katniss eventually finds her caught under a net. She cuts Rue free, but one of the boys has been lying in wait with a spear, he steps out and launches a spear at Katniss. She steps aside and looses an arrow that kills the boy instantly. When she turns, the weapon is sticking out of a shocked Rue who stands for a moment before collapsing. Katniss kneels behind Rue and cradles her on her lap. She reassures her, Rue is scared but calm. Katniss sings a lullaby and we see the trees and sky fading to white. Katniss is distraught but harvests white flowers from a meadow to lay around Rue's body. This extenuates Rue's childhood innocence and the injustice of her death. As Katniss steps away, she senses where the camera is, she looks up kisses three fingers in salute. Back in Rue's home district, the crowd is seen standing and watching the giant screens in rows surrounded by Stormtroopers. The crowd echoes Katniss's salute then turn on the guards, the watchtowers and the food destined for the capital. It is not long before the reinforcement troops and water cannon arrive to quash the riot.

Emotion is a powerful thing and, as practitioners, we need to understand and recognize the power of these emotional cognitive forces at work. To accuse someone of violence against a child is a serious and emotionally charged thing. People can be reluctant to take such a step particularly if they are not sure of their accusation. Regular child protection training, building professional confidence in logging and reporting possible indicators of abuse is vitally important. Equally, understanding that communities can be carried away by outrage and being ready to manage situations and establish facts fully and professionally with colleagues and families is important. At an individual level, managing personal emotional responses in supporting children and working with families where incidents of abuse have occurred or are occurring are also important. One does not want to convey horror and revulsion to a survivor of abuse. One may equally be required to work with a perpetrator. Part of the practice leadership role is ensuring that staff have undertaken appropriate training opportunities so that they have had an opportunity to reflect on issues of abuse and think through how they will respond to them in order that staff are more likely to present a considered and controlled response rather than an openly emotional one. Children who are survivors of trauma may need those supporting them to continue to respond in measured, non-judgemental and supportive ways for many years after periods of trauma have ceased as they work through the mental health implications of events (McMahon, 2009).

It is our emotional responses to shocking events, such as those portrayed in the film, and our outrage at the way children are treated that underpins the political will to develop a set of additional human rights specific to children. Children's rights can also be justified rationally as an essential precursor to ensuring the next generation grows up as healthy well-adjusted adults able and willing to contribute to society (Ensalaco and Majke, 2005).

Article 38 states that nations agree that children below the age of sixteen should not be recruited into the armed forces and that a child below the age of eighteen should not be involved in combat. The children in The Hunger Games are effectively placed in a combat zone and, unfortunately, this is not as uncommon in the real world as we would like Geske and Ensalaco, (2005; Save the Children, 2010).

> Children are targeted for recruitment because they are cheap, easier to control and manipulate, and because they look to adults to protect them. Usually unpaid, they are used to do tasks adults do not want to do and may also be coerced into carrying out grotesque acts of violence. (Save the Children, 2010:1)

The acceptance and enthusiasm of some of the children to participate in The Hunger Games is sadly not unbelievable. Examples of young people being drawn to participate in the conflict in Syria and the Middle East have featured in a number of prominent news stories in 2015. Children arouse less suspicion; they can therefore be exploited for purposes such as spying, acting as couriers or carrying out acts of sabotage (Save the Children, 2009:1). Their involvement in terrorist incidents made this all too visible.

Fortunately, there are few states accused of violating this article; it is more often non-governmental forces who exploit children in this way. Globally, 250,000 children were estimated to be associated with armed forces and groups (Save the Children, 2010). 'The majority of these children are aged between 14 and 18 years, but some are recruited and used from as young as seven' (Save the Children, 2009:1). However, it is interesting to note that one of the reasons cited for US reluctance to ratify the CRC was that it might compromise defence policy in having young men ready to engage in battle as soon as they are 18, a concern also expressed by the British army (Gsekey and Ensalaco, 2005). There is growing public pressure following the deaths of 18-year-olds in Afghanistan and Iraq to delay the age of entry into front-line conflict. It should also be remembered that in the D-day landings, Allied states deliberately deployed troops new to combat because they would continue to advance when experienced solders would not. Citizens need to encourage states to prosecute war crimes against children and to care for those scarred by conflict.

Article 38 states that children who have been neglected or abused in combat should receive special help to restore them.

> Children recruited into armed groups are killed, maimed, abused and exploited in the most appalling ways. They may be forced to observe or take part in atrocities, including against their own families and communities, and may be profoundly disturbed by what they have experienced. In some conflicts, particularly in West Africa, children have been drugged by their commanders before action. (Save the Children, 2010:2)

Children who have been recruited to armed groups have no access to formal education, making it hard for them to find work after the war has ended. Families and communities can view former child soldiers with fear and distrust because of atrocities. I have tried to illustrate in this part of the chapter that some of the issues raised by *The Hunger Games* are based in contemporary issues that highlight the value of children's rights; the concluding section of the chapter asks how individuals should engage with the state in respect of promoting these rights.

The individual and the state

The first of the four *Hunger Games* films establishes the underlying message of the series, that the architecture of the state, not just the Capitol, but any state, is a potentially dangerous thing. Katniss is not seeking to be involved in politics; she is not campaigning for democracy. She becomes a symbol of rebellion, not by choice but by chance. She would like to be free from state interference; she wants to be free to hunt with her bow in the forests. The final section of this chapter argues that the absence of the state interference is not necessarily a good thing. One of the roles of the state, endorsed by the CRC, should be to safeguard children's rights and this requires services fit for this purpose. Citizens have a responsibility to hold states to account through political engagement. For citizens to disengage from politics is to invite danger.

The Hunger Games reflects aspects of new liberal or 'neo-liberal' ideology. As Sue Aitken's chapter of this book explains, liberalism is a political philosophy dating back to the eighteenth century. Liberalism asserts and delineates the rights of the individual; it also defines the responsibility of the state to safeguard those rights and their responsibilities to the state. Neo-liberalism calls for individuals to be free from state interference to run their own lives at home and in their businesses (Cohen, Kennedy & Perrier, 2013). Exley and Ball (2014) identify neo-liberalism as a project to undermine the social welfare reforms to health, social care and education of the post–war era in order to allow private business and industry more scope to flourish.

Jones (2014) traced the evolution of a *new liberal* ideology to Hayek and Friedman, who shortly after the end of Second World War were writing against the prevailing international consensus of international cooperation to impose strong state controls over businesses and individuals to deliver a fairer, more caring world. Through the 1950s, 1960s and 1970s, these values drew strength from the Cold War stand-off that existed between communist and capitalist ideologies. The United States and Western Europe were seen to prosper as they allowed private enterprise, increasing freedom to generate growth and profits, while the communist stagnated economically and then collapsed politically in the late 1980s and 990s (Cohen, Kennedy, & Perrier (2013). The neo-liberal free market ideology came to forefront in the 1980s with the election of Ronald Reagan as president of the United States and Margaret Thatcher as the prime minister of Britain (Jones, 2014). In the 1990s, the worth of this ideology was apparently affirmed as communist governments began to crumble and to embrace more liberal models of trade, politics and individual freedoms. Even political parties that had championed the welfare state, such as the Labour Party in Britain, formed governments (1997 to 2010) that followed neo-liberal policies. Thus the logic of the neo-liberal ideology is a part of the 'Western' political consensus asserting that there should be less state control, less taxation and business should be allowed to offer services in a market with minimal state control. This is the focal point of the debate about how nations can manage their social welfare debts. Since 2010, Western governments have continued to liberalize trade and banking; to promote individuals' freedoms to choose services and to reduce tax burdens, while at the same time seeking to reduce government spending on health, education and social care. The Year 2016 witnessed a rise in increasingly nationalistic and protectionist voices in Europe and the United States challenging the neo-liberal internationalist consensus. Britain voting to leave the European Union and the election of Donald Trump reflect a popular view that neo-liberal freedoms may be best defended by strong nation states unfettered by international regulations, bureaucracy and migration.

In a contemporary context, would Katniss, like many from the coal mining communities of Virginia, have voted for Donald Trump in the Presidential Election of 2016? *The Hunger Games* promotes the idea that centralized state governance is a bad thing and that taxes paid to the capital are to the benefit of the do-gooder liberal elite is at the expense of those who do 'real' work. This is very close to President Trump's election campaign and inauguration speech (20 January 2017).

> For too long, a small group in our nation's Capital has reaped the rewards of government while the people have borne the cost. Washington flourished – but the people did not share in its wealth. Politicians prospered – but the jobs left, and the factories closed. The establishment protected itself, but not the citizens of our country.

Thus, while Katniss might decide not to vote for any presidential candidate, she has perhaps fuelled the political sentiment harnessed by the Trump and Brexit campaigns.

Conclusion

Many governments in the first years of the twenty-first century have sought to allow business markets to manage themselves, to allow money to circulate freely with few, if any, state-imposed restrictions. Similarly, they have encouraged individuals and families to make their own decisions about health welfare and care; to pay for their own services rather than rely on state-managed provision. This is also conducive to large businesses who would like to make money not just from dealing in foods, consumer goods, travel and entertainments but also increasingly from running health care, education and policing services. In our contemporary world, reducing state 'interference' is intended to translate into taxation reductions that benefit all. The reality is that they often benefit the better off most and the poor least (Jones, 2015; Savage, 2015).

The concern is that policies purporting to offer greater choice may leave many children more vulnerable. If the state's primary role is to enforce the law when things have gone wrong, then protecting children from harm becomes a community and family role. We should be worried that children may be left at risk because communities are nervous of intervening without the authority, training or resources of the state. We should be concerned that parents are punished and children suffer when things go wrong instead of offering support before a crisis point is reached.

It is important that the state operates within the resource limits available; however, I have tried to argue that there is a need for a strong caring state that is both able and willing to intervene on behalf of vulnerable children and respect both the UHR and the CRC. Fortunately, Panem is a fictitious state, while I share Katniss's sense of injustice at her state, I do not share her isolationist libertarian perspective that the state should simply be a 'night-watchman' (Nozick, 1974:27) responsible for policing law and order. In our world, it is important for citizens to work at interpreting the media messages they receive. They need to be active and participatory; monitoring, lobbying and voting for politicians who will work to create or maintain states that care, respect and provide for the planet's, human's and children's rights.

Having read this chapter, you might like to reflect upon the following questions:

- Rights are sometimes said to be absolute, in that they belong to everyone as part of a higher moral law: to what extent do you think this is true?

- Do you think that the poor have fewer rights than the wealthy and how might neo-liberal policies support or challenge an egalitarian distribution of wealth?

- What role can education play in addressing social disadvantage and notions of cultural capital more directly?

- Who should safeguard the rights of children and at what point should they intervene?

9

Gender, Performativity and Society:
Oranges Are Not the Only Fruit

Sue Aitken

This chapter will consider notions of the following:

- Gender identity and orientation: Butler (1993), Wilchins (2004).

- Identity politics: Spivak (1990), Kruks (2001), Wiarda (2014).

- Language and power: Fairclough (1989).

- Gender performativity: West and Zimmerman (1987).

- Queer theory: Butler (1990), Sedgewick (1990), and Halberstam (2005).

The film

Unusually this chapter does not take a film as a device to explore theory; instead, this chapter is based on a three-part TV drama first broadcast in 1990. The choice of this drama was based on its ability to allow a discussion of children and sexuality, sexual orientation and dominant cultural perceptions of 'normality'. Although set in the 1980s, the narrative highlights common and still relevant issues for children today in terms of sexual identity.

The screenplay was written by Jeannette Winterson and based on her 1985 novel of the same name. Set in an anonymous northern industrial town (Winterson herself spent her childhood in Accrington, Lancashire) and tells the story of Jess, a child adopted as a baby by a childless couple who are active members of the local evangelical Pentecostal Church. Jess's adopted mother (who is never given a name) is the dominant partner, while her husband, William, is a selective mute. From the beginning it is evident that Jess's mother believes that God has provided them with Jess in order that she may become an evangelical missionary. The three episodes tell the story of Jess's progress from child to young adult via a turbulent adolescence. Her childhood is set against increasingly conflictual expectations of who she is and how she should behave. Jess is seen as a lonely figure, home schooled until she is seven, her only contact outside of her home is with other members of her church's congregation, her only close friend being Elsie who is aged eighty-two. Jess's mother will only allow Jess to associate with those who are 'saved' by the acceptance of Jesus. When Jess meets Melanie, she knows that they can only be friends if she 'accepts Jesus' and becomes a member of Jess's church, which she does.

When Jess falls in love with, and embarks on a sexual relationship with Melanie, her family, her church and its congregation believe they must correct this aberration by performing a vengeful and violent exorcism. Convinced that her activities can only be inspired by Satan and that she is possessed by demons, her mother, the pastor and two other members of the congregation take turns to pray over the bound and gagged Jess. The exorcism is a turning point in Jess's life, as she realizes that to survive she must overtly perform the identity of an openly devout evangelical Christian while hiding her sexual orientation. In tune with the social and moral demands of the time, Jess understands that to be 'safe' she must hide her other identity, at least until she can escape home and the church.

This chapter uses episodes 2 and 3 of the drama, as Jess slowly confronts her sexuality, the reaction of her community, her past and her future while recognizing that love and support can exist beyond the confines of the parental home.

Gender, gender identity and sexual orientation

The Glory Bus and Graham (00:14:45–00:31:42)

Outside the church the pastor arrives with the new 'Glory Bus', and a new covert, Graham. Jess is tasked with 'steering him the right way', but the pastor also reminds that her body is a temple and not to give in to temptation, 'he's a good looking boy, isn't he'? Later her mother tells her, glancing at Graham, 'never mind the flesh, Jess, think of the spirit'. As Jess walks away, she whispers to Melanie, 'Trust me'.

At home, Jess's mother returns to the subject of boys, 'I saw the way you looked at Graham when he came to our church. It's only natural, a nice boy like that.' Jess rejects her mother's implicit understanding of the situation by responding, 'I wasn't looking at him, I was just saying hello. I was looking after Melanie.'

Her mother replies, 'that's different.'

Following Jess and Melanie's first sexual encounter, they are seen together looking out at the world from a window and Jess says, 'This can't be unnatural passions, can it?'

As this scene illustrates Jess's sexual orientation from the perspective of her family and her church congregation is not in question, however for Jess following her first sexual encounter with Melanie, this is less clear. It might be helpful at this point to try to unravel popular misconceptions around terminology such as sex and gender. In very simple terms, sex refers to the anatomical classification of a child at the moment of birth; whereas gender is a social construction of the actions, activities and qualities attributed to that biological label. While sex and gender may often be presented as similar but different concepts, Wilchins (2004) suggests that they are bound together in a mutually reinforcing construct. Because the term sex may often refer to an external and simple binary classification, the basis of internal understanding of what that means is of itself informed by the classification of being a girl or a boy, as Wilchins (2004:142) suggests.

'Female is to women as women is to feminine as feminine is to attraction to male.' Consequently, a disequilibrium will arise where the internal model is at odds with the external expectation, both for the individual and for the external society. As Wilchins suggests, if *any* part of these cultural links is broken, society is unnerved, whether by the manly female or the effeminate male, or an overt demonstration of same-sex love. In effect, sex classification is part of a cultural tool box that you are placed in at birth and the attributes of which are immutable. West and Zimmerman (1987) see gender as a performative practice, social structures formulating the script for the performance of being male or female. However, Butler (1993) challenges the differentiation of sex as a biological (natural) determinant from performative gender (socially constructed), suggesting that while sex may initiate the performance of gender, once initiated that performance must inevitably subsume and reconstruct the biological as social, as sex can have no meaning without gender. As Butler (1993:5) explains,

If gender is the social significance that sex assumes within a given culture ... then what, if anything, is left of 'sex' once it has assumed its social character as gender?

Can a determination of gender identity be located in the answer to the question, 'who am I'? Butler would argue that the potential responses, '*I am the person I am or want to be*'? or '*I am the person everyone else wants me to be*'? are both social constructs that orchestrate 'performativity' of gender, where choice is not an option.

Using the earlier scenes, it appears that Jess has been constructed by the external world as female and therefore her sexual orientation is not in question. Even her voiced preference of Melanie over Graham is dismissed as merely 'that's different'.

Although gender identity has been discussed from the early twentieth century (Freud, 1905; Jung, 1958), it was only in the 1950s and 1960s that gender identity became a focus within child development, largely in an attempt to discover the origins of homosexuality. At the time homosexuality was seen as both a mental disorder and a criminal act. However, the term itself was first used by Robert Stoller in 1963 when addressing an international congress of psychoanalysts in Stockholm, Sweden. In above scene, the Pastor and Jess's mother have no doubts about Jess's gender identity, she is a female adolescent and therefore must be warned of the perils of giving in to the 'sins of the flesh' with a member of the opposite sex. However, as Jess implies to Melanie, she isn't interested in Graham. Thus someone who is stereotypically gendered, whose biological sex, gender performance and gender identity neatly conjoin will reap the rewards of social acceptance. Conversely, when individuals contravene the socially accepted and constructed norms of both appearance and behaviour, society can react negatively. In recent years, the adjective 'cisgender' has been used to describe those whose conduct meets the social norms, the term adopted as a replacement for the term 'gender normative' in order to eradicate notions that its opposite, transgender, is neither normative nor natural.

However, increasingly, gender identification has become more complex than simply using a binary concept of gay or straight. The Human Rights Campaign (HRC), a US lesbian, gay, bisexual and transgender (LGBT) civil rights movement, published a report in 2012 called Supporting and Caring for Our Gender-Expansive Youth. The term gender-expansive came out of this report in an attempt to classify those individuals who did not 'identify with traditional gender roles' and who did not want or could not put their identity in a prescribed box. Paradoxically, of course, by creating a label, albeit a broad one, this term may well join the many others who exemplify identity politics.

Language and power

As discussed in Chapter 3, language and its use within society is a powerful tool of control. The power to use language is the power to endorse dominant discourses and dominant understandings of concepts (Fairclough, 1989) such as homosexuality. Thus, the terms used in the past became located in a psychiatric medical diagnosis, which prior to the 1980s offered medical conversion therapy as a curative. Homosexuality was only removed from the American Psychiatric Association's manual of mental disorders in 1973. Conversion therapy could consist of psychological aversion therapies, such as electric shocks, and/or nausea-inducing drugs. However, in 2001, the US surgeon general David Satcher issued a report stating that there was no scientific evidence that sexual orientation could be changed. Despite this, many fundamental Christian groups use biblical justification for conversion therapy describing homosexuality as a disease or, in some instances, a sin.

Fairclough (1989:84) suggests that taking ownership of language can enable the 'establishing and consolidating [of] solidarity relations amongst members of a particular social group'. However, while claiming the right to identify yourself in terms of your sexuality may bring with it notions of freedom, it also highlights complex notions of both singularity and shared understandings of that descriptor. For example, in the 1960s, it was sufficient to describe the HRC as representing the homosexual community using the term 'gay', but as this term increasingly became associated with men (usually white men), women exerted their right to be identified differently and chose to be known as lesbians. The ensuing years however saw an increasing feeling that not everyone fitted or wanted to fit into these 'labels' and that in a sense the binary division of gay/lesbian was no more helpful than that of heterosexual/homosexual. However, creating a new glossary of terms in an attempt to include every experience produced an ever-expanding identity-based taxonomy and vocabulary. However, language can also provide a positive avenue for resistance and challenge by turning an insult and pejorative, such as 'queer' into a generic celebratory and productive noun.

In Jess's evangelical community, her behaviour and conduct was labelled as sinful and the result of demonic possession and as such she could only be 'saved' by either repentance and admission of her sin or, if she continued to deny her sin, by enforced exorcism. In Jess's community, the simple binary position was described as being saved or as a sinner, but like all binaries it offered only a black and white understanding of complex experiences. Jess's love for Melanie did not replace her love for God, it simply occupied the same space. Her community however demonstrably and forcibly wanted her to choose between the two. As with the heterosexual/homosexual binary and the use of interventions such as conversion therapy, the terminology implies simple opposites, closely aligned to the right way and the wrong way to 'be'.

Heyes (2016), writing in the online *Stanford Encyclopaedia of Philosophy*, defines identity politics as a wide range of political movements and activities formed around, and by, shared experiences and injustices with the dual purpose of challenging oppressive characterizations and gaining greater self-determination. Wiarda (2014) more formally defines it as political attitudes or positions that focus on the concerns of subgroup in society. Informally, he describes it as a quest to belong.

The latter half of the twentieth century saw an explosion of political (but not necessarily Political) movements. Beginning with the Black Civil Right Movement in America, major single-identity action groups began to form in order to publicize and politicize the identification of minority group oppression, among them the Gay and Lesbian Rights Movement and post-war feminism. Many supporters saw this as echoing Spivak's (1990) notion of strategic essentialism, where accepting and participating in the existing hegemony is the only way of changing it. However, as Kruks (2001:85) comments,

> What makes identity politics a significant departure from earlier, pre- identarian forms of the politics of recognition, is its demand for recognition on the basis of the very grounds on which recognition has previously been denied.

Thus the identity within 'identity politics' is seen as the platform and spotlight for not only the personal identification of experiences of oppression but also its transformation into an aspiration for a shared and authenticated self-determination.

However, identity politics is not without its critics and their critiques, Butler (1990) argues that as identities are not fixed but flexible, single-identity politics can only be transient and ephemeral. Equally an early critique was the problematic nature of declaring a single unifying identity, as it failed to take account of dual or multiple identities and therefore potentially multiple experiences of oppression and subjugation. Holland (2005) refers to this as the myopia of identity politics, a failure to see the larger picture. Recognizing yourself as lesbian, gay, bisexual, transsexual or gender-expansive may not be the only element of your experiences and your identity; an identity may also have been forged by being black, disabled or as with Jess having a deeply felt but conflictual religious belief. One only has to look at how the broad spectrum of religious communities has struggled with accepting both clergy and lay members of congregations who proclaim or who are suspected of having an alternative gender and/or sexual identities.

Reaction to Jess's conduct (00:33:04–00:36:14)

The nature of Jess's relationship with Melanie is beginning to be recognized. At first her mother tries to control the situation by preventing Jess from seeing Melanie at Elsie's house but she does not confront Jess directly, instead she reluctantly and angrily relents and pushes away all Jess's attempts at affection. When Jess has gone, her mother ransacks here room, destroying and removing anything of Jess's she deems 'ungodly', watched by her still-silent husband William. She tells her husband, 'I'm protecting her William, its Jess I'm protecting'.

On her way to meet Melanie, she steals flowers from the graveyard to give to her. Cissy who owns the local undertakers sees her and asks where is her mother. Jess responds that 'she doesn't like me anymore'. Cissy tells Jess, 'don't be silly. It's always the same with all families. She loves you.'

As the earlier scenes indicate, Jess's sense of who she is and where she belongs is becoming confused. She tries to show her mother affection but is rejected. She is convinced that her mother doesn't like her and tells Cissy so, who repeats the accepted discourse that while all families have conflict and arguments, her mother loves her (see also Chapter 5). In Cissy's mind, that is the default position of motherhood. As discussed earlier in this chapter and earlier chapters in this book, developing a sense of self and a sense of your position in the world can be both constructed and performative. Jess wants to be loved by her mother and her church, but she loves and wants to be loved by Melanie. While she makes no attempt to disguise her relationship with Melanie, she is far from 'coming out' in public about her feelings, perhaps not able to articulate her shadow identity, she willingly performs what she perceives as her spiritual duties to God and the church.

As discussed in other chapters in this book, Bourdieu wrote extensively with regard to social and cultural capital in a socially (largely capitalist) world. Bourdieu articulated that the degree of social and cultural capital gained is matched by a need to preserve and protect that investment. However, if that capital is seen as derived from spiritual or religious 'tastes', then as Stark and Fink (2000:121) suggest, 'In making religious choices, people will attempt to conserve their religious capital'.

As noted in Chapter 2, 'taste' can result in an aversion to other lifestyles. In other words, when a spiritual investment has been made or acquired (via parental inheritance), religious dispositions have to be protected. Consequently, any activity or relationship that falls outside of the essential teachings and practices that confer full membership of the community must be challenged and corrected in order to protect the whole community. Transgressions are often met by rejection by the community in order to preserve the shared spiritual capital and prevent devaluation of the investment. Jess's mother's reactions in the scene above may be seen as both rejection of Jess herself, as well as the preservation of her spiritual position and capital within the church.

In relation to the nature and protection of spiritual capital, Megan Phelps-Roper, speaking at the TED conference held in New York in February 2017, describes how growing up in the Westboro Baptist Church in America, had for her, like Jess, created a simple binary concept of the world, the saved and the unsaved, as she describes it 'an epic spiritual battle between good and evil. The good was my church and its members, and the evil was everyone else'. Her world was narrow and unnervingly monochrome, the world outside of her own was evil, worthy only of hatred. As a twenty-first-century means of spreading the beliefs and teachings of her church, in 2009 Megan took to social media and digital evangelism, where she encountered hostility and abuse. For Megan these reactions echoed her experiences while on rallies and demonstrations she has taken part in across America, only this time her audience was global.

However, slowly amid the tirades, conversations and dialogues would emerge, still oppositional but driven by a mutual desire for better understanding, as she puts it, 'the line between friend and foe became blurred'. It was through these dialogues that Megan was empowered to ask questions and reflect on the only set of beliefs (discourses) she had ever known. In 2012, aged twenty-five, she left the church, her family and her way of life, unable to live within a community that suppressed questions and challenge. Megan rejected her ascribed spiritual capital and was in turn rejected by the Westboro Baptist Church, a mutual mismatch of Bourdieu's 'tastes' resulting in an aversion to the other's lifestyle. The real Megan and the fictional Jess both experience the construction and deconstruction of taste and lifestyle choices.

Jess and Melanie are exposed (00:38:31–00:43:39)

Following a night together in Elsie's house, Jess and Melanie accompany Elsie to church, where the pastor publicly names Jess and Melanie for committing the 'sin that dare not speak its name'. He declares to the congregation that 'these children are full of demons', Jess's protests only serve as evidence to the pastor that she is speaking the words of Satan.

When asked if she 'loves this woman (Melanie)' with the love reserved for husband and wife,

Jess replies, 'Yes! No, it's not like that.' She trades biblical references with the pastor reminding him of St Paul in Romans, chapter 14, 'I know and am persuaded in the Lord that nothing is unnatural in itself. It is made unnatural by those who think it unnatural.'

Melanie however quickly repents her sins and is led away; Jess declares her love for her, at which the pastor declares that she cannot therefore love the Lord.

Jess's friend Elsie tries to intercede but is taken ill, and in the commotion following her collapse, Jess is led away by Miss Jewsbury, a younger and marginalized member of the congregation. Miss Jewsbury takes Jess back to Elsie's house where she asks, 'Why weren't you careful Jess? Everyone could see what you were about.' When Jess declares that, 'you can't hide love'. Miss Jewsbury tells her, 'you have to learn.' Miss Jewsbury explains that Elsie had tried to protect Jess but when she became ill, she had asked her to take over. She later explains that, 'it my problem too. Loving the wrong people'

Queer theory and sexual identity

As the scene above suggests, Jess and Melanie find themselves presented with the simple binary of their church: repentance or damnation. While Melanie gives in, Jess tries to argue her case but is ignored. Later Miss Dewsbury tells her that she must be careful, in essence to hide her love.

Queer theory is a post-structural theory and paradigm that arose in the 1990s in an attempt to broaden the understanding of sexual identity, gender performance and gender politics and to relocate their study from niche subculture to mainstream lens of investigation (Butler, 1990; Halberstam, 2005; Sedgewick, 1990). As Sedgewick (1990:1) states in her introduction to *Epistemology of the Closet*,

> This book will argue that an understanding of virtually any aspect of modern Western culture must be, not merely incomplete, but damaged in its central substance to the degree that it does not incorporate critical analysis of modern homo/heterosexual definitions; and it will assume that the appropriate place for that critical analysis to begin is from the relatively decentred perspective of modern antihomophobic theory.

Frequent reference is made in queer theory to Foucault's understanding that sexual identities are social constructs that serve as the tools of power and control (Foucault, 1976). Such social constructs formulate categories of behaviour that define morality and acceptably, thus conversely their opposite can only define unacceptability and immorality. By adopting a sexual identity that contravenes these norms can lead to a sense of alienation and rejection, even danger. As De Coste (2014:75) argues,

> Foucault traced the transformation of sexuality in modern societies from a set of *practices and* relations governed by religious and secular law into a set of *identities* by norms.

However, as Savin-Williams (2014:5) argues, twenty-first-century youth 'believe that culturally mandated sexual identity labels do not correspond to the complexity and diversity of their sexual lives.' Young non-heterosexual youth astutely observe that if mainstream heterosexual youth are not required to assume a sexual identity, why should they? An indication perhaps that sexual identity and identity 'branding' can no longer be contained within single descriptors such as gay, lesbian, bi or trans.

Queer theory however is more than a study of the experiences of gay, lesbian, transsexual and transgendered individuals but is an attempt to apply a queer lens to a wider set of social experiences. Thus, queer theory seeks to remove the awkwardness and difficulty of discussing homosexuality within a heterosexual-dominated context. Where heterosexuality dominates society, any discussion is controlled by the conventions and rules set by that dominance, thus the parameters of normativity are set and alternatives will always represent marginalized groups and their transgressions. Queer theory sees the acceptance of marginalization as an approach which inevitably constructs lesbian and gay identities as separate from straight identities and emphasizes the gender rift.

In the scenes earlier, Jess and, initially, Melanie become the focus of the process of marginalization and labelling as transgressors to the moral code of the church. Using queer theory to interrogate this scenario, what we see is a powerful and omnipotent force (in this case the pastor) who has the power to elicit change or administer punishment. For Melanie the threat of punishment is sufficient to illicit change; for Jess the injustice of the charge outweighs whatever punishment is awaiting her. As the later conversation with Miss Jewsbury highlights social survival can mean secrecy, the ability to follow the rules and to hide your true allegiances. In another context, that of political dictatorship and prescriptive social performance, the state can be seen as the omnipotent force that has the power to marginalize and deliver injustice in the guise of justice and security. After her exorcism and her apparent reorientation to the true path of God, Jess speaks again to Miss Jewsbury in secret; she asks her to deliver a letter to Melanie, which at first she refused to do but eventually and reluctantly she agrees. Jess's departing remark to Miss Jewsbury is 'you've got to fight', referring to both herself and Miss Jewsbury. In essence, Jess is asking Miss Jewsbury to become part of the 'resistance'.

The National Curriculum, sexual identity and sexual orientation

The National Curriculum in the United Kingdom is 'a set of subjects and standards used by primary and secondary schools so children learn the same thing' (gov.uk website). In March 2017, the education secretary, Justine Greening, announced in a briefing paper of her intention to put Relationships and Sex Education (RSE) on to a statutory footing, subject to consultation and parliamentary scrutiny. The announcement suggested that from September 2019 all primary schools (from ages five to eleven) must teach Relationships Education; however, within her announcement were two caveats, that the parental right of withdrawal was maintained and that faith schools could continue to teach within the tenets of their faith. However, the decision to teach children beyond and outside of the science curriculum was left to individual primary school governing bodies and their head teachers, as, too, was the content (House of Commons Library Briefing paper March 2017). At key stages 3 and 4 (ages eleven to sixteen), sex and relation education is compulsory, and sits within the science curriculum. However, where the content does not fall within the science curriculum, parents have the right to withdraw their children. Within the current wording of the National Curriculum, children aged eleven to sixteen are taught about reproduction, sexuality and sexual health, 'it does not promote early sexual activity or any particular sexual orientation' (gov.uk website). Within the House of Commons briefing paper, the curriculum content suggested is 'within a broader base of self-esteem and responsibility for the consequences of one's actions'. With regard to sexual identity and sexual orientation, the policy standpoint is that teachers are able to deal honestly and sensitively with questions of sexual orientation, but the delivery should remain neutral. However, the briefing paper is somewhat opaque with regard to teaching about same-sex marriage, which is legalized under the Marriage (Same Sex Couples) Act 2013, merely referring to the reforms requiring schools to 'actively promote' British values (see also Chapter 6) and the need for further debates.

The 2017 briefing paper stands in stark contrast to the some of the political and parliamentary debates that have preceded it. At midnight on 17th November 2003 a divisive piece of legislation was repealed; Section 28 of the Local Authorities Act 1988. The content of Section 28 prohibited local authorities from promoting homosexuality or gay 'pretend family relationships' it also prohibited local councils from using their financial resources to purchase material and/or supporting projects identified as 'promoting a gay lifestyle'. It is important, however, to identify the historical context of Section 28. Following the first diagnosed case of Acquired Immune Deficiency Syndrome (AIDS) in 1983, the globe was engulfed with a panic with regard to AIDS and HIV infection. Sometimes referred to as the 'gay plague', this infection provided evidence for some that homophobia was a responsible position to take, which was validated through a biomedical discourse that homosexuality is abnormal and therefore dangerous (Black, 1986). The history of the birth and death of section 28, a period of 15 years, provides a useful backdrop to any discussion of current attitudes and practice, such as those above with regard to sex education in schools.

The birth of section 28 was ushered in during the premiership of Margaret Thatcher, a neo-liberal Conservative, by the Minister for Local Government (later, leader of the Conservative party), Michael Howard. Initially, however, what eventually became known as Section 28 was proposed in a private member's bill by Lord Halsbury in 1986. The Bill passed through the Lords on a unanimous vote.

The debate (or rather affirmation) of the second reading of Lord Halsbury's bill provided some of the peers in the chamber with an opportunity to attack and devalue gay and lesbian lifestyles. The following quotes are taken from the Hansard minutes for the debate on 18 December 1986 (Hansard 1986:331–6),

It is not designed to harass or humiliate homosexuals. They are often sad and lonely people, unable to have stable relationships, and they are, I am sure all your Lordships will agree, worthy of compassion. (Lord Campbell),

Homosexuals, in my submission, are handicapped people. The tragedy of such people is that they cannot enjoy family life and they cannot have children. If only for that reason I suppose that not many of us – perhaps none of us – would wish our children or grandchildren to grow up homosexuals (Lord Longford).

It seems very strange to me that in society today, when we spend a great deal of money and time trying to prevent physical and mental disability, in some of our schools they are promoting sexual disability (Lord Swindon).

Having passed unanimously in the House of Lords it was forwarded to the House of Commons for consideration and succeeded in passing the first stage of the legislative process (First Reading). However, it was prevented from progressing any further by the General Election of 1987. Having won the general election, the newly elected Conservative government, reintroduced Lord Halsbury's bill as an amendment to the Local Government Bill, and it became law on the 24 May 1988. While no one was ever prosecuted under Section 28, it did have the effect on schools and colleges of denying access to non-heterosexual material both in print and online, even causing the Glyndebourne Touring Opera company to abandon a production of Death in Venice (*The Guardian* online). Although Section 28 was aimed specifically at curbing the actions of Local Authority Councillors; teachers and school governors being unsure of their limits and responsibilities, playing it 'safe' by not mentioning homosexuality at all (Epstein, O'Flynn & Telford, 2003). Forrest (2000:15), writing 3 years before the repeal of Section 28, also identified the potential dangers of censoring information,

> Currently, young people are being denied the right to an education that equips them for adult life (in transgression of the law). For young gay people their enforced invisibility and the denial of access to basic relevant sex education is a breach of a human right.

Stifling the possibility of discussion and education of children and young people with regard to good sexual health was also a concern of the British Medical Association, who in 1997 called for responsible teaching about homosexuality in order to protect gay, lesbian and bisexual young people from the risk of physical and mental ill health as a result of isolation, bullying and a lack of self-esteem.

Just as Jess could not accept a personal injustice, so too were a range of organizations and gay rights charities. Stonewall, the LGBT charity, was specifically formed by political activists to fight for the repeal of section 28. All the major political parties (with the exception of the Conservative Party) and trade unions, including the National Union of Teachers, campaigned for its repeal. However, repeal would take 15 years.

Queering education

Letts and Sears (1999:1) ask the important question, 'why is sexual diversity a critical issue for elementary education?' They further ask whether the feminization of early education is linked to homophobia in schools. In the era of Section 28, the use of terms such as homosexuality, let alone terms such as 'queer', would have placed teachers, schools, governors and local authorities, if not at risk of legal prosecution, at the centre of a media backlash. However, on 19/20 August 2013, ten years after the repeal of Section 28, the *Independent*, the *Telegraph* and *Channel 4* News (online) reported that the Department for Education had been forced into investigating forty-five schools across England and Wales whose official sex education policies include clauses replicating and reviving section 28. Stephen Twigg (*Channel 4* News 20.08.2013), the then Labour Shadow Education Secretary responded by saying:

> Labour got rid of Section 28 in 2003 to ensure that schools taught about homosexuality in an open and honest way. Homophobic bullying is still too

common in schools. We must ensure that we redouble our efforts to tackle such prejudice.

Sex education in schools has been, and still is, a highly emotive subject, encompassing notions of normativity, religious belief and state interference in the private lives of citizens. As explained earlier, queer theory and the use of queer perspectives can be useful tools to unpack questions around how, who and what is taught; and in so doing help to deconstruct assumptions around childhood, sexuality and pedagogy. Queer teaching is described by Sears (1999) as the opportunity to challenge binary categorizations and to encourage critical thinking. Perhaps in this way, notions of social and educational inclusion can venture beyond race, religion and disability, and anti-discrimination policies can be equitable in their application.

Casper (1996) highlights teacher attitudes towards male cross-dressing and gender confusion. In discussions with teachers, most saw it as normal for 6-year-old boys to dress in female clothing and pretend to be princesses, dismissing it as transitory behaviour. When asked when it was no longer 'normal' however, they were less sure. Which poses the question, is the termination of that 'transitory' behaviour a consequence of natural development and personal choice or the effect of a heterosexual dominant discourse? A discourse that clearly positions male children in a different category from female children, where the framework of gender behaviour becomes increasingly narrow as children get older.

Conclusion

This chapter has attempted to provide the historical backdrop that at least in part, helps position current discourses and dispositions. Legislation in the Western world has undergone significant changes in the last half century travelling from criminalization to same-sex marriage. For many students such legislative changes have come to mean that sexual prejudice is a thing of the past (Kite and Bryant-Lees, 2016), despite continued evidence of discrimination with regard to bullying, transgender rights and disparity of employment and career opportunities. It is perhaps through a 'queering of education' that students can acknowledge the privileged position of heterosexuality in society. A factor that provides a rationale as to why all graduate practitioners need to consider this in their daily practice. Kite and Bryant-Lees (2016) suggest that it is only the teaching of the historical context of LGBT in terms of prejudice and discrimination that students can begin to identify how heterosexual privilege remains and what affects this may have on those they work with.

In the light of the above, it may assist practitioners to recognize that for some children, especially if preadolescent, sexual identity can be confusing and frightening. As described in Kurt Wicke's chapter, Harry Potter spent eleven years believing he was the abnormal one, and Jess was ultimately forced to hide her feelings until she could leave home. For many, conversations about and around sex can be socially and culturally difficult and can often be placed politically in the private sphere of responsibility rather than a public one. Thus society tends to construct parents and carers as the 'first responder' in terms of questions around sexual identity and sexual behaviour. However, practitioners need to have an awareness that subliminal messages about gender performance and gender-appropriate behaviour can destabilize, a child's sense of self-worth, as discussed in the next chapter. As already discussed earlier homophobic and transphobic bullying are a part of some children experiences. It is important therefore that practitioners understand and support children who feel different and who are treated differently.

Following on from the earlier discussion, you may want to reflect on the following questions:

- To what extent is heterosexuality institutionalized as normative behaviour?

- How useful would Kite and Bryant-Lees's suggestion be with regard to teaching the history of LGBT discrimination?

- Can teaching about the history of discrimination in general help children to understand and recognize the current existence of marginalized and 'othered' groups?

- How can practitioners ensure that personal choice and 'uniqueness' is accepted and celebrated?

PART FOUR

Becoming a Practitioner

10

Becoming a Graduate: Using All the Tools in the Toolbox: *Danny's Story*

Sue Aitken

This chapter will draw together and augment the themes and theories that run through the book. Themes such as:

- Attachment: Bowlby (1988), Field (2010).

- Transitions: Broddy (2013, Elfer, Goldschmied, and Selleck (2003), Fisher (2010).

- Identity: Cast and Burke (2002), Stets and Burke (2014), McAdams (2001), Goffman (1956).

- Communities of practice and multi-professional working: Lave and Wenger (2005), Frost, Robinson and Anning (2005).

- Praxis: Arendt (1958), Freire (1970).

Unlike the preceding chapters in this book, this final chapter will not focus on a single film or drama as the vehicle of discussion, but rather will use and expand on the ideas discussed earlier to explore their potential use in professional practice. Consequently, this chapter will use a set of scenarios that relate to a single child's experiences, offering an amalgam of many of the ideas and theoretical perspectives that you have already encountered. In so doing this chapter will also identify how some children can have complicated histories and experiences, and how understanding this can inform professional practice in the development of sophisticated, consistent and coherent responses and strategies. As the title infers, graduate practitioners working with children and families, in whatever context, need to make use of all the tools in their theoretical toolbox.

Scenario: Autumn

Danny is four years old and attends his local primary school. He currently lives with his father Matt, step mother Jane and his stepbrother Jack, who is eight. Jane works thirty hours a week as a health care assistant; she works irregular shifts, which can include early morning and late evening starts. Jane married Danny's father Matt, three years ago; Matt looks after the children when Jane is at work.

Danny's life so far has been unsettled and at times chaotic and frightening. He is Matt's son by a previous relationship and came to live with the family at two and a half years old, having been taken into care at eighteen months due to the neglect and physical abuse he received from his mother. Until located by Social Services, Matt had never had contact with Danny. At the local preschool, Danny was not meeting the EYFS emotional, social and cognitive development benchmarks for his age. Due to his background and his developmental delays, a Common Assessment Framework Action Plan (CAFAP) had been initiated. Now at school he finds it difficult to concentrate and his behaviour at school and at home can be challenging and disruptive, he still has a CAFAP in place. He has recently been diagnosed with developmental delay by a consultant paediatrician, who suggests that the likely cause is the neglect and lack of care in the first eighteen months of his life when he lived with his biological mother.

The scenario could suggest several areas of concern, both for the school and for his family. However, it is important for everyone in Danny's life to see Danny holistically and to try to disentangle simple understandings of cause and effect. Already it can be determined that Danny has had a range of professionals and services in his life; social workers within social services when he was a 'looked after' child, teachers and practitioners at school and preschool, and a paediatrician within the health service. Danny is already identified as a child who is in need of additional support to maximize his developmental potential. He has had a CAFAP since he was three years old, the Common

Assessment Framework Action Plan, is a standardized tool used to assess and plan for a child's additional needs and is designed to deliver coherent integrated multi-professional responses to meet a child's needs.

Attachment issues and safeguarding children

This first section will look at how practitioners might use their understanding of attachment, transition and identity in dealing with children with complex life histories. Chapters 4 and 5 (*The Red Balloon* and *We Need to Talk about Kevin*) both deal with attachment as a basis of understanding children's actions and needs. In *We Need to Talk about Kevin* the potential dangers of an insecure, even distorted maternal attachment is explored, while in *The Red Balloon* the potential for alternative, possibly even inanimate attachment can provide the security required for positive development. Field (2010:87) cited by Sarah Sharpe in Chapter 4 suggests that

> the forming of strong attachments and the demonstration of love, care and affection from the earliest days of a child's life … can be crucial to the child developing emotional strength and resilience.

In Chapter 5, when discussing Kevin's trajectory to mass murder, Jim Dobson writes, 'Children who exhibit symptoms of disorganised attachment may, according to Bowlby, self-harm, commit cruel and violent acts on animals, and display any lack of conscience'.

In reference to Field's proposition, Danny has had very little experience of maternal attachment, consistent love or care from his biological mother. Research shows that poorly established attachments in early childhood can have serious implications on the development of the brain, which in turn can determine the adult that children may become. The first 36 months of life are seen to be crucial in the development of what has come to be known as 'brain architecture'. The National Scientific Council on the Developing Child at Harvard University (2008:2) suggest that,

> Experiences during sensitive periods of development play an exceptionally important role in shaping the capacities of the brain.

However, while they acknowledge that genetics forms the basic platform for development, it is the environment and the experiences it offers that has a profound influence on how the brain develops. In a subsequent working paper, the Center on the Developing Child (2012) identified that timely intervention is an important indicator of future outcomes for children who have been subject to neglect and understimulation. Various studies (Fisher et al., 2000; Dozier et al., 2009; Bernard et al., 2012) have all indicated that early removal from neglect can provide substantial improvement of cognition, attention, memory, and executive functioning, provided the removal takes place between the first six and twenty-four months of life.

Danny's removal from his biological mother into foster care at eighteen months old would seem to suggest that any harm to his ability to function emotionally and intellectually, in line with social and educational expectations, may be short rather than long term. However, the need to act in a timely fashion is crucial, had Danny remained in an emotionally deprived environment for a further 6 months then the prospects for his future development could have been quite different. As referred to in Martin Needham's chapter earlier, practitioner's responses to suspicions of neglect and abuse can be fraught with both personal and profession conflict. While legislation and training together with setting policies can provide a framework for the identification and reporting of child protection and safeguarding concerns, taking the formal step of alerting the appropriate services can be a difficult but necessary decision, and this is discussed later in this chapter. Safeguarding is a broader term than child protection and refers to the promotion of a child's welfare and protection from harm. As stated in the Department for Education (DfE) document, Working together to Safeguard Children (2015c:7),

> Children are best protected when professionals are clear about what is required of them individually and how they need to work together.

In the same document, reference is made to the key tenant of the 2004 Children Act, 'the needs of the child are paramount' and that

> high quality professionals are able to use their expert judgement to put the child's need at the heart of the safeguarding system so that the right solution can be found for each individual child. (DfE, 2015c:8)

Safeguarding is everyone's responsibility, regardless of status, or professional discipline. Danny was removed from his mother's care when he was eighteen months old. Potentially, in that eighteen months he may have come to the attention of health visitors, general practitioners, concerned family members or neighbours, all of whom share the responsibility to raise concerns about Danny's welfare and development. Removal from harm however is just the first step in Danny's story; the subsequent repercussions of both his maltreatment and being taken into care will form crucial parts of future development.

Transitions and looked-after children

Transitions are discussed both in Chapters 1, 4 and 5 and refer to the process of journeying from one position, both physically and emotionally, to another. However, it is useful to look at the role transitions play in the context of unreliable attachment. In Danny's case, he has undergone several major transitions within a period of twelve months, from living with his biological mother, to living with a foster family and then to living with his biological father, his wife and her son. Under the auspices of the Children Act (1989) there lies a concept of 'permanence'. The Department of Education guidance on the Children Act 1989 (2010:12) states that permanence should offer children:

> a sense of security, continuity, commitment and Identity ... a secure, stable and loving family to support them through childhood and beyond.

Broddy (2013:1) suggests that any definition of 'permanence' must include recognition of the key qualities of family life 'including, belonging and mutual connectedness and continuity between past, present and future'. She goes on to say that in both long- and short-term placements, the focus should be a long-term view of what is the right permanence solution for the child. However, despite the prioritizing of legal permanence in the form of adoption, special guardianship orders (SGOs) and Child Arrangement orders, the uptake of permanent alternatives to foster care has been relatively low. The Department of Education statistics for looked-after children (available online at www.gov.uk) states that as at March 2016, there were 70,440 children whose care was the responsibility of a local authority Social Services. This is an increase of 3,370 since 2012. Three-quarters of these children were in foster care placements and 10 per cent of these children had experienced three or more placements in a year. During this period, only 3,000 children were placed for adoption or, as Danny was, placed with a biological parent. Special Guardianship Orders introduced in 2002 are seen as a bridge between potentially frequent and temporary foster care placements and adoption. While adoption severs all legal ties to the child's birth family, SGO's provide for contact between the child and his/her birth family, albeit subject on a limited and controlled basis.

For practitioners, notions of transition can sometimes be limited to visible and physical transitions such as entering nursery or school, moving up to another room in the setting or a different class at school. It can also be recognized in the arrival of a sibling, the death of a close relative or the breakdown of the parental relationship. However, concentration on these areas of, often inevitable, adjustment may preclude an understanding of the way prior and frequent transitions may have formulated the child's perception of change.

A child who is, or may have been, looked after by the local authority may have experienced several transitions in a relatively short period of time. To these children, change can be perceived of as a constant, a validation that life has no consistency. Consequently, the lack of an attachment figure will only exacerbate this perception of the world. As Sarah Sharpe highlights in Chapter 4, where attachment is absent or disorganized the presence of a significant 'other' or treasured transitional object can fill the void and create a sense of security and safety.

The development of the key person role (Elfer et al., 2003) and its inclusion in all EYFS settings has in part provided a mechanism for stabilizing relationships for many children. However, it could be questioned whether the local management of the key person role is not itself destabilizing, as the nominated key person may be subject to change, for a variety of reasons, as the child progresses through the EYFS. Danny is in a reception class in school and while still within the EYFS he is unlikely to have a named key person, and when he transfers to year one the provision of a key person is no longer a requirement. As cited in Chapter 4, Fisher (2010) suggests that where a child's home life is, or has been, chaotic and uncertain, there may be little evidence of resilience, thus the accommodation of new situations can become 'a thin veil between coping and collapsing'.

As discussed earlier, Danny is challenging and disruptive at home and in the classroom; for practitioners this can be difficult in terms of balancing the management of Danny's behaviour, while attempting to understanding the reasons behind it. Identifying disorganized or insecure attachment and the part transitions may play is often overlooked as managing the behaviour becomes the priority. However, taking a holistic approach can help to support rather than manage the child, in order that ultimately the child learns to manage his or her own behaviour. Providing a sense of constancy, reliability and consistency in school or early years' setting may help to alleviate the fears and trepidation of not only children such as Danny, but all children.

Identity

Identity, and a sense of self, forms part of the emotional responses to both attachment and transitional experiences. The thread of identity has occurred in several chapters in this book; in Chapter 1, Rita's journey to and through higher education traces her conscious realignment from a hairdresser to an undergraduate. Whereas in Chapter 7, Harry's self-perception, is abruptly redefined by Hagrid. For Jess, in Chapter 9, an equally significant event redefines her understanding of who she is. However, Charlie Bucket in Chapter 3 has no doubt about his identity, captured in a personal understanding of who he is; an understanding that is reinforced and recognized by his membership of the Bucket family. Outside of the family, however, he is measured and judged through wider social constructs and assumptions that are not within his control.

Underlying the construction of identity lie notions of self-perception and self-esteem, how we see ourselves and how that makes us feel (Burke and Stets, 2009). The measurement of these concepts can be difficult, especially in young children. However, towards the end of the last century Harter (1983,1985,1998) developed the Self-Perception Profile for Children. The profile asks children to answer questions relating to how they feel about themselves in five domains, which are competence at school work, in sport and games, making friends, in behaving appropriately and acceptably and how they feel about their physical appearance. Stets and Burke (2014) propose that self-esteem is composed of three dimensions: self-worth, self-motivation and agency, and authenticity.

Self-worth represents an internal human need to have a positive social worth that satisfies our desire to belong and have connectedness to others. Self-motivation and agency represent the human desire to have an effect on the environment, the ability to be in control of the forces that can affect and direct one's life. Finally, authenticity is the human search for meaning, coherence and the 'true self'. However, as discussed in Chapter 9, any attempt to construction the true self is often overlaid by externally imposed conformity to norms, values and roles which are internally managed by self-control. Thus the establishment of self-esteem is an outcome of the identity process and verification (Cast & Burke, 2002). As Stets and Burke (2014:412) state:

> An identity is a set of meanings that defines individuals in terms of the roles they occupy, the social categories or groups they belong to, and the individual characteristics that define them as unique persons.

However, as Goffman (1956) suggests, identity can be a fragmented performance dependent on time, place and audience, literally *the act of* providing and maintaining a desirable impression of oneself. As such, therefore, identities cannot be constructed as a fixed trait but should be seen as malleable and adjustable in response to maturation, context and onlookers.

Using these definitions, therefore, we can see that in terms of identity, Rita in Chapter 1 understands the meanings attached to the role of student and adjusts her behaviour accordingly to better 'fit in' with her new identity as an undergraduate. Similarly, once Harry accepts his identity as a wizard in the wizarding community, his behaviour reflects this new sense of self, but equally, on returning to the world of Muggles he realizes that a different set of behaviours are expected and once again he must perform as 'just Harry'. For Jess in Chapter 9, her sense of self is a negotiation between the competing paradigms of heterosexual and homosexual behaviour, which as an adolescent is constructed for her externally by the religious community of which she is a member.

Looking at Danny's identity in terms of his sense of self-worth, self-motivation, agency and authenticity provides a complex picture. Danny is aware that he has had three mother figures in his life, Jane, the women who has looked after him since he was two and a half; his foster mother, who he calls Maddie; and his birth mother, Sarah. However, as yet, he has not had any life story work (LSW) undertaken. LSW is considered to be an important part of a child's development of identity and, as Feast (2010) suggests, should be regarded as a right for all adopted and fostered children. Additionally, within the Statutory Guidance on Adoption, there is a focus on the importance of LSW (DfE, 2014c). However, research undertaken with adopters by Watson, Latter and Bellew (2015) indicated that the quality of the life story books for adopted children was inconstant and, at their worse, unhelpful or potentially upsetting for the child. Where the adopters were critical of the LSW provided for them, the majority believed this could have been avoided with better training for the professionals responsible for the creation of the books. Adopters also suggested that schools also had an important role to play in supporting adopted children. As their report (2015:19) suggests,

This requires better knowledge and skills on the part of school staff, of adoption generally and life stories in particular.

For most children, their life story will take the form of shared family memories supported by images (such as photographs and drawings), and artefacts that relate to their past and consequently inform the present. Essentially, these are the autobiographical tools required to develop identity. Identity itself, as McAdams (2001) suggests, comprises all the elements of narrative; that is, settings, scenes, plot and theme. While based on certain basic biological facts, they will also reflect cultural values and norms. For some children who are taken into care and subsequently adopted or placed away from the birth family, sections of these personal narratives can be missing and their past is fragmented and lacks continuity. Danny was a looked-after child, he was not adopted but placed with his biological father; therefore, LSW was not deemed useful or appropriate. However, Matt had no contact with Danny or Danny's mother before he was contacted by social services and Danny came to live with him. As Danny grows up, he is becoming increasingly aware that Jack, his stepbrother, has a history that he shares with Jane and her extended family, but he does not.

Practitioners need to be aware that children such as Danny may have difficulty with establishing self-worth as they may feel a lack of a sense of belonging or an established connection to others. So far, the events of his life have been beyond his control, which may disrupt his ability to define his true self. In this context, regardless of the permanent placement, LSW may be a useful mechanism through which Danny can start to piece together the jigsaw of his past. Holody and Mayer (1996) suggest that a 'here and now' approach to LSW will start at where the child is now, starting with the current positives in his/her life, current relationships, personal successes and interests. The study by Hooley, Stokes and Combes (2016) into the perceived value of LSW identified that LSW allowed for 'feelings to be shown, managed and normalized' but equally that difficult feelings and traumatic experiences should be explored. Additionally, participants in their study saw LSW as a useful tool in establishing attachment relationships within a safe and secure context. As Geddes and Hanko (2006:7) succinctly write:

> Memories do not remain in the past but become actions in the here and now. Behaviour is a communication and understanding the meaning of behaviour can be an invaluable tool when considering interventions.

To reframe behaviour as a communication about experiences may also be a way of defusing the impact on those practitioners working with difficult and demanding behaviour, as the behaviour can be contextualized, not as an excuse but as a mechanism of understanding.

When working with children, practitioners need to be aware that social assumptions and constructions about the nature of family structure and prior experiences can produce confusing and potentially damaging consequences for a child's sense of identity. Settings need to be mindful that families will not always consist of the stereotypical mum, dad and two children, a Christian cultural understanding, and an implicit knowledge of what Britishness may mean (see Chapter 6 for further discussion). In the twenty-first century, single-parent families, same-sex partnerships, reconstituted families, children in foster care or living with extended members of their family are a much more likely occurrence than before, as are children with alternative religious beliefs and cultural experiences. Therefore, care needs to be taken when undertaking activities that may undermine a child's sense of self-worth, creating a feeling that they are not like others and do not belong. As discussed in previous chapters and within the EYFS, children should be seen and celebrated as uniquely different.

Spring

Jane is telephoned at work to say that Matt has failed to pick up the children from school, and that he is not responding to the school's attempts to contact him. When she arrives at the school, the head teacher tells her that this was the third time it had happened and that she would, as a duty of care, have to inform social services. She also tells Jane that the children, when in Matt's care, would often be late or did not attend, and their teachers had noticed the children's clothing was often dirty and the children arrived dishevelled and unkempt. Jane takes the children to her mother's house, returns home and tells Matt to leave, which he did. Five weeks later, Danny discloses to his stepmother that his father had kicked and punched both children when he lost his temper and that sometimes he didn't feed them. Jane immediately tells the school of Danny's disclosure.

The role of the state: Safeguarding and child protection

As discussed in Chapter 3, the definition of the role of the state is often a matter of paradigm and political philosophy. Martin Needham suggests in Chapter 8 that the state has a duty of care to protect and safeguard children. In the United Kingdom, the policies and law with regard to safeguarding are devolved to each of the member nations, that is, England, Scotland, Wales and Northern Ireland. While each nation operates a different child protection system, they are all based on the same principles (NSPCC online). Safeguarding and promoting the welfare of children is defined by the Department for Education (2015c) as:

- Protecting children from maltreatment,

- Preventing impairment of children's health and development,

- Ensuring that children grow up in circumstances consistent with the provision of safe and effective care, and

- Taking action to enable all children to have the best outcomes.

When Matt failed to collect the children from school for the third time, coupled with other evidence of neglect, the head teacher, had no alternative but to inform children's social care (DFE, 2015c). Following a referral, a social worker would have been assigned to the family, the immediate task being to assess the situation and any current or potential risks to the children. Additionally, within one working day, the social worker must respond to the referrer's concerns (DfE, 2015c). Given that Matt had left the house the same day, it was deemed that the children were no longer at risk of neglect and further action would not be taken. However, on Danny's disclosure of physical abuse and neglect, a new referral would need to be made by the school. Following the second referral, the school may be asked to participate in a further assessment of the child(ren), either through an early help assessment, a child-in-need assessment (section 17 of the Children Act 1989) or a child protection enquiry (section 47 of the Children Act 1989), which would be led by a social worker.

Having been taken into care before the age of two because of maltreatment, Danny has for the second time been abused and neglected by a birth parent. In Danny's case, Broddy's (2013) notion of permanence would seem potentially at risk. Danny's current position is that he is living with a step-parent who, while having a child arrangement order, does not have parental responsibility. Parental responsibility (PR) is defined by section 3 of the Children Act (1989) as all the rights, duties, powers, responsibilities and authority in relation to a child. While all mothers are granted parental responsibility for their children automatically, fathers are not, unless they were married to the mother at the time of birth and /or are named on the child's birth certificate. Although he was not married to Danny's mother, Matt has PR for Danny as his name was on the birth certificate. Once conferred, parental responsibility cannot easily be removed; most often this can only happen where the child is adopted. However, it is possible to legally delegate responsibility for a child if a county court or family proceedings court issues a Child Arrangement Order, previously known as residence and contact orders (Children Act, 1989). Jane is named in a child arrangement order following the care proceedings which preceded Danny coming to live with them. Had she not been, then once again Danny might have been taken into care. Despite this order being in place, Jane's relationship with Danny, and Danny's relationship with Jane and Jack (his stepbrother) would have to be reassessed by a social worker. In Danny's case, the social worker observes that his relationship with Jane and Jack is mutually affectionate, and that Jack and Danny have a particularly strong bond and attachment.

However, in light of the recent disclosure and the assessments undertaken under section 17 of the Children Act, 1989, together with a child protection enquiry (section 47 of the Children Act, 1989) Danny's Common Assessment Framework Plan would now be escalated to a Child in Need plan. A Child in Need plan is a multi-agency framework that aims to provide coherent and consistent support both for the child and for the family. Typically, such meetings would be attended by the social worker attached to the case, representatives of the setting or school such as the child protection officer, special educational needs coordinator, the relevant class teacher(s) or room supervisors, possibly the school nurse or a representative of the health authority and the child's principal carer. Where age appropriate, the child(ren) may attend as well, however when this is not thought appropriate the child's views can be sought informally.

As a practitioner, whether in social work, education, care or health, the principle of working collaboratively within a multi-agency context can present its own dilemmas. Borne out of the Laming Report (2003) into the death of Victoria Climbié, the Labour Government's consultation paper, Every Child Matters (2003), emphasized the need for more effective ways of working and communicating between the agencies that have responsibility for the welfare of children. Enshrined in the Children Act (2004) is the requirement that every local authority must promote cooperation both within and between the authority and its partners and adopt a child-centred approach (Department for Children Schools and Families, 2013). The notion of a child-centred approach to working with children is discussed later in this chapter. A number of writers have suggested that it is widely accepted that collaboration and cooperation between agencies and professionals can improve the delivery and provision of children's services (Hood, 2012; Crawford, 2012; Hammick et al., 2009; Atkinson et al., 2007). In terms of meeting complex needs, as in Danny's case, there is an imperative for practitioners to work less independently and more flexibly. Practitioners need to acknowledge that complexity means more than a set of impersonal dynamics that govern cause and effect. In the context of child welfare, it is the very personal nature of the family and child experience that demands stable, respectful and trustworthy relationships from all the professionals who work with each other and the family.

Hood (2012) suggests that dealing with complex and often emotional issues can have a profound effect on the group members. As he states (Hood, 2012:11)

Any group, however constituted and for whatever purpose, will be subject to unpredictable dynamics, shaped by the interaction of diverse personal and contextual factors.

Hood further suggests that in such circumstances conflict is inevitable, especially at the beginning of a collaborative endeavour but that careful professional and organizational input can override this initial barrier to successful collaboration.

As discussed in previous chapters, notions of communities of practice (Lave & Wenger, 2005) can be useful in understanding how group dynamics, power relationships and status differences can exist within teams. Wenger (1998) points out that in using the term 'community' he is not implying that status is equally allocated or that power is shared. As Frost, Robinson and Anning (2005) discuss, interdisciplinary teams can be characterized by core–peripheral membership relations, where professional status and attendance can place some practitioners at the periphery rather than at the core. They refer in their study to a nursery nurse member of a social work team, who defined herself as 'sort of peripheral' due to her part-time work arrangements and the low professional status allocated to her by other members of the team. However, Wenger (1998) saw peripheral members as potential change agents, as they often have contact with divergent views from both inside and outside of the team, and therefore can retain the perspective of an outsider looking in, thus having the ability to recast ideas from a fresh perspective. As discussed earlier, Lord Laming's report of 2003 set in motion the statutory requirement that all the professionals working with a child must share information and collaborate across disciplines to safeguard the needs of children. It is important therefore that all practitioners, whatever their discipline, training or experience, are conscious of the need to prioritize what is best for children and families. In his 2009 progress report on child protection in England, Lord Laming quoted Sir Jonathan Sacks (2009:3), 'Children grow to fill the space we create for them, and if it's big, they grow tall'.

Lord Laming praised the effort of government in the previous six years to regularize and manage the operational needs of safeguarding and child protection practice with regard to cross-disciplinary communication and working. However, he remarked that the challenges of working across organization boundaries continued to pose barriers and that when services and staff were under pressure, cooperation efforts were the first to suffer (Laming, 2009:37).

In Danny's case, his best interests would seem to be that he remains living with Jane and Jack and that he continues attending the same school, and life, as far as possible, remains stable and consistent. If there are no criminal proceedings, then Danny and Jack can be offered psychological support immediately, such as nurture groups within school or play therapy from a trained practitioner. If criminal proceedings are anticipated, however, support may be delayed due to the need to protect evidence from the children and to ensure the viability of any future legal action.

As defined by Lord Laming, working across professional disciplines and boundaries can be difficult especially where resources and services for children are under pressure and where competing needs have to be prioritized. Therefore, it falls to practitioners in whatever context and capacity to negotiate and ensure that the best outcomes for all children are achieved.

Praxis

The term praxis is derived from the Greek word for process and often applied to the process of translating and using theory as a basis of action. Arendt (1958) in her seminal work *The Human Condition* identified that over time society had created a disconnect between academic thought, personal experiences and action. Her starting point was that theories of political philosophy would remain abstract and inert unless they could be used to make sense of real life and real experiences. However, she did not see praxis as merely the technical application of theory. Arendt saw a clear distinction between action and fabrication; by fabrication she is alluding to the use of theory as a rationale for achieving predefined ends. This description therefore may easily be applied to practice, where predefined outcomes and protocols control activity and consequently reducing professional agency. Teachers, for example, working within a prescriptive curriculum often feel that they are unable to exercise influence over subject content or ways of learning. Where praxis differs from practice is its unpredictability and its open-ended trajectory, ends which can never be fully envisaged or controlled.

Across disciplines, taking a child-centred approach allows, at least in part, the space to work with children at their own pace and in directions that interest them. As referred to earlier, nurture groups and play therapy may help children with emotional difficulties, to renegotiate and restructure how they feel about themselves and others. Psychological therapeutic work with children and adults will often adopt what Rogers (1951) referred to as client-centred therapy. However, Rodgers saw client-centred approaches (later person-centred approaches) as a tool which could be used beyond the context of personal therapy. At its core, Rogers believed that it was the quality and authenticity of relationships that rendered this approach successful. Rogers identified that three essential conditions were fundamental to the success of the therapist– or practitioner–client relationship, which were

- Congruence: the ability of the practitioner to offer an authentic transparency that does not hide behind professional or personal status; to be genuine.

- Unconditional positive regard: the ability to accept and appreciate the 'client' for who they are and the ability to listen without judgement or negativity.

- Empathy: to communicate a genuine desire to understand and appreciate the client perspectives on events and feelings.

Rogers (1969) and Rogers, Lyon and Taush (2013) later developed this approach with regard to the context of education and the relevance of the three elements listed in the relationship between teacher and learner. Rogers suggests that effective teaching requires the teacher to accept the role of facilitator and mentor rather than expert. Learning is thus differentiated from teaching, and the learner is empowered to learn from their interests, experiences and perspectives, guided rather than pushed, contextualized rather than imposed. Child-centred learning is very much a part of alternative approaches to childhood learning experiences. Approaches such as Reggio Emilia, Steiner, Montessori, Forest Schools and Summerhill, all strive to place the child at the centre of the learning experience.

In terms of Danny's situation, how might an understanding of praxis and child-centred approaches help the team of professional practitioners that currently have input into his life, ensure the best outcomes for him? In the short term, Danny is identified as having a developmental delay of approximately eighteen months. He shows no phonic awareness but is able to recognize some whole words, the English National Curriculum prioritizes the teaching of reading through phonics; in Danny's case is there perhaps scope to play to his current strengths rather than his current weaknesses?

Praxis is more than reflective practice, while a reflective practitioner may reflect upon their own role, conduct and objectives after the event; praxis is the ability to apply and use theory as a mechanism for moving the 'client' forward. Taking Rogers's three core elements of the person-centred approach: congruence, unconditional regard and empathy, practitioners need to see Danny potentially as he may see himself. Having a knowledge of the many ways in which theories may explain and describe attachment, transition and identity, may provide a basis of understanding. However, it is only when that understanding is transformed into a valuable tool that practitioners can use to reposition themselves from expert to facilitator and mentor that it becomes meaningful. Danny's lack of a coherent sense of self and his lack of resilience to change doesn't need to be met with an unempathetic reaction to his behaviour and his demonstrable lack of self-control but with a non-judgemental engagement with him that reflects a positive regard. Freire (1970) referred to praxis as informed action, meaning that every action and decision is made on the basis of a theoretical framework in an ongoing conversation and democratic relationship.

Conclusion

This chapter has considered how the theories explored and developed in the earlier chapters of this book can be redeveloped and can have a bearing on Danny's story. However, it is not, nor never could be, a finite or exhaustive recipe for effective professional practice. The most effective use for this chapter and all the previous chapters is to accept that while absorbing theory as part of an academic journey, that is not the end of its usefulness. Graduate practitioners need to take ownership of theory, in order to better understand and support children and their families The scenarios in this chapter tell the story of one child and the opportunities and barriers that might affect his life, now and in the future. However, it is worth considering, the potential variables in his story and how they might alter his trajectory. Variables, such as a different cultural background; a more complex and long-term developmental delay, such as Down's syndrome, autism or cerebral palsy or a life-shortening illness; poverty; being a more able child. In effect, every child's story is a variable on Danny's, with similarities and divergences, and should be seen and celebrated as uniquely different. As alluded to in the title of this chapter, after graduation, take the toolbox with you.

When considering the scenarios above, readers may like to consider the following questions:

- What constraints, both legal and practical, prevent practitioners from having a full knowledge of the history and circumstances of the children they are responsible for?

- Can you identify your own knowledge gaps with regard to the care, development and education of children?

- How will you develop the ability to see and use theory in your professional life to improve the experiences of children?

Concluding Remarks

Sue Aitken

The book set out to establish that popular and accessible culture can provide a starting point for a range of meaningful discussions around theory
and their application to practice. As highlighted in Chapter 1, many students
embarking on a degree programme, in whatever discipline, can feel that theory is daunting, remote and disconnected from real experiences. Many students find it hard to join up all the dots and see that ideas are rarely singular
entities but rather they offer different meanings to different people at different
times. Hopefully, over time, these ideas begin to congregate together in order
to provide students with an ontological and epistemological understanding
that informs what they believe, and how they perceive the world.

Consequently, each chapter has provided the reader with a model of how
to engage with similar ideas, in different contexts. In the planning stage, this
was very much part of the book's rationale, that each author could relate to
a specific film, which for them, created the ideal vehicle to explain complex
and often misunderstood theories through, literally, a different lens. While the
films used here perform the tasks assigned to them in theoretical terms, it is
the process of seeing and applying ideas in action that is important; the process of making connections to personal experiences, memories and knowledge not as 'facts' but as useful 'tools'. This connection then allows for an
internal reflection and engagement with ideas that may previously have been
allusive. Many of the chapters use a Bourdieuian perspective to assist the
student in uncoupling dominant discourses of truth and reality from 'common sense' and irrefutability. Such ideas can often originate from myopically
focused and personalized accounts; however, the journey to graduateness

involves the ability to reposition yourself as a sceptical, questioning professional, who has the tools and knowledge to challenge the dominant ideas in whatever discipline they work. Additionally, by using queer, and postcolonial theory to identify the oppression and discrimination of marginalized groups, the principle of 'othering' and social segregation of cultural, social or ethnic communities becomes a mechanism of control which can be applied to any group at any time.

This book's intentions are most easily explained by reference to 'intertextuality' (Kristeva, 1980); the concept of merging semiotics (de Saussure, (2013) with Bakhtin's notion of dialogism (Bakhtin, 1986) in an attempt to demonstrate how we read texts, not merely in the written form but in visual texts as well. Intertextuality therefore provides an explanation of how we engage and retain ideas from a range of texts, which then informs the readers' (viewers') understanding and meaning of subsequent texts in a constant interaction and repositioning of ideas. As Barthes (1967, 1993), suggested, meaning is not fixed by the writer in the words they write, or the images they produce – the attribution of meaning belongs to the individual consumer of the product. In this way, it is hoped that students will recognize that theory does not occupy a discrete and separate place from life, it is present in film, daily news reports and the books we read; it is present in social media, political rhetoric and daily conversations.

However, the journey doesn't end here, just before submitting this book to the publishers I watched the 2017 BAFTA-nominated film, *Lion*, starring Dev Patel and Nicole Kidman. It traces the life of a 5-year-old Indian boy (Saroo), who becomes lost and inadvertently boards a train that takes him 1400 kilometres from his family to the slums and poverty of Calcutta. Although later adopted by a childless Australian couple, as an adult, Saroo, becomes obsessed with finding his biological family or somehow finding his way home. Based on Saroo Brierley's 2013 autobiography, Saroo describes that while his childhood in Australia was happy, supportive and loving, as an adult he felt that his life had too many dead ends, fragmented by memories of a previous life and family in India.

Saroo, like Danny, in the previous chapter, has an incomplete history, one he can barely remember but without which he cannot feel whole. Saroo's understanding of his identity is unreliable and it is only by retracing and reconnecting to an earlier life can he gain a complete sense of himself. Saroo's story, like Danny's, has a sense of incompleteness, elements that are missing, elements that he needs to fully construct his identity. Practitioners need to have an awareness, as related to in several chapters of this book, that the management of processes such as attachment, transition and identity can have an impact throughout a person's life, not just in childhood. Without early intervention, support and understanding, children who experience trauma and disjointed childhoods may lack the resilience and mental strength to lead a stable life in adulthood.

Using film provides a useful backdrop for explaining, exploring and understanding childhood and practice.

References

4Children (2015), Children's Centre Census 2015. A National Overview of Children's Centres 2015. 4Children.

Abbott, M. (2003), *Family Affairs, a History of the Family in 20th Century England*, London: Routledge.

Aboriginal Act (1905) (5 EDW. VII No 14) www.slp.wa.gov.au/legislation/statutes.nsf/main_mrtitle_9579_homepage.html (Accessed 2 November 2016).

Ainsworth, M. (1989), Attachments beyond Infancy, *American Psychologist*, 44(4): 709–16.

Ainsworth, M., Bleher, M., Waters, E. and Wall, S. (1978), *Patterns of Attachment: A Psychological Study of the Strange Situation.* Hillsdale, NJ: Erlbaum.

Aldgate, J. and Jones, D. (2006), The Place of Attachment in Children's Development, in J. Aldgate, D. Jones, W. Rose and C. Jeffery (Eds), *The Developing World of the Child*, 67–96. London: Jessica Kingsley Publishers.

Allen, G. (2011), *Early Intervention: The Next Steps*, London: Cabinet Office.

Althusser, L., Balibar, É. and Bidet, J. (2014), *On the Reproduction of Capitalism: Ideology and Ideological State Apparatuses*, London: Verso.

Amiot, C. E., de laSablonniere, R., Smith, L. G. E. and Smith, J. R. (2015), Capturing Changes in Social Identities over Time and How They Become Part of the Self-concept, *Social and Personality Psychology Compass*, 9(4): 171–87.

Amnesty International (2012), *Guantanamo: A Decade of Damage to Human Rights*, London: Amnesty International Publications.

Apple, M. W. (2011), Democratic Education in Neoliberal and Neoconservative Times, *International Studies in Sociology of Education*, 21(1): 21–31.

Arendt, H. (1958), *The Human Condition*, London: University of Chicago Press.

Armitage, A., Robin B., Dunhill R., Flanagan K., Hayes D., Hudson A., Kent J., Lawes, S. and Renwick, M. (2007), *Teaching and Training in Post-Compulsory Education*, Maidenhead: Open University Press.

Aronson, E., and Mills, J. (1959), The Effect of Severity of Initiation on Liking for a Group, *Journal of Abnormal and Social Psychology*, 92(2): 177–81.

Ashcroft, B., Griffiths, G. and Tiffin, H. (2002), *The Empire Writes Back: Theory and Practice in Post-Colonial Literatures*, Abingdon: Routledge.

Atkinson, M. Jones, M. and Lamont, E. (2007), *Multi-Agency Working and Its Implications for Practice: A Review of the Literature*, Reading: CfBT Schools Trust.

Badinter, J. (2013), *The Conflict: How Overzealous Motherhood Undermines the Status of Women*. London: Picador.

Baggerly, J. N., Ray, D. C. and Bratton, S. C. (Eds) (2010), *Child-Centered Play Therapy Research: The Evidence Base for Effective Practice*, New Jersey: John Wiley.

Bagley, C. (2011), From Sure Start to Children's Centres: Capturing the Erosion of Social Capital, *Journal of Education Policy*, 26: 95–113.

Bakhtin, M. M. (1986), *Speech Genres and Other Late Essays*, in Caryl Emerson and Michael Holquist (Eds.), Vern W. Mcghee (Trans.). Austin: University of Texas Press.

Barker, C. and Galasinski, D. (2001), *Cultural Studies and Discourse Analysis: A Dialogue on Language and Identity*, London: Sage.

Barnett, A. (2016), PSPOs: Councils Using New Powers to Ban and Punish Legal Activities. Available at http://www.independent.co.uk/news/uk/politics/pspos-councils-using-new-powers-to-ban-and-punish-legal-activities-a6902256.html (Accessed 16 December 2016).

Barron, I. (2011), The Shadows of Difference: Ethnicity and Young Children's Friendships, *Race Ethnicity and Education*, 14(5): 655–73.

Barthes, R. (1967), Death of the Author, in Graddol and Boyd-Barrett (Eds), *Media Texts: Authors and Readers*, 166–70. Clevedon: Multilingual Matters.

Barthes, R. (1993), *Camera Lucida: Reflections on Photography*, London: Vintage Classic.

Barton, T. D. (2007), Student Nurse Practitioners – a Rite of Passage? The Universality of van Gennep's Model of Social Transition, *Nurse Education in Practice* 7: 338–47.

Bauman, Z. (2005), *Liquid Life*, Cambridge: Polity.

BBC (2015), Jerusalem: Palestinian Youths Stab Israeli Train Guard. Available at http://www.bbc.co.uk/news/world-middle-east-34777393 (Accessed 11 November 2015).

Bentham, J. (1791), *Panopticon or Inspection House*, Dublin: Payne.

Bentham, J. (2009), *Panopticon: Or the Inspection House*, Montana: Kessinger Publishing.

Benyon, J. and Solomos, J. (1987), *The Roots of Urban Unrest*, Oxford: Pergamon Press.

Bergin C. and Bergin D. (2009), Attachment in the Classroom, *Educational Psychology Review*, 21: 141–70.

Bernard, K., Dozier, M., Bick, J., Lewis, E., Lindhiem, O. and Carlson, E. (2012), Enhancing Attachment Organization among Maltreated Children: Results of a Randomized Clinical Trial, *Child Development*, 83(2): 623–36.

Berndt, T. and Keefe, K. (1995), Friends' Influence on Adolescents' Adjustment to School, *Child Development*, 66(5): 1313–29.

Bernstein, B. (2000), *Pedagogy, Symbolic Control and Identity: Theory, Research, Critique*, Oxford: Rowman and Littlefield.

Black, D. (1986), *The Plague Years: A Chronicle of AIDS, the Epidemic of Our Times*, New York: Simon and Schuster.

Blair, T. (2006), BBC interview, 31 August 2006. www.news.bbc.co.uk/1/hi/5301824.stm (Accessed 10 June 2016).

Bloom, M. and Horgan, J. (2015), The Rise of the Child Terrorist: The Young Faces at the Frontlines. *Foreign Affairs*. Available at https://www.foreignaffairs.com/articles/middle-east/2015-02-09/rise-child-terrorist (Accessed 8 August 2016).

Bolton, G. (2010), *Reflective Practice: Writing and Professional Development*, London; Sage.

Bombèr, L. (2007), *Inside I'm Hurting; Practical Strategies for Supporting Children with Attachment Difficulties in Schools*, London: Worth Publishing.

Bombèr, L. (2011), *What about Me? Inclusive Strategies to Support Pupils with Attachment Difficulties Make It through the School Day*, London: Worth Publishing.

Booth, J. (2004), UK Sleepwalking into Stasi State. Available at https://www.theguardian.com/uk/2004/aug/16/britishidentity.freedomofinformation (Accessed 10 June 16).

Bourdieu, P. (1977), *Outline of a Theory of Practice*, Cambridge: Cambridge University Press.

Bourdieu, P. (1984), *Distinction: A Social Critique of the Judgement of Taste*, Cambridge, MA: Harvard University Press.

Bourdieu, P. (1986), *Distinction: A Social Critique of the Judgement of Taste*, London, Routledge.Bourdieu, P. (1990), *The Logic of Practice*, Oxford: Polity Press.

Bourdieu, P. (1991), *Language and Symbolic Power*, London: Polity Press.

Bourdieu, P. (1993), *Sociology in Question*, London: Sage.

Bourdieu, P. (1997), The Forms of Capital in A. H. Halsey, H. Lauder, P. Brown, and A. Stuart Wells (Eds), *Education; Culture, Economy and Society*, 46–58. Oxford: Oxford University Press.

Bourdieu, P. (1998), *Practical Reason: On the Theory of Action*, Cambridge: Polity Press.

Bourdieu, P. (2010), *Distinction: A Social Critique of the Judgement of Taste*, London: Routledge.

Bourdieu, P. and Passeron, J. C. (1977), *Reproduction in Education, Society and Culture*, London: Sage.

Bourdieu, P., Poupeau, F. and Discepolo, T. (2008), *Political Interventions: Social Science and Political Action*, New York: Verso Books.

Bourdieu, P., Calhoun, C., Lipuma, E. and Postone, M. (Eds.). (1993). *Bourdieu: Critical Perspectives*. Chicago: University of Chicago Press.

Bowlby, J. (1951), *Maternal Care and Mental Health*, Geneva: World Health Organisation.

Bowlby, J. (1969), *Attachment and Loss*, vol 1., London: Pimlico.

Bowlby, J. (1977), The Making and Breaking of Affectional Bonds. I. Aetiology and Psychopathology in the Light of Attachment Theory. An Expanded Version of the Fiftieth Maudsley Lecture, Delivered Before the Royal College of Psychiatrists, 19 November 1976. *British Journal of Psychiatry*, 130 (3): 201–10.

Bowlby, J. (1988), *A Secure Base: Parent–Child Attachment and Healthy Human Development*, New York: Basic Books.

Bowles, S. and Gintis, H. (1976). *Schooling in Capitalist America*, Vol. 57. New York: Basic Books.

Brain, C. and Mukherji, P. (2005), *Understanding Child Psychology*, Cheltenham: Nelson Thornes.

Bray, J., Lee, J., Smith, L. and Yorks, L. (2000), *Collaborative Inquiry in Practice; Action, Reflection and Making Meaning*, London: Sage.

Brierley, S. (2013), *A Long Way Home*, Melbourne: Viking.

Briggs, A. R. J., Clark, J. and Hall, I. (2012), Building Bridges: Understanding Student Transition to University, *Quality in Higher Education*, 18(1): 3–21.

British Medical Association (1997), *School Sex Education: Good Practice and Policy,* London: British Medical Association, Board of Science and Technology.

Broddy, J. (2013), Understanding Permanence for Looked After Children: A Review of Research for the Care Inquiry, *The Care Inquiry*. Available at https://thecareinquiry.files.wordpress.com/2013/04/understanding-permanence-for-lac.pdf (Accessed 12 March 2017).

Bronfenbrenner, U. (1979), *The Ecology of Human Development*, Cambridge, MA: Harvard University Press.

Bronfenbrenner, U. (2005), *Making Human Beings Human: Bioecological Perspectives on Human Development*, London: Sage.

Brooker, L. (2008), *Supporting Transitions in the Early Years*, London: Mcgraw-Hill Education (UK).

Brookfield, S. (2011), *The Power of Critical Theory for Adult learning and Teaching*, Berkshire: Open University Press.

Brown, J. (2016), *NEET: Young People Not in Education, Employment or Training*, London: House of Commons.

Brown, S., Armstrong, S. and Thompson, G. (1998), *Motivating Students*, London: Kogan Page.

Brubaker, R. and Cooper, F. (2000), Beyond Identity, *Theory and Society*, 29(1): 1–47.

Burdman, D. (2003), Education, Indoctrination, and Incitement: Palestinian Children on Their Way to Martyrdom, *Terrorism and Political Violence*. 15(1): 96–123.

Burke, P. J. and Stets J. E. (2009), *Identity Theory*, New York: Oxford University Press.

Burman, E. (2008), *Deconstructing Developmental Psychology*. 2nd ed. Hove: Routledge.

Burr, V. (2002), *The Person in Social Psychology (Psychology Focus)*, Hove: Psychology Press.

Butler, J. (1990), *Gender Trouble: Feminism and the Subversion of Identity*, London: Routledge.

Butler, J. and Salih, S. (2004), *The Judith Butler Reader*, Malden, MA: Blackwell.

Butler, J., Laclau, E. and Zizek, S. (2000), *Contingency, Hegemony, Universality: Contemporary Dialogues on the Left*, London: Verso.

Byron, T. (2008), *Safer Children in a Digital World: The Report of the Byron Review: Be Safe, Be Aware, Have Fun*. Available at http://Dera.Ioe.Ac.Uk/7332/7/Final%20report%20bookmarked_Redacted.Pdf.

Cairns, K. (2006), *Attachment, Trauma and Resilience*, London: BAAF.

Cameron, D. (2011), Troubled Families Speech, London: Cabinet Office.

Casey, L. (2013), Working with Troubled Families. *Families, Relationships and Societies*, 2(3): 459–61.

Cast, A. D. and Burke, P. J. (2002), A Theory of Self Esteem, *Social Force*, 80(3): 1041–68.

Center on the Developing Child at Harvard University (2012), The Science of Neglect: The Persistent Absence of Responsive Care Disrupts the Developing Brain. Working Paper No. 12. Available at www.developingchild.harvard.edu. (Accessed 12 March 17).

CHANNEL 4 (2017), Schools Accused of Reviving Anti-Gay Sex Education Policies. Available at www.channel4.com/news/schools-revive-old-anti-gay-sex-education-policies (Accessed 22 February 2017).

Charlie and the Chocolate Factory (2005), [Film] Dir. Tim Burton, USA: Warner Bros.

The Children Act (1989). Available at www.legislation.gov.uk/ukpga/1989/41/introduction (Accessed 23 March 2017).

The Children Act (2004). Available at http://www.legislation.gov.uk/ukpga/2004/31/contents (Accessed 23 March 2017).

Children of the Corn (1984), [Film] Dir. Fritz Kiersch, USA: Angeles Entertainment Group.

Children's Rights Alliance for England (2014), State of Children's Rights in England: Review of Government Action on United Nations' Recommendations for Strengthening Children's Rights in the UK, London: Children's Rights Alliance for England.

Chivers, T. (2014), Psychopaths: How Can You Spot One? *Daily Telegraph*. Available at http://www.telegraph.co.uk/culture/books/10737827/Psychopaths-how-can-you-spot-one.html (Accessed 12 June 2016).

Civil Rights Movement (2016), FAQ: UK Citizens and CCTV Privacy Rights. Available at http://www.civilrightsmovement.co.uk/faq-uk-citizens-cctv-privacy-rights.html (Accessed 12 October 2016).

Cleaver, H. (2006), The Influence of Parenting and Other Family Relationships, in Aldgate, J., Jones, D., Rose, W. and Jeffery, C. (Eds), *The Developing World of the Child*, London: Jessica Kingsley Publishers.

Cohen, D. and MacKeith, S. (1992), *The Development of Imagination: The Private Worlds of Childhood*, London: Routledge.

Cohen, R., Kennedy, P. T. and Perrier, M. (2013), *Global Sociology*, 3rd edn, Basingstoke: Palgrave Macmillan.

Cohen, S. (2002), *Folk Devils and Moral Panics*, London: Paladin.

Colebrook, C. (2002). *Gilles Deleuze*. London: Routledge.

Collins, J. and Foley, P. (2008), *Promoting Children's Wellbeing: Policy and Practice*, Bristol: Policy Press.

Collins, S. (2009), *The Hunger Games*, London: Scholastic

Committee for Investigating the Causes of the Alarming Increase of Juvenile Delinquency in the Metropolis (1815), Report of the Committee for Investigating the Causes of the Alarming Increase of Juvenile Delinquency in the Metropolis, London: J. F. Dove.

Connolly, P. (2004), *Boys and Schooling in the Early Years*, Abingdon: Routledge Falmer.

Coppock, V. and McGovern, M. (2014), Dangerous Minds? Deconstructing Counter-Terrorism Discourse, Radicalisation and the 'Psychological Vulnerability' of Muslim Children and Young People in Britain, *Children and Society*, 28(3): 242–56.

Coutant, A., De la Ville, V., Gram, M. and Boireau, N. (2011), Motherhood, Advertising, and Anxiety: A Cross-Cultural Perspective on Danonino Commercials. *Advertising and Society Review*. 12(2): 1–19. Available at http://vbn.aau.dk/en/publications/motherhood-advertising-and-anxiety(3037f8d6-2085-41de-9f53-d9d1a2c583aa).html (Accessed 12 February 2016).

Cowdery, R. and Knudson-Martin, C. (2005), The Construction of Motherhood: Tasks, Relational Connection, and Gender Equality, *Family Relations*, 54(3): 335–45.

Crawley, J. (2005). *In at the Deep End*, London: David Fulton Publishers.

Creme, P. and Lea, R. (2005), *Writing at University: A Guide for Students*, 2nd edn, Maidenhead: Open University Press.

Crossley, N. (2012), Social Class, in M. Grenfell (Ed.), *Pierre Bourdieu. Key Concepts*, 2nd edn, 87–99. London: Routledge.

Crossley, S. (2015), The Troubled Families Programme: The Perfect Social Policy, Crime and Justice Briefing Paper 13. Available at https://www.crimeandjustice.org.uk/sites/crimeandjustice.org.uk/files/The%20Troubled%20Families%20Programme%2C%20Nov%202015.pdf (Accessed 12 April 2016).

Cullberg, J. (2008), *Crisis and Development*, 5th edn, Copenhagen: Hans Reitzel.

Dalley, G. (1996), Community Care and the Meaning of Caring, in *Ideologies of Caring*, 1–25. London: Macmillan.

Daniel, B. and Wassell, S. (2002), *Assessing and Promoting Resilience in Vulnerable Children*, London: Jessica Kingsley.

Daniels, H. (2006), *Vygotsky and Pedagogy*, Oxon: Routledge.

Datler, W., Ereky-Stevens, K., Hover-Reisner, N. and Malmberg, L. E. (2012), Toddlers' Transition to Out-of-Home Day Care: Settling into a New Care Environment, *Infant Behaviour and Development*, 35(3): 439–51.

David, T., Goouch, K., Powell, S. and Abbott, L. (2003), Birth to Three Matters: A Review of the Literature, DfES Research Report Number 444. Nottingham: Queen's Printer.

De Coste, J. (2014), Toward a Theory of Rural Queer Studies, in J. S. Kaufman and D. A, Powell (Eds), *The Meaning of Sexual Identity in the Twenty-First Century*, 73–86, Newcastle upon Tyne: Cambridge Scholar Publishing.

de Fina, A. (2011), Discourse and Identity in T. A.V. Dijk, (Ed.), *Discourse Studies: A Multidisciplinary Introduction*, 2nd edn, Thousand Oaks, CA: Sage Publications.

De Saussure, F. (2013), *Course in General Linguistics*, R. Harris (Trans.), London: Bloomsbury.

Deer, C. (2012), Doxa, in M. Grenfell (Ed.), *Pierre Bourdieu. Key Concepts*, 2nd edn, London: Routledge.

Delebarre, J. (2016), NEET: Young People Not in Education, Employment or Training. *Parliamentary Briefing Paper Number, 6705*.

Deleuze, G. and Guattari, F. (1987), *A Thousand Plateaus: Capitalism and Schizophrenia*, Brian Massumi (Trans.), Minneapolis, MN: University of Minneapolis.

Department for Children Schools and Families (2013), *Working Together to Safeguard Children: A Guide to Interagency Working to Safeguard and Promote the Welfare of Children*, London: HMSO.

Department for Education (1996), *Education Act*, London: HMSO.

Department for Education (1998), *The Education (Compulsory School Age) Order*, London: HMSO.

Department for Education (2004), *The* Children Act, London: HMSO.

Department for Education (2010), *The Children Act 1989 Guidance and Regulation Volume 3: Planning Transition to Adulthood for Care Leavers*, London: HMSO.

Department for Education (2014a), *Advice on the Admission of Summer Born Children*, London: HMSO

Department for Education (2014b), *Statutory Framework for the Early Years Foundation Stage: Setting the Standards for Learning, Development and Care for Children from Birth to Five*, London: HMSO.

Department for Education (2014c), *Statutory Guidance on Adoption for Local Authorities, Voluntary Adoption Agencies and Adoption Support Agencies*, London: HMSO.

Department for Education. (2014d), *Children's Social Care Innovation Programme*, London: Department of Education.

Department for Education (2015a), *The Prevent Duty: Departmental Advice for Schools and Childcare Provider*, London: DFE.

Department for Education (2015b), *What to Do If You're Worried a Child Is Being Abused: Advice for Practitioners*, London: HMSO.

Department for Education (2015c), *Working Together to Safeguard Children: A Guide to Inter-Agency*, London: DFE.

Department for Education (2016), *Children Looked After in England (Including Adoption) SRF41/2016*. www.gov.uk (Accessed 11 March 2017).

Derrida, J. and Moore F. C. T. (1974), White Mythology: Metaphor in the Text of Philosophy, *New Literary History*, 6(1): 5–74.

Department of Children Families and Schools (2008), *Explanatory Memorandum to the Childcare (Exemptions from Registration) Order*, London, DFCS.

Di Giorgio, C. (2009), Application of Bourdieuian Theory to the Inclusion of Students with Learning/Physical Challenges in Multicultural Settings, *International Journal of Inclusive Education*, 13(2): 179–94.

Dick, P. K. (1956), *The Minority Report in Fantastic Universe*, New York: King-Size Publications.

Donzelot, J. (1997), *The Policing of Families*. Baltimore, MD: John Hopkins University Press.

Dowling, M. (2010), *Young Children's Personal, Social and Emotional Development*, London: Sage.

Dowling, M., Gupta, A. and Aldgate, J. (2006), The Impact of Community and Environmental Factors, in J. Aldgate, D. Jones, W. Rose and C. Jeffery (Eds), *The Developing World of the Child*, London: Jessica Kingsley.

Dowty, T. (2008), Pixie-Dust and Privacy: What's Happening to Children's Rights in England? *Children and Society*, 22(5): 393–9.

Dozier, M., Lindhiem, O., Lewis, E., Bick, J., Bernard, K. and Peloso, E. (2009), Effects of a Foster Parent Training Program on Young Children's Attachment Behaviours: Preliminary Evidence from a Randomized Clinical Trial, *Child & Adolescent Social Work Journal*, 26(4): 321–32.

Draper, J., Sparrow, S. and Gallagher, D. (2009), Crossing the Threshold: Students' Experiences of the Transition from Student to Staff Nurse, Nurse Education Today Conference, 8–10 September 2009, University of Cambridge.

Du Gay, P., Evans, J. and Redman, P. L. (2000), *Identity: A Reader*, London: Sage.

Dunn, J. (2004), *Children's Friendships: The Beginnings of Intimacy*, Oxford: Blackwell.

Durkheim, E. (1951), *Suicide: A Study in Sociology* [1897]. Translated by J A Spaulding and G. Simpson. Glencoe, IL: Free Press.

Dweck, C. (2007), *Mindset: The New Psychology of Success: How We Can Learn to Fulfil Our Potential*, London: Ballantine Books.

Dworkin, G. (2014), Paternalism, *Stanford Encyclopaedia of Philosophy*. Available at http://plato.stanford.edu/archives/sum2014/entries/paternalism/ (Accessed 15 September 2015).

Easton, D. (1985), Political Science in the United States: Past and Present, in J. Farr and R. Seidelman (Eds), *Discipline and History: Political Science in the United States*. Repr. (1993), Ann Arbor: University of Michigan Press.

Educating Rita (1983), [Film], Dir. Lewis Gilbert, United Kingdom: Acorn Films.

Eisenstaedt, N. (2012), Poverty, Social Disadvantage and Young Children, in L. Miller and D. Hevey (Eds), *Policy Issues in the Early Years*, London: Sage.

Elfer, P., Goldschmied, E. and Selleck, D. (2003), *Key Persons in the Nursery: Building Relationships for Quality Provision*, London: David Fulton.

Emanuel, L. (2005), *Understanding Your Three-Year-Old*, London: Jessica Kingsley.

Ensalaco, M. and Majka, L. C. (2005), *Children's Human Rights: Progress and Challenges for Children Worldwide*, Lanham: Rowman and Littlefield.

Entwistle, N. (1998), Motivation and Approaches to Learning: Motivating and Conceptions of Teaching, in S. Brown, S. Armstrong and G. Thompson (Eds), *Motivating Students*. London: Kogan Page.

Epstein, D., O'Flynn, S. and Telford D. (2003), *Silencing Sexualities in Schools and Universities*, Stoke on Trent: Trentham Books.

Erikson, E. H. (1965), *The Challenge of Youth*, Garden City, NY: Doubleday.

Erikson, E. H. (1971), *Identity: Youth and Crisis*, London: Faber and Faber.

Exley, S. and Ball, S. (2014), Neo Liberalism and English Education, in D. Turner and H. Yolcu, *Neoliberal Education Reforms: A Critical Analysis*, New York: Routledge.

Fahlberg, V. (1985), *Attachment and Separation*. British Agencies for Adoption and Fostering, Practice Series: 5.

Fanon, F. (1967), *Black Skin, White Masks*, Sidmouth: Pluto Press.

Fanon, F. (2008), *Black Skin, White Masks* (new edn), London: Pluto Press.

Farrell, F. (2004), *Why Does Literature Matter?* New York: Cornell University Press.

Feast, J. (2010), Access to Information: Progress and Perils, *Adoption and Fostering*, 34(3): 74–9

Feeley, M. M. and Simon, J. (1992), The New Penology: Notes on the Emerging Strategy of Corrections and Its Implications, *Criminology* 30(4): 449–74, Available at: http://scholarship.law.berkeley.edu/facpubs/718

Field, F. (2010), *The Foundation Years: Preventing Poor Children Becoming Poor Adults. The Report of the Independent Review on Poverty and Life Chances*, London: Cabinet Office.

Fielding, M. and Moss, P. (2011), *Radical Education and the Common School: A Democratic Alternative (Foundations and Futures of Education)*, London: Routledge.

Fisher, J. (2010), *Moving on to Key Stage 1: Improving Transition from the Early Years Foundation Stage*, Maidenhead: Oxford University Press.

Fisher, P. A., Gunnar, M. R., Chamberlain, P. and Reid, J. B. (2000), Preventive Intervention for Maltreated Preschool Children: Impact on Children's Behaviour, Neuroendocrine Activity, and Foster Parent Functioning, *Journal of the American Academy of Child & Adolescent Psychiatry*, 39(11): 1356–64.

Forrest, S. (2000), Difficult Loves: Learning about Sexuality and Homophobia in Schools, in M. Cole (Ed.), *Education Equality and Human Rights: Issues of Gender, 'Race', Sexuality, Special Needs and Social Class*, London: Routledge Farmer.

Fortuna, K., Baor, L., Israel, S., Abadi, A. and Knafo, A. (2014), Attachment to Inanimate Objects and Early Childcare: A Twin Study, *Frontiers in Psychology*, (5)486. Available at http://www.ncbi.nlm.nih.gov/pmc/articles/PMC4033092/ (Accessed 23 March 2016).

Foucault, M. (1972), *The Archaeology of Knowledge and the Discourse on Language*. London: Routledge.

Foucault, M. (1976), *The History of Sexuality Volume 1: An Introduction*, London: Allen.

Foucault, M. (1977a), *Discipline and Punish. The Birth of the Prison*, London: Allen Lane.

Foucault, M. (1977b), The Discourse on Language, in H. Adams and L. Searle (Eds), Rupert Swyer (Trans.), *Critical Theory Since 1965*, Tallahassee, FL: Florida State University Press.

Foucault, M. (1995), *Discipline & Punish: The Birth of the Prison*, New York: Vintage Books.

Foucault, M. (1995), *Discipline and Punishment*, New York: Vintage Books.

Foucault, M. (1996), The Eye of Power, in M. Foucault and S. Lotringer (Eds), *Foucault Live: Collected Interviews, 1961–84*, New York: Semiotext.

Freire, P. (1970), *Pedagogy of the Oppressed*, London: Penguin.

Freud, S. (2011), *Three Essays on the Theory of Sexuality*, J. Strachey (Trans.), Eastwood: Martino Publishing.

Frey, C. (2016), *Revealed: How Facial Recognition Has Invaded Shops – and Your Privacy*. Available at http://www.theguardian.com/cities/2016/mar/03/revealed-facial-recognition-software-infiltrating-cities-saks-toronto (Accessed 12 October 2016).

Friedman, M, (2002), *Capital and Freedom*, Chicago: University of Chicago Press.

Frith, S. (1985), The Sociology of Youth, in M. Haralambos (Ed.), *Sociology: New Directions*, Ormskirk: Causeway.

Fritz, G. (2015), Imaginary Friend, *Brown University Child and Adolescent Behaviour Letter*, 31(5): 8.

Frost, N., Robinson, M. and Anning, A. (2005), Social Workers in Multidisciplinary Teams: Issues and Dilemmas for Professional Practice, *Child and Family Social Work*, 10(3): 187–96.

Fuentes, A. (2011), *Lockdown High: When the Schoolhouse Becomes a Jailhouse*, London: Verso.

Gad, C. and Hansen, L. K. (2013), A Closed Circuit Technological Vision: On Minority Report, Event Detection and Enabling Technologies, *Surveillance & Society*, 11(1/2): 148–62.

Garland, D. (2001), *The Culture of Control: Crime and Social Order in Contemporary Society* , Chicago: University of Chicago Press

Geddes, H. (2006), *Attachment in the Classroom: The Links between Children's Early Experience, Emotional Wellbeing and Performance in School*, London: Worth Publishing.

Geddes, H. and Hanko, G. (2006), *Behaviour and the Learning of the Looked After and Other Vulnerable Children*, London: National Childrens Bureau.

Gellman, S. A. (2005), *The Essential Child: Origins of Everyday Thought*, New York: Oxford University Press.

Gerhardt, S. (2014), *Why Love Matters: How Affection Shapes a Baby's Brain*, 2nd edn, London: Routledge.

Giddens, A. (1991), *Modernity and Self Identity: Self and Society in the Late Modern Age*, Cambridge: Polity Press.

Giddens, A. (2006), *Sociology*, 5th edn, Cambridge: Polity.

Giddens, A. and Sutton. P. W. (2013), *Sociology*, 7th ed. Oxford: Polity Press.

Giles, H. and Powesland, P. F. (1975), *Speech Style and Social Evaluation*, London: Academic Press.

Gillies, V. (2005), Raising the 'Meritocracy': Parenting and the Individualization of Social Class, *Sociology*, 39(5): 835–53.

Gleason, T., Sebanc, A. and Hartup, W. (2000), Imaginary Companions of Preschool Children, *Developmental Psychology*, 36(4): 419–28.

Goddard, T. (2012), Post-Welfarist Risk Managers? Risk, Crime Prevention and the Responsibilization of Community-Based Organizations. *Theoretical Criminology* , 16(3): 347–63.

Goffman, E. (1956), *The Presentation of Self in Everyday Life*, New York: Doubleday.

Goldson, B. (2011), *Youth in Crisis: Gangs, Territoriality and Violence*, London: Routledge.

Goleman, D. (1995), *Emotional Intelligence*, London: Bloomsbury.

Gopnik, A. (2013), *The Philosophical Baby: What Children's Minds Tell Us about Truth, Love and the Meaning of Life*, London: Bodley Head.

Gordon, A. (2008), *Ghostly Matters: Haunting and the Sociological Imagination*, 2nd edn, Minnesota: University of Minnesota Press.

Gordon, M. M. (1964), *Assimilation in American Life: The Role of Race, Religion and National Origins*, New York: Oxford University Press.

Granot, D. (2014), Teacher–Student Attachment and Student School Adaptation: A Variable Centered and Person Centered Analytical Approaches, *American Journal of Educational Research*, 2(11): 1005–14.

Gregg, D. (2010), *Family Intervention Projects: A Classic Case of Policy-Based Evidence*, London: Centre for Crime and justice Studies.

Grenfell, M. (2012), Interest, in M. Grenfell (Ed.), *Pierre Bourdieu. Key Concepts*, 2nd edn, London: Routledge.

Grover, S. (2012), Child Soldiers as Victims of 'Genocidal Forcible Transfer': Darfur and Syria as Case Example, *International Journal of Human Rights*, 17(3): 411–27.

Gsekey, M. B. and Ensalaco, M. (2005), Three Prints in the Dirt: Child Soldiers and Human Rights, in M. Ensalaco and L. C. Majka (Eds), *Children's Human Rights: Progress and Challenges for Children Worldwide*, Lanham: Rowman and Littlefield,

The Guardian (2003), Section 28 Gone … but Not Forgotten, 17 November 2003. Available at https://www.theguardian.com/politics/2003/nov/17/uk.gayrights (Accessed 20 February 2017).

The Guardian (2015), Shocking Images of Drowned Syrian Boy Show Tragic Plight of Refugees, Available at http://www.theguardian.com/world/2015/sep/02/shocking-image-of-drowned-syrian-boy-shows-tragic-plight-of-refugees (Accessed 10 November 2015).

Halberstam, J. (2005), *In a Queer Time and Place: Transgender Bodies, Subcultural Lives*, New York: New York University Press.

Hall, S. (1992), The Question of Cultural Identity, in S. Hall and B. Gieben (Eds), *Formations of Modernity. Understanding Modern Society*, Cambridge: Open University/Polity Press.

Hall, S. (1993), Cultural Identity in Question, in S. Hall, D. Held and T. McGrew (Eds), *Modernity and Its Futures*, Cambridge: Cambridge Polity.

Hall, S. (1994), Cultural Identity and Diaspora, in P. Williams and L. Chrisman (Eds), *Colonial Discourse and Post-Colonial Theory: A Reader*, New York: Columbia University Press.

Hall, S. and du Gay, P. (2011), *Questions of Cultural Identity*, London: Sage Publications.

Hammick, M., Freeth, D., Copperman, J. and Goodsman, D. (2009), *Being Interprofessional*, Cambridge: Polity Press.

Hancke, G. P., de Carvalhoe Silva, B. and Hancke, G. P. Jr. (2013), The Role of Advanced Sensing in Smart Cities, *Sensors* 13(1): 393–425. Available at http://www.ncbi.nlm.nih.gov/pmc/articles/PMC3574682/ (Accessed 14 July 2016).

Hansard (1989), *House of Lords Debate on the Local Government Act 1986 (Amendment) Bill*. London: Hansard, 483 cc310–38Hare, R. D. (1998), The Hare PCL-R: Some Issues Concerning Its Use and Misuse, *Legal and Criminological Psychology*, 3(1): 101–22.

Harkness, S., Gregg, P., Macmillan, L. (2012), *Poverty: The Role of Institutions, Behaviours and Culture*, Bath: Joseph Rowntree Foundation.

Harris, J. R. (1998), *The Nurture Assumption: Why Children Turn Out the Way They Do*. Free Press. Available at http://emilkirkegaard.dk/en/wp-content/uploads/The-Nurture-Assumption-Why-Children-Turn-Out-the-Way-They-Do-Revised-and-Updated-Judith-Rich-Harris.pdf (Accessed 2 November 2015).

Harry Potter and the Philosophers Stone (2001), [Film] Dir. Chris Columbus, United Kingdom: Heyday Films.

Hartas, D. (2014), *Parenting, Family Policy and Children's Well-Being in an Unequal Society: A New Culture War for Parents*, Basingstoke: Palgrave Macmillan.

Harter, S. (1983). Developmental Perspectives on the Self-System, in E. M. Hetherington (Ed.), Handbook of Child Psychology. 275–385. New York: John Wiley.

Harter, S. (1985). Competence as a Dimension of Self-Evaluation: Toward a Comprehensive Model of Self-Worth. *The Development of the Self*, 2: 55–121.

Harter, S. (1998). The Development of Self-Representations, in W. Damon and N. Eisenberg (Ed.), *Handbook of Child Psychology: Social, Emotional, and Personality Development*, 553–617. Hoboken, NJ: John Wiley.

Haydon, D. and Scraton, P. (2000), Condemn a Little More, Understand a Little Less: The Political Context and Rights' Implications of the Domestic and European Rulings in the Venables-Thompson Case, *Journal of Law and Society*, 27(3): 416–48.

Hayek, F. A. (2006), *The Constitution of Liberty*, London: Routledge Classics.

Hebdige, D. (1979), *Subculture: The Meaning of Style (New Accents)*, Abingdon: Routledge.

Henderson, M. (2012), A Test of Parenting Strategies, *Sociology*, 47(3): 542–59.

Herman, E. S. and Chomsky, N. (1988), *Manufacturing Consent: The Political Economy of the Mass Media*, New York: Pantheon.

Heyes, C., (2016), Identity Politics, *Stanford Encyclopedia of Philosophy* (Summer edn), Edward N. Zalta (Ed.). Available at https://plato.stanford.edu/archives/sum2016/entries/identity-politics (Accessed 13 February 2017).

Heywood, C. (2001), A *History of Childhood: Children and Childhood in the West from Medieval to Modern Times*, Cambridge: Blackwell.

Holland, K. (1999), A Journey to Becoming: The Student Nurse in Transition, *Journal of Advanced Nursing*, 29(1): 229–36.

Holody, R. and Maher, S. (1996), Using Lifebooks with Children in Family Foster Care: A Here and Now Process Model, *Child Welfare*, 75(4): 321–35.

Home Office (2016), *Hate Crime, England and Wales*. Available at https://www.gov.uk/government/statistics/hate-crime-england-and-wales-2015-to-2016 (Accessed 12 February 2017).

Honeybone, P. and Watson, K. (2006), *Phonemes, Graphemes and Phonics for Liverpool English*, London: Education Committee of the Linguistics Association of Great Britain.

Honeyman, S. (2007), Gingerbread Wishes and Candy(Land) Dreams: The Lure of Food in Cautionary Tales of Consumption, *Marvels & Tales*, 21(2): 195–215.

Hood, R. (2012), Complexity and Integrated Working in Children's Services, *British Journal of Social Work*, 44(1): 27–43.

Hooley, K., Stokes, L., & Combes, H. (2016). Life Story Work with Looked After and Adopted Children: How Professional Training and Experience Determine Perceptions of Its Value. *Adoption & Fostering*, 40(3): 219–33.

Hope, A. (2009), CCTV, School Surveillance and Social Control, *British Educational Research Journal*, 35(6): 891–907.

Hope, A. (2015), Governmentality and the Selling of School Surveillance Devices, *Sociological Review*, 63(4): 840–57.

House, R. (Ed.) (2011), *Too Much Too Soon? Early Learning and the Erosion of Childhood*, Stroud: Hawthorne Press.

House of Commons (2017), Sex and Relationship Education in Schools (England), Briefing Paper 06103, 2 March 2017, www.researchbriefings,files,parliament.uk (Accessed 9 March 2017).

Human Rights Campaign. *Supporting and Caring for Our Gender Expansive Youth* (2012), www.assets.hrc.org//files/assets/resourcs/Gender-expansive-youth-report-final.pdf (Accessed 13 February 2017).

Hume, D., (1987 [1742]), Essays Moral, Political, Literary, E. F. Miller (Ed.), *Indianapolis, Lib Fund*. Available at http://www.econlib.org/library/LFBooks/Hume/hmMPL4.html (Accessed 18 September 2015).

The Hunger Games (2012), [Film] Dir. Gary Ross, USA: Color Force.

Illich, I. (1971), *De-schooling Society*, Harmondsworth: Penguin Books.

The Independent (2013), The Return of Section 28: Schools and Academies Practising Homophobic Policy That Was Outlawed under Tony Blair. Available at http://www.independent.co.uk/news/uk/politics/the-return-of-section-28-schools-and-academies-practising-homophobic-policy-that-was-outlawed-under-8775249.html (Accessed 22 February 2017).

The Independent (2016), Theresa May 'Will Campaign to Leave the European Convention on Human Rights in 2020 Election', 29 December 2016.

Irwin, S. and Elley, S. (2011), Concerted Cultivation? Parenting Values, Education and Class Diversity, *Sociology*, 45(3): 480–95.

Jackson, S. (2012), Foundations for Learning: Foundation Degrees, Learner Identities and Part-Time Learners, *International Journal of Continuing Education and Lifelong Learning*, 5(1): 107–24.

Jalango, M. (1987), Do Security Blankets Belong in Preschool? *Young Children*, 42(3): 3–8.

James, A. and James, A. (2012), *Key Concepts in Childhood Studies*, London: Sage.

James, A. and Prout, A. (1997), *Constructing and Reconstructing Childhood*, London: Routledge.

Jarvis, M. (2004), *Psychodynamic Psychology: Classical Theory and Contemporary Research*, London: Thomson Learning.

Jarvis, M. and Chandler, E. (2001), *Angles on Child Psychology*, Cheltenham: Nelson Thornes.

Jenks, C. (1996), *Childhood*, London: Routledge.

Johnson, E. P. (2001), 'Quare' Studies, or (Almost) Everything I Know about Queer Studies I Learned from My Grandmother, *Text and Performance Quarterly*, 21(1): 1–25.

Johnson, E. P. and Henderson, M. G. (2005), *Black Queer Studies*, Durham: Duke University Press.

Jones, D. S. (2014), *Masters of the Universe: Hayek, Friedman, and the Birth of Neoliberal Politics*. Priceton: Princeton University Press.

Jones, O. (2012), *Chavs: The Demonization of the Working Class*, London: Verso.

Jones, O. (2015), *The Establishment*, London: Verso.

Jung, C. G. (1958), *The Undiscovered Self*, Princeton: Princeton University Press.

Jupp, E. (2013), Enacting Parenting Policy? The Hybrid Spaces of Sure Start Children's Centres, *Children's Geographies*, 11(2): 173–87.

Kafka, F. (1919), In the Penal Colony, in Kafka, *The Complete Stories (1971)*, New York: Schocken Books.

Kamau, C. (2013), What Does Being Initiated Severely into a Group Do? The Role of Rewards, *International Journal of Psychology*, 48(3): 399–406.

Katz, L. G. (2011), Current Perspectives on the Early Childhood Curriculum, in R. House (Ed.), *Too Much Too Soon? Early Learning and the Erosion of Childhood*, Stroud: Hawthorne Press.

Kauffman, L. A. (1990), The Anti-Politics of Identity, *Social Review*, 20(1): 67–80.

Keating, C., Pomerantz, J., Pommer, S. D., Ritt, S. J. H., Miller, L. M. and McCormick, J. (2005), Going to College and Unpacking Hazing: A Functional Approach to Decrypting Initiation Practices among Undergraduates, *Group Dynamics: Theory, Research, and Practice*, 9(2): 104–26.

Kehily, M. J. (2003), Consumption and Creativity, in M. J. Kehily and J. Swann (Eds), *Children's Cultural Worlds*, Milton Keynes: Open University.

Kiernan, K. E. and Mensah, F. K (2011), Poverty, Family Resources and Children's Early Education Attainment: The Mediating Role of Parenting, *British Education Journal*, 37(2): 317–36.

Kite, M. E. and Bryant-Lees, K. B. (2016), Historical and Contemporary Attitudes towards Homosexuality, *Teaching of Psychology*, 43(2): 64–170.

Klaus, M. and Kennell, J. (1982), *Parent–Infant Bonding*, 2nd edn, St Louis, MO: C. V. Mosby.

Klerk, V. D. (2013), Initiation, Hazing or Orientation? A Case Study at a South African University. *International Research in Education* 1(1).

Kottak, C. P. (1994), *Anthropology: The Exploration of Human Diversity*, 6th edn, New York: McGraw Hill.

Kristeva, J. (1980), *Desire in Language: A Semiotic Approach to Literature and Art*, New York: Columbia University Press.

Kruks, S. (2001), *Retrieving Experience: Subjectivity and Recognition in Feminist Politics*, Ithaca, NY: Cornell University Press.

Laclau, E. and Mouffe, C. (2001), *Hegemony and Socialist Strategy: Towards a Radical Democratic Politics*, London: Verso.

Laing, F. (2011), A Parents Challenge to New Labours Early Years Foundation Stage, in R. House (Ed.), *Too Much Too Soon? Early Learning and the Erosion of Childhood*, Stroud: Hawthorne Press.

Lambirth, A. (2007), Challenging the Laws of Talk: Ground Rules, Social Reproduction and the Curriculum, *Curriculum Journal*, 17(1): 59–71.

Laming, Lord (2003), The Victoria Climbié Report, London: HMSO.

Laming, Lord (2009), The Protection of Children in England: A Progress Report, London: HMSO.

Lareau, A., (2003), Unequal Childhoods: Race, Class, and Family Life, Berkeley: University of California Press.

Latner, J. D., Rosewell, J. K. and Simmonds, M. B. (2007), Childhood Obesity Stigma: Association with Television, Videogame and Magazine Exposure, *Body Image*, 4(2): 147–55.

Lave, J. and Wenger, E. (2005), *Situated Learning: Legitimate Peripheral Participation*. Cambridge, England, and New York: Cambridge University Press.

Le Grand, J. and New, B. (2015), *Government Paternalism: Nanny State or Helpful Friend*, Princeton: Princeton University Press.

Leach, P. (2011), The EYFS and the Real Foundations of Children's Early Years, in R. House (Ed.), *Too Much Too Soon? Early Learning and the Erosion of Childhood*, Stroud: Hawthorne Press.

Lehman, E., Arnold, B. and Reeves, S. (1995), Attachments to Blankets, Teddy Bears, and Other Nonsocial Objects: A Child's Perspective, *Journal of Genetic Psychology*, 156(4): 443–59.

Letts, W. J. and Sears, J. T. (1999), *Queering Elementary Education: Advancing the Dialogue about Sexualities and Schooling*, New York: Rowman and Littlefield.

Levine, E. and Tamburrino, M. (2014), Bullying among Young Children: Strategies for Prevention, *Early Childhood Education Journal*, 42: 271–8.

Lewis, G. H. (1978), The Sociology of Popular Culture, *Current Sociology*, 26(3): 1–160.

Lippert, R. (2015), Thinking about Law and Surveillance. *Surveillance and Society*. 13(2): 292–94.

Lion (2016) [Film], Dir. Gareth Davis, USA: See-Saw Films.

Livingstone, S., Haddon, L., Görzig, A. and Ólafsson, K. (2011), *Risks and Safety on the Internet: The Perspective of European Children. Full Findings*, London: London School of Economics.

Loader, I. (1997), Thinking Normatively about Private Security, *Journal of Law and Society*, 24(3): 377–94.

Locke, J. (1689), *Two Treatises of Government*, London: Awnsham Churchill.

London School of Economics (2011), *Reading the Riots*, London: London School Economics.

Lowe, R. (2004), Childhood Through the Ages, in T. Maynard and N. Thomas (Eds), *An Introduction to Early Childhood Studies*, London: Sage.

Luke, A. (1986), Linguistic Stereotypes, the Divergent Speaker and the Teaching of Literacy, *Journal of Curriculum Studies*, 18(4): 397–408.

Lukes, S. (2005), *Power: A Radical View*, 2nd edn, Basingstoke: Palgrave Macmillan.

Lyon, D. (2013), *The Electronic Eye: The Rise of Surveillance Society*, Oxford: Open University Press.

Lyon, D. (2015), The Snowden Stakes: Challenges for Understanding Surveillance Today, *Surveillance and Society*, 13(2): 139–52.

Malekpour, M. (2007), Effects of Attachment on Early and Later Development, *British Journal of Developmental Disabilities*, 53(105): 81–95.

Mannheim, K. (1928), Competition as a Cultural Phenomenon, in K. H. Wolff (Ed.), *From Karl Mannheim*, New Brunswick and London: Transaction Publishers.

Marcia, J. E. (1980), Identity in Adolescence, *Handbook of Adolescent Psychology*, 9(11): 159–87.

Markus, H. and Nurius, P. (1986), Possible Selves, *American Psychologist*, 41(9): 954–69.

Marr, L. (2006), The Social Construction of the New Student, *Learning and Teaching in Action*, 2(4): 14–17.

Maslow, A. (1970), *Motivation and Personality*, 3rd edn, New York: Harper and Row.

Mayall, B. (2015), Intergenerational Relations: Embodiment over Time, in L. Alanen, L. Brooker and B. Mayall (Eds), *Childhood with Bourdieu*, Basingstoke: Palgrave Macmillan.

McAdams, D. P. (2001), The Psychology of Life Stories, *Review of General Psychology*, 5(2): 100–22.

McAdams, D. and McLean, K. (2013), Narrative Identity, *Current Directions in Psychological Science*, 22(3): 233–8.

McLaren, H. (2009). Using 'Foucault's Toolbox': The Challenge with Feminist Post-Structuralist Discourse Analysis. https://www.academia.edu/25522700/Using_Foucault_s_toolbox_the_challenge_with_feminist_post-structuralist_discourse_analysis accessed 15 February 2017

McLuhan, M. (1967), The Medium Is the Massage: An Inventory of Effects with Quentin Fiore. *Nueva York: Bantam*.

McLuhan, M. (1967), *Understanding Media*, London: Sphere.

McMahon, A. Foulkes, P. and Tollfree, L. (1994), Gestural Representation and Lexical Phonology, *Phonology* 11:277–316.

McMahon, L. (2009), *The Handbook of Play Therapy and Therapeutic Play*, 2nd edn, London: Routledge.

Mill, J. S. (1865), *On Liberty*, London: Longman Green.

Minority Report (2002), [Film] Dir. Stephen Spielberg, USA: Cruise Wagner Productions.

Mitchener-Nissen, T. (2014), Failure to Collectively Assess Surveillance-Oriented Security Technologies Will Inevitably Lead to an Absolute Surveillance Society, *Surveillance and Society*, 12(1): 73–88.

Molesworth, M., Nixon, E. and Scullion, R. (2009), Having, Being and Higher Education: The Marketisation of the University and the Transformation of the Student into Customer, *Teaching in Higher Education*, 14(3): 277–87.

Mouffe, C. (2005), *On the Political*, London: Routledge.

Moullin, S., Waldfogel, J. and Washbrook, E., (2014), *Baby Bonds: Parenting, Attachment and a Secure Base for Children*, London: Sutton Trust.

Mythen, G., Walklate, S. and Khan, F. (2009), I'm a Muslim, But I'm Not a Terrorist: Victimisation, Risky Identities and the Performance of Safety, *British Journal of Criminology*, 49 (6): 736–54.

Nagel, M. (2009), Mind the Mind: Understanding the Links between Stress, Emotional Well-Being and Learning in Educational Contexts, *International Journal of Learning*, 16(2): 33–42.

National College of Teaching and Leadership (NCTL) (2014), *An Introduction to Attachment and the Implications for Learning and Behaviour*. Available at http://researchspace.bathspa.ac.uk/id/eprint/5134 (Accessed 14 September 2017)

National Curriculum. Available at https://www.gov.uk/government/publications/national-curriculum-in-england-framework-for-key-stages-1-to-4 (Accessed 18 August 2016).

National Scientific Council on the Developing Child (2007), The Timing and Quality of Early Experiences Combine to Shape Brain Architecture: Working Paper No. 5. www.developingchild.harvard.edu (Accessed 12 March 2017).

Nettle, D. and Romaine, S. (2000), *Vanishing Voices: The Extinction of the World's Languages*, Oxford: Oxford University Press.

Noddings, N. (2012), The Caring Relation in Teaching, *Oxford Review of Education*, 38(6): 771–81.

Norris, C. (2003), From Personal to Digital: CCTV, the Panopticon, and the Technological Mediation of Suspicion and Social Control, in D. Lyon (Ed.), *Surveillance as Social Sorting: Privacy, Risk and Digital Discrimination*, London: Routledge.

Nozick, R. (1974), *Anarchy, State and Utopia*, Oxford: Blackwell.

Nozick, R. (2001), *Anarchy, State and Utopia*, Chichester: Wiley-Blackwell.

O'Connor, J. (2011), Applying Bourdieu's Concepts of Social and Cultural Capital and Habitus to Early Year's Research, in T. Waller, J. Whitmarsh and K. Clarke (Eds), *Making Sense of Theory and Practise in Early Childhood: The Power of Ideas*, Maidenhead: Open University Press.

O'Connor, R. (2016), Greater Manchester Council Ridiculed for Salford Quays Swearing Ban. Available at http://www.independent.co.uk/news/uk/home-news/manchester-council-ridiculed-for-salford-quays-swearing-ban-a6909086.html (Accessed 29 June 2016).

O'Neill, M. and Loftus, B. (2013), Policing and the Surveillance of the Marginal. *Theoretical Criminology*. 17(4): 437–54.

Oates, J. and Grayson, A. (2004), *Cognitive and Language Development in Children*, Oxford: Wiley Blackwell.

The Omen (1976), [Film] Dir. Richard Donner, USA: 20th Century Fox. *Oranges Are Not the Only Fruit* (1990), [TV Programme] BBC TWO 10–24 January 1990

Oyserman, D. (2004), Self-Concept and Identity, in M. Brewer and M. Hewstone (Eds), *Self and Social Identity*, Oxford: Blackwell Publishing.

Pal Sian, K. (2015), Spies, Surveillance and Stakeouts: Monitoring Muslim Moves in British State Schools, *Race Ethnicity and Education*, 18(2): 183–201.

Parliament UK, (2017), Homophobia in Sport: Report of the Culture, Media and Sport Committee of the House of Commons. www.parliamnet.uk/cmscom (Accessed 13 March 2017).

Parties and Election in Europe. Available at http://www.parties-and-elections.eu (Accessed 10 February 2017).

Passman, R. H. (1977), Providing Attachment Objects to Facilitate Learning and Reduce Stress: Effects of Mothers and Security Blanket, *Development Psychology*, 13(1): 25–8.

Payne, G. (2000), *Social Divisions*, Basingstoke: MacMillan Press.

Pearson, G. (1983), *The Hooligan*, London: Macmillan.

Phelps- Roper, M. (2017), TED Conference Speech.6 March 2017. Available at https://www.ted.com/talks/megan_phelps_roper_i_grew_up_in_the_westboro_baptist_church_here_s_why_i_left (Accessed 10 March 2017).

Placa, V. L. and Corlyon, J. (2016), Unpacking the Relationship between Parenting and Poverty: Theory, Evidence and Policy, *Social Policy and Society*, 15(1): 11–28.

Plomin, R., DeFries, J. and Fulker, D. (2006), *Nature and Nurture during Infancy and Early Childhood*, Cambridge: Cambridge University Press.

Podesta, J. (2014), Habitus and the Accomplishment of Natural Growth: Maternal Parenting Practices and the Achievement of 'School-Readiness', *Australasian Journal of Early Childhood*, 39(4): 123–30.

Portes, J. (2016), The Troubled Families Programme Was Bound to Fail – and Ministers Knew It. Available at https://www.theguardian.com/commentisfree/2016/oct/18/troubled-families-programme-ministers-data (Accessed 4 November 2016).

QAA (2014), Subject Benchmark Statement, Early Childhood Studies. Available at http://www.qaa.ac.uk/en/Publications/Documents/SBS-early-childhood-studies-14.pdf (Accessed 2 November 2016).

Rabbit-Proof Fence (2002), [Film] Dir. Phillip Noyce, USA: Miramax.

Raffo, C., Forbes, C. and Thomson, S. (2015), Ecologies of Educational Reflexivity and Agency – A Different Way of Thinking about Equitable Educational Policies and Practices for England and Beyond? *International Journal of Inclusive Education*, 19(11): 1126–42.

Rawolle, A. and Lingard, B. (2013), Bourdieu and Educational Research. Thinking Tools, Relational Thinking, Beyond Epistemological Innocence, in M. Murphy (Ed.), *Social Theory and Education Research. Understanding Foucault, Habermas, Bourdieu and Derrida*, London: Routledge.

Read, V. (2014), *Developing Attachment in Early Years Settings: Nurturing Secure Relationships from Birth to Five Years*, 2nd edn, Abingdon: Routledge.

Reay, D. (2000), A Useful Extension of Bourdieu's Conceptual Framework? Emotional Capital as a Way of Understanding Mothers' Involvement in Their Children's Education? *The Sociological Review*, 48(4): 568–85.

Reay, D. (2004), It's all Becoming a Habitus: Beyond the Habitual Use of Habitus in Educational Research, *British Journal of Sociology of Education*, 25(4): 431–44.

The Red Balloon (Le Ballon Rouge) (1956), [Film] Dir. Albert Lamorisse, France: Films Montsouris.Reif, A., Rosler, M., Freitag, C., Schneider, M.,

Eujen, A., Kissling, C., Wenzler, D., Jacob, C., Retz-Junginger., Thome, J., Lesch, K. and Retz, W. (2007), Nature and Nurture Predispose to Violent Behavior: Serotonergic Genes and Adverse Childhood Environment, *Neuropsychopharmacology*, 32: 2375–83.

Rhee, K. (2008), Childhood Overweight and the Relationship between Parent Behaviours, Parenting Style, and Family Functioning, *Annals of the American Academy of Political and Social Science*, 615(1): 11–37.

Riley, P. (2010), *Attachment Theory and Teacher Student Relationships*, Abingdon: Routledge.

Rogers, C. (1951), *Client Centered Therapy: Its Current Practice, Implications and Theory*, Boston: Houghton Mifflin.

Rogers, C. (1969), *Freedom to Learn*, New York: Merrill.

Rogers, C. and Lyon, H. C. (2013), *On Becoming an Effective Teacher: Person-Centered Teaching, Psychology, Philosophy, and Dialogues*, Abingdon: Routledge.

Romaine, S. (1994), *Language in Society, An Introduction to Sociolinguistics*, Oxford: Oxford University Press.

Ronson, J. (2011), *The Psychopath Test: A Journey through the Madness Industry*, London: Riverhead Books.

Root-Bernstein, M. (2009), Imaginary Worldplay as an Indicator of Creative Giftedness, in L. V. Shavinina (Ed.), *International Handbook on Giftedness*, 599–16, Amsterdam: Springer.

Rose, J. (2006), *Independent Review of the Teaching of Early Reading*, London: Department of Education and Skills.

Rose, W. (2006), The Developing World of the Child: Children's Perspectives, in J. Aldgate, D. Jones, W. Rose, and C. Jeffery (Eds), *The Developing World of the Child*, London: Jessica Kingsley.

Rubin, K., Coplan, R., Chen, X., Buskirk, A. and Wojslawowicz, J. (2005), Peer Relationships in Childhood, in M. Bornstein and M. Lamb (Eds), *Developmental Psychology: An Advanced Textbook*, 5th edn, Hillsdale, NJ: Erlbaum.

Rubin, K., Coplan, R., Chen, X., Bowker, J., McDonald, K. and Heverly-Fitt, S. (2015), Peer Relationships, in Bornstein, M. H. and Lamb M. E. (Ed.), *Developmental Science: An Advanced Textbook*, 7th edn, Hove: Psychology Press.

Rutter, M. (1972), *Material Deprivation Reassessed*, Harmondsworth: Penguin Books.

Rutter, M. (1981), *Maternal Deprivation Reassessed*, 2nd ed. Harmondsworth: Penguin Books.

Said, E. W. (1979), *Orientalism*, London: Penguin books.

Said, E. W. (1993), *Culture and Imperialism*, London: Vintage.

Sanders, S. and Spraggs, G. (1989), Section 28 and Education, in C. Jones and P. Mahoney (Eds), *Learning Our Lines: Sexuality and Social Control*, London: Women's Press.

Santayana, G. (1998), *Life of Reason*, New York: Prometheus Books.

Sartre, J. (2003), *Being and Nothingness: An Essay on Phenomenological Ontology*, Abingdon: Routledge

Savage, M. (2015), *Social Class in the 21st Century*, London: Penguin Books.

Save the Children (2010), *Child Soldiers – and Other Children Used by Armed Forces and Groups*. Available at http://www.savethechildren.org. uk/sites/default/files/docs/Child_soldiers_policy_brief_1.pdf (Accessed 2 November 2015).

Savin-Williams, R. C. (2014), The New Sexual Minority Teenager: Freedom from Traditional Notions of Sexual Identity, in J. S. Kaufman and D. A. Powell, (Eds), *The Meaning of Sexual Identity in the Twenty-First Century*, Newcastle upon Tyne: Cambridge Scholar Publishing.

Schilt, K. and Westbrook, L. (2009), Doing Gender, Doing Heteronormality, Gender Normals, Transgender People and the Social Maintenance of Heterosexuality, *Gender & Society*, 23(4): 440–64.

Schon, D. (1984), *The Reflective Practitioner: How Professionals Think in Action*, New York: Basic Books.

Schwab, G. (2010), *Haunting Legacies: Violent Histories and Transgenerational Trauma*, Chichester: Columbia University Press.

Sedgewick, E. K. (1990), *The Epistemology of the Closet*, Berkeley: University of California Press.

Shiloh, I. (2009), No Exit: Motherhood as Hell in Lionel Shriver's *We Need to Talk about Kevin*. Paper presented at a conference on Gender and Diversity, University of Maastricht, March 2009.Available at http://www.academia.edu/ 1206148/No_Exit_Motherhood_as_Hell_in_We_Need_to_Talk_about_Kevin (Accessed 12 December 2015).

Shriver, L. (2003) *We Need to Talk about Kevin*, London: Serpent's Tail.

Simon, B. (2005), The Return of Panopticism: Supervision, Subjection and the New Surveillance, *Surveillance & Society*, 3(1): 1–20.

Simon, J. and Feeley, M. (2003). The Form and Limits of the New Penology. *Punishment and Social Control*, 2: 75–116.

Skeggs, B. (1997), *Formations of Class and Gender: Becoming Respectable*, London: Sage.

Skinner, B. F. (1969), *Contingencies of Reinforcement: A Theoretical Analysis*, New York: Appleton-Century-Crofts.

Smale, B. and Fowlie, J. (2011), *How to Succeed at University*, London: Sage.

Smidt, S. (1998), *A Guide to Early Years Practice*, London: Routledge.

Smidt, S. (2006), *The Developing Child in the 21st Century: A Global Perspective on Child Development*, London: Routledge.

Smith, M. K. (2001), Community, *Encyclopaedia of Informal Education*. Available at http://www.infed.org/community/community.htm (Accessed 8 February 2016).

Social Exclusion Task Force (2007), *Reaching Out: Think Family Analysis and Themes from the Families at Risk Review*, London: Cabinet Office.

Social Mobility Commission (2014), Britain, Elitist? London: Social Mobility Commission. Available at https://www.gov.uk/government/publications/elitist-britain (Accessed 2 August 2016).

Spivak, G. C. (1990), *The Postcolonial Critic*, Abingdon: Routledge.

Stainton Rogers, R. and Stainton Rogers, W. (1992), *Stories of Childhood: Shifting Agendas of Child Concern*, Toronto, ON: University of Toronto Press.

Standards and Testing Agency, (2012). Assessment and Reporting Arrangements Year 1 phonics screening check available online at www.education.gov.uk/ publications.

Stark, R. and Fink, R. (2000), *Acts of Faith: Explaining the Human Side of Religion*, Berkeley: University of California Press.

Stets, J. E. and Burke, P. E. (2014), Self Esteem and Identities, *Social Perspectives*, 57(4): 409–33.

Sunwolf and Leets, L. (2004), Being Left Out: Rejecting Outsiders and Communicating Group Boundaries in Childhood and Adolescent Peer Groups, *Journal of Applied Communication Research*, 32(3): 195–223.

Swartz, D. (1997), *Culture & Power: The Sociology of Pierre Bourdieu*, Chicago: University of Chicago Press.

Tajfel, H. (2010), *Social Identity and Intergroup Relations*, Cambridge: Cambridge University Press.

Tatz, C. (2006), Confronting Australian Genocide, in R. Maaka and C. Anderson (Eds), *Indigenous Experience: Global Perspectives*, Toronto, ON: Canadian Scholars Press.

Taylor, A., Pacinini-Ketchabaw, V. and Blaise, M. (2012), Children's Relations to the More-than-Human World, *Contemporary Issues in Early Childhood*, 13(2): 81–5.

Taylor, E. and Rooney, T. (2016), *Surveillance Futures: Social and Ethical Implications of New Technologies for Children and Young People*, Abingdon: Routledge.

Taylor, M. (1999), *Imaginary Companions and the Children Who Create Them*, Oxford: Oxford University Press.

Taylor, M. and Mottweiler, C. (2008), Imaginary Companions: Pretending They Are Real but Knowing They Are Not, *American Journal of Play*, 4(2): 4.

The Telegraph (2013), Britain's Homophobia Needs to Be Tackled before We Turn to Russia's. Available at http://www.telegraph.co.uk/women/womens-life/10254992/Britains-homophobia-needs-to-be-tackled-before-we-turn-to-Russias.html (Accessed 22 February 2017).

Them (2006), [Film] Dir. David Moreau, France and Romania: Eskwad.

Thomas, L. (2012), *Building Student Engagement and Belonging in Higher Education at a Time of Change: Final Report from the What Works? Student Retention and Success Programme*, London: Paul Hamlyn Foundation.

Thomas, L., Jones, R. and Ottaway J. (2015), Effective Practice Design Directed Independent Learning Opportunities, Higher Education Academy. Available at http://www.qaa.ac.uk/en/Publications/Documents/Effective-practice-in-the-design-of-directed-independent-learning-opportunities.pdf (Accessed 22 May 2015).

Thomas, P. (2009), Between Two Stools? The Government's 'Preventing Violent Extremism' Agenda, *The Political Quarterly*, 80(2): 282–91.

Tizard, B. (1991), Working Mothers and the Care of Young Children, in A. Phoenix and A. Woollett (Eds), *Social Construction of Motherhood*, London: Sage.

Townsend, P. (1979), *Poverty in the United Kingdom, A Survey of Household Resources and Standards of Living*, Harmondsworth: Penguin.

Trump, D. J. (2017), Presidential Inaugural Speech. Available at https://www.theguardian.com/world/2017/jan/20/donald-trump-inauguration-speech-full-text(Accessed 28 January 2017).

UN General Assembly (1948), UN Declaration of Human Rights (217 [III] A), Paris: United Nations.

UN General Assembly (1948), *Universal Declaration of Human Rights*, New York: United Nations.

UN General Assembly (1989), *Convention on the Rights of the Child*, United Nations, Treaty Series, 1577: 3.

UN General Assembly (1989), *UN Convention on the Rights of the Child*, New York: United Nations.

UNICEF (1989), *Convention on the Rights of the Child*, New York: United Nations.

Usborne, E. and de la Sablonnière, R. (2014), Understanding My Culture Means Understanding Myself: The Function of Cultural Identity Clarity for Personal Identity Clarity and Personal Psychological Well-Being, *Journal for the Theory of Social Behaviour*, 44(4): 436–58.

Valdre, R. (2014), *We Need to Talk about Kevin*: An Unusual, Unconventional Film: Some Reflections on 'Bad Boys', between Transgenerational Projections and Socio-Cultural Influences, *International Journal of Psychoanalysis*, 95: 149–59.

van Dijk, T. A. (1996), Discourse Power and Access, in Caldas-Coulthard, C. R. and Coulthard, M. (Eds.), *Texts and Practices: Readings in Critical Analysis*, London: Routledge.

van Gennep, A. (2010), *The Rites of Passage*, London: Routledge.

Van Rosmalen, L., Van der Veer, R. and Van der Horst, F. (2015), Ainsworth's Strange Situation Procedure: The Origin of an Instrument, *Journal of the History of the Behavioural Sciences*, 51(3): 261–84.

Vandenbroeck, M. (2007), De-Culturalising Social Inclusion and Re-Culturalising Outcomes, *Early Childhood Matters*, 108: 7–10.

Vandenbroeck, M., Roets, G. and Snoeck, A., (2009), Immigrant Mothers Crossing Borders: Nomadic Identities and Multiple Belongings in Early Childhood Education, *European Early Childhood Education Research Journal*, 17(2): 203–16.

Village of the Damned (1960), [Film] Dir. Wolf Rilla, United Kingdom: MGM British Studios.

Vogler, P., Crivello, G. and Woodhead, M. (2008), Early Childhood Transitions Research: A Review of Concepts, Theory, and Practice, Working Paper No. 48. The Hague, The Netherlands: Bernard van Leer Foundation.

Voss, B. L. (2005), Sexual Subjects: Identity and Taxonomy in Archaeological Research, in E. C. Casella and C. Fowler (Eds), *The Archaeology of Plural and Changing Identities*, New York: Springer.

Vuorisalo, M. and Alanen, L. (2015), Early Childhood Education as a Social Field; Everyday Struggles and Practices of Dominance, in L. Alanen, L. Brooker and B. Mayall, (Eds), *Childhood with Bourdieu*, Basingstoke: Palgrave Macmillan.

Wacquant, L. J. D. (1989), Towards a Reflexive Sociology: A Workshop with Pierre Bourdieu, *Sociology Theory*, 7: 26–63.

Waddington, P., Stenson, K. and Don, D. (2004), In Proportion: Race, and Police Stop and Search, *British Journal of Criminology*, 44(6): 889–914.

Walkerdine, V. (2014), Communal Beingness and Affect: An Exploration of Trauma in an Ex-Industrial Community, *Body and Society*, 16(1), 91–116.

Walkerdine, V. (2015), Transmitting Class across Generations Theory and Psychology, 25(2): 167–83.

Walkerdine, V., Lucey, H. and Melody, J. (2001), *Growing Up Girl: Psychosocial Explorations of Gender and Class*, Basingstoke: Palgrave.

Walsh, S. (2002), Construction or Obstruction: Teacher Talk and Learner Involvement in the EFL Classroom, *Language Teaching Research*, 6(1): 3–23.

Walton, S. (2013), Care Plan Sees Dystopian Future Arriving Early, *The Scotsman*, 8 May 2013.

Watson, D., Latter, S. and Bellew, R. (2015), Adopters' Views on Their Children's Life Story Books, *Adoption and Fostering*, 39(2): 119–34.

Watson, J. B. (1924), *Behaviorism*. New York: People's Institute Publishing.

Weisberg, D. and Gopnik, A. (2013), Pretense, Counterfactuals, and Bayesian Causal Models: Why What Is Not Real Really Matters, *Cognitive Science*, 37(7): 1368–81.

Wen, N. J., Herrmann, P. A. and Legare, C. H. (2016), Ritual Increases Children's Affiliation with In-Group Members, *Evolution and Human Behaviour*, 37(1): 54–60.

Wenger, E. (1998), *Communities of Practice: Learning, Meaning, and Identity*, Cambridge: Cambridge University Press.

Wenger, E., McDermott, R. and Snyder, W. (2002), *Cultivating Communities of Practice*, Boston: Harvard Business School Publishing.

West, C. and Zimmerman, D. (1987), Doing Gender. *Gender and Society*, 1(2): 125–51.

Wiarda, H. J. (2014), *Political Culture, Political Science and Identity Politics: An Uneasy Alliance*, London: Routledge.

Wilchins, R. (2004), *Queer Theory, Gender Theory: An Instant Primer*, New York: Alyson Publications.

Willy Wonka and the Chocolate Factory (1971), [Film] Dir. Mel Stuart, USA: Wolper Pictures.

Wilson, R. and Pickett, K. (2010), *The Spirit Level: Why Equality Is Better for Everyone*, London: Penguin.

Winnicott, D. (1953), Transitional Objects and Transitional Phenomena – A Study of the First Not-Me Possession, *International Journal of Psycho-Analysis*, 34(2): 89–97.

Winnicott, D. (1971), *Playing and Reality*, London: Tavistock Publications.

Wood, D. (1988), *How Children Think and Learn*, Oxford: Blackwell.

Woodhead, M. (2006), *Changing Perspectives on Early Childhood: Theory, Research and Policy*, Paris: UNESCO.

Young, J. (1999), T*he Exclusive Society: Social Exclusion, Crime and Difference in Late Modernity*, London: Sage.

Young, R. J. C. (2001), *Postcolonialism: An Historical Introduction*, Oxford: Blackwell.

Zimmerman, B. J. (2000), Attaining Self-Regulation: A Social Cognitive Perspective, in M. Boekaerts, P. Pintrich and M. Zeidner (Eds), *Handbook of Self-Regulation*. Burlington, MA: Elsevier Academic Press.

Zimmerman, B. J., Bandura, A. and Martinez-Pons, M. (1992), Self-Motivation for Academic Attainment: The Role of Self-Efficacy Beliefs and Personal Goal-Setting, *American Educational Research Journal*, 29(3): 663–76.

Zournazi, M. (2002), Navigating Movements: An Interview with Brian Massumi, in M. Zournazi (Ed.), *Hope: New Philosophies for Change*, Annadale, NSW: Pluto Press.

Index